SIDNEY J. FURIE

SIDNEY J. FURIE

Life and Films

DANIEL KREMER

UNIVERSITY PRESS OF KENTUCKY

Scholarly publisher for the Commonwealth,
serving Bellarmine University, Berea College, Centre College of Kentucky,
Eastern Kentucky University, The Filson Historical Society, Georgetown College,
Kentucky Historical Society, Kentucky State University, Morehead State
University, Murray State University, Northern Kentucky University, Transylvania
University, University of Kentucky, University of Louisville, and Western
Kentucky University.
All rights reserved.

Editorial and Sales Offices: The University Press of Kentucky
663 South Limestone Street, Lexington, Kentucky 40508-4008
www.kentuckypress.com

Frontispiece: Courtesy of the Everett Collection. Unless otherwise noted,
photographs are from the author's collection.

Library of Congress Cataloging-in-Publication Data

Kremer, Daniel, 1984–
  Sidney J. Furie : life and films / Daniel Kremer.
     pages cm — (Screen classics)
  Includes bibliographical references and index.
  ISBN 978-0-8131-6596-7 (hardcover : alk. paper) —
  ISBN 978-0-8131-6598-1 (pdf) — ISBN 978-0-8131-6597-4 (epub)
  1. Furie, Sidney J. 2. Motion picture producers and directors—Canada—
Biography. I. Title.
  PN1998.3.F865K84 2015
  791.4302'33092—dc23
  [B]   2015026559

This book is printed on acid-free paper meeting
the requirements of the American National Standard
for Permanence in Paper for Printed Library Materials.
∞

Manufactured in the United States of America.

Member of the Association of
American University Presses

To my mother and my aunts, who, during my childhood,
were dispatched to find and purchase the offbeat movies
that I requested they give me as gifts for birthdays
and holidays (of which *The Ipcress File* was one)

Contents

Illustrations follow page 194

Foreword

Sidney J. Furie will no doubt always be known as an American filmmaker, but England and his native Canada can also lay claim to him. Although he is remembered these days for his more commercial Hollywood films, such as *The Appaloosa, Lady Sings the Blues, Little Fauss and Big Halsy*, many would claim that his strongest work was done in England in the sixties (*The Leather Boys* and *The Ipcress File*). Canadian film historians note the contribution he made to the early days of Canadian cinema in the fifties. This is all to say that Furie has led at least three lives in his long and illustrious career.

The 1950s was not a terribly auspicious time for a young Canadian aspiring to make feature films. There was no film industry to speak of. But, undaunted, a generation of future filmmakers gravitated, perhaps ironically, to the nascent form of television. The Canadian Broadcasting Corporation is where Canadians like Norman Jewison, Ted Kotcheff, Silvio Narizzano—and Sidney Furie—got their start. And more ironically, all of them followed exactly the same career path. After their early CBC days, they emigrated to England, where they established their careers and made their names. Then each made the cross-Atlantic trip again, this time to the mecca of Hollywood.

Sidney Furie was perhaps the most ambitious of these for that time, however, as he is the only one who, before he left, made full features, two brightly innocent, naive works that captured the rhythms and voice of a generation. Through the very act of directing these films, he staked his claim and left an indelible mark on my country's cinematic history. *A Dangerous Age* and *A Cool Sound from Hell* acted as his calling cards when he arrived in England, and they led almost immediately to the successes of *The Young Ones* and *The Leather Boys*. But it was with *The Ipcress File* that Furie jumped into the front ranks of filmmaking, and its success led to Los Angeles and a long and enduring career.

Too restless to be classified as a true auteur by critics, Furie was most often considered a fine craftsman who, much like his contemporaries

Jewison and Kotcheff, applied his skills to a wide range of films and genres. Stylish, forceful, creative, and imaginative, Furie joins a long list of Hollywood professionals from an earlier era who were content to step behind a camera and let the story tell itself.

It remains a wonder to behold that he started making striking, bold, and of-the-moment feature films in Canada when the only game in town was the short films being made by the NFB. Furie and his films captured a country struggling to establish its identity. That he went on to such an exemplary career makes this book all the more important.

Piers Handling
Director
Toronto International Film Festival

Prologue

Opening the Furie File

This is the first book ever written about Sidney J. Furie, a filmmaker who, in varying quarters, has been branded a wizened old hack, a journeyman, and an industry stalwart on a woeful losing streak. But also, sometimes in the same breath, he has been identified as a visual virtuoso, a pioneer in his home country of Canada, an auteur, and a marginalized film artist unaccountably neglected by cineastes, historians, and film scholars. Intriguingly, the polar extremes of these contradictory claims suggest a paradox. The statement "I am writing a book about Sidney Furie" beckons the question "Which Sidney Furie?" because the sundry nature of his work leaves one breathless. One thing is certain: for a man who has enjoyed as lengthy, eclectic, and impressive a career as Furie's, he has heretofore never been seriously covered in any depth whatsoever. Indeed, he has often been dismissed outright. This book, then, becomes a fresh appraisal rather than a reappraisal.

As the author of this book, I have had to build the foundations of my Furie scholarship nearly from the ground up. My intent is to fill the gap and draw attention to Furie's rich body of work, because his prolific career extends beyond a randomized selection of titles; it suggests a filmmaker with identifiable stylistic and thematic trademarks. His work engenders many workflows and movements, including early Canadian independent cinema, the British New Wave, the New Hollywood, American studio filmmaking, the Hollywood blockbuster wave in the eighties, and the direct-to-video assembly line in the nineties and the first decade of the current century. For his involvements in the latter two, connoisseurs of cinema have indicted him and cast him aside, but it would be disingenuous to favor this knee-jerk verdict, because it overlooks how his career has been a broad evolutionary journey. It would be equally disingenuous to overlook how the man himself has evolved in conjunction with his work.

Furie is not neglected wholesale, nor has anything overshadowed his individual moments of career glory. If the cognoscenti have written him off, his list of individual achievements speaks for itself, and his chief defenders and enthusiasts are filmmakers rather than academics, historians, and scholars. As cinematographer Stephen Burum told me in his interview, "As far as I'm concerned, a book on Sidney is so long overdue because he is one of the three best staging and camera directors I've ever known. The other two are Brian De Palma and Francis Coppola." The British Film Institute has recognized Furie's BAFTA (British Academy of Film and Television Award) Best Picture Award–winning *The Ipcress File* (1965) as one of the one hundred best British films ever made. Martin Scorsese has named *The Entity* (1982) the fourth scariest horror film ever made, ranking it above even *The Shining, The Exorcist,* and *Psycho.* Peter Tscherkassky's *Outer Space,* an experimental short film that sent shockwaves through the international film community in 1999, extensively incorporated footage from *The Entity.* Stanley Kubrick acknowledged taking cues from Furie's *The Boys in Company C* (1978) for his own *Full Metal Jacket,* going so far as to use Furie's Marine drill instructor actor R. Lee Ermey as his own film's Marine drill instructor and to employ a dual-structured narrative balanced between boot camp and battlefield. Quentin Tarantino has spoken admiringly of the peculiar pacing in Furie's *Hit!* (1973), and his British New Wave masterpiece *The Leather Boys* (1963), one of my own personal favorite films of all time, is still regarded as a key work of kitchen sink realism. And I have not even mentioned the critical and commercial impact of *Lady Sings the Blues,* which *Time*'s Richard Corliss named one of the "Top 25 Important Films about Race."

In 1956 Toronto, twenty-three-year-old Sidney J. Furie walked onto the set of what was to be his debut feature film, *A Dangerous Age.* His withering confidence had been reaffirmed with the comforting recall of trade secrets picked up from the pages of Lillian Ross's book *Picture,* a publication that served as Furie's ad hoc "film school" in an age when film schools were rarefied entities isolated on the West Coast of the United States. *Picture,* now considered a landmark book of its kind, details the production of John Huston's 1951 film adaptation of Stephen Crane's *The Red Badge of Courage.* As it so happens, I believe that Stephen Crane shares a few significant things in common with Furie. For inasmuch as Crane was considered a paragon among American writers, adored by Hemingway and many of his contemporaries, he built much of his career on writing self-described "potboilers" and on occasional journalism as a means of stability. When one looks at his entire body of writings, it is only select works that stand out as aesthetically and historically meaningful, while a large portion of it was written for food and shelter, by his own admission.

This fusion in a life's work is one of extreme delicacy, and anyone who makes a livelihood involving any creative pursuit internalizes the fragile yin and yang between personal art and the demands of commerce. This conceit is, by now, a cliché. Furie, like others, is the first to admit, of his creations, that "some were made for love and others were made because I needed a job to support a huge family."

Stephen Crane once wrote, "Do not weep, babe, for war is kind," a sentiment later broadened (and perhaps completed) by legendary director John Ford's claim that "filmmaking is war." Samuel Fuller echoed the sentiment on his own accord. However, if you put that all together, you discover that filmmaking is, somehow, kind, even in the ironical sense that Crane intends. When one looks at Furie's life, he becomes nothing if not a testament to the truth of this compacted summary equation. His good fortune in the industry is enough to make any cub moviemaker yearn for it.

When the Director's Guild of Canada presented Sidney J. Furie with its Lifetime Achievement Award in 2010, it published a rare interview with him in its magazine, *Montage*. The title of the piece was nothing if not perfect: "Born to Film." When I read this title, I immediately thought of being seated in a restaurant with Sidney and his wife, Linda. Sidney aggressively takes a corner seat with a choice vantage point that scopes out the entire joint. With his kino-eye ever functioning, he often instructs me, "Remember, if you can, always get a restaurant seat that matches where you would put the camera if you were shooting a master shot of the location." Walking through a Beverly Hills mall, he explains the thrills of shooting in anamorphic wide screen and uses the food court there as a point of visual illustration. Although he may have been "born to film," he certainly was not born for publicity and putting himself "out there." It took a fair amount of convincing for him to agree to cooperate in the writing of this book.

One sunny and otherwise ho-hum afternoon in the fall of 2012, I received my first message from Sidney. About five months prior to this, I had written a lengthy article about his body of work, published on a blog. Startlingly, this first message read, "Haven't you anything better to do?" I read it at least three times. Again and again, the words echoed in my head.

"Haven't you anything better to do?" The blood drained out of my face as those words echoed through my synapses. As it turns out, actress Margot Kidder had shared my article with him on the set of the picture he was shooting just a few months before, *A Pride of Lions*. Even though I later learned that his initial message to me was sent sarcastically and in the spirit of self-deprecating humor, at the time I panicked and considered the question carefully. Later that same night, I was confronted with a similar question by my friend and ex-professor Paul Sylbert, an Academy Award–winning production designer who happened to be an old acquaintance of Sidney's from their days together at Paramount. Paul questioned me not because he doubted Sidney's talent, but because an endeavor like a book requires a reader's initial intrigue, which should be later compounded by sustained interest and loyalty to the text. What made Sidney J. Furie's story worth a whole book?

A cursory glance at Sidney J. Furie's eclectic résumé clearly reveals that he has dabbled in every genre in narrative cinema: musical, horror film, war film, biopic, Western, espionage thriller, drama from the school of kitchen sink realism, romantic comedy, romantic drama, action thriller, courtroom drama, screwball comedy, crime film, superhero film, melodrama, and so forth. Each film is a rapid departure from the previous one, and his genre-hopping has given him certain chameleon qualities and a career that laughs in the face of monotony. Chameleon filmmakers tackle sundry forms and styles, and the best of them braid the same thematic threads, yielding work that is singular and customized, with individual efforts that stand as director testaments. They often operate under the academic and critical radar relative to other directors who develop more perceptible stylization within consistent forms and genres. Finding the connecting fibers in these cross-genre works may strike one as a difficult task, but a slightly closer look reveals that Furie consistently examines a revolving door of themes, such as wounded masculinity, male collective group dynamics, duty and personal commitment, and the disparity between life's winners and losers.

Furie is most known for his visual style, having one time been faulted for "being the most obsessively clinical of modern directors" and making films that were "more interesting visually than dramatically." His brave and innovative use of mise-en-scène and, by extension, anamorphic wide screen, the "Scope" aspect ratio, challenges the often paradoxically restraining conventions of its usage. Furie's shot choices are more often than not elegant, deliberate, evocative, and calculated to heighten a given scene's dramatic intent in unexpected ways. His packed compositions also make for a more proactive viewership. From *The Young Ones* (1961) onward, Furie shoots most of his films in anamorphic widescreen, so there are many such examples to which I will refer in later chapters. He uses cinematic language eloquently and efficiently, standing among many directors who prove that an actor's contribution can be amplified with the way a camera is used. The dolly away from Rita Tushingham in a key point-of-view shot in *The Leather Boys* immediately leaps to mind. His sophisticated *découpage* (a French term with no exact equivalent in English, meaning "the choice of shots and their arrangement") also makes his work one-of-a-kind.

Yet, at the same time, one can imagine many an upright film scholar blanching at the mention of some of his later-career titles. Beginning in the late eighties and early nineties, he directed the Rodney Dangerfield vehicles *Ladybugs* and *My 5 Wives,* a pair of Dolph Lundgren action films, and the widely ridiculed *Superman IV: The Quest for Peace.* He is also responsible for *Iron Eagle* and two of its sequels. The old Hollywood adage claims, "You're only as good as your last hit." My own brother's immediate question to me was a valid one: "Does one mortgage true worth in this case by appraising the art along with the purely commercial ventures? How do you reconcile the stratified nature of the work when you're implicitly expected to examine all the films under the same lens?"

I also had a very personal stake in the case of Sidney J. Furie, as a filmmaker and as a film writer. One of my own first teenage amateur film projects mimicked a shot from *The Ipcress File.* It was undoubtedly the first shot from any film that I ever stole, and the first visual index to which I ever paid homage in my own work; it was the "eyeglass p.o.v." from the parking garage trade-off sequence.

Around age eleven, I caught an afternoon showing of *The Ipcress File* (1965) on Bravo. Yes, I am speaking of Bravo as it was circa 1995, when I could catch obscure gems like Albert Finney's *Charlie Bubbles* (1968), Irvin Kershner's *The Luck of Ginger Coffey* (1964), and Jack Gold's *The Bofors Gun* (1968), as well as established classics like Antonioni's *Blow-Up,* Andrei Tarkovsky's *Andrei Rublyev,* and Truffaut's *The 400 Blows.* All of the films I had seen on television around that time helped to define and open the door to a brand of cinematic language to which I had not been accustomed. For me, *The Ipcress File* was a top-tier example of artistry in this early cinema education, as valuable to me as the Antonioni, Tarkovsky, or Truffaut films.

In my reply to Sidney's original e-mail, I also essentially responded to the question that friend and mentor Paul Sylbert later posed to me. It ultimately took very little concerted effort to convince both Sidney and Paul of the endeavor's worth, although Sidney was never really looking to be convinced of my intentions. When he called me on the phone the day after our initial cyber exchange, we shared a good laugh about our introduction. Although Sidney has granted very few interviews throughout his career, has done little publicity for his films, and has saved no memorabilia of special note, his demeanor is complementary to the deep humanism he injects into even the genre pieces that often cannot afford such luxuries. Curiously a very private individual, Sidney opened himself up to me, and this book was thankfully born, as a biography and an analytical examination of Furie's directorial sensibility, one that French director and writer Bertrand Tavernier once referred to as "the most identifiable in the business."

As much as I want to take the reader through Furie's history in his own voice, I also seek to provide analysis of his work on a film-by-film basis: the triumphs, the various critics' lambastings, the same critics' love letters, the on-set struggles, the trade secrets, and the enduring secrets to Sid's success that have kept him working consistently for more than fifty years as a filmmaker. Sidney claims that he has not had a single unhappy day in the industry and that he never rued any of his projects or perceived career missteps. He is a testament to the fact that war is kind, filmmaking is war, and filmmaking is indeed "kind" (wink, wink). In even the roughest patches, he has surfed that fragile yin and yang that wrecks and ruins most artists, who cannot reconcile the demands of the balancing act. Whether one accepts or dismisses the claims made in this book about Sidney Furie's value as an artist, he still deserves attention for making work that is individual and often very unique. This book is a stab at giving the man and his corpus a fair shake. He deserves his day in court, and I believe it is long overdue.

Chapter 1

The Boy in His Own Company

It burned slowly, the script. But it was loud. The flames themselves were noiseless, but the rebel yell that the blackening pages symbolized made quite a tremendous din. Those who did not murmur were quieted to amazement by the chutzpah of the man who lit the match, the one who did the proverbial "honors." It was an "honor" because everyone hated the script, but no one really had the wherewithal to voice such an opinion, let alone act it out in such a manner. After all, they were in the employ of a stern, shoot-from-the-hip producer with an imposing physique, who, if he himself did not find the script high-quality, ventured simply to cash in on what it represented. The content—good, bad, or indifferent—embodied that most coveted of things: it was trendy. Now, it was all up in smoke.

The dark, olive-skinned *chutzpahdik,* one of the new reputed hotshots on the British film scene, was heard to bellow, "That's what I think of the script!" It was the first morning of shooting. There were other copies of that same script around, not that they would ever really come to use them . . . at least in that version. There would be rewrites, lest more public burnings should occur.

Every subsequent day of work, there were more rebel yells, in varying volume. Much to the beleaguered producer's chagrin, the whole thing was undergoing metamorphosis. It had been hijacked from a snazzy, quicksilver little B picture, a freely admitted imitation of something else, into something unusual, strange, arty, something that went on to nab major filmmaking awards and honors at the end of the year. The spy film had been elevated to the level of art. People fight the unknown, and the producer Harry Saltzman fought tooth and nail the upstart director he had hired. And so it went with director Sidney J. Furie and Saltzman on *The Ipcress File,* in the fall and winter of late 1964.

7

Furie never lost his moxie after his troubling sojourn with the maddened Saltzman. In fact, he never left home without it, and everyone with whom he has worked has remembered that about him, perhaps most of all. Remembrances of Sidney J. Furie, across the board, involve the words "energy," "dexterity" and "efficiency."

From his earliest youth, the need to make feature films was an obsession. There were no salad days spent directing theater, nor a lengthy tenure directing episodic television. While in college, at Carnegie Institute of Technology in Pittsburgh, Furie drew scoffs and derision when he staged an original one-act play entitled *The Young Don't Cry*, complete with background music. Future Beverly Hills Playhouse director Milton Katselas was among Furie's classroom peers. Theater professor Charles Moore stood up and turned to his students. "You're all laughing," he told them, "but Sidney wants to direct movies . . . and that is what he is going to do." And so the die was cast.

In May 1950, at Vaughan Road Collegiate High School in Toronto, Furie made his directorial debut, a production of John Patrick's play *The Hasty Heart*, a drama about the friendships among the patients at an army hospital in Burma. It was the first time a student had been given the opportunity to direct one of the school's stage productions, as this was a task usually left to the teacher. At the eleventh hour, the actor cast in the role of Yank, the character Ronald Reagan played in Vincent Sherman's 1949 film, came down with the mumps. In the grand tradition of the classic backstage movies of the thirties, Furie himself stepped into the role to salvage the production. During the first act, the confused actor playing the role of Blossom launched into his third-act lines. The woebegone student director improvised around his fellow actor's erroneous readings, proclaiming with a concealed wink-wink, "Blossom's not well. His mind is going, and we've got to restrain him," thus gently returning him to his first-act material.

"That was the first time I ever used improvisation," Sidney Furie remembers with a nostalgic laugh. It could indeed be considered a harbinger, as he later used improvisation extensively in large-scale film productions long before most studio directors dared to attempt such a thing. Furie shot *The Leather Boys*, *Lady Sings the Blues*, and other films in sequence to capitalize on building characters from the ground up and shaping the course of his stories with the performers' in-the-moment invention.

"My father once told me, 'I'm a dental technician and you have to work at a bench your whole life. I don't have time for lunch. If you make movies, you won't have to sit at a bench. You'll be able to go out to lunch, you'll have days off because you can't shoot every day, and you'll have a better life.'"

Sholom Joseph "Sidney" Furie was born in the downtown College Avenue section of Toronto on February 25, 1933, and grew up as an only child. Claims Furie, "No one ever called me Sholom. I was always Sidney, for some reason. I sometimes wonder if I should have kept the original name. Directed by Sholom J. Furie has a ring to it." Only when he moved away to college was the name on the birth certificate officially changed to Sidney Joseph Furie. Sidney's mother, Ann (née Tawil), and father, Samuel Furie, two Polish-Jewish immigrants, lived together as teenage sweethearts in the Polish village of Krinick, the population of which was predominantly Jewish. The Furie family, whose name is of French origin, had emigrated to Poland from France in 1840, after a series of pogroms occurred, coinciding with a blood libel known as the Damascus Affair, which included the ritual murder of a monk and the resulting accusation of eight prominent Damascus Jews. Those eight were imprisoned and tortured, and the Jews in Damascus bore the immediate brunt of the violent aftermath, but European Jews felt a very considerable impact. The repercussions of the Damascus Affair led to mass migration of Jews from their hostile homelands to other more hospitable nations. Ottoman authorities received support from England, Austria, and France for the systematic imprisonment, torture, and murder of their Jewish population; therefore the backlash proved to be the most palpable in these countries. Though hard evidence of persecution is lacking concerning the Furie ancestry, it is fair to assume that the Furie family's migration from France to Poland resulted from these events.

Ann Furie's maiden name, Tawil, has Sephardic Jewish origins in Syria, North Africa, and/or Iraq. Little is known about the background of Furie's mother beyond these few known facts, since precious little documentation exists of her family. Her own birth was undocumented, and thus her age was debatable, unknown even to her dying day. Her headstone, however, gives March 25, 1912, as her birthdate, making her about sixteen at the time of marriage to Samuel.

Samuel Furie's father, Yitzhak Furie, a pious man throughout his life, attended daily morning services at Krinick's synagogue. Samuel, who rejected his family's Jewish traditionalism, first arrived solo in Toronto in

1930, after marrying Ann. He was turned away from the United States; the last wave of American immigration had long since closed, in the early 1920s. Having a married sister in Montreal but wishing not to live in what he perceived as a strictly Francophone city, Samuel Furie set himself up in Toronto. He soon raised enough money from rolling cigars to import his new wife from Krinick to Toronto. Around the time of his son Sholom/Sidney's birth three years later, Samuel Furie took up a career as a dental technician. Both Samuel and Ann were fluent in Russian, Polish, Hebrew, and Yiddish, but they never spoke anything but English after arriving in Toronto, albeit with predictably heavy accents.

The year of Sidney Furie's birth coincided with a key event in Toronto Jewish history: the Christie Pits Riot of August 16, 1933, in which anti-Semitic and xenophobic "Swastika clubs" actively harassed the poor and working-class Jews at the Willowvale Park playground during a community baseball game, resulting in a skirmish. After this incident, Jewish Canadians seldom suffered other violent, widely reported altercations.

Although he attests to growing up in a loving, nurturing household, Furie admits that being the only child had its disadvantages, most of all a loneliness that was only to be expected. At age ten, when one of his school comrades, Elliot Collins, would boast to him about his "career" as a child radio actor, Furie evinced an interest in the same pursuit. He had been acting all along anyway, when left alone to his own devices; he resorted to inventing scenarios around a running ensemble of custom-made characters to quell his feelings of isolation. Through receiving an occasional child role in Canadian radio dramas, Furie first entered the world of his eventual calling. Acting did not keep him for very long, however.

"I remember sitting in a barbershop, hearing how Canadian soldiers had been shot down at Dieppe," says Furie, speaking of the 1942 Allied raid on the northern coast of France. Beyond this, one of Furie's most indelible memories is one that still troubles him today. On February 16, 1943, he laid eyes on screenwriting legend Ben Hecht's full-page notice in the *New York Times,* which brought Nazi Germany's worsening crimes against Jews front and center in the national consciousness. It read simply, "For Sale to Humanity: 70,000 Jews, Guaranteed Human Beings at $50 a Piece."[1] It was followed by another on August 30: "We All Stand before the Bar of Humanity, History and God . . . we will all be judged bloodguilty if we do not create the machinery to save the Jewish people of Europe." So introduced the wrinkle, the wet blanket, in the young Furie's newly sorrowed life. Throughout most of his childhood until then, he had found himself rapt in the joys of moviegoing. Now, harsh realities that the young Furie deeply internalized bled into his escapism with the newsreels that followed feature presentations. "I still recall seeing the first newsreels of the bodies in the camps," Furie says, his solemnity still potent as ever. "I knew I could never escape it. It's the darkest part of me. It is the shadow that has hung over me my entire life."

Although anti-Semitic intolerance and bigotry never directly plagued Furie's childhood in Toronto's upwardly mobile Cedarvale neighborhood, the Holocaust had an immeasurable effect on how he perceived the world from an early age. "What a great way to be set up for life! To know unspeakable horrors can be committed on a people of which you're part. For a sensitive person, the world is ugly, tough and not fair. I was very sensitive, very emotional, always reacted to things very strongly. Movies gave that ugly world that I knew the only happy ending. If you took that away, I don't know what I would have done growing up, knowing the horrors of the Holocaust. It was a very delicate balance." Cinephilia spawned early, and so did designs on the future. When Furie caught a showing of Victor Fleming's *Captains Courageous* (1937), starring Freddie Bartholomew and Spencer Tracy, in Niagara Falls around age six, it proved a formative experience. "My mother claims I left the theater saying that I wanted to be a movie director. I don't recall saying those exact words, but I just knew that I wanted to make movies."

Samuel opened the dental technician firm Posen & Furie with friend and associate Harry Posen, relocating at least three times during Sidney's early years. Posen & Furie Dental Laboratories Limited & Design still exists today in Toronto, as Dental Services Group of Toronto, under different management. Around the time the firm was established, Samuel and Ann Furie befriended podiatrist Dr. Oscar Brewton and his wife Leona "Madame" Brewton. The Brewtons, a black couple, had moved from Emerson, Ohio, after World War I to establish the Comfort Clinic of Podiatry on Yonge Street in downtown Toronto. Despite the social pressures at the time, the unabashedly progressive Furies never succumbed to a second thought about keeping them as social friends. "On *Lady Sings the Blues*," says Furie, "I'd be in meetings where everyone in the room was black. Of course I couldn't see myself and there were no mirrors. And a white person would come in and I'd think, 'God, they look pale!' That unassuming attitude is really spurred from being Canadian and growing up as the son of people like my parents. As a Canadian, I had little conception of all the racial troubles in the United States. We would just think, 'Why?' It seemed absolutely barbaric to us that, just south of the border, people were that backward."

Sidney Furie wanted to attend Upper Canada College, a prep school, for his high school education, seduced by the beauty of its facilities and the prospect of living independently away from home. However, owing to a strict Jewish quota at the time, he was not admitted, and he wound up attending Vaughan Road Collegiate beginning in 1947. "Vaughan Road was something like a New York City high school. It felt like every other student there was a juvenile delinquent." By the time he entered, he had started to consider a future in making feature films on a practical level. Playing hooky on Fridays was not an uncommon practice, as this was the day when new movies would arrive at the local Village Theater on Spadina Road in Toronto's Forest Hill Village. Contrary to the expected consequences of such a habit, Furie maintained good grades and eventually graduated near the top of his class.

Around that time, there had been a contest in the *Toronto Star* concerning ideas for a new Canadian flag. Furie saw one of the suggestions offered, a joke, as assuming a much larger meaning for the Canadian status quo. It was "the stars and stripes of Canada limited." Furie explains, "All the products in those days were Canada Limited. Heinz Ketchup of Canada Limited, Proctor and Gamble of Canada Limited. So, the stars and stripes of Canada Limited was a bitter bit of humor about our Canadian inferiority complex." The prevailing attitude was, If you're so good, why aren't you down in the States?

Movies and the world in which they were made were decidedly far away from the constipated, provincial Toronto that mythologized the movies. To them, movie stars were gods. "I remember my father pointing to some guy and saying, 'See him? He's in Hollywood movies!' It turns out that he had only been an extra, but he was still so impressed with the fact he was in a movie! You could see him briefly in the background in *Blossoms in the Dust,* with Greer Garson and Walter Pidgeon." Later, actor Sean Sullivan, Furie's friend and fellow movie buff, related his story of meeting actor Farley Granger backstage at the Royal Alexander Theater. Jostled in wonderment, Sullivan imparted a key bit of firsthand testimony to his younger friend: "Farley Granger actually went to the toilet just like we do!" Furie swears this exchange is true.

Though Furie now remembers such incidents and exchanges with nostalgia, they highlighted his motives for breaking out of Toronto after graduating from high school, while most of his friends and peers were attending the University of Toronto. The scope of his ambitions somewhat diluted when he selected the theater department of Pittsburgh's Carnegie Institute of Technology (now Carnegie Mellon University), in lieu of the University of Southern California and the University of California–Los Angeles, the only schools of the time that offered any film curriculum. Nonetheless, just the privilege of going away to school was enough. "It meant more money that had to be spent, trips back and forth, and all to encourage something that had no employment office and no guarantee of a job after it was all over. It goes to show you how totally without pressure my upbringing was."

At Carnegie Tech, Furie joined the Jewish fraternity Beta Sigma Rho, where he was elected the social chairman and shared a room for a time with future actor Alan Oppenheimer, who later starred in supporting roles in *In the Heat of the Night* and *Little Big Man*. "My father Fritz Friedlaender was Sidney Furie's fraternity brother at Beta Sigma Rho," says Dan Friedlaender, now a university film instructor himself. "He was three years Furie's senior and he remembered him as 'the hotshot from Toronto' because he had a notoriously confident sense of himself. My dad knew of his ambition to become a filmmaker, and he made it seem to me that it was known throughout the fraternity. Everyone apparently called him 'the hotshot.'"

Matriculating in the autumn of 1950, Furie opted to major in theater as a playwright because the student directors at Carnegie Tech had to also study as actors. His playwrighting instructor, Arthur Wilmert, who gained fame for translating and adapting *Antigone* for Broadway, "pounded" three-act structure into his students. "Wilmert preached that it was the best and, really, the only way to tell a story that would resonate with an audience, and also with aesthetes." Playwrighting majors in the early fifties could never totally distance themselves from curriculum dedicated to the art of directing, however, even if the attempt at distance was deliberate. Early on, Furie performed in a number of the school's productions, his most substantial role being "Tommy" in a freshman-class rendition of Eugene O'Neill's *Ah, Wilderness!* (Mickey Rooney had played the same part in Clarence Brown's 1935 film adaptation.) As his college years wore on, he shied away from the limelight in favor of smaller walk-ons (a Citizen of Venice in *The Merchant of Venice* and Call Boy/Sam in Clifford Odets's *Golden Boy*). By the time graduation loomed, he had retreated to mostly backstage work (as stage manager for Pirandello's *Six Characters in Search of an Author* and prop man for *The Corn Is Green*). Furie explains that the dwindling allure of his thespian ambitions went hand-in-hand with a dwindling interest in stage work in general: "My brain was always on movies movies movies."

Because his four years at Carnegie Tech coincided with the advent of Marlon Brando and the height of the Stanislavsky craze, Furie had Barry Farnol to instruct him on the ins and outs of the Method. In between these lessons on three-act structure and homilies about the new messianic figures of the Stanislavsky school, Furie took bus excursions to New York on a regular basis to catch the films and plays that expanded his education. Vincente Minnelli's *The Bad and the Beautiful* (1952) was a key text in this regard. "I saw that film over and over and over again when it was out in theaters," says Furie. "I would stay for many showings of it in a row. It was a formative experience because it was the only movie I could see on the subject of moviemaking, and what directors do, and what producers do, with people using big film equipment. This is all without mentioning the movie's story itself." As he neared graduation, *On the Waterfront* (1954) hit movie theaters. "If *The Bad and the Beautiful* primed me for greatness, *On the Waterfront* changed everything. It cannot be underestimated. The story truly meant something to me, and Brando was unspeakably, untouchably good. I dreamed of working with him one day." And over ten years later, he realized this goal.

While a student in Pittsburgh, Furie got himself into hot water when he started dating a girl from Squirrel Hill, a predominantly Jewish section of Pittsburgh, after meeting her at a mixer. "Rachel," a Pittsburgh native attending an all-girls school in North Carolina, dated Furie over the protests of her father, who believed that all theater students were homosexuals and Communists. When Furie clandestinely took a trip to visit her down in North Carolina, he arrived with the intention of eloping. Later, Furie's first feature film, *A Dangerous Age* (1957), told the tale of this misadventure in more precise terms. He never married "Rachel," and the whole affair did not end well, as is recounted in the film.

After graduating with a bachelor of fine arts degree, Furie returned to Toronto, cocksure in his presumption that he could walk into the Canadian Broadcasting Corporation headquarters and score a job. "It was on Jarvis and Carlton Streets. In those days, the hookers were below and the actors were above." Those who worked within the building affectionately referred to it as The Kremlin. When he entered, he was sent to the office of Gene Holman, the head of public affairs. Looking at the fresh-faced Furie, Holman informed him that he personally had nothing to offer him. However, on the basis of his education and the fact that he had bothered to return to Canada after getting a degree in the United States, Holman turned him over to Peter Francis, the CBC's head of film purchasing. Francis took a shine to the dark, handsome kid, and he handed him the task of screening two hundred Hollywood B movies. From this collection, Furie was told to select thirty to show on CBLT, the local Toronto station, for its afternoon *Movie Matinee* program. Officially, his job title was continuity writer, as he also was entrusted with providing spoken intros and outros for the films when they were shown.

Of these two hundred B movies, Furie recalls, "Many of them opened with 'Robert L. Lippert Presents' and a lot of them were directed by Andrew L. Stone. And Neville Brand acted in a lot of them. When these films shot interiors on sets, they were the worst damn sets you ever saw, and you could always tell where the lights were. And the lighting was always too hot. When they weren't using sets, they shot on real locations, usually around the streets of Los Angeles." Sitting in a cubicle watching two hundred low-budget movies was Furie's film school, along with the repeated viewings of *The Bad and the Beautiful* and reading Lillian Ross's *Picture*, the book that told the behind-the-scenes story of the making of John Huston's *The Red Badge of Courage*.

After successfully completing this job, Furie returned to Peter Francis for more work. The result was the first piece of celluloid the young aspiring filmmaker ever directed. Flown to the Muskoka Lakes area in Ontario to shoot a public service announcement about how to build a campfire and properly extinguish it, Furie then returned to Toronto to hear the bellyaching of angry, jealous CBC editors. "He's just a continuity writer! How did this kid get to direct something? We've been waiting to direct something well before this kid ever got here!" Other jobs surfaced. Soon, Furie was working as a writer, director, and occasional actor for live programs, such as *On Camera* and *The General Motors Theatre,* under the aegis of Sydney Newman, the supervisor of drama production and then one of the key figures at the CBC. *On Camera* was a half-hour show created for the purpose of encouraging Canadian writers, in that it provided an outlet for domestic television plays. Furie's contemporaries at the CBC then included future directors Norman Jewison, Harvey Hart, Silvio Narizzano, and Ted Kotcheff. Today, Kotcheff still credits Sydney Newman as his mentor.

Furie dated many young women when he returned to Toronto in glory, as a talent enlisted for steady employment in Canadian television. His specific memory on this matter is not especially vivid, but in June of 1956 he married Sheila Hiltz, the daughter of a businessman in the linen supply trade who also owned a dry-cleaning establishment. "We met at a party and we dated, and we did what kids did after having dated for awhile in that period: we got married. It was an Orthodox wedding. Her family was much more observant than my own, and they had a notice of the wedding published in the *Toronto Jewish News*." One of Furie's closest friends from the CBC, actor Don Borisenko, this time stepped into the role of best man.

Furie said of his new wife, "She couldn't have been happy when she found out that a nice, cushy job at the CBC couldn't hold me. I never stopped setting my sights on the 'impossible dream' of feature filmmaking."

Chapter 2

Colonizing a Wilderness

If I ask, "What is the tragedy of Canadian cinema?," what answer comes
to mind? That Mary Pickford, Mack Sennett, Sidney Furie and Norman
Jewison have all left this fair country of ours?
—*Pierre Véronneau, "Canadian Film: An Unexpected Emergence"*

Martin Knelman poses a pervasive question in his book *This Is Where We
Came In: The Career and Character of Canadian Film.* "How can one
explain that Canadians have been content to exist for most of the twentieth
century without films of their own, while living next to a country whose
movies have culturally colonized the world?" As a Toronto-born would-be
filmmaker striving to make things happen for himself and for his prospective projects in the largely complacent Ontario of the 1950s, Sidney Furie
quickly found himself up against a wall, thanks to popular habits bred by
both national apathy and self-deprecation on a grand scale. Knelman continues, "The theater chains and distribution companies were mostly con-
trolled by foreign interests, which meant that even if a good Canadian film
did get made, there was no way of guaranteeing it a chance to reach audiences."[1] The National Film Board of Canada, for its part, seemed to exclusively sponsor animated and live-action narrative shorts, and
documentaries of no more than an hour in length.

Many separate claims have been made as to which film and, by exten-
sion, which filmmaker set up shop first in the virtual wilderness of
Canadian cinema in the 1950s and 1960s. As Toronto International Film
Festival director Piers Handling writes, "Our best talent, people like
Norman Jewison, Ted Kotcheff, Sidney Furie, Silvio Narizzano and Arthur
Hiller, all moved into television, before leaving the country to make feature films, and their fortunes, elsewhere. An entire generation of our young
filmmakers left due to an unhospitable production climate, leaving a huge
gap."[2]

The generation to which Handling alludes has been termed in other sources "the lost generation of Canadian filmmakers,"[3] or rather "the men that got away." As a result, the fifties was "a decade of erratic production, magnificent short films and departing directors," with the answer to the question "Who was the trail-blazer, and with what film?" appearing difficult to answer. Handling writes, "The only exception was Sidney Furie, who before leaving in 1959 [sic], never to return, made two fresh, low-budget features."[4] In 1956 and 1957, Sidney J. Furie defied the odds stacked against a would-be Canadian independent filmmaker in producing *A Dangerous Age* with Canadian money, with Canadian actors, with a Canadian crew, well before others produced films that they claimed were the first such effort. Not only did Furie achieve this, but, unlike William Davidson, who made *Now That April's Here* independently in Ontario in 1958, he also got the films distributed outside of Canada.

Ted Kotcheff, one of Furie's contemporaries at the CBC, remembers, "Sidney was one of our real crackerjack writers. You could rely on him in the clutch. But he was restless. He really wanted to be directing . . . and beyond that, he really wanted to be making feature films."

The first original script Furie wrote for the CBC was a roman à clef, the story of two Canadian college students who are in love and wish to marry. They cross the American border and plan to return home to present their parents with a fait accompli. Their mutual fear of marriage and commitment manifests itself in a variety of ways throughout their twenty-four hours of trying to outsmart their surrounding elders to accomplish this bold, daring scheme. When the two kids come up against a female registry clerk who realizes that the underage Nancy's birth certificate is forged, they find themselves on the run from the police, the college authorities, and Nancy's parents. Framed around the couple's thwarted attempt, the script was closely based on Furie's own misadventure in attempting to marry "Rachel" while attending college in Pittsburgh.

The CBC agreed to produce it as a television play under the title *The Runaways* but declined his request to direct the show. Under the direction of Henry Kaplan, the *Philco Playhouse* production, starring New York import Burt Brinckerhoff, was aired in September 1956. Although handsomely paid one thousand dollars for his writing, which was a sizable sum for a novice CBC writer in those days, Furie lamented the results. He itched to see the script succeed as a feature-length production. With no public funds available, however, this proved a tall task.

I don't remember if people thought I was crazy for wanting to do it on my own. I didn't care then, and I don't care now. I had seen those two-hundred B movies for Peter Francis. I saw where they put the lights. It didn't look tough. I had been an assistant to the producer on a synch-sound set, for a documentary about the Canadian Army, so I knew what to do for sound. I had seen the big movie about making movies, *The Bad and the Beautiful*, many times over. I read Lillian Ross's *Picture*. I knew what I had to do.

Venturing to New York as he often did, Furie cast Ben Piazza, a twenty-one-year-old California-born Actor's Studio graduate who had just made his professional off-Broadway debut in the play *Too Late the Phalarope*. Piazza went on later to a career as a character actor in television and popular films such as *The Bad News Bears* (1976), *The Blues Brothers* (1980), and *Mask* (1985). Starring opposite Piazza was Anne Pearson, a bright-eyed nineteen-year-old who was then fresh off a supporting turn in a Broadway production of Arthur Laurents's *A Clearing in the Woods* (which closed on February 9, 1957, after only thirty-six performances); she disappeared from film and television after her star role in *A Dangerous Age*. When Furie's father agreed to invest twenty-nine thousand Canadian dollars of his life savings in the production, a National Film Board sound recordist and the cinematographer Herb Alpert were recruited for the technical ends. Additional funds were raised from friends and other contacts, with three thousand dollars being the largest from one of these contributors. Beginning on August 9, 1957, Furie shot in just nine days in near-total secrecy. The negative of the newly retitled *A Dangerous Age* was delivered to a Toronto laboratory that had never processed 35mm motion picture film before.[5] This was only the dawn of the chronic grief the budding filmmaker was to encounter.

As Furie mounted the editing of the film, his wife Sheila informed him that he was about to become a father. With this life-altering disclosure, the film-in-progress's success became all the more necessary. With an eighty-six-minute first assembly edit of *A Dangerous Age* completed in September 1957, Furie's struggle to give the film life was far from over. When he announced the film's completion to the Toronto press on November 26, 1957, he declared his intention to make one Canadian feature film per year. Of *A Dangerous Age,* he told columnist Jack Karr, "I said nothing about the movie while it was in production simply because I wanted to get it finished and not have it blow up in my face."[6] For his follow-up, he pursued adapting John Gray's controversial play *Bright Sun at Midnight,* about the suicide of a Canadian ambassador to Egypt, which was then being staged at Toronto's Crest Theatre.

When one of Samuel Furie's friends, a man who had connections in the world of film distribution, agreed to look at the film, which by then had been trimmed down to a length of sixty-nine minutes, the verdict could have scarcely been more discouraging: "Throw it in the garbage! It will never play in any Canadian theater. Save yourself some aggravation." Though he was hopeful of selling the film, Furie was realistic about its prospects, telling the *Toronto Star,* "It's not an epic but I think it's a good entertainment feature for the double bills."[7] Making the rounds in New York by hauling the print from office to office, he encountered Irvin Shapiro (who pronounced his surname Sha-pie-roh). Shapiro ran a distribution outfit called Films Around the World, which developed specialized theaters for foreign films. Shapiro helped to end the American boycott of German films after World War II. He agreed to pay half of thirty thousand dollars for the picture in partnership with Eliot Hyman, president of Seven Arts.

Shortly after the birth of his son Daniel on January 31, 1958, Furie took a 35mm print in his suitcase to sell the film in London. Silvio Narizzano, a chum from the CBC who had emigrated there to work for Granada Television, invited Furie as his guest for the duration of his stay. Narizzano informed him that Granada owned theaters in London independent of the two main British distribution circuits ABC and Rank. When Narizzano himself screened *A Dangerous Age* for the Granada buyer, Furie was not present. When the film was recommended for pickup, Ingram Fraser of Films de France, another distributor that imported foreign films, agreed to represent it on Rank's Gaumont circuit. Flying Sheila and newborn son Daniel over to join him in London, Furie spent a number of months in 1958 unsuccessfully trying to score a second picture there. Around this time, he chanced to meet Kenneth Harper, a producer who greatly admired *A Dangerous Age* and respected Furie as a ripe young talent to keep an eye on. Although he had nothing to offer him at the time, Harper played a key role in Furie's life some years later.

With a one-thousand-dollar profit from his American sale, Furie reimbursed his father for the original twenty-nine-thousand-dollar cost of production and watched as the movie was taken to the Cannes Film

Festival Market, which was then only in its second year. "No one came to that screening," says Furie. "I had that empty feeling in the pit of my stomach. I was returning back from Cannes feeling discouraged, but the people on the plane with me asked me about my picture. They looked it up in the English papers and that was the first time I saw the title of one of my films printed anywhere." Opening on England's Gaumont circuit on September 22, 1958, *A Dangerous Age* was double-featured with a J. Arthur Rank adventure film quite ironically titled *Sea Fury* (1957).

"The review in London's Sunday Times was the best. 'Only 24 years old, but what a filmmaker!' I'll never forget those words." Although the film did draw reviews that were often incongruous raves, the most reasoned ones came from people like Penelope Houston, who reviewed it in the British Film Institute's *Monthly Film Bulletin*. She conjectured that it was "probably the first Canadian feature to rate serious criticism," adding that, "as a first film, and from a country where so little has been done in the feature field, *A Dangerous Age* seems distinctly encouraging." In *Films and Filming*, Peter John Dyer called the picture "simple and unpretentious." Citing its "honesty, enthusiasm, courage and freshness" did not soften Dyer's candor in also branding it "amateurish, immature and thin." However, he ended his review respectfully stating, "Above all, I suppose, I like its independence." In *Sight & Sound*, Derek Hill called it "a welcome film" that "cost rather less than most British second features." However, Hill's hopeful claim that the film's London success "already encouraged a serious consideration of the possibilities of feature production in Canada" could not have been further from the truth, as its director was to rediscover later.

Another reviewer wrote about Canada giving chances to a young director, whereas in reality, Furie had to take what he could get. Although receiving favorable notices at the Venice and Cannes Film Festivals, *A Dangerous Age* still failed to find a Canadian distributor. In the United States, Hyman and Shapiro eventually sold the film in November 1959 to the Chicago-based Modern Film Distributors on a "states-rights basis" (i.e., sold to individual U.S. states for exhibition in theaters as a second feature). Today, its status in Canadian film history is one of respect rather than renown. Few know or care enough to acknowledge it as a milestone in the country's national cinema. It was, however, programmed regularly on Canadian public television throughout the 1970s, later to be preserved by the Canadian National Film Archive.

The quick turnaround and birth of *A Dangerous Age* are all the more remarkable for having been completed at a time when John Grierson, one of the fathers of the Canadian film industry, had long since fallen from grace, having relocated to Paris in 1947 after being implicated in an espionage scandal for which he was brought before the Kellock-Taschereau Royal Commission hearings ("Our McCarthy hearings," Piers Handling calls them).[8] Grierson's answers before the commission were curt and evasive, and his dismissal from questioning blackened his reputation for some time. This, among other things, had driven Grierson's high aspirations for the future of Canadian cinema into the ground. Meanwhile, the other Canadian cinema luminary, Budge Crawley, labored away at the NFB producing avant-garde short and documentary films. Though the contributions of both are substantial and their heroic status is rightfully guaranteed in Canada, no precedent had been set by either of them for Furie to follow.

Canadian film scholar and critic Gerald Pratley acknowledges *A Dangerous Age* as "an honest little picture" that "holds an important place in the development of English-language films in Canada."[9] Technically, it is a ragged, flawed film, prone to flubbing eyeline, screen direction, and rules of staging for camera. However, it deflects these flaws with a robust sense of purpose. Furie knows the story he wants to tell and is incredibly economical about the whole affair, keeping himself in check to tell it straight and without much in the way of ornament. Beyond its technicality as a Canadian picture, it is a film with a distinct Canadian character. Canadian film historian Steve Gravestock keenly observes that because *A Dangerous Age* ends with a large, proud title card stating "Made in Canada," "One gets the sense that if the film were American, David and Nancy probably would have succeeded in their quest."[10] Even though the film is based on Furie's experience in the United States and there is no explicit mention of Canada in the dialogue, it is still possible to read the film as a text about what it means to be shortchanged in the disenfranchised Canada of the time. In his tense encounter with a gruff, cowboy-like lawman who puts a wrinkle in the couple's plans to elope, the "gentle Canadian" David lectures him about Magna Carta and attempts to reason with him on the matter. For his trouble, he is smugly and dismissively referred to as "Smart Boy" for the rest of the picture, and the officer curtly deems their quest "a case of hot pants." Even before David and Nancy's troubles foment, they are sabotaged by the terminally small-minded people they encounter, such as the post office clerk who asks if David would not prefer to buy stamps instead of a marriage license, then laughs heartily at his dead-on-delivery attempt at humor.

In Furie's mind, *A Dangerous Age* is set in a country that, at that point in history, "could have died from quaint." And if the figures that David and Nancy encounter are not so, they are colorless or hidebound. When met with failure at the end, as Nancy dumps him for the benefit of her concerned parents, David takes with him a piece of soil as a souvenir. "As a writer," the character says, "this pain ought to do me some good." The pain, ultimately, is in being a "think-big Canadian" kept on a short leash in the Canada of the 1950s, crippled by Weltschmerz (defined by the *Merriam-Webster Unabridged Dictionary* as "mental depression or apathy caused by comparison of the actual state of the world with an ideal state; sentimental pessimism") and the provinciality of a stiff-necked class of people with no sympathy for those who see beyond their station in life. Although Furie's most pervasive theme did not begin to emerge until his next picture, the addled, anxiety-ridden David's struggle to assert himself as a man to the various figures casting doubts on his intentions helped pave the way toward a larger thematic concern. Marriage is the means by which David can be recognized as a man rather than a boy. More than that, it is the means by which he can break out of his by-the-book Canadian cage.

A lack of response from Hollywood talent scouts and lack of interest in Canada made Furie rather glum about his future in the film industry. As a living example of the hope for a Canadian independent cinema, *A Dangerous Age* had failed to set the disenfranchised country on fire, in spite of the film's modest success abroad. He now had a firmer grasp of the staggering odds stacked against him in his ambitious attempts to galvanize a base of English Canadian feature filmmakers. With a new family to provide for, there was now a sense that his efforts had to translate into practical results. That his work had been rejected by the spectators that mattered most to his future made him consider an alternate career path.

Knowing a friend who had gone to Harvard Law School after likewise getting a bachelor of fine arts degree, Furie applied to Osgoode Hall, the oldest and, at that time, the only law school in Toronto. Scoring an interview in the spring of 1958, he was told that his degree in drama did not properly qualify him. "I was stunned. I pleaded to this guy, 'But my buddy got into Harvard Law with a bachelors of fine arts! I was a drama student! Lawyers need to be dramatic, right?' That showed me I had to get out of

Canada, somehow, because there was that whole Canadian mentality again . . . always the fear that we were not going to measure up, that we weren't going to be good enough. It's what we grew up with." He then applied to Hebrew Union College in Cincinnati, Ohio, with the intent of entering the Reform rabbinate. According to Furie, many of his boyhood heroes growing up were the Reform rabbis he came to know personally from his family's local synagogue. When he arrived in Cincinnati for the interview, though, he was outwardly warned off. "This guy at Hebrew Union told me, 'You make movies and shows, right? You can touch more lives doing that than standing in front of a crowd as a pulpit rabbi giving a sermon.' It was a very forward statement. He didn't even waste any time trying to get to the bottom of why I might have wanted to become a rabbi. It was an in-and-out appointment."

His last option seemed more of an open door. "I had a friend whose father was a builder. He said to me, 'We have an option on six lots in North Toronto and we're going to build some houses.' And I have always known that if I built those houses, I'd be super rich today. Even if you were stupid and built houses in the Toronto of then, you would have been rich by the mid-seventies." Needless to say, Furie demurred. He realized that a once-bitten-and-twice-shy attitude about the profession in which he had the most training and experience failed to make practical sense. He went back to the drawing board . . . and back to the CBC.

Not all efforts on *A Dangerous Age* were in vain, as Furie soon discovered. As reward for the very act of completing a feature-length independent picture, United Artists Television hired him to direct episodes of the Canadian Western adventure series *Hudson's Bay,* a saga about fur trappers starring Hollywood actor Barry Nelson. The producers of the show were grousing that the director of the first six episodes, Alvin Rakoff, had been taking more days than necessary to complete his shooting. Remembers Furie, "The first episode of the show I did, they gave me three days to do it, and I had the footage back to them in two, because I was looking to impress them. They told me, 'Take three days but do close-ups.' I had done the whole thing in medium shots to save time." Eventually, Furie came to helm twenty-nine episodes, throughout 1957 and 1958. The time on *Hudson's Bay* became the bedrock of Furie's filmmaking education, because he met his most valuable mentor while working on those episodes.

Eugen Schüfftan, a German-Jewish refugee of the war who at the time was around age sixty-five, was a veteran cinematographer who had shot feature films in Hollywood, France, Italy, and elsewhere. "He taught me everything. He taught me ways of cheating shots in ways that I have driven script girls and camera operators nuts over the years." Known for inventing an optical process for special effects that had revolutionized the industry, Schüfftan and his bag of shooting tricks informed Furie's workflow. One of these tricks included reversing the actors in a two-shot and changing the background mise-en-scène to make viewers think they were seeing another side of a room. This allowed the director to save valuable lighting and setup time. Although relatively advanced in age, Schüfftan's surprising vigor inspired everyone on the set, especially the young director. "If we had to get to the top of a hill or climb some rocks to get a shot, he was always the first to the top, and he would sprint up there," says Furie. Schüfftan went on to become the cinematographer of *The Hustler* (1961).

The assistant director on these shows was Tommy Thompson, who later became a member of Robert Altman's stock crew. Altman, at the time, was shooting the show *Whirlybirds* in California for the same production company. The executive producer of both shows, Dick Steenberg, once told Furie, "I've got two guys working for me, you and Altman, who are going to make it in this world." Television producer Carey Wilber spoke of Furie to the Canadian press with abandon: "That kid has so much talent, it's positively frightening. I'll lay any odds that within five years he'll be one of the biggest names in the film business."[11] Wilber, learning that Furie was a favorite director among the cast and crew of *Hudson's Bay*, offered him the chance to "pinch-hit," as it were, as director for his ailing television drama *Troubleshooters* (for which Robert Altman had also directed episodes), starring Keenan Wynn as the ringleader of a construction crew that specializes in difficult and often dangerous projects. For reasons that are unclear, Furie never rendered any services on the series, which was canceled after only a year on the air.

With his father's investment in *A Dangerous Age* fully returned, and a fatherly confidence affirmed, the reticent Furie set his sights on another Toronto-based feature-film project. Thinking that somehow he had shortchanged his first film's commercial potential for Canadian audiences and exhibitors, the director vowed in an unpublished interview with cub reporter Clive Denton that he would never again make "a film with so few selling angles." He compared *A Dangerous Age* unfavorably to Nicholas Ray's directorial debut *They Live by Night*, a 1948 noir about a "23-years-young" convict on the lam with the woman who becomes his lover, stating that he should have had his character David rob a service station. "The public likes a bit of crime with their sociology,"[12] he told Denton. With this, Furie abandoned his earlier plans to translate John Gray's earnest, topical play *Bright Sun at Midnight* to the screen for his next project and proved that his learning curve was indeed swift. It was at least partly out of this would-be epiphany that his follow-up effort, *A Cool Sound from Hell*, was born.

Furie was a semiregular in the nascent jazz and Beat subcultures in Toronto during his time at the CBC. Speaking of his Toronto social life, Furie recalls, "Culturally, there wasn't a whole lot in 1950s Toronto, but there was always Clem Hambourg's. I was there a lot. How that place stayed open, I'll never know." Furie is referring to the House of Hambourg, an all-night jazz club. Clement "Clem" Hambourg, a London-born musician and promoter, opened the now-defunct establishment with his wife, Ruth, in 1946. CBC composer Phil Nimmons, a Juilliard graduate who provided the score for *A Dangerous Age* and ultimately did the same for *A Cool Sound from Hell*, also frequented. Remembers Nimmons, "Musicians would play at other clubs like Towne Tavern or the Silver Rail. After they played their sets there, they would come to House of Hambourg and jam for hours on end. People would sit there and hang till sunrise. [Jazz legends] Oscar Peterson and Maynard Ferguson were two of the visiting artists."

Another popular hangout existed at the home of Bill Davis, a variety show director at the CBC. Frequenters of his get-togethers included Furie, future experimental filmmaker jazz guitarist Ed Bickert, painter Harold Town, Michael Snow (a painter in those days), and a parade of other artists and musicians. Snow and Furie were early veterans of Graphic Associates Films, Toronto's first private animation studio, founded by animators George Dunning and Jim McKay. Graphic Associates opened its doors circa 1950 to produce documentary and short subjects. It folded in 1956 and closed its doors. Michael Snow remembers, "I was in the animation department while Sidney was working as a crew member on their Canadian military documentary." This 1955 documentary was Furie's first experience with sync-sound production.

Beyond this superficial familiarity, it was Furie's own involvement with a drug-running hipster girlfriend that most profoundly informed his scripting. Sometime in 1954, a friend of Samuel Furie's, a member of the Royal Canadian Mounted Police, alerted him that his son was dating a girl who was under surveillance for her illicit activities. "This happened about four years before I married Sheila, just around the time I first got back to Toronto from Pittsburgh. I knew this girl from these all-night jazz circles. My dad, needless to say, was very worried about the whole thing, but just told me to be careful. The club in the movie is based on Hambourg's and the main character in the film is based on me, even though the real story is nowhere near as lurid as the movie story. But *A Cool Sound from Hell* is just as autobiographical as *A Dangerous Age*."

With all of this informing the backdrop of this proposed new film, another roman à clef, Furie embarked on a script, fueled by a fresh proclivity toward more provocative, action-oriented storytelling. Initially titled *The Young and the Beat*, *A Cool Sound from Hell* tells the tale of a postcollege "little-boy-lost" named Charlie, Furie's new avatar, who is seduced into a soul-crushing world of Beat poets, all-night jazz, and drug-running. Behind Charlie's corruption is a sexy young woman named Steve, who has an overzealous taste for a good time and an open disregard for words like "love." By the end of film, Charlie is humiliated and beaten down by these Beats. He realizes that his happiness rests with the nice, straight-arrow girl Debbie, who has pined away for him while he has agonized over trying to figure himself out.

While the drug angle proved to be its most provocative element, the script (which opens with a voice-over stipulating that the film was made "not to shock but to inform") also granted him the opportunity of countering critics' allegations that he cowered away from exploring the sexual fears and desires of the young couple in *A Dangerous Age*. In response, *A Cool Sound from Hell* provided a freer depiction of (suggested) sex between couples "living in sin" with no strings attached. Gerald Pratley, considering *A Cool Sound from Hell* in this historical context, writes, "Few films at the time, even those from Hollywood, touched on young, unmarried couples living together."[13]

A surfeit of Beat-speak, a dense slang with an inflective affectation, saturates much of the dialogue. Characters refer to each other colloquially as "dad" or "cat" and liberally use hip idioms like "Endsville" (meaning "the ultimate") and "crazy" (meaning "cool") in sentences that often end in the slang directive "man." "People may look at that part of it as campy nowadays, but that is really how people talked in that world," Furie says, defending the dialogue's realism and fidelity to the era. "Frankly, I even used to talk that way a bit."

As with *A Dangerous Age,* Furie once again crossed the border on an expedition to find a New York–trained actor who could step into the shoes of the Charlie character, preferably one who studied under Lee Strasberg. His earlier mention of Nicholas Ray's *They Live by Night* proved ironic (and perhaps a self-fulfilling prophecy) when he wound up casting Ray's son Anthony "Tony" Ray, an Actor's Studio–trained performer, in the lead role of Charlie. The dark, intense Tony Ray had been submerged in acting work throughout 1958 in both television roles and John Cassavetes's directorial debut *Shadows.* Despite his "Introducing" credit in *A Cool Sound from Hell,* Ray had previously played small roles in Anthony Mann's *Men in War* and his father's *The True Story of Jesse James.* He also understudied for Timmy Everett in Elia Kazan's production of William Inge's *The Dark at the Top of the Stairs.*

"I must say that Sid's view of the Beats is not the one I remember," says Tony Ray. "I don't know much about the Toronto scene, but the New York Beat scene was segregated. The artists were one group, and the druggies were a separate cult. The two actually didn't mingle all that much." Of Toronto at that time, he observes, "I felt the city had been built before it had a need for it. There were tall buildings and nobody on the streets. All it had was just a couple good places to eat and some good jazz." When agreeing to do *A Cool Sound from Hell,* Ray had to exercise his contractual leave of absence from a daytime soap opera called *Search for Tomorrow.*

Continues Ray, "Cassavetes was able to work around the soap, which had a rehearsal time of 8:00 to noon, with a noon airtime. John knew I got another film in Canada, so he had to bite the bullet and continue to work around all that." Ray remembers precious little of his time shooting *A Cool Sound from Hell,* but acknowledges one thing as indelible:

> When I arrived in Toronto, Sid would show up where I was staying, at this shared apartment, on a daily and sometimes multidaily basis. He was omnipresent, very intent on coaching me about every aspect of the day's work, because I still felt incredibly unprepared stepping onto this set. I also always felt the locations were too dark. But at that point, I hadn't met a director who was as omnipresent as that. I also remember riding in a car with Sid when he would go to visit his newborn son. He seemed to juggle it all pretty effectively. I admired him for it, actually.

Plumbing the *Hudson's Bay* casting pool, Furie brought on actors from episodes he had directed to fill out the rest of his cast. Writing more speaking parts into *A Cool Sound from Hell,* as well as scenes with extras, meant that Furie's budget would see a definite increase from *A Dangerous Age,* and his father this time scored him fifty thousand Canadian dollars for the picture. Selecting a union crew also influenced the price-tag hike. On top of that, Furie also wished to employ a more mobile camera, and he itched to use the real streets of Toronto. Future Canadian feature filmmaker Don Owen, then a stagehand and apprentice writer at the CBC, played an uncredited Beat poet and occasionally acted in the capacity of assistant director. He reduces the whole affair to "an imitation Hollywood B-movie" that was made with the excuse that Furie "just wanted to go to Hollywood."[14]

Shooting on a ten-day schedule commenced at Julian Roffman's Meridian Film Studios in November 1958, as Roffman himself was shooting *The Bloody Brood,* another picture about the Toronto branch of the Beat Generation. Roffman's story, though set predominantly in Beat clubs, lent itself more to genre classification and revolved around a "thrill murder" perpetrated by a Beatnik drug peddler. Meridian, built inside the old Community Theatre building on Woodbine Avenue, just south of Mortimer Avenue, had been involved with creating prefeature theater advertisements, documentaries, short subjects, and television programs before expanding into feature films. On *The Bloody Brood,* Roffman was directing a young, unknown Peter Falk in the murderous lead. Tony Ray, for his part, does not recall his friend Falk's presence in Toronto. "It could have been because we were each focused on our individual pictures," Ray reasons.

Tony Ray, described in Patrick McGilligan's book on Nicholas Ray as sweet, volatile, and at times a hell-raiser, cruised all-night bongo parties with James Dean as a teenager. Attending these functions had an additional purpose: Nick was using young Tony ("a Plato of sorts," referring to the Sal Mineo character in *Rebel without a Cause*)[15] to woo Dean to play the lead in his film. In Tony Ray's own words, "I wet my teeth with the Beats, because Dean and I hung out for quite some time in New York and Los Angeles. The two of us, with Marty Landau and others, would hit up Jerry's, a New York bar on 54th and Sixth, not to mention the Five Spot with Stan Getz in the Village, and Birdland." Later, Ray's time as a Broadway actor and understudy also inducted him into circles that were never too far from the one that Charlie starts to inhabit in Furie's film. "Those were all-night benders with artists, actors, writers, musicians," continues Ray. The actor's time working under the aegis of Cassavetes on *Shadows* trained him in the finer points of shooting in public spaces without permits, as Furie was equally apt to do. There was but a single schedule conflict involving Tony Ray's involvement with John Cassavetes's *Shadows*. When Furie needed to reshoot a couple scenes, he had to negotiate a return for Ray that did not interfere with the Cassavetes schedule.

According to Furie, the *Cool Sound* cast and crew were largely unaware of Tony Ray's headline-making affair with stepmother Gloria Grahame, which ended his father's second marriage in 1952. Furie himself had been only peripherally aware of these messy personal matters.

Sheila Furie gave birth to their second son, Noah, on January 16, 1959, right at the outset of editing. By the spring of 1959, Furie moved his base of operation to a studio-cum-lab off Toronto's Dundas Street West. In April, as *A Dangerous Age* was to be shown at the Toronto Film Society, Clive Denton observed that he was "glad the Film Society had chosen to present *A Dangerous Age*" but that he was "pissed off that nobody else had shown interest in it."[16] During weekdays, the inundated (but newly popular) director worked from eight in the morning to six-thirty at night shooting *Hudson's Bay,* then spent the evening at his typewriter fixing the next day's script. He spent only weekends completing *A Cool Sound from Hell.* While Denton sat shadowing him in the editing room, Furie expressed concern that an actress was showing the outline of a breast rather markedly in an unedited scene he was running. On his next personal project, *During One Night,* in 1961, Furie shed his prudishness about on-screen nudity.

Upon the completion of *A Cool Sound from Hell* in November 1959, a month after Julian Roffman delivered his final cut of *The Bloody Brood,* Furie flew again to London to sell and distribute his picture. Dudley Sutton, a British actor who later became a close friend, says, "I didn't know Sid at the time, but he told me later about how he literally hauled these cans of film around SoHo on his own looking for a distributor for *A Cool Sound from Hell.*"

When he took the negative to Ingram Fraser at Films de France, hoping for a pickup that repeated the one for *A Dangerous Age,* Furie was introduced to a striking, swarthy man of forty-one named Kenneth Rive, the son of a German cameraman. Rive, a onetime child actor, grew up in Berlin and set up Galaworld Films in 1952 to distribute mostly foreign-language films. Among other things, he was credited for first exhibiting *The 400 Blows* to British audiences. "Ken was always very well turned out, and wore a boutonnière," says Furie, adding that "a top hat or a bowler wouldn't have been unbecoming to his ensemble." Rive immediately agreed to purchase the distribution rights for *A Cool Sound from Hell,* for sixty thousand pounds, and Furie's father once again made his money back. Galaworld released the film to British theaters in February 1960, to some critical acclaim and respectable box office considering its status as a B picture.

Britain's *Monthly Film Bulletin,* while branding the film "too reminiscent of similar ventures in its thin and routine plot," observed that Furie "promisingly combines a sensitive awareness to atmosphere with a feeling for contemporary dialogue and mood" and found the photography to be "suitably harsh and evocative." In the *Sunday Times,* Dilys Powell counted the film's "immaturity and reliance on gimmicks" as deficits and its "ingenuity, style and surprising sensitivity" as assets. Though Canadian film historians and those involved remember the other reviews as approving, those reviews are nowhere to be found today in print. It is fair to assume that not many existed in the first place, because of the film's status as a second feature. *Films and Filming,* however, did mention *A Cool Sound from Hell* in a 1962 profile piece about Furie, as a means of defining him as a filmmaker that exuded youth and vitality.[17] Writing about the film as an important piece of his own country's cinematic history, Gerald Pratley remarks, "Lively and knowingly, this low-budget, homemade-looking film captures [the character's] mood and feelings, and those of the people around him."[18]

Don Owen is less upbeat about the final product, however. In 2005 he told his biographer Steve Gravestock, "I know what [*A Cool Sound from Hell*] is like. I've seen it. I'm in it. I'm so glad it's lost. I'm so relieved."[19] Tony Ray, composer Phil Nimmons, and most of the other cast and crew members never were able to see the final product upon completion.

A Cool Sound from Hell had been a missing piece from any serious study of Furie's work since its initial release. Finding a copy originally proved impossible, as source materials for it, both film prints and negative, had long since vanished, even though Internet vendor sites like Barnes & Noble and Best Buy offered a DVD of generic NASA space shuttle footage that falsely claimed to be the film. The Library of Congress possessed only a record of its previous existence. The Canadian National Archives, while having restored and housed a print of *A Dangerous Age,* had nothing what-soever on *A Cool Sound from Hell.*

The odds continued to stack more and more against the film's having survived intact. Don Owen's printed claims attested to this, while Ted Kotcheff told me that Piers Handling, a leading authority concerning films shot in Toronto, had exhausted his search for it as well. Other Internet sources likewise used the word "lost" to designate its status.[20] It had van-ished without a trace, its memory clouded by decades of disinterest that made forgetting a foregone conclusion. The only remnant was a British Pathé newsreel that captured the queue around the block at a London the-ater showing *Saturday Night and Sunday Morning* advantageously paired with *A Cool Sound from Hell.*

On May 1, 2013, the British Film Institute, responding to a search request, returned with news that they had located the master picture nega-tive in their vaults. The elements had not been touched in more than fifty years. Upon inspection, which followed a sequence of convoluted legal wrangling that attempted to determine where the film's copyright rested, the BFI reported that the negative had shrunk and bore some scratches. Thankfully, the acetic level on the film tested at P1, the lowest level. The bad news was that the magnetic sound track and one of the 35mm reels had gone missing. A search was conducted in the BFI's vaults. Without the sound and a part of the story, these newly located materials would be of little to no use.

Months passed as the BFI searched. By the fall of 2013, the magnetic sound track (a revised mix track dated June 29, 1959) and the missing reel were found, both having been misfiled under the title *The Beat Generation.* When an anonymous Canadian donor stepped up to finance the preserva-tion and restoration, 6,267 feet of film could be processed, digitized, and restored. The following notes on the film are based on the DVD created from this restoration.

Continuing somewhat where *A Dangerous Age* left off, *A Cool Sound from Hell* is Furie's first unclouded inquiry into a recurring theme in his subsequent work, that of wounded masculinity and male inadequacy. It might even be a master index for this thematic thread, which resurfaced various times in different forms as Furie matured as a film director. As the picture progresses, Charlie, aimless by his own admission, is left powerless in the grip of the woman aptly named Steve, who wears not only a man's name but also the proverbial pants in the relationship. Charlie's addled intentions of marriage are a half-hearted, misguided attempt to marry his "square" moral compass to a new lifestyle choice that is at odds with such traditional morality, rather than to literally marry the girl representing that new lifestyle for reasons of personal commitment. In this Hell, exemplified most by the characters' local rathskeller hangout and the Toronto Beat scene in general, "marriage" is a foreign concept reserved for "squares," and Charlie's free mention of it reveals that a true, irrevocable nature has been suppressed by the woman who has remade him in her image. It is to Steve that the increasingly rattled Charlie owes his descent into the depths of the movie's Hell, where he is beaten to a pulp, cuckolded, turned into a drug-runner, and left at the curbside.

In *A Cool Sound from Hell,* the two women, the reckless and feckless Steve and the upright and uptight Debbie, are the assertive figures, the only ones confident in their positions on things, and to a fault. Though Debbie is loosely involved in the Beat life, mostly because of a dilettante interest in jazz, she avoids becoming mired in it, as she sees Charlie do, and keeps boundaries. Charlie, who surreptitiously shares her values but meekly folds under pressure, lacks the sense of self that both of the film's women possess.

The picture's devolution into high camp during its set-piece finale, a dangerous skydiving expedition aboard a small passenger plane, works in perfect rhythm with the film's sense of thematic direction. Charlie can only come to his senses and assume his true identity, enough to finally assert himself, when Steve and her posse orgiastically unleash an onslaught of Beat-speak into the dialogue and laugh in the face of imminent death, almost at the risk of becoming cartoons. That it takes such histrionics to awaken the wounded male is telling of Furie's own position, that such rehabilitation is possible but not probable. Very few (if any) of Furie's other wounded males so easily realize and reclaim themselves as Charlie does by the final fade-out.

Both *A Dangerous Age* and *A Cool Sound from Hell* are centered around young people in trouble, and this is another staple of Furie's subsequent work. While *A Dangerous Age*'s David is assertive and knows what he wants, it is only his technical manhood (and would-be bride Nancy's technical womanhood) that is questioned and belittled. That story, therefore, is left in the hands of destiny rather than the character's control. The case is the opposite in *A Cool Sound from Hell,* as Charlie voids his persona to favor the dangerous woman for whom he lusts. Fascinatingly and quite oddly, other early Canadian independent films were comparable in their examinations of wounded masculinity, in varying degrees, especially Claude Jutra's *A tout prendre* (1963), David Secter's *Winter Kept Us Warm* (1964), Don Owen's *Nobody Waved Good-bye* (1964), and Donald Shebib's *Goin' down the Road* (1970).

Although still unpolished and somewhat crude, Furie's visual sense started to mature with *A Cool Sound from Hell*; there is a quantum leap forward from the quaint but awkward style of *A Dangerous Age*. The director attributes his learning curve to the time spent under the tutelage of Eugen Schüfftan on *Hudson's Bay*. Furie has peppered *A Cool Sound from Hell* with often elaborate dolly shots, refracted compositions (featuring early experiments with the style used in *The Ipcress File*), and consistent image depth. Various sequences, like the "midnight jazz-blasting motor rave" (in which a synchronized group of Beatniks speed around Toronto's late-night streets in their convertibles to clobber sleeping "squares" with loud jazz) and the downtown pickup sequence (in which Charlie, enlisted to pick up drugs for the jonesing Tenor Sax Man, is tailed by a narcotics detective to Toronto's Union Station), stand out as centerpieces. Likewise, a slow dolly down a row of dazed Beatniks from the perspective of the narcotics detective is effective.

The film, then, is a clear bridge from Furie's days at the CBC to his emergence as a successful feature film director in England. Although flawed and, at its worst, cravenly moralist, the film exudes a vigor, a raw ambition, and a youthful impetuosity often present in the best filmmakers' less-than-perfect debut films, even though this was Furie's second. Upon seeing the film for the first time in more than half a century, Furie found himself flabbergasted. Shortly after viewing it with his wife, Linda, he phoned to express how proud he was seeing it today. "I was a crazy kid making *A Cool Sound from Hell,* and it's written all over every frame," he said.

Tony Ray and Phil Nimmons, when furnished with new DVD copies of the film, were likewise flooded with memories and a strange mix of emotions, as well as gratitude that they were finally able to see it after having been denied the opportunity decades earlier. Says Tony Ray, "The storyline was better than I remembered and Sid was a better filmmaker than I remembered. I always felt unprepared in that role, but in seeing the film for the first time, I must credit Sid for getting what he needed from me. He was a very good director." Says Nimmons, "It was quite a rush to see the film. Sidney was quite the creative visionary and, in retrospect, prophetically way ahead of the times. It was good fortune to be associated with his distinctive creativity."

As for Canada, things did not even begin to improve until well over a decade later. Eugene Walz writes in the introduction of the book *Canada's Best Features:*

> Furie's decision to make a Canadian feature came out of nowhere. Ten years earlier, the Film Producers Association of Canada, expecting the government to impose restrictions on American film profits in Canada similar to those enforced by France, Italy, Australia and other countries, was poised to expand into feature filmmaking from the modest documentaries and promotional films that were their stock-in-trade. Hollywood, however, was not about to relinquish a penny of the $17 million it earned in Canadian movie theaters that year. American studios did not want rival producers to get a foothold in what they considered to be part of their domestic market. Shrewdly, the MPAA proposed a "Canadian Co-operation Project." It effectively eliminated the possibility of independent Canadian feature films for ten years. The MPAA cooperated by promising to film some features in Canada and by agreeing to introduce Canadian sequences and subjects into Hollywood films and to make more short films, newsreels, and radio broadcasts about Canada. Feature were made over the course of the agreement. And references to Canada in American films, as Pierre Berton detailed in his book Hollywood's Canada, were laughably and insultingly inaccurate.[21]

Robert Fulford (the nom de plume of Canadian film critic Marshall Delaney) once remarked that a generation of English-speaking Canadians grew up believing that the smartest among them would eventually graduate from Canada,[22] which is precisely what Furie did. On Saturday, January 30, 1960, he uprooted himself, his wife, and his two sons, and headed for London, where the film industry had already been friendlier to him. Fellow directors Lindsay Shonteff, Silvio Narizzano, and Ted Kotcheff followed in his wake.

Nor was he moving there creatively empty-handed. Furie was gearing up for a new project, a serious drama that he wrote upon first returning from England in early 1958 following the sale of *A Dangerous Age*. He set up a deal with a producer named Jack Lamont, whom he met in the office of his newly acquired New York agent Jay Sanford. Lamont bought the air tickets that Furie and his family used to relocate, promising to set them up at a prominent London hotel, whereupon he would deliver the money and a deal for the project. Provisionally titled *The 25th Mission* and set in World War II–era England, Furie's drama told the story of an American World War II bomber pilot, a young virgin from Pittsburgh named David, who is petrified at the thought of dying on his last bombing mission without ever having been with a woman. It is set over a single night in which the awkward, bashful David goes AWOL and has a series of misadventures trying to make things happen in that department. In the midst of this, he falls in love with a sweet young barmaid named Jean.

Furie later decried his issues making films in Canada, admitting to the press in January 1962, "I wanted to start a Canadian film industry, but nobody cared. There's no pattern of distribution and nobody had any money to put up." Gerald Pratley accused Canada of "unforgivable neglect" in its treatment of the young filmmaker. In Pratley's article, Furie lamented that "the services [in London] are inferior to ours" and that "we miss our families deeply" before conceding that the United Kingdom "is a wonderful place to live."[23]

He relates that years later, while visiting Toronto after an extended absence, he spotted a key technician from his early features begging for change on the street. "This guy was skilled labor, not just some buddy of mine hanging out on set who turned on a light, or someone who fiddled around a bit with the footage. In any other country, he could have easily gotten work in the film industry. But there he was, still in Toronto all those years later, homeless and accosting people on the street." Truly, sometimes reality's symbolism can be so apt as to provoke discomfort.

One day, when things looked better, Furie would return.

Chapter 3

Making a Name in London

He made a very good impression in those days, being friendly, direct and not afraid to say that love makes the world—and the movies—go round.

—*Clive Denton, describing Furie in 1959*

"I was stranded at the Westbury Hotel . . . with a wife and two kids."

Furie was referring to the fact that, once he arrived in England, producer Jack Lamont failed to turn up with the money to finance *The 25th Mission*. The wait was agonizing, with no income to ensure his ability to stay in England longer than two weeks. "It was like *Waiting for Godot*. It's still one of my most stressful memories." Desperate, he gave *The 25th Mission* to his newest contact, Kenneth Rive at Galaworld Films, who appreciated the quality of the writing but was, as a distributor, not yet situated to actually produce films. When he knocked on Kenneth Harper's door, the producer had nothing to offer him. Other than Silvio Narizzano, Furie's London contacts were still rather limited, but the success of his two Canadian independent features on the British theatrical circuit made him somewhat hopeful that he could overcome the crisis. *A Cool Sound from Hell* had only begun its theatrical run at the West End's Berkeley Cinema. That, however, was not enough, and Furie's luck was running out fast. He was ready to chuck it and return home to Toronto defeated.

The young director's salvation, a deus ex machina, resulted from a serendipitous meeting between two people uninvolved in his unfolding drama. At the Pinewood Studios Bar, the favorite networking spot in town for those in the film industry, producer George Fowler sat down one night for a drink with assistant director Fred Slark, a Brit who had worked as Furie's assistant director on *Hudson's Bay* and *A Cool Sound from Hell*. Slark emigrated to Toronto in 1958 to work briefly at the CBC and had returned to his home country only a year before Furie's January 1960 arrival. Fowler was a production manager who, thanks to producer David E. Rose, was on the threshold of graduating to full producership. Rose had raised a cache of money to shoot a series of "genre quickies," many of them cheap Hammer Studios–influenced horror potboilers. Sealing a deal with United Artists in New York to distribute the films as exploitation double features, he entrusted Fowler with the task of pulling together a creative team for the pictures. The only thing that eluded him was a willing director.

"I know a director who would gladly take the job," Slark volunteered.

"I've only got £5000 in the budget for a director," Fowler said, encoding the information with a producer's veil of coy.

"He'll do it for £3500," Slark replied.

And with that, Furie scored *Doctor Blood's Coffin*, his first director-for-hire job on a feature-length motion picture. It was also his first film to be shot in color, from a script by Nathan "Jerry" Juran, now most known for having helmed *Attack of the 50 Foot Woman* (1958). Hazel Court, one of the English horror's most famous "scream queens," headed up the cast. The twenty-five-thousand-pound budget was certainly minuscule, but the financial pittance and the resulting challenges provided an ideal training ground for breeding and building Furie's resilience and resourcefulness.

With *The 25th Mission* put on indefinite hold, Furie never again heard from Jack Lamont, who resurfaced only once more in the industry with an obscure low-budget thriller called *Stranglehold* (1962).

The thirty-five-hundred-pound godsend allowed Furie to rent a house on Peel Street, near Notting Hill Gate. One of his neighbors there was future Academy Award–winning director John Schlesinger, who lived three doors down and had not yet directed a feature. Schlesinger had vaguely established himself as a documentary filmmaker with a series of short subjects, including the award-winning *Terminus*. Like Furie, Schlesinger had gotten his start in television, in a variety of positions, including second-unit director for *Danger Man* and exterior decorator for *The Four Just Men*. "John and I were friendly as neighbors, and we connected in that we both wanted to be making real movies. He was the first person I met who made no mystery of the fact he was gay. He was out and proud in 1960."

In the spring of 1960, after a cursory session of rewriting Juran's script, shooting on *Doctor Blood's Coffin* started in Cornwall, along England's southern tip, with interiors at Walton Studios in Surrey. Within ten days, the entire film was in the can.

One of Furie's most vivid memories of working on *Doctor Blood's Coffin* was meeting his camera operator, future director Nicolas Roeg. "He was the only person on the crew reading the *Times* of London. In those days, that was the upper-class paper. The best word to describe him then is sardonic, with his public-school accent, but he was a very sweet guy, and quite brilliant in conversation." Roeg's advice to Furie, who was itching to make *The 25th Mission*, was simple: "Just be happy with the movies they gave you. It's good practice! Who gives a damn?" So impressive was the young Roeg's presence on a movie set that, at this early stage of their career, future A-list directors Richard Lester and Joseph Losey remarked, "We'll be working for him one day."[1]

Says Roeg, "The first word that leaps to mind when you mention Sidney is movie-mad. He was obsessive about movies, constantly talking about movies, whereas I guess, in those days, I wasn't quite concerned with the cinema as much as all that. We were certainly friendly, but it never really extended much beyond the set. I admired him because it was marvelous seeing someone who truly loved what he was doing."

For bringing in *Doctor Blood's Coffin* on schedule and under budget, Fowler rewarded Furie with more pictures to direct. Of making *The Snake Woman*, another Hammer Studios–influenced horror tale, this time in black and white and budgeted at an even skimpier seventeen thousand pounds, Furie has two vivid memories: "We had a boiler room at Walton Studios, and all the sets were built inside each other. You peeled one off, you had the next set. And you peeled that one off, you had the next. It was like working in television again. Then, I also got in trouble with the unions because I shot in the rain with the extras. They just slapped me on the wrist and told me to never do it again." *The Snake Woman* was completed in a record six days; Roeg returned this time as an uncredited second-unit photographer.

Of making *Three on a Spree*, a fourth remake of the classic *Brewster's Millions*, budgeted at twenty-three thousand pounds and completed in twelve days, the director now has no memory. Fowler and Rose completed one more quickie picture, a sex comedy called *Mary Had a Little . . . ,* shortly after Furie departed their company. Among the three Furie directed, there is early evidence of a keen attention to camera and blocking that typified his later output. Although original reviews of the films magnified their occasionally shoddy production values, *Doctor Blood's Coffin,* with its skewed deep-focus perspectives and unexpectedly memorable set pieces; *The Snake Woman,* with its moody monochrome; and *Three on a Spree,* with its studied compositions and sometimes dynamic mobile-camera reveals, all saw Furie steadily building his skills, despite working with what seemed less-than-premium material.

Although *Doctor Blood's Coffin* has earned a formidable reputation among fans of B-movie classics and low-budget horror, it is still best to weigh the three Fowler-produced quickies as sketch-pad exercises for Furie, during what was perhaps the most formative year of his career. Though enlisted strictly as director-for-hire on these projects, Furie's sensibility and thematic fascinations do surface, being no less present than in later, personally engineered endeavors. *Doctor Blood's Coffin,* with its story of illegal human medical experiments in an abandoned small-town tin mine, features Kieron Moore as a twisted physician who literally takes his male psychosis underground while proving inept in attempts to woo (and impress) nurse Hazel Court. Hence, the movie's obligatory "monster" is a superficially normal, but of course duplicitous, red-blooded young man, a rather unlikely candidate for "mad doctor." The screwball comedy *Three on a Spree* features Jack Watling as another of the director's hapless males who is made a eunuch by money and by a variety of women who work different angles.

In April 1961, after his triple stint with George Fowler, Furie learned that Kenneth Rive was now finally in the market to produce films, having transformed his distribution outfit Gala into a production company. "Do you still want to do that picture about the virgin pilot?" Rive asked Furie. Digging out *The 25th Mission,* the story of the bomber pilot who doubts his manhood and looks to settle the problem before becoming a casualty of the war, Furie applied a few minor rewrites and prepared to mount his first personal picture in his new adopted country.

"The first thing we need to do is give it another title," announced Kenneth Rive. "*The 25th Mission* makes it sound too much like a war picture. We need something maybe a bit sexy."

Budgeted at fifty thousand pounds and shot in sixteen days, once again at Walton Studios, at the tail end of the studio's nearly sixty-year existence, the newly renamed *During One Night* reunited Furie with Don Borisenko and Sean Sullivan, two of his closest Canadian friends. Borisenko, who had been the best man at Furie's wedding, likewise left Canada, not long after starring in Lindsay Shonteff's *The Hired Gun,* an independent Western shot on an Ontario ranch throughout 1960.

Furie wrote both roles with Borisenko and Sullivan in mind, leaving him to hold auditions for the lead female role of Jean, the barmaid with whom the meek bomber pilot David falls in love over the course of a single evening. Of the two primary candidates, Susan Hampshire and Jackie Collins, Hampshire was cast as Jean while Collins was given a supporting role. "It was a lovely set, but lighting took forever because the lighting crew took their jolly old time," Susan Hampshire remembers. "They would light all morning and then we'd have only had a limited amount of time to get the shots done. Sometimes, it was only enough for a single take."

Furie stages much of the action with elaborate camera movements that open scenes, often allowing them to continue as long takes (some of which clock in upwards of four minutes). This was done out of necessity. "I quickly learned that I was better off fitting stuff into one camera set-up. We had tea breaks in the morning, tea breaks in the afternoon, and there was no such thing as overtime. The Electrical Trades Union didn't like overtime because, no joke, in those days they were unabashedly Communist." Daily call-time for the crew would be 8:00, with a break from 12:30 to 2:00. Lights would go out at 6:00, and everyone would reconvene for the same thing the next day. Often, the crew made a habit of going harder than tea, heading to Walton's workman's bar for pints at midday. A studio luncheon club that served a gourmet smorgasbord provided another key distraction.

Susan Hampshire corroborates, "Each take seemed to run about ten minutes long, so we really had to master the script, and I do know that the unions in those days were very strict. I felt very much out of my depth, and I was always frightened. But I would go home exhilarated."

During One Night completed a three-film cycle that started with *A Dangerous Age* and *A Cool Sound from Hell.* All three are essays on the meaning of manhood. This time, frontal female nudity was added as a marketing ingredient. "That was the fashion for small art films then," says Furie. "The European pictures Gala picked up for distribution all had that kind of nudity. It was not uncommon, but it was new to me. *During One Night,* though, was made strictly for the art-house, not for the B-movie circuit." Also added to the mix this time was the dicey subject matter of male impotency, a very pointed theme that literalized, in boldest terms, Furie's thematic focus on male inadequacy and wounded masculinity.

Reviews across the board were ambivalent. *Box Office* magazine branded it "a somber, never-sensationalized-for-sensation's-sake study"

When the film arrived in the United States in February 1962, it was promptly condemned by the Catholic National Legion of Decency. Calling the Legion's bluff, the American distributor Astor Pictures retitled the film to the more sexploitation-friendly *Night of Passion*. The *Los Angeles Times* referred to it as "dreary" and "interminable," while the *Los Angeles Herald-Examiner* called the technique "choppy" and the characterizations "self-conscious."

The film opens with the real emasculation of a supporting character. When their jet is hit by enemy fire, the protagonist's copilot is wounded and thereby rendered sexually useless. In the next scene, he sits in an infirmary bed revealing to our hero that he is likewise a virgin and that stories of his sexual conquests told directly before his injury were lies concocted for self-aggrandizement. He is vulnerable for the first time, to a member of his own sex. When it is mentioned later that this character has committed suicide, one man's literal emasculation and resulting death makes Furie's main character impotent. After a couple of sexual misadventures in which the character fails to perform, he meets the lovely young barmaid Jean, who, as an ad hoc therapist, helps to rehabilitate him. She comes the closest but likewise fails. With the help of a military chaplain in disguise, played by Furie's old Toronto buddy Sean Sullivan, he is able to stage a scene that will function as his panacea—a scene in which he experiences a faux near-death. Now hopeful of his future, he flies his twenty-fifth mission, as Jean's loving eyes look skyward, optimistic that he will return safe. In the film, the fate of their relationship is left in question. The leather-bound copy of the shooting script that Furie still personally owns reveals a more definitive ending, which flashes forward to a married David and Jean walking down a row of veteran's graves with an infant. In the script, like *A Cool Sound from Hell*'s Charlie, he survives his wounded male self and lives to tell of it. As in *During One Night,* death is a potential consequence of being unsure of oneself in life.

The film is well constructed and handsomely mounted, with World War II aerial footage leased from the Crown Film Unit seamlessly woven into the film by editor Antony Gibbs. While putting the finishing touches on *During One Night* with Gibbs, who was about to depart for the greener pastures of Tony Richardson's Woodfall Films, Furie received a call from an old friend:

"Hi, Sid, it's Kenneth Harper."

"Ken! Long time no hear!"

"How would you like to do an MGM musical?"

"What the hell are you talking about? There aren't any more MGM musicals! They're gone with the wind!"

"Well, we've got to do this Cliff Richard and The Shadows picture." He was referring to one of the hottest acts in England. "The writers I've got for it want to do a Mickey Rooney/Judy Garland *Babes in Arms* kind of story and then work Cliff's pop stuff into that."

"So it's actually a rock 'n' roll picture?"

"In a way. In another way, it's like *Babes in Arms*. The kids put on a show to save their youth club from a greedy developer."

Furie paused to think things over. He had never done a musical, and one needed money and songs and dancers and lots of manpower to make a musical happen. Knowing he probably would not get the opportunity again any time soon, this was perhaps incentive enough.

"And you want me to direct?"

"Yes. It needs your youth."

He laughed. "My youth? What does *that* mean? You think I've got some to spare?"

"Well, we're calling it *The Young Ones*. You're a young director. You have that young energy. You'll get it right."

In Furie's formative filmmaking "textbook," Lillian Ross's *Picture,* MGM producer Arthur Freed is quoted as saying, "In musicals, we don't have any of those phony artistic pretensions." So signifies the leap that Furie took from directing *During One Night,* a personally engineered art-house film, to being hired for *The Young Ones,* a musical with no apparent aspirations toward high art.

In retrospect, the director was realistic in discussing his own appeal in the eyes of producers like Harper. "I didn't know it at the time, but I was a well-known commodity," says Furie. "I didn't know what that meant then, but those quickies set me up as a competent director who worked cheap and didn't bump heads with authority."[2] *The Young Ones* as a title, though, could not have been more suited to Furie, a "young one" director whose previous pictures dealt with specifically young themes and young dilemmas.

Beyond any of these factors, Harper took a shine to Furie as a hungry young talent, giving him an unusual amount of space to make a number of crucial creative decisions. He also gave the still obscure director his biggest budget yet, the initial sum of one hundred thousand pounds, funded through the Associated British Picture Corporation. The first line of business was to meet Harper's writing team, Peter Myers and Ronald Cass, who were both involved as scribes for West End revues, and whose responsibilities for *The Young Ones* extended beyond dialogue and story. With the Cliff and The Shadows tunes as a foundation, a curious mix of two musical styles ultimately made up the soundtrack, which featured a lineup of splashy MGM-style ensemble numbers for which Myers, a lyricist, and Cass, a composer, were responsible. Remembers Furie, "Myers was a Hollywood musical and Broadway show buff. He had all these LPs and all this stage and screen memorabilia. It was like a museum of sorts."

In their juxtaposition of classic MGM-style numbers with Cliff Richard and The Shadows tunes, Harper, Myers, and Cass were able to covertly woo family audiences over to rock 'n' roll, still a suspect form of entertainment at the time. "For the public, we sort of eased them into it," says Cliff Richard, who was later often lauded for his wholesome, clean-cut appearance. "And it became acceptable to moms and dads. It opened up my career so much. It was like an overnight change. One minute, I was a rock 'n' roll phenomenon. The next minute, I was an all-around entertainer."[3] That said, the rock 'n' roll pedigree really crystallized when the Elvis songwriting team of Roy Bennett and Sid Tepper provided two songs for use in *The Young Ones,* including the title song, which was later appropriated for the 1980s television show *The Young Ones.* Since it was custom for the Elvis pictures, directed by veterans, to pit age against youth, Myers and Cass also threw this formula into the stew, lending to it a more classical Rodgers & Hart–influenced style.

Because Cliff Richard had hastily signed a three-picture contract the year before with producer Mickey Delamar at the production company Alva Films, which produced Richard's screen debut *Serious Charge* (1959), Harper arranged a necessary payout of ten thousand pounds. This released the star to headline the much more substantially budgeted *The Young Ones* and placed him under a three-movie contract with Harper. Broadway choreographer Herbert Ross, a future film director and then the resident choreographer at the American Ballet Theatre, was Harper's choice to stage the numerous dance numbers. According to many sources, including Cliff Richard's biography, an agog Ross recommended the unknown Barbra Streisand for the lead female role.[4] After Harper flew to New York to see her perform and returned thinking she was wrong, the part eventually went to Rhodesian-born dancer Carole Gray. As Stephen Glynn writes in

The British Pop Musical: The Beatles and Beyond, "It was felt that, while pretty, she was not an unduly threatening presence to Cliff's female following and, while talented, she would not upstage the star."[5] In fact, Gray's singing voice was ultimately dubbed by singer-actress Grazina Frame. Herbert Ross himself later directed Streisand in two films, *The Owl and the Pussycat* (1970) and *Funny Lady* (1975).

While *The Young Ones* was short on story, with its done-to-death "let's put on a show" Andy Hardy formula, Cliff Richard's popularity made a hit a foregone conclusion. "Expectations were very high because Cliff was hot," says Furie.[6] British stage and screen star Robert Morley, a portly character actor traditionally typecast as pompous British gentlemen, was cast as the Cliff character's uncle, a member of the Establishment intent on closing the prized youth club that the film's young ones aspire to save.

Production got under way at Elstree Studios in Borehamwood on May 29, 1961, just months after the birth of Furie's third son, Jonathan. Although the picture's higher budget tier was not germane to Furie's low-budget training, he adapted to the new demands in flying colors. Of the work schedule, Furie recalls, "Yes, there were of course more tea-breaks and resulting delays, and while this new crew went to the pubs for their pints, I could sneak into the executive dining room with the senior staff of the picture, either for whiskey or wine." The clean-cut Cliff Richard resisted immersing himself in the recreational rivers of alcohol and tea that formed around the collective.

For his part, Richard was most anxious about appearing alongside the more experienced Morley, given his "reputation for not suffering fools gladly."[7] Richard had appeared in two pictures before, both released in 1959: Terence Young's drama *Serious Charge* and Val Guest's adaptation of Wolf Mankowitz's Horatio Alger-esque stage musical *Expresso Bongo*, neither of which truly challenged Richard or expanded his acting prowess. "Morley loved the movie because his kids were thrilled he was acting with Cliff Richard," Furie remembers. Says Cliff Richard, "I'm sure he didn't have respect for me as an actor, because I wasn't one, but his thoughtfulness to me as a person was quite a lesson." When Richard would blow his lines, Morley would accept the blame ("I'm awfully sorry, Cliff, you'll have to excuse an old dodderer like me, but I've made a mistake").[8] Although the climate was amicable, decades later, Morley's son, critic Sheridan Morley, famously urged prospective audiences to "imagine Liberace as King Lear" when referring to Cliff Richard in his nineties stage musical *Heathcliff*.[9]

One day, as heavy rainfall spoiled the shooting of a planned exterior, the production manager preemptively announced a cancellation of the rest of the day's work. As the crew picked up to go home, Furie erupted. "I never lost a day's shooting in my life and I'm not going to lose one now!" In response, he staged an improvised scene with his young performers in an interior space, the backdrop revealing the rain falling against a bank of window panes. For many of the cast members, this was their first film, and improvising a scene was something no one was used to. Although this type of display in front of the crew was rare, it confirmed their director's low-budget-trained pluck.

As photographed by veteran Douglas Slocombe, the distinguished lighting cameraman Furie respected as the "slowest lighter" of his directing career, *The Young Ones* became Furie's entry into shooting CinemaScope, something that became a trademark in his work of the subsequent three decades. The lenses, as per standard, were leased from 20th Century Fox, which still owned the major interest in wide-screen processes at that time. Instead of using it simply to compose, Furie experimented with the extra screen space in various ways, including framing shots in drastic Dutch angles, clouding the lens with red Vaseline during a solo love ballad, and using a split screen of eight multicolored oblong panels to present eight different characters simultaneously getting ready for a night on the town. Stephen Glynn, in his book on the history of the British pop music film, refers to the latter as the picture's "boldest cinematic moment" in that "each addition is matched to the rhythm of the music, providing a visual octave, a metonymic keyboard. Sound and vision synergize, demonstrating how music plus colour equals entertainment."[10] Indeed, in this moment, *The Young Ones* becomes the purest of cinema.

Under Furie's and Herbert Ross's guidance, Cliff Richard attested that he "put more work into the rehearsals than he did for the entire shooting schedule of *Expresso Bongo*," adding that "Sidney Furie is a man I admire. He is like everyone else here—so patient with me. If anything goes wrong, there is a smile and a discussion to put it right."[11] The relationship between Furie and Ross, however, proved to be polite but not so friendly. No direct animosity was directly displayed between them, but their exchanges were curt and fraught with undercurrents of spite on Ross's part.

Furie posits that, from the day Ross arrived, the spiteful choreographer wished he had been hired as the director. "I was grateful to have him, but he was bitchy and would barely say hello to me in the morning. I was a kid. He was older, had worked on Broadway, had gone to Hollywood, and I hadn't. My credits would have been *Doctor Blood's Coffin* and *Snake Woman*." Furie describes how, much later, Kenneth Harper told him that, during the shooting of *The Young Ones,* Ross said something to the effect of "Who is this unsophisticated Canadian kid? He's not going to last in the business." Furie, for his part, knew he had job security, because Harper, resolute in his hiring decision, had involved him early on in working with the writers and planning the musical numbers. Years later in Hollywood, however, an all-smiles Ross complimented Furie on *The Ipcress File* after its 1965 opening.

By the time of picture wrap in mid-August 1961, the £100,000 budget had ballooned to £230,000, owing not to any fault of Furie's, but rather to a miscalculation by Kenneth Harper, who had underestimated final costs. "They wouldn't have asked me back to do *Summer Holiday* or *Wonderful Life* if that had been my fault," Furie says. Opening at London's Warner Theatre in Leicester Square on December 13, 1961, then opening nationally in January 1962, *The Young One* received overwhelmingly positive reviews, with the trades reporting that the film "was fairly packing them in straight from release." Paul Dehn of the *Daily Herald* led the pack with unqualified zeal: "I pick my words as cautiously as I sink my boats: this is the best-screen musical ever to have been made in England." Nina Hibbin of the *Daily Worker* sang these praises almost verbatim in proclaiming it "easily the best British musical I've seen," while the usually measured *Monthly Film Bulletin* labeled it "rare and robust." Critics placed much of the credit for the film's success on Furie's shoulders, though David Robinson of the *Financial Times* took exception to the film's "derivative choreography" and "timid shooting," which he felt made the film resemble "a Hollywood film of the forties (though that in itself is not bad)." The *Sunday Times* critic wrote, "*West Side Story* hasn't arrived from the Americans yet, but until then, this picture, with its lively musical showmanship, will do just fine." Furie's memory of the latter review is his most vivid.

The Young Ones became the second-highest-grossing film at the box office that year, behind only *The Guns of Navarone,* with Cliff Richard topping the list for the ten most popular film stars at the 1962 British box office, followed by Elvis Presley and Peter Sellers. Today, the soundtrack remains the pop star's best-selling album, having topped the UK charts for six weeks in early 1962, selling an unprecedented 110,000 copies in that time. It then spent ten months in the top ten. The title track, paired with The Shadows' "We Say Yeah," entered number one on the singles charts, with an advance record order of 524,000 copies. By March, sales had exceeded 1 million pounds, with 2.5 million in international sales.

In the United States, Paramount Pictures, who cared not about the film's box-office returns in England, purchased the American rights to the film, deleted sixteen minutes, and retitled it *Wonderful to Be Young!* for a tie-in to Burt Bacharach's song of the same name, and opened it in October 1962. American prints feature Bacharach's tune over the opening credits, in lieu of the "Friday Night" number. Despite this indignity, Paramount nevertheless launched an ambitious campaign to introduce Cliff Richard to American audiences, with Cliff and The Shadows performing live hour-long shows before selected screenings. Touring during the Cuban Missile Crisis did not bode well for this flourish of showmanship, as even the largest theaters failed to fill even half their seats during this period. Richard never again toured the United States with The Shadows.

Narratively a throwaway picture, *The Young Ones* is a spunky bubble-gum musical to its core, complete with an appropriately garish title sequence. To his and the film's credit, Furie still manages to customize the film by injecting it with unexpected doses of personality, especially as demonstrated in some of its more audacious moments (the eight-panel split screen being key among other such flourishes); thus, although it qualifies as studio-produced "fluff," it is no less perceptible as the work of its director, even at this early juncture in his career. As to this question of perceptible authorship, *The Young Ones* as "fluff" certainly eclipses, for example, the Doris Day pictures *The Thrill of It All* (1963) and *Send Me No Flowers* (1964) as directed by Norman Jewison early in his own career. Historically, the film is in some ways important for setting a pace and a standard for British musicals centered around rock idols, especially Richard Lester's *It's Trad, Dad* (1962), Michael Winner's *Play It Cool* (1962), Lance Comfort's *Live It Up!* (1963), John Boorman's *Having a Wild Weekend* (1965), and Richard Lester's game-changing *A Hard Day's Night* (1964). In a 1993 television interview, Cliff Richard posited, "Because we did our films our way, what could the Beatles possibly do, other than do it our way, or say 'We don't want to do it that way?'"[12] The following year, Clive Donner used a similar narrative formula to *The Young Ones,* adding a dose of British realism to create the rock musical drama *Some People* (1962).

Most suspect to the film's detractors, however, is its conspicuous timidity relative to the other youth pictures and musicals of its time, which had deliberately rendered it more family-friendly. As *Daily Telegraph* critic Patrick Gibbs "would have preferred [the characters] to find the cash with the help of a cosh, flick knife or bicycle chain," Stephen Glynn observes that Richard's Nicky character never even attempts as much as a good night kiss and "is respectful to the point of chasteness, a leading man reminiscent of Gene Kelly. . . . Here is a utopia free of Newtonian principles *and* of teenage promiscuity."[13] British film scholar Robert Shail identifies the movie as "a plea for greater understanding of the lives of young people" but complains that it "drains Richard of any connotations of youth rebellion or sexuality, which his following might have implied."[14] Years later, especially upon the Beatles' arrival at the cinema, this perceived drawback proved to be the nail in the coffin for the Cliff Richard pictures.

Be that as it may, the propitious reception of *The Young Ones* provided the needed, fabled "big break" for Sidney J. Furie, who was now a name director in the British film industry. With the paycheck, he was able to buy his first home, a small townhouse in Roehampton, a suburban district in southwest London. As his hit picture continued to incite positive press, public goodwill, and lines around theater blocks, Kenneth Rive was luring Furie back to make another film for Gala. It could once again be one of his own choosing. In reading scripts that Gala owned, the director became enamored with one commissioned by Rive, penned by a socialist author.

On a chilly, rainswept evening in November 1961, Furie attended a performance of Thomas Murphy's controversial play *A Whistle in the Dark* at the Apollo Theater in the West End. Known to many as "that violent Irish play," the production starred Patrick Magee, Michael Craig, Oliver McGreevy, Derren Nesbitt, and Dudley Sutton, who hailed from a Royal Academy of Dramatic Art training. "We kicked all the polite plays out," says Sutton, proudly.

The following week, Sutton received a call from his agent, Jimmy Fraser, who informed him in a wry deadpan, "I'm sending you to see this film director who is rather like a Beatnik. If you go to an interview and he's sitting on the floor and he hasn't shaved, it's probably the director." Undeterred by this admonition and even enticed by its suggestion, Sutton proceeded to meet Sidney Furie at his Galaworld Films office in SoHo, knowing instantly that they would become very good friends. Furie promptly presented him with a script. "I was very political in those days," says Sutton, "and I was passionate about the abolition of capital punishment. When I was a kid, they'd always announce executions on the radio, and there was always a glint of approval in everyone's eyes, and I thought it was monstrous. I grew up having actual nightmares of men being hanged. Then, here was Sid handing me Stuart Douglass's script for *The Boys*. It was in the stars."

Written by British socialist Stuart Douglass as a spec script and sold immediately to Gala, *The Boys* tells the story of four young "teddy boys" who stand accused in court of murdering a night watchman for a service station's cashbox. Under rigorous cross-examination, witnesses paint a conflicting account of the night in question, the events of which are told in separate flashbacks and photographed from different perspectives. As these variations emerge, so do details about the boys' home life, in a London tenement of the Kings Cross slums. This courtroom drama with a dash of kitchen sink realism was Kenneth Rive's first foray into producing more mainstream pictures, after having worked exclusively in the tight corners of imports, art-house, exploitation, and soft-core sex pictures. Christened with newfound street credit, Galaworld backed Furie as the shepherd leading the company toward respectability. As insurance, Furie headlined the film with distinguished thespians Robert Morley, Richard Todd, and Sir Felix Aylmer and rounded out the cast with other performers from *A Whistle in the Dark* (he used nearly all of the cast members of this play in future films, as well).

The success of *Room at the Top, Saturday Night and Sunday Morning*, and *A Taste of Honey* had spurred the evolution in British cinema that was about to occur over the ensuing years, attracting United Artists to set up shop full-time in London that year. Other modest British realist films, such as John Schlesinger's *A Kind of Loving*, fared prodigiously well against more prestigiously budgeted pictures' box office of the previous year. As directors grew ever more restless in confining themselves to the constantly redefined boundaries of good taste, British realist films came to represent a level of potency that transcended such limiting criteria. British directors now found their truth in a take-it-to-the-streets method of capturing potent dramatic images, which appropriated the Italian neorealist tactics of Roberto Rossellini, Luchino Visconti and Vittorio de Sica. "There's no question that when we all saw *Saturday Night and Sunday Morning*, a new world was born," says Furie. "I mean, that was like Rossellini all over again. I mean, that had a reality and a grittiness. And, on top of that, it was a highly successful film financially."[15] As an aspiring British realist director, Furie had come to know many members of the Woodfall Films team, including its creative director Tony Richardson, who was toiling away on the edit of *Tom Jones* (1963) with Antony Gibbs. Furie remembers visiting a dejected Richardson, who informed him with grim resolve that *Tom Jones* would be a disaster (ultimately the film took home Academy Awards for Best Picture and Best Director, thanks to innovative editing and its liberated sexual attitudes).

When *The Boys* went into production in April 1962, Morley's courtroom scenes were grouped into one stretch and executed first, so as to free the actor for his commitment to *Nine Hours to Rama*, which was mounting production in India. Quite often, there was only time for a single take of each setup. This method also made it often too easy for the cast and crew members to lose track of what part of the script was being shot. "This will make the cutting room more interesting,"[16] Furie remarked on set, reflecting on how rewarding it would be to see it all in correct order for the first time. Shooting access for an actual courtroom had been denied to Furie and Rive, so an exact replica of the Old Bailey No. 4 court was built at Elstree Studios. For the sake of realism, to heighten the illusion that the shots were from actual courtroom proceedings, Furie demanded that the set be built with solid walls (as opposed to the "wild" movable walls usually constructed).

A correspondent for *Films and Filming*, Barrie Pattison, remarked in his piece that the "casually dressed" Furie looked "less like a director with seven features to his credit than anyone else on the Elstree set, but there was no doubt who was in charge." Pattison also observed that "it was disappointing to [Furie], in a way, that his biggest success had been a straight entertainment film like *The Young Ones*. *During One Night* is still his favourite."[17]

Robert Morley was fresh from his experience with Furie on *The Young Ones*, and the four young actors collectively playing the title role took note of the esteemed veteran actor's generosity of spirit. Dudley Sutton recalls that Morley would often bellow, "Don't put the camera on me, Sidney. Put it on the children, they need it!" "Robert Morley was a very sweet man. But Richard Todd was a mean little shit," says Sutton, explaining, "There is this big fat close-up on me when I realize I have to be hanged. Richard Todd, who was playing the prosecuting attorney, refused to come read with me. He sat in his dressing room. Morley was so outraged that he refused to ever speak to Todd again. So Morley sat by the camera and read the scene with me. He knew how hard it was as a young actor to be on the edge of tears in this tight close-up. He understood that and he respected the film, and wanted to give me the respect he thought I deserved. Richard Todd was just too grand for that."

Furie explains, "Richard Todd was rather stiff and a wee bit uptight. I think he was in disbelief that there were actors around like Dudley. I got on well with him. He was by-the-book and I respected him for what he was, as I loved Dudley for what he was. But if there was friction, it was because the personal chemistry didn't mix."

Although there was little else in the way of acrimony on the set, there were still bones to pick about certain details. When the courtroom scenes wrapped, the crew moved to the Kings Cross location in London, to shoot inside a real working-class flat. Dudley Sutton's arrival to this new set was, at first, not a happy one: "I arrived when the art department was busy painting the walls so that it looked filthy. They were tattering the place, making the slats show and all that. I went fucking spare. Sid said 'What's the matter?' and I just started in saying, 'I'm not going to work on a set with this kind of bourgeois view of working class people! That place was perfect when we walked in!' And just like that, Sidney got rid of them. The set decorators had to clean the whole place up and they were furious. I loved him for that." Furie provided room for the invention of the actors, as when Sutton decided that his character would clean his fingernails with a switchblade, after having seen an actual teddy boy do it firsthand.

With the film in the can, Cliff Richard's band The Shadows was brought on to compose the film's score. Their instrumental main theme became a popular single. Reviews of the film were middling, with the *Sunday Times* calling its experimental repetitive flashback structure "monotonous." *Sight & Sound* called it "an accomplished piece of filmmaking," admitting to the film's "undeniable grip" in that it "constantly absorbs, constantly has one guessing as to its final outcome, and constantly entertains, even if it's not so honest and not so impartial as it thinks it is." Yet, *Sight & Sound* still questioned the film's validity as a truly serious work, musing that it was "nothing so much as a directorial exercise of sorts—a display of technique." *Films and Filming*'s Peter John Dyer posited that "Furie is not being especially profound or original, yet it's hard to think of many directors who have given more economical or decently matter-of-fact attention to the stresses set up by poverty."

The film works as a dry run for the flashback structure later used in Furie's *The Lawyer* in 1970, with its *Rashomon*-style representations of the varying testimonies given in court. *The Boys* scores most outside the courtroom, especially in its gritty and often beautiful use of real locations. The use of the Kings Cross tenement is particularly striking. There, Furie often opts to use natural light to shade his actors. His confident use of CinemaScope, his second application of it following his first foray in *The Young Ones,* is perhaps most worthy of note, in that he seeks to use every inch of the screen space in many shots. "Sidney and the cameraman Gerry Gibbs spent a lot of time puttering around with framing," Dudley Sutton recalls. "Sid wanted the picture-perfect frame, and it's a shame because when it comes on television here in England, all that hard work is lost."

As a hybrid of courtroom drama and kitchen sink realism, *The Boys* provided a stepping stone to Furie's follow-up picture, *The Leather Boys.* Author Robert Murphy writes in *Sixties British Cinema,* "With its interminable interrogations and repetitive flashbacks, the film tends to drag on, but this is easily forgiven for the unpatronizing view it presents of British working-class life and the sympathy it extends to these not particularly attractive victims of society. By the end of the film Robert Morley is able to sum up a position which the audience, if not the court, would endorse."[18]

With the release of *The Boys* came a few sober appraisals of Furie's current market value as a director worthy of serious consideration. *Films and Filming* said, "Given time and opportunity, Furie might well turn out to be a director of weight. Currently, he seems to be feeling his way, would appear to be testing his resources." *Sight & Sound* posited that "Furie's unfussy, functional style of direction underline the impression of a likable, confident talent of no great personal distinction, yet one which is undoubtedly on the threshold of self-discovery and maturity of conscience."[19] Indeed, the director was positioning himself for a personal coup. Meanwhile, Furie, Dudley Sutton, and their wives became close social friends following the release of *The Boys;* the two of them often went to movies together and would meet up for dinner and drinks on a regular basis. "There was no one else in London like Dudley," Furie says. "He was a ticking time bomb, and I mean that as a compliment."

Chapter 4

Man's Favorite Sport

We can't have too many fads and fancies as I'm sure you'll understand.
—*Gran in Gillian Freeman's novel* The Leather Boys

Now looking to support a wife and three sons and ever hopeful for that next job, Furie speedily accepted the offer to direct the next Cliff Richard vehicle, *Summer Holiday*. Furie had developed a mutually invigorating working relationship with producer Kenneth Harper, and the two high-tailed to the Greek islands to prep the picture in the spring of 1962. Soon after returning home, Furie jumped at the prospect proffered by producer Raymond Stross, of adapting *The Leather Boys*, a controversial novel by Gillian Freeman about two working-class young men in a motorcycle fraternity whose camaraderie and devotion to each other begins to extend beyond the platonic. That one of these characters was a newlywed trapped in a loveless marriage conformed with something Furie had expressed in the previous June issue of *Films and Filming*, that he was "interested in moving away from the teenage themes" of *The Boys*, to a film "dealing with the problems of young married people."[1] This narrative fascination stemmed, perhaps, from the burgeoning but expected growing pains in his marriage to wife Sheila, at least in some small part. In Furie's hands, *The Leather Boys* turned out to be a sort of half-sequel to *A Dangerous Age*, one that pondered what would have happened had the David and Nancy of that film succeeded in tying the knot.

Gillian Freeman had written the original novel responding to bisexual publisher Anthony Blond's request for a "Romeo and Juliet novel" about two working-class gay characters. Says Edward Thorpe, Gillian Freeman's longtime husband, "In that way, the novel really was a prototype for *Brokeback Mountain*. Anthony Blond wanted a gay love story between two otherwise normal everyday boys." Because Freeman was under strict contract at rival publisher Longmans Green, she was obliged to adopt a droll pen name, one that inverted the pseudonym of preeminent nineteenth-century novelist George Eliot. When it was discovered that Eliot George was in fact a pseudonym for Freeman, many falsely hypothesized that Freeman had used the name to distance herself from the novel's incendiary content.

Fred Slark, the stalwart assistant director who had by now worked with Furie on every film beginning with *A Cool Sound from Hell*, had worked under Raymond Stross the previous year. It is fair to surmise that Slark, who sold Furie to George Fowler on *Doctor Blood's Coffin*, also sold Furie to Stross on *The Leather Boys*. Having a look at Furie's previous youth pictures, including *A Dangerous Age* and *The Young Ones*, Stross realized that Furie would be able to meet the challenges of *The Leather Boys*. Stross's previous projects, which included 1961's *The Mark* (which tackled child molestation) and 1963's *The Very Edge* (which examined a married couple's response to the wife's rape) were in the vanguard of fresh cinematic adventurism. Even if these were B pictures in the grand scheme of things, the pedigree of artistic risk was no less solid.

Bowing out of *Summer Holiday* opened up the director's chair to the debuting Peter Yates, a Brit who cut his teeth as an assistant director on large Hollywood productions like *The Inn of the Sixth Happiness* and as an episodic television director on shows like *The Saint*. He later directed hits like *Bullitt, Breaking Away,* and *The Dresser.* Before Yates took the reins, *Summer Holiday* was offered to the BBC directing prodigy and future British film auteur Ken Russell. Russell detested the script and declined, but he later made his feature-film debut with *French Dressing* (1964) under Kenneth Harper's producership.

The chief drawback of accepting the position with Stross rested in the fact that *The Leather Boys* worked on a tighter budget; thus there would be less pay for the director, whereas *Summer Holiday* had offered him substantially more. This aspect most startled Sheila Furie, who urged him to reconsider in favor of the higher paycheck. Furie was deaf to this appeal for many reasons, one being that he did not wish to be pigeonholed early on as "the Cliff Richard director." Another cause for alarm was that Kenneth Harper had warned Furie about Raymond Stross, who openly deemed himself a creative element of the crew, often to the chagrin of many of the directors under his employ. After the box-office success of *The Young Ones*, however, Furie was confident in his ability to assert directorial command in the event of being second-guessed. The potential risks were all ones that Furie was willing to venture. Winning the gamble meant high yield, as success on this project would certainly mean a gateway to more serious pictures.

The adaptation had been reframed to focus slightly more on the married couple Reg and Dot, though the homosexuality component remained present. The film now told the story of Reg and Dot as two cheery, foolhardy kids from working-class backgrounds who get married young and, as per the cliché, learn that marriage is not what it is cracked up to be. Reg is naive and rather dull-minded but no less decent and dependable, while the ineffectual Dot is materialistic and arrested in adolescence. When it appears as if Reg's recently widowed grandmother might need to be moved into the old-age home she dreads, Reg is the only member of his family who is prepared to move heaven and earth to save her from that fate. He even suggests that he and Dot move in with her, much to Dot's unveiled protestations. This puts a damper on the marriage, even when Reg finds his granny a lodger in the form of his new friend Pete (renamed from the novel's Dick). When Reg has a feud with Dot and moves out, he moves in with Pete, where they nonsexually share a bed (and much of everything else) and become inseparable. Reg finds solace from his crumbling marriage in this friendship but does not see what the audience can clearly see, that the gay Pete has designs on him. In a departure from the gay-themed films of the time, however, Pete is depicted as generous and indeed lovable, and the relationship between Reg and Pete is depicted as genuine, even though the two see the relationship somewhat differently. It is only the husband-wife relationship that is given short shrift.

Then married to actress Anne Heywood, the "colorful" Stross often insisted on casting her in previous and subsequent projects. It was in fact Heywood who first recommended the novel to her husband. Because *The Leather Boys* centered around its three young protagonists, Stross did not at any time make Heywood's casting a condition, nor was it even suggested. Instead, responding to the wave of praise surrounding Tony Richardson's *A Taste of Honey,* he contacted the agent of the newly established Rita Tushingham, who had achieved a breakthrough with the lead role in her debut picture. Astoundingly, Richardson had chosen her from a casting pool of two thousand young women. Like others, the Royal Court–trained Tushingham was bewitched by Stross's comportment and self-presentation and recalls that "Raymond was always beautifully turned out. His hair was always beautifully coiffured, to a degree I had never seen in any man up to that time."

The rest of the cast was filled out by Dudley Sutton, Colin Campbell, a newcomer to feature films who had been a child actor at the BBC, and Gladys Henson, a veteran character actress of sixty-five, who played Reg's widowed grandmother faced with spending the rest of her days in an old-folks home.

"When Sid first told me about the project, he told me that it was about a young couple with marital problems, so I naturally assumed I'd be playing the part of the husband," says Dudley Sutton, chuckling. "Then he tells me no, that I'm playing this gay boy, and I just thought, 'Oh shit!'" Sutton, however, despite fear of the obvious stigma surrounding actors playing homosexual characters, strongly connected with this provocative aspect of the story in the same way he had connected to *The Boys* with its position on capital punishment. It would be another five years before homosexuality was decriminalized in England; in 1962 the only filmic references Brits had for homosexuals had been Murray Melvin's sympathetic art student in *A Taste of Honey* and, especially, *Victim,* a "social thriller" about Dirk Bogarde as a lawyer pursuing a blackmailer who targets homosexuals. Sutton considers what originally beckoned him to the role of Pete: "Even though I'm not gay, I had a deep concern for gay friends of mine at the time who were being put in prison, beaten, blackmailed, and all that. Most of them went to New York because there was less prejudice there than there was in London. When I got the role of Pete, I wanted to shatter the stereotype by not mincing around and doing the campy, limp-wristed stuff. And Sid, bless him, thought that was right on."

Indeed, at the time of its conception, the film's sense of individuality and freshness hinged on the risk Sutton took to humanize Pete beyond any posturing or caricaturing. Continues Sutton, "I hated *Victim.* I thought it was shit. The title really said it all, didn't it? All homosexual are just pathetic victims. And I wanted to see a gay character who wasn't an art student or a hairdresser or something one would expect. I wanted to play a gay character who was much like any other man. He was just some guy in love, an average bloke." Sutton's improvised dialogue for Pete was based on a crew of merchant navy men he had known as a mechanic in the RAF. These navy men often took boats to Cape Town with "queens" below deck. They would tell Sutton stories speaking with "this bogus, high-speed pseudo-American accent." Seeing this characterization actualized, Furie enthusiastically gave Sutton free rein.

Furie, who gravitated toward further experimentation with British realism after the modest release of *The Boys,* was up to the task of adapting Freeman's material, but he immediately knew that a great deal of work would have to be done to Freeman's adaptation. Her shooting script, mirroring her own source novel, was written in dense Cockney dialect, emphasizing that it was first intended as the project's Bible.

Budgeted at one hundred thousand pounds, *The Leather Boys* went into production in October 1962. By that time, as predicted, Furie had gone head-to-head with Stross during preproduction over the director's unorthodox process, one that was later modified and pioneered by British independent Mike Leigh. Tushingham, whose memories fully concurred with Furie's, remembers, "The book read well, but in script form, it didn't flow as it would or sound like these kids would really talk." Because of this, Furie used the rehearsal period to workshop dialogue that was improvised around the intent of each scene. Script girl Helen Whitson would keep track of which bits of improvisation were deemed workable, and the script's dialogue was rewritten based on these notes.

Says Edward Thorpe, "Gillian really didn't like that Sidney was changing all the dialogue. She rather thought that the dialogue she had written was better than what they had improvised." Furie and Freeman never went to war over this contention, though, and remained civil and even friendly throughout the rest of production. According to Thorpe, Freeman found him amusingly impulsive and prone to saying things that raised eyebrows. "She came home one day and told me that Sid told her that he was a Communist," Thorpe says, laughing. Dudley Sutton, however, says, "I thought for a long time that Sid actually was a red . . . and then, when I met him again some years later in the eighties, and he was praising Margaret Thatcher, I thought decidedly not."

Creative discontent with the young director came not just from Gillian Freeman, but from other angles. At one point during this rehearsal process, while the actors ad-libbed a scene in a small theater space, Stross arrived unannounced to have a look at what they were doing. Remembers Dudley Sutton, "I hated him being there because it was sort of a sacred space, and we were very close-knit while reworking on the whole thing. It was a distraction." Sutton's ire was incited when the tendentious Stross interrupted a rehearsal by shouting at Sutton "You're not being queer enough! Queen it up!" The actor proceeded to take him by force and push him through the doors, stridently ordering him to stay away and keep out of directing his performance.

"Dud, you've just ruined your career!" Furie exclaimed in amazement, half-laughing at the frustrated actor's audacity. Furie later went to visit Stross, who was beside himself, to quell his hysteria over Sutton's behavior. "Sid told me he went upstairs to Raymond's office and told him, 'For 90 pounds a week, we've got a genius playing that character!'" He continued to passionately back the actor on his decision to play the role without the usual gay affectation. Stross, biting both his tongue and the bullet, acquiesced and accepted his conviction. Dutton insists that Stross "wanted a dirty movie, a snide movie about a couple of fags, as he saw it."

Sutton fortified his friendship with Furie when he showed up for work one morning with a black eye. He explained that while defending a short Jewish guy being victimized by a pair of toughs at a local pub, he received the contusion as a souvenir. "This guy was known as The Count and some lads were having a go at him. Like a fucking idiot, I had to say 'Pick on someone your own size!' I showed up the next day with a shiner and Sid just looked at me and shouted, 'Jesus, Dud, what the fuck happened to your eye?' I told him what happened, which was completely true, and he just paused and said, 'Hmm, Jewish guy, huh? Great, Dud! Thank you!' It was the first time I learned that Sid was Jewish. He was grateful I had done that."

Despite the fact *The Leather Boys* was only her second film, Tushingham also found herself stunned by her director's manner. With his slicked-back hair and endearing braggadocio, Furie's air of youth and cool were as sure as the weather. "He would show up to work in jeans and a sweater, which was a stark contrast to Desmond Davis and Basil Dearden. Basil was an excellent director but very 'old guard.' He would show up in a suit and tie, with a very fine upper-crust public-school accent, and we worked off the script religiously. Tony Richardson was freer to a certain extent on *A Taste of Honey,* but we wouldn't really improvise at all. Sidney was special because he really wanted every single line to be fresh."

According to Sutton, during an actual take, Furie would turn his back and concentrate purely on the sound of the dialogue. The need was to block everything else out beforehand, with the goal of capturing dialogue as if he had actually been eavesdropping on a real conversation. At the end, after yelling "Cut," he would turn to Chic Waterson, the camera operator. If Waterson nodded, he would have the take printed. "I was actually very impressed with that," Sutton said. "He had this intense desire to make everything look real, and then sound real, and gave concentration to both individually."

When news of the Cuban Missile Crisis hit the set on Monday, October 15, 1962, Tushingham clearly recalls Furie cancelling the rest of the day's shooting and announcing to the cast and crew, "You can all go home! We're not going to be here tomorrow! Go home to your families!" Says Tushingham, "I vividly remember the poor hairdresser was crying and in such a hurry." The cast and crew reconvened about four days later, with the world still hot amid the international crisis.

Much of the film was shot in and around the Ace Café, a "sprawling, seedy petrol station café near the London terminus of the M1,"[2] which had become the Mecca for leather-clad London motorcyclists. Located on North Circular Road near Brent Junction, the café had been the epicenter of a number of brouhahas the previous year. Scare tactics, however, were often at the heart of a fresh stream of news stories about "teddy boys" and juvenile delinquents reputed to be rampaging the streets about town, with the café identified as their base of operations. The Ton-Up Boys, the most "infamous" among the Ace Café's cyclist clientele, made regular headlines when they stood accused for a variety of transgressions, mostly for charges like disorderly conduct and violations of the noise ordinance.

"At first I was quite scared about going to shoot at the Ace Café, with all these people I knew telling me it wasn't safe and that we'd get into trouble shooting there," says Dudley Sutton. "But then we get there, and it's just a bunch of nice blokes who love motorbikes. All the Ton-Up Boys stuff in the papers was always more of the same bullshit. People were afraid of the leather and the motorcycles, never the actual people in the leather and on the motorcycles." Indeed, in one of these news stories, one of the Ton-Up Boys, a young man of eighteen named Harry Martin, spoke firsthand of this prejudice on behalf of his mates: "People are always blaming us for causing trouble. But we keep to ourselves and the Ace is our café. There's bound to be a bit of noise but no rowdiness. We were arrested for the simple reason that we wear leather jackets."[3] Although the filmmakers were likewise warned by many about the café's less-than-stellar record with the law, these warnings went unheeded for many reasons. Beyond calling out newspapers for their journalistic propaganda, Furie desired the utmost authenticity. Indeed, shooting at the Ace Café played out without much in the way of incident or controversy. The patrons, including those who appeared to be the most fearsome, assisted the cast and crew as unpaid background players. Furie even took their advice, as when one morning one of them pointed to Colin Campbell's pants and exclaimed, "You'd never find an Ace boy wearing them jeans!"[4] So agreeable and comfortable was it that Furie took to shooting there whenever he saw fit.

Ultimately, this way of working led Furie to adapt uniformly to a more guerrilla style of shooting. In 1993, Furie recalled, "It was an era of don't-fake-anything. People just went about their business. The Brits weren't going to show you they were interested. They would just walk through the shot, and they wouldn't look at the camera. You would do your shooting in the café itself, where nothing was roped off. And wherever we went, no one bothered us. We'd go to tough areas near the docks, too."[5]

For Reg and Dot's wedding near the beginning of the film, they leave the church and board a London transit bus in lieu of a festooned car. "We couldn't afford to rent out a bus, so a real transit bus came and we just got on and shot the scene. And then, at the end of a take, we'd get off and a car would run us back for another take on another bus."[6] When they were shooting Reg and Dot's honeymoon at Butlin's Holiday Camp in Bognor Regis along England's southern coast, youthful hijinks ensued. Rita Tushingham remembers, "It really was a very young set, so when something happened like Dudley Sutton getting hold of the Billy Butlin statue and dunking it in the pool, it was not out of character. People were eating, because you could see the people swimming in the pool through the glass wall, and all of a sudden you just saw Billy Butlin's head descending to the bottom. It was just hilarious being at a place like Butlin's with a lot like ours. It was one of those times in life when you felt young, invincible and all that."

The only discontent in the cast was Colin Campbell, who hated Furie's allegiance to improvisation and disliked Dudley Sutton for throwing him off balance with his departures from the workshopped script. "I never stuck totally to the script we reworked in rehearsal, and it mixed him up," says Sutton. "Rita and I got on like a house on fire, however." Fencing with Stross over this matter also persisted, but active interferences were, thankfully, limited.

Production wrapped in December of 1962 and editing was finished four months later, but the film controversially did not reach British theaters until almost a year later. *Variety* reported on February 5, 1964, that *The Leather Boys* had "become a talking-point, sight unseen, in the current hassle about independent producers claiming a raw deal from the two major circuits,"[7] the circuits being ABC and Rank. *Films and Filming* editor Peter G. Baker recounted a "silly" comment from "a film salesman who shall remain nameless" who said, "*The Leather Boys* is a jolly fine film; difficult to sell though, because motorbikes are out. Most youngsters can afford cars these days."[8] This pathetic excuse was made funnier and more disingenuous in light of a previous news item in the August 1963 issue of the magazine. It revealed that the Federation of British Film Makers had started an investigation to discover why theater chains were routinely shafting independent productions in favor of booking theater dates for larger productions financed (even in part) by ABC or the Rank Organisation. It was stated in bold terms, "The situation for independent filmmakers is serious." In October, *Films and Filming* reported that Board of Trade's Cinematograph Film Council had censured the circuits and suggested breaking everything up into booking groups in order to temper the chains' monopoly. Other temporary casualties of this monopoly included the Clive Donner–directed, Harold Pinter–scripted *The Caretaker* (1963) and Basil Dearden's *A Place to Go* (1963), which also starred Rita Tushingham.

Says Rita Tushingham, "I think they were really worried about its content. I want to say they were ashamed of the movie. *The Leather Boys* was a little independent production and it didn't have the advantages other bigger movies like *Victim* had. It was strange for us when it wasn't being released and we had to wait all that time, because we never thought about it while we were doing it. It was so natural for us."

In the United Kingdom, it was released on the ABC circuit in March of 1964, with a West End premiere. The British reviews were complimentary, if slightly cautious. *Observer* critic Penelope Gilliat began her review in plain speech: "Mr. Furie and Mr. Sutton have made a film about loneliness." She then proceeded to give Dudley Sutton what he still calls "the best review of my career." *Films and Filming* applauded the "careful and observant direction of Sidney Furie." The film was a financial success at the British box office.

When *The Leather Boys* arrived in the United States in November 1965, distributed by R. Lee Platt's Allied Artists (only opening after the success of Furie's second post–*Leather Boys* picture, *The Ipcress File*), the reviews were mostly raves. It was the first of Furie's films to arrive in America uncompromised. Brendan Gill of the *New Yorker* called the film "one of the best films of the year, and one of the very few pictures I've ever seen that I, though a born Mr. Fixit, didn't feel tempted to tamper with in any way." Gill also wrote with complimentary abandon that "the chief hero of the occasion is the director, Sidney J. Furie." In the *New York Times,* A. H. Weiler observed that Furie and the cast had "managed to elicit honesty and genuine tenderness and humor from their simple drama." Richard Schickel in *Life* opened his review stating, "Sidney J. Furie is an offbeat movie director. I mean that quite literally," but he stated that *The Leather Boys*'s "sputtery, fitful rhythm" was "artfully achieved." Ironically, he then compared the film favorably to "the over-praised Canadian study of demi-delinquency, *Nobody Waved Good-bye,*" of course not mentioning—nor perhaps even realizing—that Furie had pioneered the still meager Canadian independent cinema scene within which *Nobody Waved Good-bye*'s director Don Owen operated. Schickel felt in general that Furie had "kept his balance, neither sensationalizing nor sentimentalizing, trying always to see with his own fresh eye. I think it will wear well." The rest of the reviews were similar.

Commercial success, despite the wealth of good reviews, was not something *The Leather Boys* achieved Stateside, where today the film is obscure and seldom mentioned alongside other landmark British realist pictures. In 1966 it was nominated for a single Golden Globe Award, for "Best English-Language Foreign Film," a prize captured by John Schlesinger's *Darling* (1965). The film does have a legacy, however, especially in England, where it is considered a classic of its kind. Clips from the film were prominently featured in the music video for the Smiths' *Girlfriend in a Coma,* and a still of Colin Campbell in *The Leather Boys* provides the cover image for their single "William, It Was Really Nothing."

Novelist Michard Arditti, in the foreword of the 2014 reprinting of *The Leather Boys* (which, for the first time, is credited to Gillian Freeman sans pseudonym), writes that both the novel and the screen adaptation of *The Leather Boys* "played a vital part in liberalising British attitudes to homosexuality."[9] Robert Murphy writes in his book, "What makes the film remarkable is its refusal to impose facile, artificial solutions on the problems of the young. Reg is left with nowhere to go at the end of the film because there is nowhere for him to go until he wakes up to the changes that are going on around him."[10]

Dudley Sutton never worked with Furie again; he spent the rest of the decade dealing with an alcohol problem that temporarily crippled his career. He speaks only in superlatives when remembering his outings with the director. "I liked working with Sidney Furie better than anyone I've ever worked with, and that list includes Ken Russell, Fellini, Derek Jarman and Sally Potter. It was so thrilling to go to work, because it was open, and there was a trust, and we trusted what we came up with in the story. It was a dynamic process, which you don't get very often."

The Leather Boys remains perhaps Furie's best and most resonant film from a narrative, stylistic, and emotional standpoint. The staging of scenes and moments, like the confrontation after the grandfather's funeral and the dolly away from Rita Tushingham at the Ace Café, minted Furie as a director with an expressive camera. It is also his most progressive from a social and political standpoint. In an age of de rigueur films like Basil Dearden's *Victim,* in which Dirk Bogarde's homosexual character is more conceptual, a topical political instrument rather than someone for whom we develop human sympathy, Furie never allowed even the most discreet allusions to pervasive and often insidious homosexual stereotypes. Pete's homosexuality is never thematically overdrawn; it is a single point in a larger story, rather than an unbearably heavy focal point around which the film single-mindedly revolves. This would have weighed the story down. His character can feel wounded without becoming pitiful or the butt of some covert joke.

The Leather Boys also crystallizes the theme Furie tirelessly developed over the years in *A Dangerous Age, A Cool Sound from Hell,* and *During One Night.* When Reg and Pete go to the seaside and half-interestedly pick up two flighty females, the sequence is directed in both camera and performance to suggest the whole ordeal as a charade. Beyond any homosexual undercurrent or consideration of Furie's wounded male psyche, the film examines the outermost boundaries of platonic male friendship. It effectively probes how intense and elastic such a relationship can be and mines the gray area between platonic and erotic. This is something seldom considered in other films, which often take either one tack or the other. Thematically beyond the surface-scratching of *A Dangerous Age,* the early inquiries of *A Cool Sound from Hell,* and the literalization of *During One Night, The Leather Boys* is rich in the filmmaker's ability to realize the theme's deeper complexities. He again tackled the complexities of male bonding in *Little Fauss and Big Halsy* (1970).

In 1993, Ace Café historian Mark Wilsmore spearheaded an annual event to mark the closure of the original Ace Café, along with a book and a film documenting its history. This yearly gathering proved more and more popular, until it became something resembling a major event. His ambition to reopen the café as a motorcycle hangout was ultimately realized on September 6, 2001. Rita Tushingham, Dudley Sutton, Colin Campbell, and Gillian Freeman were there for its ribbon-cutting. "There was a priest there, and a vicar there and the whole thing was blessed," recalls Tushingham. "*The Leather Boys* is memorialized there. All these people with their motorcycles were so happy to have the place back again, and grateful to us for immortalizing it on film."

Furie confessed to *Sight & Sound*, "I've made so many films like *The Leather Boys*, where I have been trying desperately to make at least the details believable while knowing all the time that there was a hard central nugget of untruth in the materials I had to work from, which would compromise things in the end."[11] If one is to accept that statement, his next project selection took him even further away from the elusive truth for which he was searching, so much so as to lampoon the pursuit of it. Although pegged to direct a film adaptation of Frank Norman's *Fings Ain't Wot They Used t'Be*, a Lionel Bart–scored West End stage musical about spivs (petty criminals) and teddy boys that had been directed on the stage by Joan Littlewood,[12] his real follow-up was a glossy movie about the movies—or, more appropriately, the dream factory.

Harsh English winters were perhaps most responsible for Furie's reassuming the director's chair on the third Cliff Richard musical, *Wonderful Life*. Under Peter Yates's direction, the previous entry in the series, *Summer Holiday*, rose to become the second-highest grosser at the 1963 British box office.

Wonderful Life offered what seemed to be a pleasant excursion, or rather escape, to the Canary Islands during the coldest, most unforgiving months in England. "Ken Harper took me out, wined me and dined me, and he loved only the best wine, and cigars. He told me about the Canary Islands and did this really convincing song-and-dance. 'Come on, you owe me. We'll have fun.' By the end of that, who wouldn't accept?" Before Furie knew it, he was in and around Las Palmas de Gran Canaria, scouting locations.

Peter Myers and Ronnie Cass contrived another "let's-put-on-a-show" formula story recycled from previous Cliff Richard vehicles, which had in turn recycled them from classic MGM musicals. This time, moviemaking was the focal point of the shenanigans. Cliff and The Shadows play a group of stewards who are thrown off a ship after short-circuiting the liner's electrical circuits. In a dinghy, they row to the shore of a tropical island, where, seeking work and wandering the desert, they happen upon a veiled damsel in distress mounted atop a camel. Managing to "rescue" her, Richard (in the role of "Johnny"), discovers that he has just ruined a scene in a movie being shot by big-time director Lloyd Davis. Johnny is given the job of stunt man for a cowardly star, and his mates are hired to play chamber quartet mood music on the set. Enlisting the help of the cameraman, they surreptitiously make their own movie while pretending to rehearse Jenny, the pretty lead actress with whom Johnny predictably falls in love. When both movies are separately made, each one is only half-good. When director Davis learns what his young counterparts have done, he cuts the two movies together and emerges with one terrific movie.

Susan Hampshire was floated by Furie for the role of Jenny, because he had happily worked with her on *During One Night.* Walter Slezak, a veteran of classic Hollywood films like *Lifeboat, The Pirate,* and *The Inspector General,* was cast in the role of blustery film director Lloyd Davis, the new incarnation of the Robert Morley character type in *The Young Ones*—that is, the "old fogey" antagonist in the classic youth-versus-experience struggle. In the fashion of *The Young Ones,* the villain reconciles with the heroes in the end.

As Furie started to make preparations for his stay in the Canary Islands, he received a call from producer Walter Shenson, who dangled a tempting offer in front of his nose. "I remember where I was sitting in the bedroom of my house in Roehampton when Walter Shenson called to offer me *A Hard Day's Night,*" says Furie.[13] Because the director had already signed a contract for *Wonderful Life* and could not break free, Shenson then approached Richard Lester, with whom he had worked on *The Mouse on the Moon* (1963), and the rest is history. Facts, memories, and halfhearted regrets be as they may, Furie certainly did not wish to continue churning out rock musicals for the rest of his tenure in England. Nevertheless, *A Hard Day's Night* came back to haunt him, the Cliff Richard team, and their latest project around release time.

Shooting commenced in January 1964. In March, *Films and Filming* correspondent Brian O'Brien quoted Furie as saying, "You can make any kind of film you want here. There are mountains, palm trees, barren deserts and huge sand dunes, scrub, lush green fields, donkeys, camels, horses, Cadillacs, Vespa scooters. And the sun never stops shining."[14] The veracity of this last claim is highly questionable, since the crew was often chasing the weather while shooting various sequences. Because of weather issues, a production that normally would have taken three weeks wound up taking nearly three months. Cliff Richard remembers, "For the first couple days, everything was fine when we filmed in a place called Masapalomas. And then when we came to do the close-ups the next day, it had rained and everything was black. It looked more like a Welsh mining village than a tropical island. So we waited and waited, and when the rain eventually stopped, the sand took four days to dry out and regain its color. Our stint there was terrible."[15]

As a result of these setbacks, the production went over budget, in the end skyrocketing from £350,000 to somewhere in the vicinity of £750,000. In the midst of all this, Harper considered uprooting production to Puerto Rico.

Susan Hampshire's experience was largely negative. She explains, "Sidney seemed very agitated all the time, because I think he was under a great deal of pressure. He was a completely different human being than he had been [on *During One Night*]. He couldn't say anything cross to Cliff under any circumstances, because Cliff had his entourage, and his people were on the set every day. But with me, I think because he knew me, he could be rather abrupt and unpleasant."

There to assuage Furie's grief was choreographer Gillian Lynne, who went on to an illustrious career staging the dance in such hit stage shows as *Half a Sixpence, Cats,* and *The Phantom of the Opera.* Gone were the power struggles between Furie and choreographer Herbert Ross while making *The Young Ones.* Furie speaks of Lynne with considerable affection: "She was a joy and a true collaborator. She could get anyone to dance, because she is one of the most inventive, incredible people."[16] Susan Hampshire agrees that Lynne was the production's much-needed boon: "Gillian was a ball of energy, and was lovely just to be around. Everyone adored her." *Wonderful Life* provided her first movie experience.

Another valuable "technical star" of *Wonderful Life* turned out to be the newly perfected motion picture zoom lens. Its inventor, Pierre Angenieux, received a technical award from the Academy of Motion Picture Arts and Sciences in 1964. With BBC cameraman Ken Higgins as cinematographer, Furie was later invited to a filmmaker's symposium to screen the final film and demonstrate the expansive and often lavish use of the lens. "We went a little crazy with using the zoom lens on that picture," says Furie, grinning with the fond memory of how the novelty appeal of this "new toy" inebriated his muses and induced using it to excess. "Almost the entire opening twenty minutes of the movie are elaborate zoom-outs. They oohed and ahhed over it at the time though, believe me."

The centerpiece of *Wonderful Life* is certainly the boisterous, thirteen-minute "We Love the Movies" detour sequence, an inventive variety-show-style affair in which Cliff and The Shadows breezily parade through set piece after set piece gussied up as Chaplin, Fairbanks, Valentino, Jolson, Garbo, Astaire, the Marx Brothers, and others, charting the entire history of the movies from the silent era all the way up to James Bond. Requiring more than sixty costume changes, the sequence suggests a structural anarchy suited to a film that affectionately sends up the act of moviemaking. In fact, the first word that comes to mind at the mention of *Wonderful Life*—a film suffused with an unabashed love of movies like few others—is "infatuated."

On July 2, 1964, the film received a "Royal Premiere," with Princess Alexandra and her husband, Sir Angus Ogilvy, the vice chairman of the Association of Youth Clubs Expansion Campaign Fund, in attendance. It opened at the box office the next day, receiving lukewarm reviews. In the film's most laudatory notices, *Film Daily*'s Edward Lipton called it "a thoroughly enjoyable picture" that "should be exploited so that adults see it too. Hip grown-ups will appreciate it even more," while the *Motion Picture Herald* praised Furie's "apt direction," declaring that "the movies as an institution have been taken apart, drawn and quartered in a most delightful and unexpected way in the guise of a British rock 'n' roll film." *Box Office* opined that it had "all the freshness, gaiety and enthusiasm" with dancing that was "certainly the best that has been seen in any British musical." *Films and Filming*, however, called it "a sad little picture. It's so square. The musical numbers both sound and for the most part look like Hollywood of the forties." *Variety* commented, "Sidney J. Furie is an on-the-ball director but he has a tough struggle with some of the material at his disposal" and lamented that "tighter editing would have kept the tempo at highest pitch."

Within three days of the general release of *Wonderful Life*, Richard Lester's *A Hard Day's Night* was unleashed into British theaters, royally trumping any chance the comparably old-fashioned Cliff Richard vehicle had to turn a profit. According to Richard, it took seven years for *Wonderful Life* to make its money back. "*Wonderful Life* was a flop, a disaster from the word go," the pop star later said. The titanic overall effect of the Beatles at the box office proved too much to handle for Cliff Richard's future screen ventures. Continues Richard, "The Beatles were doing films that were really avant-garde movies at the time. We were trying to do films that were one step from *The Young Ones* and *Summer Holiday,* but they were not different enough."[17] Explains Susan Hampshire, "I didn't want to do *Wonderful Life*. I was sort of persuaded to do it by my agent. Then, I was given a hard time by the press when it was released."

Seen today, *Wonderful Life* does have its merits. On a purely cinematic level, it is a more exciting film than *The Young Ones.* The film is an exuberant pastiche of various movie musical number styles, blending the swooning rock-idol love ballads of Elvis Presley pictures (in the "Do You Remember" and "In a Matter of Moments" sequences), the extended meta-musical detours reminiscent of MGM productions (in "We Love the Movies" and "Imagination"), the beach-blanket-bingo-style numbers of the Avalon-Funnicello movies of the time (in "On the Beach"), and the garish, hyperkinetic numbers reminiscent of the later Jacques Demy operettas (in "Working Together"). Movies are the essence of life itself in *Wonderful Life,* and the title reflects this. The eponymous "wonderful life" is clearly life as it exists in the movies, while the mission of the heroes is to make the "wonderful life" of the film-within-the-film more wonderful by covertly musicalizing it. The affected Andy Hardy–esque narrative model of the previous Cliff Richard musicals is subverted, as the moviemaking dream factory and its irresistible magic assume almost religious heights in *Wonderful Life.*

The crane-mounted tracking shot toward the end of the "On the Beach" sequence, approximately thirty minutes into the film, inaugurates a favorite visual trope used and reproduced in many shots throughout the film—the reveal of film equipment via a backward dolly. The background dancers finally approach the foreground as the number reaches its crescendo, and the audience becomes conscious of the lighting sources as glaringly reflected off the actors' faces and bodies. Only moments later, the lighting sources themselves become visible in the foreground. In the moments between, one is deliberately taken out of the action at hand, suddenly becoming hyperaware of its artifice. The sequence's staging allows for a fleeting moment of reflection, causing the digesters of the images to awaken startled and disoriented. *Wonderful Life,* though ostensibly a quick throwaway picture, offers Furie at his most sly and witty. He has packed the film with insider's humor (sometimes approaching postmodernism) and a joie de vivre that is rare for such an enterprise. It also more closely approximates Furie's admitted influence, Stanley Donen's *Give a Girl a Break!* (1953).

Sight & Sound wrote that the Cliff Richard musicals collectively have "more life and spirit than any British musical one can think of since the heyday of Jack Buchanan and Jessie Matthews."[18] A compliment like this could not subdue the vicissitudes of *Wonderful Life*'s troubled production, nor could it subdue the angst of seeing history repeat itself. This time, the American distributor Paramount deleted a full thirty minutes from the original British version and retitled it *Swingers' Paradise.*

Chapter 5

Through a Glass Refracted

The Wild Angles Picture Show

Insubordinate. Insolent. A trickster.
—Harry Palmer's B-107 profile in The Ipcress File

Furie returned from the Canary Islands to discover he was invited to a special prerelease screening of Joseph Losey's *King and Country,* starring Dirk Bogarde. Losey was still riding high from his critical success with *The Servant* the year before, and his follow-up was hotly anticipated. Furie had shrugged off the two Cliff Richard pictures by that time, feeling they had served their purpose as preliminary name-makers. Although his industry track record was established, his critical reputation had failed to solidify by the outset of 1964, as he begrudgingly struggled to rise above the rank of journeyman. One evening, a call from a reporter at the *Evening Standard* confirmed Furie's worst suspicions on the matter.

"Nat Cohen recently called you, Sidney Furie, a 'has-been.' Would you care to comment on that remark?" Cohen, an eminent producer known mostly for the popular *Carry On* series, was then the head of the British production company Anglo-Amalgamated (later to dissolve with Associated British Picture Corporation under EMI).

Furie, with brio, fired back: "That's funny. How can I be a 'has-been'? I haven't even been a 'been' yet!"[1] Furie's angst, however, went deeper. His irritated impatience over the delayed release of *The Leather Boys* coexisted with a confidence that critical detractors who had yet to be won over by his efforts would soon realize his value as a serious filmmaker.

The Losey screening drove thorns further into Furie's side. At the end of *King and Country,* the notoriously petulant Losey asked the people present for their reactions, expecting them to fall in line with praise and sycophantic choruses.

"Well," Furie began, responding to Losey's soliciting of reactions, "the direction was great, and the film is really well done, but it was the script that had problems for me, to be honest. The script didn't quite work for me." As Furie broke down his specific issues with the writing, Losey, in ill-mannered form, interrupted his young critic.

"Who exactly are you?" Losey testily asked Furie.

"I'm Sidney Furie, I'm a director."

"Is that so?" Losey responded, now connecting a face with a name he had seen printed in passing. "And what have you directed?"

"Why would that matter?"

"I'd just like to know," said Losey. Hesitating slightly, Furie recounted a few of his directing credits and assured Losey that his comments were made with the best of intentions.

"A director who has directed nothing is criticizing *my* film!" Losey exclaimed. At that moment becoming persona non grata, Furie backed down and retreated from the event. As a result, Furie has to this day never held advance screenings for friends or fellow filmmakers. "It always puts everyone in a terrible position, and hardens the pride of filmmakers with too much ego." His status in the eyes of established filmmakers like Losey, as "a director who hadn't directed anything," was about to change in a very big way, with *The Leather Boys* and especially his next film, *The Ipcress File.*

First serialized in the *London Evening Standard* before being published by Hodder & Sloughton Press in July 1962, *The Ipcress File* was haircare entrepreneur Charles D. Kasher's break-in to the movie business. Kasher had, throughout the 1950s, patented and developed Charles Antell's Formula No. 9 as a lanolin-based cure for baldness. (Antell was Kasher's mother's maiden name.) His extended commercials for his product became a prototype for what later became known as the infomercial. When Kasher first took *The Ipcress File* to the United Artists New York offices to pitch it as a movie property, it was there that he met Harry Saltzman, a producer whose name was firmly associated with both Tony Richardson's Woodfall Films and the increasingly popular James Bond franchise. Based in London, Saltzman made many such trips to United Artists in New York, because the Bonds and most of the Woodfall projects were set up through them.

Saltzman's attraction to *The Ipcress File* was spurred by a hunch that he could fashion a separate series of spy films, likewise adapted from popular novels, into products that would be cheaper to finance than the Bonds and just as easy to sell on the international film markets. The spy film had fast become a hot commodity after the lucrative release of *Dr. No*, and Saltzman felt that resigning himself solely to the 007 franchise was limiting further possible business opportunities centered around the current boom. This was to be a completely different enterprise, independent of his Bond partner Albert "Cubby" Broccoli. The seasoned producer would also annex many members of the Bond series technical team to helm this new slate of pictures.

When resident Hammer Films screenwriter-producer Jimmy Sangster became aware that Saltzman was on the hunt for an interesting young director who could deliver a quality movie on the cheap, Sangster recommended that he have a look at *The Leather Boys*, which had just received the cover treatment in the January 1964 issue of *Films and Filming* magazine.[2] Furie had by now vaguely regretted declining producer Walter Shenson's offer to direct the first Beatles picture, *A Hard Day's Night* (1964). Says Furie, "I know now, and I did know then, that I could not have done what Richard Lester did on that picture. If I made it, sure, it would have been Alun Owen's script, but it wouldn't have been anything near that end result." Regardless, when *A Hard Day's Night* became a smash hit that put Richard Lester on the A-list, Furie's dream to make a picture that would lure Hollywood into making him an offer to direct larger pictures was again renewed.

He knew this breakthrough was not to come with Kenneth Rive's production of *Devil Doll*, another film in the illustrious tradition of mad-ventriloquist horror pictures, a la Michael Redgrave's classic turn in *Dead of Night* (1945). Nonetheless, when Rive offered Furie the task of directing, he accepted. He had three sons, and his wife was now carrying their fourth child. When *The Ipcress File* came his way, however, he stepped down during preproduction, as he had on *Summer Holiday*, recommending old CBC pal Lindsay Shonteff for the job. Furie remained on much of the picture as an uncredited producer when Rive asked him to supervise Shonteff, whose rookie status in England rendered him an unproven risk. "I had done low-rent horror already, with *Doctor Blood's Coffin* and *Snake Woman*," says Furie. "*Devil Doll* didn't excite me because directors are naturally looking to do something they've never done before. A spy picture, on the other hand, did excite me." Harry Saltzman's name was also a hook. He was a hitmaker, a showman, a marquee name just as prominent or larger than many directors, having produced *Saturday Night and Sunday Morning,* one of Furie's favorite films upon his arrival in England.

Ken Adam, who had just previously designed the sets for *Dr. Strangelove, or How I Learned to Stop Worrying and Love the Bomb* (1964) as well as for two of the first three Bond pictures, was hired early in preproduction as production designer. "When Harry decided that he wanted to do *The Ipcress File* like a 'Poor Man's Bond,' we attacked him on that," says Adam. "Sidney, Michael Caine and myself, we all ganged up on him and told him that it should be an anti-hero, not a Poor Man's Bond."[3] The then-unknown actor chosen as the film's star, Michael Caine, adds, "It was not even to be a competition with Bond. It was never another suave spy. It was more like a real spy, the kind of ordinary guy who you wouldn't look at twice walking down the street. It was a 'spy as victim' versus 'spy as hero' sort of mentality."[4] Robert Murphy writes in his book *Sixties British Cinema* that the film "depended for its success less on its plot than on the novelty of Caine's Harry Palmer and an espionage world characterized by grimy offices and cracked cups rather than luxury apartments and expensive nightclubs."[5]

The Ipcress File was to be lensed in Techniscope, a cost-effective two-perforation process that delivered a CinemaScope-sized image without the use of expensive anamorphic lenses, while also circumnavigating the licensing costs associated with proper CinemaScope. Essentially, it provided the allure and prestige of wide screen, furthering the illusion of an "event picture," but for less money. Though Furie had recently used the process on *Wonderful Life,* there were a number of limitations with Techniscope. Because projection of the image involved a slight blow-up, grainier resolution and gritty color definition were by-products of its cost-effectiveness. Universal in the late sixties was fastidious in using the process on many of its anamorphic wide-screen pictures, even prompting then-fledgling film critic Roger Ebert to note the studio's adherence to it and to observe its drawbacks ("Universal shouldn't be so cheap")[6] in a 1968 review of Ralph Nelson's *Counterpoint.* The upcoming Bond film, *Thunderball* (1965), was to be lensed more lavishly with proper Panavision, putting into perspective Saltzman's vision of *The Ipcress File* as the Poor Man's Bond. Fortunately, the Techniscope luster worked in favor of *The Ipcress File,* giving the picture a depressed, washed-out edge as a complement to its overcast cityscapes.

Informed that Saltzman was flying to Hollywood to put together additional financing on the film, Furie learned that his producer had effectively cast the lead role, a protagonist for whom the novel provided no name. Furie accepted Saltzman's offer to direct and agreed to meet with the producer and his chosen star upon his return to London.

Despite being at least somewhat well-connected in the London film scene at the time, Furie had never once chanced to meet Harry Saltzman before discussing *The Ipcress File*. Years before, however, in 1961, Furie had encountered Albert "Cubby" Broccoli on board a plane from London. Both were en route to the United Artists offices in New York. "Cubby was always a gentleman, unlike Harry, who was somewhat gruff. I remember asking Cubby on the plane how his current film was looking, which was then *Dr. No*. I think I was finishing the editing of *Doctor Blood's Coffin* or *Three on a Spree* or one of the other cheapies I did for United Artists. He told me, 'Our career is over. The movie is a disaster.' This is before John Barry came in with his music score. Cubby and Harry were suicidal before John Barry came onto the picture."

Furie might not have known Saltzman, but he gradually became aware that he did indeed know the man Saltzman had cast as *The Ipcress File*'s nameless protagonist. "I used to frequent The White Elephant, which was this private dinner club," Furie remembers. "I'd see Terence Stamp always there with this other blonde guy who wore glasses, and they were rather chummy and always had these pretty girls at their table, and they were always laughing. And I sort of hated him at the time. Sometimes, I would get a bit drunk and tell whomever I was with, 'I want to punch that guy in the face.' I guess I was jealous. And here I was now sitting down with Saltzman and, of all people, Terry Stamp's partner-in-crime." Furie later learned that the blond, bespectacled man in question, Michael Caine, happened to be Stamp's flat mate and best friend. "When we met, I said, 'I've got to confess, when I used to see you at the White Elephant with all those girls, I wanted to slug you.' And knowing Michael, that's the best thing you could have said. The worst would have been, 'I'm a great admirer of your work.'"

Says Michael Caine, "Harry had seen me in a supporting role in *Zulu*, and one night, I was having dinner with Terry Stamp, and Harry sat down with his family across the room and saw me. He then had a note sent over to me with a waiter saying, 'Would you have coffee with me afterwards?' and I of course agreed."[7] A seven-year contract with Saltzman and the leading role in *The Ipcress File,* a novel that Caine coincidentally happened to be reading at the time, resulted from that serendipitous meeting—no screen test or any further consideration required. Caine, still an unknown, relished such a lucrative offer, after having spent the previous twelve years struggling in the business. His £4,000 income on *Zulu,* which the actor had already exhausted, increased overnight to £100,000, and soon he was enjoying posh dinners at restaurants like Les Ambassadeurs with his new employer.

"My character in *Zulu* was an aristocrat," Caine continues, "so I looked at Harry sideways and said, 'You saw my character in *Zulu* and you thought of me for the spy in *The Ipcress File?* And he just said, 'Yes, I just think you'd be good in it.' I think he liked the fact that I wore glasses. He liked the idea of a spy with glasses. And I really loved the character, because he was insolent."[8]

Prior to Caine's fortuitous casting, both Christopher Plummer and Richard Harris had been approached for the role. Plummer, who at that point had only been cast previously in supporting roles, turned down Saltzman's offer in favor of a well-paying lead role in *The Sound of Music,* and Harris, whose star had risen after Lindsay Anderson's acclaimed *This Sporting Life* (1963), turned it down in favor of Sam Peckinpah's troubled production *Major Dundee,* in which he starred opposite Charlton Heston. Harris later regretted this decision. *Ipcress* screenwriter W. H. "Bill" Canaway suggested the relatively lesser known Harry H. Corbett, who had just ascended to leading-man status with two films, Muriel Box's *Rattle of a Simple Man* and Duncan Wood's *The Bargee* (both 1964). Corbett played a key supporting role in Alexander Mackendrick's *Sammy Going South* (1963), Canaway's only previous screenwriting credit (based on his own novel).

The immediate question: the name they would give to *Ipcress* novelist Len Deighton's anonymous hero for the film version. "Harry and I agreed that the character's name had to be boring," Caine reported, "so I immediately said 'Harry,' and then realized what I had just said, and I backpeddled and said, 'Oh, I'm sorry, Harry, I didn't mean anything by that.' And he just said, 'It's alright, my real name is Herschel.'"[9] Caine then remembered a boy named Palmer with whom he attended school in Marshall Gardens, claiming he was "the most boring boy" he had ever met. "That's it," said Saltzman, "We'll call him Harry Palmer."

Saltzman set the film's budget at six hundred thousand pounds. Dennis

Selinger, Caine's agent and a close personal friend of Harry Saltzman, assisted in the casting of the film's supporting players, including the key roles of Palmer's mutually distrusting superior officers Colonel Dalby and Colonel Ross, played by Nigel Green and Guy Doleman, respectively. Green had likewise been recruited from *Zulu,* and Doleman, a New Zealander, had already established a respectable career in the Australian film industry. Doleman performed double duty for Harry Saltzman at the time of production, appearing also in the Bond production *Thunderball,* which was shooting simultaneously on a neighboring stage at Pinewood Studios. One of the roles that had not been cast before Furie's arrival was that of Jean Courtney, the alluring female agent at the Ministry of Defence who keeps tabs on Palmer and, in classic spy-literature tradition, beds the hero. Joan Collins and Carol White auditioned for both Furie and Saltzman for the role eventually given to Sue Lloyd, who had up to that time acted only in scattered television.

No sooner had preproduction started than Saltzman's acrimony toward Furie began steadily building. Composer John Barry, who was hired well before shooting commenced, remembers clearly, "[Saltzman] told people at the start: 'I'm gonna hold this guy's hand all the way through.' He would say to Sidney himself: 'You just shoot the stuff. I've got Peter Hunt to put it all together.'"[10] From early on, the crusty Saltzman, a formidable dealmaker with little to no aesthetic sense, railed against his director's style affectations.

Furie, with alarming candor, made his ongoing displeasure with the script known on a constant basis, as others associated with the project lodged complaints about the project's quality as reflected in the writing. An epidemic of insecurity broke out. Demands for a major rewrite and a near-overhaul followed, with scripter James Doran later enlisted to alleviate W. H. Canaway's considerable workload. Writers Lukas Heller, Lionel Davidson, Ken Hughes, and Johanna Harwood provided additional work on the script, without screen credit. (Harwood had scripted *Dr. No, From Russia with Love,* and the Saltzman-produced Bob Hope vehicle *Call Me Bwana.*) Saltzman saw Furie as an insolent young upstart and found it impossible to "hold his hand" through the production as he had originally planned. When he word of Furie's unorthodox methods filtered down from *Leather Boys* producer Raymond Stross, he feared that he had hired a renegade who would be difficult to rein in. The Bond films had built the franchise around scrupulously "stable" directors like Terence Young and

Guy Hamilton, neither identified as "artistic" directors. Saltzman had counted on a journeyman of their ilk.

Charles Kasher, the book's original owner and the film's executive producer, pleaded to Furie before shooting commenced, "This script is garbage. You've got to save it." Michael Caine specifically used the word "codswallop" to describe the text he had been given. Kasher acted as taskmaster in improving the subpar writing. Together, they became what Furie referred to as a "brain-trust," explaining that Kasher "knew nothing about movies, but he was so wise."

The film's ironclad September 21, 1964, start date could not be pushed back, and Saltzman had no time in which to hire another director to make him feel more secure. He had slated *The Ipcress File* as a British-American coproduction between J. Arthur Rank and a Hollywood studio, on a base of financing totaling $460,000. When Columbia, the film's original American backer, reneged on its investment promise, having been reluctant to originally commit to the project owing to a lack of starpower, Saltzman immediately filed a lawsuit against the studio on September 24, 1964. An out-of-court resolution was reached eight days into production, on October 12. Saltzman recruited Universal to step in and fill the Hollywood studio vacancy. Saltzman invested his own money during the time it took for the American money to reach the production, to ensure that work on the film would begin on the designated start date. A Universal Pictures representative, Ernie Nibbs, was assigned to the production and dispatched to monitor their activities on behalf of the studio.

"Saltzman was a bull in a china shop," Furie claims. "Like a lot of people who move mountains, you have to be rough, tough and gutsy. I do have to say that the movie would not have gotten made without him and his devotion to seeing it through, considering the problems with Universal, no matter how much I fought with him during the making of it. And boy, did we fight!" Saltzman's uncertain hope that Furie's previous success with films like *The Young Ones* and *The Leather Boys* would repeat itself were often, in his eyes, shanghaied by Furie's penchant for heavy style. "Harry was a very meat and potatoes guy. His idea for *Ipcress* was all based in Bond, straight-on, no cinematic style whatsoever."

Tremendous, plaguing doubts about the script sent continued waves of doubt and anxiety through Furie and his team. Michael Caine recalls, "The driver picked me up for the first day of shooting and asked me if I was an actor in the movie, and if I had read Len Deighton's book. When I told him I was the lead in it, he told me, 'The whole thing is a load of rubbish, isn't it?' Then, when I arrived on set, Sidney had everyone gather around. He asked if anyone had any matches, and I smoked at that time, so I handed mine over. Sidney took the script, lit the match, looked at everyone and said, 'Here's what I think of this script' and set the match to it. That was his copy of the script, so he asked if anyone had another copy to consult after he had burned his own, so I gave him mine. But it was a gesture, an illustration. It was a hell of a way to be christened into being the lead in a film."

Says Furie, "I was very depressed always when we started shooting, thinking that it was going to be really lousy and I didn't know what to do, so I told myself I would come up with a style of shooting that is different. I put shoulders across the screen, I shot up at things, I shot down, just to make it different, to give it ambiance. It was done out of insecurity, with a little cognac spiked in my morning coffee to give me courage."[11]

Production designer Ken Adam claims, "Harry was still convinced, despite Sidney's and everyone's protestations, that we were still making a Bond picture." Adam cites a specific example of Saltzman's misguided outlook: "I designed Nigel Green's office in the film. I found this very tall room in this Edwardian house in Grosvenor Square and I thought, 'Wouldn't it be interesting to have this military disciplinarian sitting behind a desk with a bust of a famous general like Wellington or Caesar sitting in front of one of these big casement windows?' And Harry had told me earlier that whatever I needed for this office set, whether it be a large supercomputer or other gadgets to fill up the entire space, I would get whatever I wanted. I asked Sidney Furie about my idea and he told me to give him ten minutes. He went out, thought about it for a bit and then returned telling me he loved the idea. I arrive on that set to shoot that morning, and Harry Saltzman arrives, and he sees this mostly empty set, and he just went ape."[12]

Furie was in favor of that 28–30 Grosvenor Gardens office set from early on. "It was negative space, and you can do a lot with that photographically. Ken Adam and I both fought for that vision." Later in the shooting day, Adam claims that Saltzman told him that the right decision had been made regarding that set. Curiously, he did not approach Furie to tell him the same.

Fights during the first three weeks of shooting were daily, if not hourly. Saltzman started going head-to-head with Furie with reckless abandon, chastising him, often screaming at him in front of most everyone present.

Emotions ran high, putting many of the cast and crew on edge. Strange camera angles and general audacity ruled the dailies with defiance. There were canted frames, deliberate focus-blurs and objects obstructing any clear view of the action, all of which wantonly broke Saltzman's rule of stylistic inconspicuousness. Furie was attempting to fragment the wide Techniscope frame in various patterns, penetrating the things native to the shooting environment with his lens. The whole movie, a daredevil exercise in the cinema of paranoia, was being shot as if it were being observed by a third party who was constantly hiding and spying. The audience would become eavesdroppers, as if the agenda was highly classified and the cameraman did not have clearance. An entry on the curriculum vitae of the film's cinematographer, Otto Heller, suggested that he was well suited to the strategy of using a camera to spy and eavesdrop, having previously shot Michael Powell's classic *Peeping Tom* (1960).

Saltzman had no frame of reference for what he was seeing: a half-realized romantic conversation in a government office shot through the thin metal dials of a desktop paper-bin, a character in the backseat of a car framed through the vehicle's hood-ornament, an approaching figure framed through a just-expired parking meter, a character's disembodied head framed in an upper quadrant of the screen while a shoulder and backside fully occupy the other three quadrants. Furie was caught in an effort to actively unnerve the audience, but all these machinations made the increasingly cantankerous Saltzman consider firing Furie, although the crew always made their day in good time. In fact, the film was never in danger of going over schedule. Nevertheless, as far as Saltzman could see, the film was being hijacked; it was no longer the straightforward genre picture he had envisioned. He convinced himself that he was overseeing a flat-out profit deterrent, some ungraceful punk's experimental film project.

The harried producer confided in production manager Denis Johnson that, when editor Peter Hunt (who had been on vacation after having edited *Goldfinger*) returned and saw the rushes for *The Ipcress File,* he would concur that Furie needed to be fired. Furie knew he was on thin ice. Word quickly leaked concerning Saltzman's plans. Meanwhile, pages were steadily being rewritten every day, and Furie would instruct lighting cameraman Otto Heller to take longer than usual to light the sets while they waited for the new pages to arrive. "The writers would be working all night long without sleep, and into the next day, trying to get us the pages we would shoot for the day," Furie recalls. "We would be lighting a staircase for three hours sometimes, and you'd see the staircase in the film for maybe a few seconds."

The script soon departed with abandon from the novel on which it was based. Len Deighton's original manuscript had scenes set in Lebanon and on an atoll during a U.S. atomic weapons test. These, among other elements, were completely excised from Doran and Canaway's script. They whittled it down to stage it solely in London, defining it more as a character piece for the phlegmatic Palmer. It now told the story of a domestic spy, a self-styled gourmet with glasses and an irreverent sense of humor, who is charged with tracking down a missing scientist, in a longer chain of missing scientists who have ceased to function after receiving a "brain drain" at the hands of an enemy brigade seeking to render them intellectually useless. (The *Ipcress* of the title refers to "Induction of Psychoneurosis by Conditioned Reflex under Stress.")

Saltzman could not have been at all thrilled when Furie freely admitted to a *Sight & Sound* magazine journalist that the film would be a "thoroughly uncommercial film." Furie was printed in the magazine's winter 1964–1965 issue as saying, "You wouldn't think that you could make an uncommercial film about spies these days, but I think I'm doing it!"[13] One day, another in a series of heated arguments between Saltzman and Furie at a shooting location in Shepherds Bush ended when Saltzman literally ripped the script out of Furie's clutches. This time, Furie walked off the set in tears, boarding a No. 12 bus bound for Marble Arch. "It was the oddest walking-off-a-set I've ever seen," claims Michael Caine, smiling broadly. "Everyone just kind of looked around asked, 'Where's Sid?' Harry and I got into his Phantom 6 Rolls Royce and chased this No. 12 bus down Bayswater Road, screaming to the bus driver, 'Stop the bus, you've got our director on there!'"[14] Eventually, the two of them got Furie back to the set and the day's shooting continued, as relations between the producer and the director now fell cold, silent, and spiteful.

"I did know it was good stuff I was getting," Furie claims. "I'd see Peter Hunt's assistant Nick Stevenson and he'd always be excited and say, 'What have you got for me today?!' He found what I was doing interesting and original, and I think most people did."

Michael Caine observes, "Harry and Sid were so different, you could just look at them and know it. Harry was old. Sid was young. Harry wore proper suit and tie. Sid wore blue jeans, sweaters and a jacket. I could go on." Furie conjectures, "I also didn't have that thing that I heard Terence

Young had. When Harry would do the same with him at the beginning of their working relationship, Young had that dry British humor, a kind of sardonic wit, and was able to charmingly tell him, 'Oh yes, that's wonderful, Harry. Now be a good boy and piss off, would you.' I never had that thing. I just told him to fuck off without the humor."

As the chemistry of headstrong director and irascible producer continued to make for incessant on-set tension, Michael Caine, whom Saltzman considered a friend being taken under his wing, approached his producer to respectfully confront him about his behavior toward their director. "I said, 'Harry, for God's sake, lighten up a little bit. Don't lean on people so much.' He looked at me, and almost looked confused, and said, 'Did I lean on him?' I was amazed: 'Did you lean on him?! The way you were going on, the poor guy looked like he was about to have a nervous breakdown.'"[15]

When Peter Hunt returned from his post-editing R&R, he ran all of the dailies of *The Ipcress File*. Hunt, at that point, had edited *Dr. No, From Russia with Love,* and *Goldfinger* for Cubby Broccoli and Saltzman. To both men, he stood firm as one of their most credible and trusted confidants and was later granted the opportunity to direct the Bond film *On Her Majesty's Secret Service* (1969) for them. Immediately after screening the footage, Hunt phoned Saltzman, telling him simply, "Don't fire Furie! Kiss him! This is the most brilliant footage I've ever seen!" To further his conviction that Furie's stylistic choices and shooting style were working, he edited together a sequence in which Furie had managed to catch a marching band in the background behind Nigel Green, who marches in step with their military tempo. It was a "grabbed" shot that any other director would have forgone. This shot is followed by a dialogue between Green and Guy Doleman, carefully intercut with their closed umbrellas stepping with them in motion.

"Harry just looked at that sequence I cut together, looked at me, smiled, nodded and said, 'Good, keep going,'" Peter Hunt remembers. "Once I assured him it would be a good film, he started getting confident." Although Saltzman's hopes for the film were lifted, his ill feeling toward Furie continued throughout the rest of the production, and combat turned into something more closely resembling cold war. "Saltzman was a terrible bully towards Sid, and could be toward others," continues Hunt. "I don't know why he carried this on with him. Everything was this intense battle of wills between the two of them."[16]

"I really have Peter Hunt to thank," says Furie. "Once Peter told Harry that it was good and that everything would be alright, he left me alone the rest of the shoot."

"The film had all these little touches. There was a shot when I was walking up the stairs," says Caine, "and the camera was on the next landing up. I looked up and I asked Sidney, 'Why's the camera up there? Is someone going to jump down from there or something?' and he said 'No, but I want people to think there is.' It was always fascinating to see where they'd put the camera next. It was like film school for me as well."

One of the most agreeable working relationships on the troubled set developed between Furie and Otto Heller, a Czech-born cinematographer whose narrow escape from Nazi-occupied Europe mirrored that of Furie's television-days mentor Eugen Schüfftan. Furie originally approached Heller with caution, knowing that he had shot his previous films with high-key facial lighting that was scrupulously even, with little mood or contrast. "I told him not to light like that, with the high-key. I couldn't stand seeing people's faces perfectly lit. I told him to give it some definition and mystery. He just told me it would be his pleasure, and then explained that he had been asked by previous directors to light that way. He didn't prefer that look. It also made it easier that we shot the exteriors on overcast days, and in London at that time of year, that was never difficult."

The Techniscope process also often proved frustrating and often challenging. Considering that a Techniscope frame of film took up only two perforations versus the usual anamorphic four frames, on the off-chance a hair or fiber got caught in the camera gate, it would take up the entire vertical aspect of a frame. On regular CinemaScope, a hair in the gate would be simply a little flickering fiber at the very bottom of a frame. In addition to headaches like these, the camera operator Brian Elvin could never see the left side of the frame because of Techniscope limitations on the reflex viewfinder. Heller and Elvin had to keep checking in with the lab. They would call Peter Hunt to confirm that the leftmost parts of the frame were up to par. A hair or fiber in the gate, however, immediately pointed to a reshoot, and ate away schedule time.

Universal Pictures's "Man in London" Ernie Nibbs remained relatively staid throughout much of the shoot, even when the "Saltzman-Furie War" flared at its most vitriolic. Universal Pictures, for its part, demanded a number of action set pieces, and one of them added to the script was a confrontation outside the Royal Albert Hall. The scene involves a scuffle between Harry Palmer and Housemartin (Oliver MacGreevy, an alumnus of *The Leather Boys*), the bald henchman to one of the nefarious figures in the film. It was outside the Royal Albert Hall that Nibbs finally spoke up, and with rancor. Furie chose to shoot the action through the telephone booth that Palmer leaves in the first moments of the sequence. The red metal beams of the phone booth boldly segment the screen, with the action happening mostly in longshot. Occasional cut-ins with a longer lens offer a fragmentary and almost impressionistic view of the hand-to-hand violence.

Nibbs, who had stomached Furie's more "arty" directorial flourishes up to that point, became incensed with using the same established style to shoot one of the action sequences his employers had mandated. "He just lost it and said, 'That's not how you shoot a fight sequence! No one shoots a fight sequence like that! You can hardly see anything! You've got to get in there and get the action!'" Caine remembers, laughing. "Sid just turned to him and said, 'No, that's how you shoot a James Bond fight sequence. We're trying to do something different.' And that's how it came to pass, and Nibbs just had to take the piss, as we say."

Memos were soon being passed down from Universal Pictures executives, in which they took Saltzman and his crew to task for casting a hero wearing glasses. "Why is Palmer wearing glasses? Is he short-sighted?" Caine surmises that he was the first bespectacled leading man to come along in the wake of silent comedy star Harold Lloyd, remembering that "when Harold Lloyd came to London a couple years after, he took me out to dinner, because I sort of carried the torch from him as he saw it. He told me that I probably gave guys who wear glasses more good press than perhaps anyone in history. A lovely man."

In response to a scene in which Palmer cooks a meal for the Sue Lloyd character, Courtney, a Universal memo dated January 11, 1965, reads simply, "Cut the scene with the guy cooking." Says Caine, "Sid showed me the note and it said something like, 'People are going to say he's a fag. John Wayne wouldn't cook anything for anybody. He looks like a faggot cooking.' It was hysterical. They were so panicked." Len Deighton himself had written that into the novel's character, because he himself was a great cook and wrote his own weekly food column in the *London Times*. Ultimately, the cooking sequence stayed in the film, much to the American studio's chagrin. The fact that the lead character was a gourmet additionally gave license to executive producer Charles Kasher, the entrepreneur who had originally bought the rights to Deighton's novel, to product-place kitchen gadgets he was marketing to the public, such as his then-cutting-edge InstraBrewer Coffeemaker. "In Bond films, there were cars with jets coming out with poison gas," continues Caine, "And then, here I am as Harry Palmer coming along with a trolley in a supermarket buying button mushrooms."

"I didn't think Harry would have any reason to carry on this hatred of me after picture-wrap," says Furie. "But, somehow, don't ask me how, I was wrong. I was just trying to make a good movie. All the stuff he hated was done while saying, 'You know, the picture will go down the drain, but they'll remember what I did with it.' It's what I had to do to fight back. I tried anything, and everything. It was a long, bitter fight. I won most of it but I lost the battle on the final brainwashing scene. Instead of the big, gimmicky set and James Bond effects, I wanted a little room and no gimmicks. But it does not detract from the film for me."

Furie's son Daniel remembers *The Ipcress File* as the first set he ever visited of his father's. "When we were in the Canary Islands for *Wonderful Life,* we never visited the set where Dad was working. We were on the beach there the whole time, and for all we knew it was a vacation. I remember a big birthday party for Charles Kasher at Pinewood Studios on the brain-drain set, and there was a cake covered with gold chocolate coins. It was the first time I really gotten a sense of what it was my father did." As to his two eldest sons, Furie adds, "Dan and Noah were pros by the time they ever set foot on the *Ipcress* set, even as little kids. Before that, I would always take them to see the films I wanted to see. I mean, I took them to *Lawrence of Arabia* when it came out. Dan must have been no more than four or five." Dan Furie corroborates, "*Lawrence of Arabia* and *Von Ryan's Express* were two of my favorite films growing up as a little kid. He never took us to Disney movies. My mom took us to those. But suffice it to say, those were the seeds of my own love of film."

Principal photography on *The Ipcress File* wrapped on December 11, 1964, with additional "pick-up" shots completed on January 20, 1965. The last scene shot was the film's finale, inside the abandoned warehouse set at Pinewood. No sooner did shooting end than Saltzman brought John Barry in to score the film. Barry had risen as another stalwart member of the Saltzman-Broccoli trust, cemented when he rescued *Dr. No* from an over-the-top Stan Kenton–esque theme. Saltzman's orders to John Barry during the scoring of the film could scarcely be clearer: "You are not to meet with

Sidney Furie!" However, once he saw the film cut together, Barry aptly compounded the film's often surreal style with a score to match the offbeat visuals, all on his own accord. In large part, Barry employed an instrument called the cimbalom, a Hungarian zither, which lent to the film an ethereally ominous eastern European sound.

"That fight scene outside of Albert Hall was like two ants on a mound fighting," John Barry observes. "And the music I wrote for that was slow arpeggios on the cimbalom, with these strange chords, and it created a totally different effect. We would never have done that sort of thing if we hadn't have been coming off the Bond movies."[17] Says Furie, "I just moved on when Saltzman told John Barry not to meet with me to discuss the score. You know, what can you do? Then, one day, John Barry calls me on the phone and tells me, 'I've finished the score. Can you meet me at the Pickwick Club in a couple hours?'" The Pickwick Club, on Great Newport Street off Charing Cross Road, was owned by Wolf Mankowitz, a playwright and screenwriter in his own right. Mankowitz also happened to be the man who introduced Harry Saltzman to Cubby Broccoli. "So, John and I met at the Pickwick Club that afternoon, and we sat at a table there, and he hummed me the entire score," Furie fondly remembers. "He did all the background parts, the orchestrations—he hummed everything. The people at the other tables applauded."

"There were huge rows about the music," Michael Caine recalls. "I think Harry literally wanted ersatz Bond, and when he heard all this foreign stuff, which was, again, like everything else, the antithesis of Bond, he thought, 'Christ! What's this?' But you could talk Harry around anything. He always hated everything when he first heard it or saw it. He used to wait for people's approval."[18]

Says John Barry, "After I'd written the theme, I went to the cimbalom player John Leach and he played it for me on the cimbalom, letting all the tones ring out. Sometimes when you play the cimbalom, you deaden the tones, but I said, 'Let them carry on,' so it got that very distinctive sound which I wanted for the film."[19] The eerie mood conveyed by the film's score, with its warped twang, suited the film perfectly in Furie's and Caine's eyes, and it did eventually meet Saltzman's approval. It remains one of Barry's most beloved scores to this day. In 2013, the eerie strains of the main theme opened the whole of the three-part BBC documentary *The Sound of Cinema: The Music That Made the Movies*. Posits the documentary's host-narrator Neil Brand, an accomplished composer himself, "To my mind,

John Barry's title music for the Cold War thriller *The Ipcress File* is one of the finest ever written. In his hands, the music becomes another character. It captures the appeal of Michael Caine's character, and promises that the film will entertain us as well as chill us."[20]

One day, as the release of the film neared, Harry Saltzman told Caine of his recent executive decision: to put the actor's name above the title on the poster and in the credits. "And I said, 'Gee, Harry, that's great. You mean, you thought I was good in it?' He said, 'No, it's just that, if I don't think you're a star, who the hell else is going to?'"[21] Caine had, upon the completion of his role in *The Ipcress File,* exhausted one of the films in the six-picture contract he had signed with Saltzman. If the film proved successful, Harry Palmer sequels would be imminent. But before the film's release, Peter Hunt took a dinner engagement with director Lewis Gilbert, who was looking for an actor to cast in the lead role of his newest film, an adaptation of Bill Naughton's novel and stage-play *Alfie.* The part had been performed on the London stage by Caine's roommate Terence Stamp, who had shown absolutely no interest in taking the role in the film. At Hunt's beckoning, Gilbert was given a secret screening of the final workprint of *The Ipcress File.* Hunt felt strongly that Caine would be an ideal fit because of how the actor's affable presence helped carry every scene. Gilbert agreed with Hunt's recommendation, and Caine started work on *Alfie* in August 1965, as did cinematographer Otto Heller, nabbed by Gilbert after *The Ipcress File.*

The final cut of *The Ipcress File* was first shown in privacy at the Woodfall screening suites on March 15, 1965, after it had been invited as one of the two official British entries at the Cannes Film Festival, next to Sidney Lumet's *The Hill,* starring Sean Connery. Surprisingly, the festival committee invited Richard Lester's Woodfall production *The Knack . . . and How to Get It,* starring *Leather Boys* alumnus Rita Tushingham, as an additional in-competition picture. United Artists had been keen to dump it as a double feature alongside a Western only on the condition Woodfall provided UA with theatrical reissue rights to *Tom Jones.* The Cannes jury special invite dramatically justified Woodfall's loyalty to the film.

As a contender for the Grand Prix du Festival International du Film (the equivalent of the Palme d'Or between 1964 and 1974), Saltzman, Furie, and company packed up for the south of France, where Saltzman threw one of his notoriously extravagant Cannes parties. Saltzman made a point to inform Furie that he was not invited. Furie remembers, "This is how much he carried on his personal vendetta against me. It proved he was a grudge-holder, but I didn't care at the time. I was young. I spent the evening with Cy Harvey and Bryant Haliday of Janus Films, laughing over drinks over the fact I hadn't been invited to the party for my own film, like I could really give a shit. And we had a wonderful evening together." Haliday had appeared as an actor in Lindsay Shonteff's *Devil Doll* the previous year, which Furie had come close to directing.

Olivia de Havilland headed the jury that year. Up until the last moments of deliberation, Lumet's *The Hill,* Masaki Kobayashi's *Kwaidan,* and *The Ipcress File* had all been favored to take the Palme d'Or. The jury's other members included Rex Harrison, documentarian François Reichenbach, producer Goffredo Lombardo, and novelist-filmmaker Alain Robbe-Grillet. It took the de Havilland jury six hours to reach their final decisions, with *The Knack . . . and How to Get It* capturing the main prize, much to everyone's surprise. Richard Lester, flanked by John and Cynthia Lennon, accepted the award in person. Lester's prowess with creative montage and "zany" editing in *The Knack* was analogous to Furie's prowess with creative framing, composition, and shot fluidity in *The Ipcress File,* so the difference between the winning film and Furie's film was one of stylistic focus.

Slightly crestfallen but grateful to have had the Cannes experience after *The Leather Boys* had been unceremoniously passed over for invitation, Furie learned at one of the final night's festival parties, from actress Joanna Shimkus, the then-girlfriend of Michelangelo Antonioni, that the Italian master found his film one of the most brilliant works of its time. Antonioni had told Shimkus that Furie had a "great cinematic eye." The year after, in Los Angeles, Furie chanced to dine with François Truffaut and producer Kenneth Rive, the man who first imported the French master's films to England before bankrolling Furie's *During One Night* and *The Boys.* Truffaut literally applauded Furie for *The Ipcress File* upon his arrival at the restaurant. "Knowing Antonioni and Truffaut's responses, that was better than getting the Golden Palm to me. Being respected by one's fellow artists, the ones you look up to, is the greatest of all rewards." Additionally, it was later revealed that French author and filmmaker Alain Robbe-Grillet was one of the jurors who fought in favor of *The Ipcress File*'s taking the prize over Lester's film, which he dismissed, *à la Français,* as a "trickstery trifle."[22]

On July 2, 1965, *The Ipcress File* opened at Leicester Square Theatre, with ticket lines queueing around the block. "Michael and I were on our way to the Pickwick Club to have dinner during the film's first showing," says John Barry. "Michael had me ride by the theater, and we saw these people waiting to get in, and he turned to me and said something like, 'God knows how people get a nose for a movie. An unknown actor in a film with a weird title gets this line!' But it was a massive hit."[23]

Despite Furie's comment to *Sight & Sound* that his ambition was "to make a cultural wow that was a commercial flop," the box office for *The Ipcress File* was solid and the British reviews were largely raves, though the *Times* faulted the film's second half as "irritatingly obscure." The *Sunday Telegraph* praised Michael Caine, insisting that his performance "installs him as the first mod conman of the new British crime wave." The *Evening Standard* echoed the admiration for Caine and stated that the film "is everything that James Bond is not, and all the better for it." The film opened in New York and Los Angeles on August 2. Its successful release in the U.S. boded so well for Furie that, on November 8, 1965, *The Leather Boys* was finally given its first American release, purchased by R. Lee Platt for Allied Artists, after having been passed over eighteen months previously.

In 1967, Michael Caine confessed to *Playboy* that the film's Stateside success surprised him. "I suppose I underestimated the intelligence of the audience, which people in show business do all the time. We made *The Ipcress File* very cheaply, expecting, if we were lucky, to break even or make a little profit. I thought it would be a rather specialized movie."[24]

Newsweek called the film "the thinking man's *Goldfinger*," claiming that it was "funnier by far than any of the 007 films, and more rewarding too." Bosley Crowther of the *New York Times* extolled the film, saying it was "as classy a spy film as you could ask to see," calling attention to its "fast, fluid, candid shooting" and finally observing a "Techniscope setting of London . . . full of rich and mellow colors." The *New Yorker* called it "an admirable thriller in every respect." *Time* labeled it a "tingling, no-nonsense suspense yarn." Hollis Alpert in the *Saturday Review* called the film "the very model for suspense entertainment." *Sight & Sound,* fast becoming Furie's biggest fan among the critics, remarked in a 1965 issue that "Furie is always on the point of becoming one of the best directors we've got."[25]

Upon seeing the film, the exasperated Billy Wilder famously exclaimed, "The director can't shoot a scene without framing it through a fireplace or the back of a refrigerator."[26] Furie laughs when being reminded of this: "It's funny, I don't remember anything in the film shot through a fireplace or the back of a refrigerator, but that was thrown back at me for years, even after I quit using that style." In their two-volume text *50 ans de cinéma américain,* Bertrand Tavernier and Jean-Pierre Coursodon remark that Furie as a director earned distinction for being "possibly the most recognizable in the profession" in terms of style, and in turn they acknowledged his "bizarre, comic-strip-inspired framing."[27]

Caine's and Furie's stars skyrocketed after the film's release. Furie received a call from producer Martin Ransohoff, who had founded and then presided over the production company Filmways, which had established a distribution deal with MGM. Ransohoff had just completed *The Cincinnati Kid* with Norman Jewison, and he offered Furie a three-picture deal and a first-class ticket to Hollywood to work on a project then titled *Day of the Arrow,* an occult-themed thriller adapted from a novel by Robin Estridge (under the nom de plume Philip Loraine), to star Kim Novak. The movie was to be filmed on location in Dordogne, France, with interiors to be shot at MGM British Studios.

> I arrived at the airport in Los Angeles, where they put me up at the Beverly Wilshire. The first night there, I was invited to a special screening of *The Sandpiper* at the Director's Guild. Liz Taylor and Richard Burton were there, and I remember being excited about that. Afterward, we all went out to Ciro's on the Sunset Strip, and I remember seeing sweaters tied around people's necks at this place, and just found the whole scene really elite. It felt good to be where I was aiming to go for years. I waited to be invited to Hollywood. I didn't just want to go with nothing, with no name for myself, and hope everything would somehow turn out alright. In my mind, I had to be given the invitation, so I went to England first.

That said, Furie and his family still maintained their home in Roehampton, and they did not officially emigrate to the United States until late 1967.

The Ipcress File went on to receive five British Academy Film and Television Awards (BAFTA) nominations. It took home three awards, including Best British Film (with the prize going at that time to the director), Best Art Direction (Ken Adam), and Best Colour Cinematography (Otto Heller). "Harry Saltzman went up to receive my award for Best Film," says Furie, "and he said something like, 'I'm accepting this award for Sidney Furie, who's in Hollywood.' And the thing is that he never gave it to me! He kept it as if it were his own! So that says more about him than anyone could ever say."

In the years since, *The Ipcress File* has lived a rich legacy, having been named to the British Film Institute's Top 100 British Films list (it is currently number 59 on the list). Over eight hundred thousand British viewers tuned in to watch *The Ipcress File* when it was screened on BBC2 in early 2015. It is still the film with which Furie's name is most associated in the annals of film history, and the one that has enjoyed the most influence, having justifiably put the still-young director on the map. When Furie visited the set of Francis Ford Coppola's *One from the Heart* with producer Gray Frederickson in 1981, he was introduced to the film's cinematographer, Vittorio Storaro. "I said, 'Hello, I'm Sidney Furie, I'm a director' and he cut me off and said, 'You don't have to tell me who you are. I've stolen from you!' He explained that when *The Ipcress File* came out, all of them in Italy were so influenced by the mood and the style of it that it gave them the freedom to try things. And he went on to do *The Conformist,* and not that that film is really anything like *Ipcress,* but I recall thinking when seeing it at the time, 'Gee, this all looks a bit familiar.'"[28] Even Palmer's signature glasses see their reincarnation in the *Austin Powers* film series.

The "brain-draining" process depicted in the film has also been examined in academic articles, mainly involving psychiatry. For instance, in a book exploring transcranial magnetic stimulation (TMS), author Dr. Nick Begich explicitly references *The Ipcress File,* giving specific credence to the type of brain-drain and mind-control (Induction of Psycho-Neuroses by Conditioned Reflex under Stress) used in the film. The director shrugs and apathetically accepts this footnote: "That was the part of the movie that I liked the least, because I thought it looked fake."

The Ipcress File is an espionage potboiler cum art film where the tradecraft is austere but strangely never uninvolving. The film succeeds in establishing, in a very specific sense, a "world of the film." Within its sober, deeply impersonal milieu of "cold hard British efficiency," where government forms carry comedically arcane names like B107, TX82, L101, and T104, even a small metal nameplate reading T108 is affixed to the backrest of a public bench in a brief but unexpectedly important shot. Special attention is also paid to the numbers and letters on license plates. The overcast, encoded world of the film is a vast, pencil-pushing negative space in which a striking number of objects are ascribed a dehumanized, seemingly arbitrary bureaucratic cipher. A cabal of dapper and dour men have codified everything, ensuring that all has been made official, often enigmatically so. Its gloomy color palette and eerily forlorn tonal quality is demonstrative of an exceptionally strong directorial voice and evokes a downbeat postwar, pre-Swinging London. *Film International* writer Gary McMahon writes, "Downbeat details are stretched to the anamorphic proportions of magic realism, including one of the greatest shots in British cinema that finds abstract expressionism in a lampshade."[29]

The film's humor, considering all this, is well-placed, well-timed, applied in right doses, and endowed with a droll, entirely British tenor. Palmer's barbed wit (and Caine's deft delivery of it) gives the film a human center as such a thing can truly exist in this sober, efficient world in which it is set. Palmer is a working-class movie hero very much in the spirit of the times. Considering the lone Palmer character's implicit disdain for authority figures, the film could almost be considered a British "Angry Young Man" drama set curiously in the espionage world. This aspect also seems ironically to speak to the film's behind-the-scenes troubles in a canny yet inadvertent way. Gary McMahon keenly quips in his 2012 journal article about the film, "Sidney J. Furie's B107 would read like Harry Palmer's, as read by Palmer's seething new boss Dalby: 'Insbordinate. Insolent. A trickster.' And when Green's character read the riot act to Caine's Palmer, he must have come close to echoing Saltzman's sentiments about the infuriating Furie. If director Terence Young was Connery's model for playing Bond, Furie could be a Canadian model of Palmer's Cockney insubordination." McMahon wraps up his academic study of the film by stating, "That film schools now screen *The Ipcress File* as a paragon of what can be achieved with widescreen composition . . . goes a long way to substantiating why this is one of Britain's finest films. Every scene is seen refracted."[30]

Many of Furie's films reveal an understanding of the instability and outright treachery of human male relationships. Andrew Sarris, in his book *The American Cinema: Directors and Directions, 1929–1968,* writes of the film's "father fixation ending with its battered hero in the position of choosing which pater to perforate" and how it "adds a new dimension to the sick cinema."[31] In *The Ipcress File* a traditional male movie hero is virtually stripped down into a bespectacled everyman who cooks gourmet meals for female dates and is vulnerable for an unusually lengthy stretch of the film's third act. In perhaps one of the sexiest seduction scenes in movie history, it is the female love interest who makes the first move, by taking the eyeglasses off her male partner while the picture itself goes out-of-focus. This table-turning of sexual roles and sexual expectation was radical at the time of release and remains radical today.

"I still think it's Sidney's greatest film," says Michael Caine. "And the film is certainly one of my personal favorite films of all the stuff I've done." To this day, Furie and Caine meet up annually in Las Vegas for a charity function held on the joint birthday of Caine and Quincy Jones, both born on the same day in 1933 just minutes apart from each other. "Years later, a woman came up to me at a function," says Michael Caine, "and she said, 'I used to be a spy, you know, and that film you made was the only one I ever saw which showed really what it was like. I spent more time sitting in cars waiting for people to come out of houses than anything else I ever did.'"

In the decade following the film's release and rise to prominence, Saltzman continued a smear campaign against Furie, consisting of claims that editor Peter Hunt had completed directorial duties on *The Ipcress File* and that Furie had been fired early on in production. Hunt and others involved in the production have vehemently denied all such claims. The film spawned two sequels, *Funeral in Berlin* and *Billion Dollar Brain,* neither of which reached the great success of the original film. Needless to say, Furie was not approached to direct them; those tasks were handed to Bond journeyman Guy Hamilton and future auteur Ken Russell.

Furie first arrived in Hollywood the weekend of September 4, 1965, having leased Soupy Sales's Beverly Hills home at 619 Arden Drive. Only twenty-four hours after his arrival, he was interviewed for the *Los Angeles Times* by staff writer Philip K. Scheuer. His first couple of months in Hollywood were spent working with British novelist Norman Bogner on a rewrite of *Day of the Arrow,* which had been retitled *13*. A script penned by Robin Estridge, the author of the novel on which the film was being based, had been prepared in advance, and this provided the source material to which Furie and Bogner applied alterations. When Ransohoff resisted Furie and Bogner's changes, many of which were drastic, and demanded that they stay faithful to Estridge's original draft, Furie left the project and hunted for something else to direct as his Hollywood debut. Less than a year later, Bogner hit the *New York Times* best-seller list with the novel *Seventh Avenue.* For his part, Ransohoff exhausted two other directors, including Arthur Hiller and Michael Anderson, before finally settling on British veteran J. Lee Thompson, whose previous credits included *The Guns of Navarone* and *Cape Fear.* The final film, eventually released under the title *Eye of the Devil,* starred David Niven, Deborah Kerr, and newcomer Sharon Tate.

Furie then found himself attached to direct a Bernard Girard script entitled *Eli Kotch,* a breezy heist comedy. While at a meeting at Columbia Pictures to discuss the project with Girard and Tony Curtis, who was then to star in the film, Curtis, who had suggested Furie for the project, having been enthusiastic about *The Ipcress File,* invited the director to his home in Bel-Air. "He told me to follow him up to his house," Furie recalls. "He had a Rolls Royce Cornish convertible, and I had a rental car Mustang, and at that time he was married to Christine Kaufmann. When I got there, I remember thinking, 'Oh my God, look at how they live!' It was opulent and just true Hollywood to me. I was just a boy from Canada by way of England, so it was rather alien to me then." Once again, Furie eventually left the project when producer Carter De Haven vetoed proposed changes to Girard's script. Girard himself stepped in as director, and the film was released as *Dead Heat on a Merry-Go-Round,* starring James Coburn in the role originally intended for Curtis, who had walked away from the project because of a salary dispute.

After his fall-out with De Haven and Girard, Furie was sent the script of *Funny Girl,* which he promptly turned down. "They weren't even close to talking about Streisand for *Funny Girl* at that point, and the script was a disaster. I had been one of about a dozen directors they had offered that one to." He also declined *The Slender Thread* (1965), which was eventually made starring Sidney Poitier under the direction of a debuting Sydney Pollack. "The producer Steve Alexander and his wife, Shana, who wrote the article the script was based on, came to my place in Beverly Hills to try to convince me to do it. I was just really turned off by the idea of a suicide hotline thriller." Shirley MacLaine, given the power to choose the director for her next picture, pursued Furie to direct her in the romantic caper *Gambit* (1966), in which she eventually costarred with Michael Caine under the direction of Ronald Neame.[32]

After his short tenures working under Ransohoff, Girard, and De Haven, Furie returned to his London home in Kensington in the fall of 1965. He received the script for *The Appaloosa,* adapted by first-time screenwriter (and future director) James Bridges from a 1963 paperback by Western author Robert MacLeod. Universal purchased the property in

December 1964, while *The Ipcress File* was still in production. At that early point in his career, Bridges, then twenty-eight years old, had only received credit for writing five episodes of *Alfred Hitchcock Presents*. Marlon Brando, cornered into a five-picture contract at Universal, had unsuccessfully tried to rally both Elia Kazan and George Stevens to direct the picture. Kazan was not answering phone calls at that time, and Stevens, having been in ill health on the set of his star-studded, big-budget *The Greatest Story Ever Told* (1965), decided he could not handle the strain of another picture so soon.

Brando's five-picture contract with Universal precipitated from the studio's corporate overlord MCA buying out of Brando's bankrupted Pennebaker Films in 1962, after the star's directorial extravagance on *One-Eyed Jacks* (1961) and his own father's reckless financial dealings had exhausted the fledgling production company's resources. The contract made Brando spiteful, and performing in the contract pictures chronically reminded him that he had sold himself into creative indentured servitude. In exchange, Brando was guaranteed continued income for his father, courtesy of MCA, and a $270,000 salary for each picture in the contract. He also received shares in MCA.

With an offer to direct *The Appaloosa*, Furie's bells finally chimed in approval. "All I heard was Brando and I said, 'I'm in!'" Although he was Furie's acting idol from seeing *On the Waterfront* numerous times, Brando had continually earned a reputation as box-office poison in the intervening years. Furie, for his part, claimed to have been mostly ignorant of the failure of Brando's previous four films. "What I wanted to bring out in the picture was the old Brando," Furie meditated in a 1966 *Los Angeles Times* article. "I wanted the Brando that preceded all the pictures he had done in the last five years."[33]

When Furie accepted the job, MCA head Lew Wasserman had the project's title changed (not for the last time) to *Southwest to Sonora*. Brando hated this decision and, in classic ornery style, arranged for a mariachi band to wander the Universal Studios backlot playing an ad hoc original tune entitled "Southwest to Sonora" in an effort to annoy the studio brass. Even though the change back to *The Appaloosa* was eventually made, press releases continued to refer to the project as *Southwest to Sonora*, and that title was kept for the film's overseas release. Midway through shooting, the press also referred to it as *Cocatlan*.

In a January 23, 1966, article in the *New York Times*, then journalist (and future Paramount executive) Peter Bart writes, "Universal Pictures decided to team two incendiary personalities, Marlon Brando the actor and Sidney J. Furie the young director, in a western called *Southwest to Sonora*. Hollywood's reaction was one of morbid fascination. 'They'll never get the picture made,' said one well-known producer. 'The only question is which guy will land the first punch.'"[34] Since the financially disastrous MGM megaproduction *Mutiny on the Bounty* (1962), which nearly toppled the studio, Brando had found his career at sea, cast in a series of projects about which he cared little or not at all.

Many, including Brando's personal secretary Alice Marchak, thought the experience of directing the Western epic *One-Eyed Jacks* (1961) and the ensuing battle with Paramount over the final cut of the film had left the actor demoralized, disillusioned with his own success, and largely apathetic regarding his future in film acting. According to Brando biographer Peter Manso, Brando would run his finger down the list of his own films, mumbling "Pain" when he came to each "good" film he had made. As he came to each of the "trashier" endeavors, he would muttered either "Alimony" or "Indians." Manso writes, "It was his way of telling that the negligible movies had been made simply for money."[35] Thus, he lent his name to dead-on-arrival productions like *The Ugly American* (1963), *Bedtime Story* (1964), and *Morituri* (1965). Among students of acting, however, his name was still gold-standard, although his working reputation was questioned owing to his unpredictable and often obnoxious behavior on sets. Such behavior on *Mutiny on the Bounty* set the production back months, leaving its flustered directors, the departing Carol Reed and the arriving Lewis Milestone, to pick up the pieces in delivering what had become an unwieldy epic. Its troubles extended even beyond its intolerably unruly star. After that film tanked at the box office, critics commonly branded his selection of starring roles erratic and his performances in them lazy, uninspired, even sleepwalking.

Furie found Bridges's script deficient but not hopeless or without potential, and he was assured by agent Jay Kanter, who helped put the deal on the picture together, that he would be allowed to work with its writer to improve it. "Overall, action and dramatic structure were lacking in the first draft," Furie remembers. The project was also the producing debut for Alan Miller, an MCA agent turned producer in the recent MCA-Universal merger. Miller, who was equally excited to be working with "Brando the Legend," had been duly warned by many of his colleagues about Brando's disruptive conduct. The prospects, despite the promise of Furie's rising star, did not look rosy. An inexperienced rookie producer, a recalcitrant star with a history of tantrums with directors, a director fresh to Hollywood, and a troublesome script did not cast a particularly auspicious oracle.

Nonetheless, the first step for Furie was to meet his star, and so their fateful meeting was arranged. To Furie, it was something akin to a meeting with a Greek god, a private audience with the titan of modern cinema acting. Walking into the room where Furie awaited a legend, Brando opened with unqualified bluster.

"Well," Brando revved up, "I'm doing this thing because it's in my contract. Why are *you* doing it?"

"Because I wanted to work with you," Furie meekly responded, still in astonishment that he was in the room with one of his heroes.

"Oh come on," Brando sputtered impatiently, "Don't give me that shit!"

Looking back, Furie is more clearheaded about how he should have navigated this treacherous terrain: "He had no idea of his standing. None! I should have taken a different tack. I should have said, 'Listen, I know the script isn't the greatest, but I think the two of us together can improve it and make it something good.' He couldn't have had much of a first impression of me based on that, because he was so disillusioned at that point in his career."

"What makes you think you know what actors are all about," Brando countered to the director that his agent and handlers had built up as cinema's newest enfant terrible, whose war with Harry Saltzman had surfaced as industry gossip.

"Well, you don't want to work for anyone except Kazan, and you can't get Kazan," Furie fired back.

"We don't even have a script!" Brando fired back.

"We started *Ipcress* without a script too, and that's done pretty well."

"Bullshit!"

Furie learned soon enough that Brando would have full script approval regarding the rewrites. From his perspective, it was a small price to pay for directing a Brando picture, and he was at least given some latitude for reworking the material, whereas with both *13* and *Eli Kotch,* such efforts were quickly shot down.

The Appaloosa tells the story of Matt Fletcher, a saddle tramp who wanders into a border town in the American Southwest atop a beautiful appaloosa horse. He proceeds directly to the town church, where he repents of years of sin and resolves in his prayers to live a moral, decent life that will allow him distance from the past. While inside, however, he is harassed by an angry bandito named Chuy Medina, who falsely accuses him of improper conduct with his mistress Trini. Retreating to his friend Paco's nearby homestead, he is immediately rampaged there by Chuy and his men, who steal his appaloosa and humiliate him in front of Paco's family. Venturing into unfamiliar and unfriendly territory to regain the appaloosa, his personal symbol of a new life of repentance, humility, and civility, Matt only humiliates himself further and is almost killed in an arm-wrestling match involving deadly scorpions that are poised on both sides to sting the loser. After befriending an old Mexican man, who is accidentally killed in the crossfire of a gun battle, Matt positions himself to eliminate his tormentor and regain the prized horse in a patch of snow-covered hills—his last kill before permanently stowing his gun, and his past, away.

"I wanted to continue the style of unusual camera angles that I had developed and established for *The Ipcress File,* especially when the character actually ventures forth on the journey to get the horse back," says Furie, "and I had Russ Metty as a visual collaborator. I loved his camerawork in *Touch of Evil.*" Russell Metty was the quintessential Universal Pictures journeyman cinematographer. He had shot everything from the Douglas Sirk melodramas to *Spartacus* to *Bringing Up Baby* and had lensed close to a hundred films for Universal alone, often working on as many as six pictures a year. He had just completed shooting *Texas across the River,* another Western for Universal, starring Dean Martin, near San Diego. "Metty was an interesting character," Furie remembers. "When I first met him, he tried to come off as boorish, like a hick or a redneck, almost trying to hide the fact that he was artistic. I got the feeling he came from an environment where it was a sissy to be creative. I tried to explain the style I was going for, and he paused, thought about it, looked back up at me, would say something gruff and just kind of went right into working that way with me. I really liked the guy, but he wanted to think of himself as 'just folks' and saw himself more as a technician . . . someone who works with his hands."

The unusual *Ipcress* style Furie had consigned to this particular Western must have, to some extent, broken the methodical Metty out of a more ho-hum reflex. "He went crazy when I wanted to use the Arriflex, because he was strictly Mitchell BNC." The Arriflex was a lightweight and more supple alternative to the Mitchell BNC, a large and cumbersome camera, the use of which had been popularized in major Hollywood studio feature filmmaking since the 1930s. "That's how old-school and classically trained he was." Furie also took issue with Metty's assuming what he deemed an overactive role in the composition of the shots. Later, when Furie published a filmmaker editorial entitled "Hollywood Misses Its Cue" in the Sunday Calendar section of the October 9, 1966, *Los Angeles Times*, it gave him a chance to air his grievances vis-à-vis the Hollywood studio filmmaking working style to which he was attempting to adjust as a young filmmaker having just emigrated from England. Before asserting that the director "is responsible for the composition of the scene, the placement of his actors and the kind of camera angle he believes is essential for a particular scene," Furie writes, "In England, they call the cinematographer the 'lighting cameraman' because that is what he does. After I have picked the camera angle and rehearsed my actors and then the camera movements with the camera operator, the only thing left for the lighting cameraman to do is light. I have heard that in Hollywood if you take on this kind of responsibility, you will be told, 'I'm the cameraman, and you're the director; you do your job and I'll do mine.' I've never heard that kind of reaction in England because if a cameraman ever said that to a director he'd be removed from the picture."[36] Furie, clearly frustrated that he had to struggle for his license to extend the *Ipcress* visual style into *The Appaloosa*, also lamented the restrictive equipment used on Hollywood productions, citing the advancements made with the handheld camera despite popular resistance to its usage in mainstream moviemaking.

The director received a quick rebuttal to his editorial, published in the same paper a week later, written by a galled Herb Aller, then the executive secretary of the local motion picture machine operators union and later the executive director of the International Photographers Guild. Aller's response, in which he criticized Furie for "laying the blame on the cinematographer" and for attempting to claim authorship for the director alone, was both vitriolic and indignant. "Respect is earned not muscled," Aller writes. "Furie would be wise to devote his time to the script, for it may be that he'll go out the way he came in—with no class." Furie's reputation as an enfant terrible in no short supply of chutzpah was cemented, as he sought to redefine the extent of a director's role a few good years before Andrew Sarris and auteur theory rose to more visible prominence. Aller likewise posited that "Kazan, Logan and others have entered the motion picture industry and entrusted themselves into the hands of many distinguished American cinematographers" and that "the net result has been successful, artistically and monetarily."[37]

As a filmmaker who had stated to a journalist on an *Ipcress File* shooting location in London that he felt he was "beginning to mature as a creative artist," Furie believed that the next logical step was to define for himself a sense of creative autonomy beyond the customary limitations relegated to a Hollywood director. As a "young gun" sounding a "rebel yell," he wanted total control of his films' images and was, even in 1966, already preparing to break out on his own terms within a stubborn industry that never prided itself in yielding to new ways of operating, at least at that time. But who can say whether Furie's jeremiad endeared him to the craftsmen on whose behalf Aller was speaking? In the Hollywood of 1966, many aligned with Aller, who believed that things such as handheld technique were "hardly suitable for good picture-making." Decades later, in 1997, Furie was admitted to the Local 600 camera operators union. He carries a union card to ensure that he can personally see to the operating task at hand, if need be. "I love flashing that card if someone says, 'You can't operate!'"

"I will say that no one could light day-for-night like Russ Metty could," says Furie. "Like Otto Heller, I asked him to light the film without the usual studio high-key lighting, and he provided that in spades. I was trying to establish a style and needed to be in control of that." Incidentally, future Academy Award–winning cinematographer Bruce Surtees acted as Metty's camera operator.

While Furie, producer Alan Miller, cinematographer Russell Metty, and the art directors were sent to scout locations in Wrightwood, California, and Antelope Valley, near St. George, Utah, the makeup team, led by Phil Rhodes, were working with Brando on developing a special look for his character in the film. "He was originally supposed to be Mexican in the film," said Rhodes. "So I made him up the way he thought a Mexican should look. I was always one for prosthetics, artificial teeth, artificial eyelashes, suck his cheeks in, bring his cheekbones out. I thought he looked fantastic. But he also wanted a moustache, which made him look like Charlie Chaplin." Rhodes quickly received a call from a Universal executive, lambasting him for his "campy" makeup job. "I just said, 'It's not my fault. I just took my directions from him.' And by that point, he had fallen in love with how he looked."[38] Rhodes was told that it was now his job to talk him out of it. The prevailing opinion among most people was that he looked like Genghis Khan. Brando was so angry about the whole affair that he threatened to not wear any makeup at all, which is ultimately what came to pass (with the exception of a faux full beard, which is "shaved" after the story's first movement). The character was rewritten from being a Mexican to being an American in Mexico.

From the socially conscious, politically active Brando, one question persisted throughout James Bridges's rewrites: "How can we make this thing more about the struggle of American Indians?"[39]

Martin Landau had auditioned for the key role of the villainous Chuy Medina, eventually given to John Saxon. "Landau almost had it, and he was so good at his audition," recalls Furie. "But Saxon just barely edged him out because he had these flashing teeth, and could do that kind of menacing smile from ear-to-ear." Anjanette Comer, who had just finished a lead role in Tony Richardson's *The Loved One*, was cast in the female lead as Trini, in a role for which Pat Quinn had been briefly discussed and passed over on Brando's say-so. "I will not work with anyone with whom I am emotionally involved" was the indignant star's explanation. Meanwhile, during the two months Furie was able to revise the screenplay, Brando incessantly suggested to Furie that they turn the film into a plea for the plight of American Indians.

Shooting commenced in October 1965. Furie remembers, "When we started shooting, he would often not feel like filming in the afternoon. What he would do as an excuse was paunch out his belly over his pants and then act like he could not get his pants buttoned up." Alan Miller, who was constantly trying to inject the star with enthusiasm at whatever cost (much to Brando's annoyance), had wrongly presumed that the horror stories of shooting with Brando were largely apocryphal. Furie formulated a means by which they could continue shooting for the rest of the day. "We would let Marlon go. He used to get out of school early, and I'd shoot his double Paul Baxley from behind, and get all that coverage. The next morning, we would get Brando's close-ups and just kind of quickly pop him into the scene in order to make the day."

Brando, meanwhile, had his afternoons free and would have women flown to location on a private jet. Both Furie and screenwriter James Bridges used the same terms to describe the type of women who would appear for Brando's amusement. "They were 'exotic-types.' There's just no other way to say it," says Furie. "None of them were particularly attractive, really. So, in the afternoon, after the filming would exhaust his patience for the day, he just go off with these women, and I, as the director, had to keep pushing forward the best way I knew how. He questioned everything, even if the full crew was there and we had five minutes of sun left to finish a scene. It gets you down sometimes but he was gutsy and tremendously creative."[40]

John Saxon remembers an early exchange between himself and his costar. "I told him, 'You know, I might steal this picture out from under you, Marlon.' All he said was, 'Be my guest.'"

As during the making of *The Ipcress File*, the script for *The Appaloosa* was being reworked every single day of shooting, and the crew would have to wait on pages to be delivered by the overburdened Bridges, who was fueled by the fact that everyone seemed "very excited" by the dailies. After the script had been delivered to Furie and producer Miller's satisfaction, Bridges returned to Los Angeles, only be summoned back within forty-eight hours. "I got a hysterical call from Alan," he explained. "I rushed back to set, and was met when I got off the plane by Alan and Sidney. They told me that Marlon was now refusing to play any of the scenes as written. He was just going crazy. They told me, 'There is this scene we are shooting tomorrow and you've gotta rewrite it!' They gave me notes." That night, Bridges retired to his hotel to write three different versions of the same scene, in hopes that Brando would approve at least one of the three. "Script conferences were not constructive. Soon enough, it became all about discussing what Marlon would accept, as opposed to what was the right thing to do with the story."[41]

Says Furie, "I had a deep respect for Brando and you will never hear me knock him. He would walk up to me and say, 'I've got an idea for this. If you don't like it, you don't have to use it,' and most of the time we did do it his way. The worst I could say is that he'd put up a fuss sometimes and question everything, even when we were losing light or under extreme time pressures." Brando would also take his own stab at writing scenes solo, then would often struggle to remember his new lines. Furie claims that they ultimately used virtually everything that Brando created on the spot. "He'd always attack the big speeches. He loved to mess around with the speeches."[42]

The Pollyanna-ish antics of Alan Miller, who was constantly looking to lavishly placate the rebellious star, were reportedly driving Brando to madness. James Bridges remembers, "He would approach Brando in this patronizing way, and say, 'Jim has just done this brilliant scene. You've gotta read this.' Brando would fire back, 'What do you want me to do with this? Play it as written?' and Alan would say, 'Oh, it's brilliant, Marlon. It's just brilliant.' Brando just looked away and shook his head, 'Well, I don't think it's very brilliant, Alan,' and he refused to play it like that."[43]

Furie took a different tack, asking Brando to work with Bridges on scenes. "I would want them to collaborate on things," Furie explains. "It seemed to be a way to resolve a lot of the situations." So Bridges retired with Brando to the star's trailer while Furie and Metty, under the gun as always, lined up the next shot. Bridges then suggested that Brando improvise the scene himself while putting on his makeup, and Bridges would take dictation as the actor spoke the new freshly improvised lines. Taking down every word the actor mouthed verbatim, he handed the result back to Brando to read. Brando then announced he was unhappy with this version as well. "I said, 'Marlon, I didn't write that. You did. It's exactly what you said,'" Bridges remembers. Brando responded by throwing the script up in the air. Finally fed up with Brando's game, Bridges announced he would be returning to Los Angeles that afternoon. Brando's response was to grab Bridges by the collar, lead him by the hem of his coat and walk him out the door. "He then gave me a little shove on the ass with his foot," claims Bridges. "It wasn't violent, but I was pissed. I turned, looked back at him, and was about to say something when he interrupted, 'You're the only one here with any integrity.'"[44]

The studio issued a press release on December 13, 1965, stating that a second writer, Roland Kibbee, had been brought in on *The Appaloosa* to fill in for Bridges on additional rewrites. Bridges was gratefully relinquished from the project and left the set in the middle of the night. After his departure, at five weeks of shooting, the production decamped from St. George, Utah, to Indio, Utah, because of heavy rains. "I think Bridges was just upset because Brando changed a lot of stuff in his script with my approval," says Furie. "The script just had a lot of problems. Dramatically, there were just no meat and potatoes. So we had to bring on Kibbee to fix a lot of the stuff. It wasn't really especially collaborative with Kibbee. He was a more detached presence than Bridges, just there to work and not to grow emotionally attached. I think Bridges really cared more about his involvement because it was his first film script."

Bridges, in a letter to his friend actor-screenwriter-producer Jack Larson, wrote that Brando's stance on Furie was that he was a verifiably talented director but one that he could not fully trust. Brando's double Paul

Baxley assured Brando on no uncertain terms that the footage looked impressive. The running joke throughout the shooting, however, in reference to Furie's wild angle style, was something to the effect of "Where's this guy going to put the camera next? Up the horse's ass?"

Furie remembers a particular incident of "One-Eyed Jack vs. Kino-Eyed Sid" that he feels speaks to a healthy actor-director relationship between himself and Brando. "You know," begins Furie, "when you keep resentment towards actors and crew members hidden and inside, you get to hate. My policy has always been that it's always best to get it out there, because it's not healthy to keep it hidden. Things build and coldness and hatred on a movie set is never a good thing. I had it out with Marlon up in Wrightwood in the San Bernadino Mountains, during the shoot-out at the finale of the film, with all the snow on the ground. He said something nasty to me, I don't remember really what it was specifically. It resulted in a shouting match. But I recall he got on his horse and we were going to get the shot. I just looked up at him and, as serious as anything, just told him, 'Boy, you just don't give a shit about anybody, do you?' He immediately started laughing out loud, and I do mean out loud. He got down off his horse and gave me a hug, and we went about the rest of the day's shooting. He loved my honesty for having called him on it, and that I was not just patting him on the head and just accepting the abuse and clamming up after this shouting match."

Although Brando rarely attended the dailies, word was still filtering down from many in the cast and crew once again about how visually innovative and imaginative Furie's shots were, and how impressively staged everything was.[45]

James Garner, who was shooting *Duel at Diablo* sixty miles away in nearby Kanab, Utah, came to the set of *The Appaloosa* one day to visit Brando, with whom he had costarred in the 1957 film *Sayonara*. A false yarn has been spun that Michael Caine visited the set and Brando asked him his impression of Furie as a director. When Caine replied that he found him to be "an excellent director," the indignant Brando deemed that "he couldn't direct traffic." "That story is a lot of rubbish," says Caine. "First of all, I was never there even for a minute on *The Appaloosa,* and in the second place, when I did meet Brando, he never said a single negative thing about Sid."

"Everyone working on that picture had such respect for Marlon," Furie says. "I mean, how could you not have respect for the guy? He was Marlon

Brando! The thing is that he had no self-respect. I always say that he was a thoroughbred, and the studios were racing him at state-fair with the kind of stuff they were putting him in."

Furie's final and most lasting memory of Brando, however, was at the most unlikely of places.

> Wrap parties on movies in that time were real events. They were happenings. No one expected that Marlon would be at the wrap party. He had no reason to be there. But everyone's spouses had flown in for this thing, and suddenly, there we see Brando landing in a helicopter, dressed like he showed up for a high school dance. He showed up at the wrap party, and he danced with all of the wives and girlfriends of the cast and crew members, who were starstruck. "Who's your husband? Oh, the prop guy?" That's the kind of guy he could be. He could be a good boy, a total mensch. In my heart and mind and soul, that is the real Brando.

Editor Ted Kent, another Universal journeyman, had already begun his assembly cut of the film when production wrapped on May 13, 1966. "I was so impressed with Kent's editing of the film that I hardly ever entered the editing room," remembers Furie.

The September 14, 1966, premiere of *The Appaloosa* opened to somewhat respectable business but then flatlined at the box office before making a profit. *Newsweek* noted "Furie's mania for weirdly mannered camera angles," adding parenthetically, "you spend half the time peering round, over or under obstacles behind which the action is strategically placed." Philip Scheuer of the *Los Angeles Times* took umbrage with the stylized direction and camerawork and the "somnambulistic" acting of Brando. Pauline Kael was the most scathing: "Poor Marlon Brando! Here he is trapped inside still another dog of a movie. Failure was guaranteed by Mr. Brando's weird interpretation of the hero and by Sidney J. Furie's equally weird direction. Not for the first time, Mr. Brando gives us a heavy-lidded, adenoidally openmouthed caricature of the inarticulate, stalwart loner." She keenly ended her review, stating, "If he is trapped, it is not by others but by himself." Others attacked only Brando's performance; Arthur Knight stated in the *Saturday Review* that he "underplays to the point of monotony," and *Variety* noted a "shortage of thrills and a strange lack of color in the Brando character."

Bosley Crowther of the *New York Times* was slightly more respectful but also aired his own grievances with the work. "To be quite blunt about it, it is on the bold, pretentious side. It does radiate rather strongly the kind of glossy pictorial style and the taste for elaborate camera angles that Mr. Furie used effectively in his first hit, the London-made *The Ipcress File*. And he does permit Brando to play an aging saddle tramp with something of the same ostentation he showed in his own previous Western *One-Eyed Jacks*." One critic, Barry Rohan of the *Chicago Tribune*, wrote admiringly of the cinematography, calling the film "a routine Western almost made memorable by sparkling camerawork that brings everything to life." In its best notice, Clyde Leech of the *L.A. Herald Examiner*, proclaimed that Brando had been given "one of the best roles he's had in a very long time" and that, pictorially, *The Appaloosa* was "a singularly beautiful motion picture." William Wolf of *Cue* observed that "the big boon is handsome, creative direction by Sidney J. Furie. He has made it a good visual job." *Film Daily*'s Mandel Herbstman wrote, "[Furie] guides the action along with mounting force. His evocation of images shows sure imagination."

In many ways, *The Appaloosa* could be considered as much of a follow-up to *One-Eyed Jacks* as it is to *The Ipcress File*. Besides the obvious parallel, that both *One-Eyed Jacks* and *The Appaloosa* are Westerns starring Marlon Brando, the penitent Matt Fletcher character is a descendant of *One-Eyed Jacks*'s Kid Rio. As Tony Thomas writes in *The Films of Marlon Brando*, "It is another of his brooding, tortured, simple men, and, as in so many of his other films, a man suffering brutal physical treatment."[46] Having been inexplicably tamed after a life of misdeeds only vaguely alluded to, Matt Fletcher longs for a civil, peaceful life. He is first seen riding into a Mexican village to stop at its church. When the character's process of atonement, a visit to the priest to confess his sins and a prayer offered at the church's altar, is interrupted, so is the film, making for a careful stylistic break. The "*Ipcress* style" becomes more perceptible and more audacious as we follow the character through the land that his adversary knows intimately and presides over with a sense of power and security. These are uncertain territories for the Brando character. He journeys into the "lion's den" to retrieve the symbol of his atonement, the appaloosa horse he has inherited. The dense visual language of Furie's pictures magnifies the film's building dramatic tensions by defining these uncertain spaces with precarious camera placement. The eye is also teased into viewing impending danger and violence from what seem to be safe, shadowy hiding places in the immediate vicinity.

As in *The Ipcress File,* the effect is cumulative, with meanings realized in the gestalt only as the story progresses. Critics who applauded the style in *The Ipcress File,* for evoking a palpable sense of voyeuristic tension, did not generally know what to make of all this style in *The Appaloosa* only one year later, thinking it anomalous within the confines of an American Western. Though many accused the director of affectation and his technique of inconsonance, both function beyond simply revealing new ways of seeing a scene. On one level, Richard Schickel observed that "Furie's search for the odd angle is, finally, the most suspenseful element in the movie: what will he think of next?" However, Schickel's claim that "searching for dubious visual novelty when they should have been searching for his character drove Brando crazy"[47] is an embellishment, since Brando had little awareness of Furie's methods as the action was being staged. A claim like "it drove the critics crazy" is significantly more apropos.

Even the occasional unobstructed shots struck many as ostentatious, frustrating critics such as the *Los Angeles Times*'s Phillip K. Scheuer, who wrote, "Style is fine in its way, but not when it takes precedence over content." By default, the director was perceived as continuing a singular and dangerously specific visual style that worked in favor of one film, a paranoid thriller, but seemed strained, irritating, and forced in the trappings of another. Gerald Pratley, a *Variety* writer who often championed the Canadian film industry and Canadian filmmakers (including expatriates like Hiller, Jewison, Kotcheff, and Furie), considered *The Appaloosa* a "transitional picture" for its director, referring to it as the struggling follow-up effort necessary to make the jump from the artistically freeing British methods of picture-making, in which the young Furie reveled, to the contrasting Hollywood of the 1960s, which funneled motion-picture production into more rigid methods. Moreover, sequences such as the arm-wrestling match involving the deadly scorpions and the later shoot-out at the hacienda, are taut, arresting in imagery, and adroitly paced.

A particular incident that took place a decade after the release of *The Appaloosa,* accounted in Peter Manso's biography of Marlon Brando, is one that Furie does not remember and semirefutes. The story: Furie ran into Brando in London sometime in the late sixties. Brando was surprisingly friendly, saying, "I thought you were a phony, a liar, a double-crosser.

I discovered you've got the great visual sense of good directors. Let's do another film." Furie, without batting an eye, allegedly responded, "Never!"[48]

"I never would have said 'Never' to him. If he would have wanted to work with me again, I would certainly have done it again. I, for one, thought as the director of the film that his performance in *The Appaloosa* was pretty damn good, and in the end, that's what matters."

In the interim between picture wrap on *The Appaloosa* and its U.S. release in September 1966, Furie had chanced to meet a towering character actor named Brad Dexter through producer Joe Schoenfeld, who had just started representing Furie through the William Morris Agency. Dexter, who had been married to Peggy Lee for eight months in 1953, had made a career as a burly and imposing presence in films throughout the fifties and sixties, including *The Asphalt Jungle, Last Train from Gun Hill,* and *The Magnificent Seven.* On May 10, 1964, Dexter made headlines by saving Frank Sinatra from nearly drowning in Hawaii, during the shooting of *None but the Brave.* Although the press originally reported that Sinatra had indeed drowned, he only came dangerously close to drowning. After costarring together in another film, *Von Ryan's Express* (1965), Sinatra showed his appreciation for Dexter's valor by giving his brawny savior his own film to produce under the Sinatra Enterprises banner. The resulting film put an abrupt and bitter end to the relationship between Dexter and Sinatra, and that film was Furie's follow-up film after the rough-and-tumble battles fought on *The Ipcress File* and *The Appaloosa.*

During the shooting of *The Appaloosa,* Furie's wife, Sheila, gave birth to their fourth child, Simon. As Furie's Hollywood career showed no sign of slowing, *Canadian Cinematography* magazine said of the newly hot director: "A great many people have asked if Furie wants to come back to Canada to make films." Furie answered, "I would travel anywhere to make a film if I believed in that film. I don't care where it's being made."[49] It was a diplomatic response, and it scarcely suggested homesickness. To Gerald Utting of the *Toronto Star,* around the same time, he was more brusque: "Despite all the work we did in Toronto, and the hopes we had for it, there's really no more reason for Toronto to have a movie industry than Cleveland."

Quickly apparent was the fact that Furie and Brad Dexter worked astonishingly well as collaborators. "Throughout my whole career," Furie claims, "I have always had someone to bounce things off. Brad Dexter, Harry Korshak, Rick Natkin, Kevin Elders, Gary Howsam, Greg Mellott . . . I've always had a partner in my endeavors to act as a sounding board.

Brad Dexter was really the first of these figures. He had a simpatico about him, and we just immediately synched."

Canadian filmmaker Paul Lynch, a personal friend of Sidney Furie's, speaks fondly of Dexter as "the guy I'd often see in movies of the 50's who would twist people's heads off. He was quite tall and in films like *Violent Saturday,* he'd play the character who would shoot people for fun and all that kind of stuff. He was quite a presence." Dexter himself is quoted in 1962 as saying, "I love playing heavies. It's the best-written character."[50] In Dexter's *Los Angeles Times* obituary, his friend, air force comrade, and fellow Serbian Karl Malden remembered, "Brad was always outspoken." Dexter reigned at Sinatra Enterprises that year as "executive vice-president in charge of motion picture production," which entailed finding movie properties in which Sinatra could star and putting the deals on them together.

Following the back-to-back fusillade of raging production battles Furie had waged with Harry Saltzman and Marlon Brando, he was hoping that making *The Naked Runner* would return him to a decidedly less strained method of working. The first meeting with Sinatra went as well as it could. Sinatra had starred in two flops, including *Marriage on the Rocks* (1965) and *Assault on a Queen* (1966), which lost considerable amounts of money for Warner Bros. and Paramount, respectively. They also both reflected poorly on Sinatra, whose Sinatra Enterprises Productions had shepherded both films into existence. Sinatra had acquired the rights to the novel *The Naked Runner,* written by British novelist Arthur Bell Thompson under his pen name Francis Clifford. Thompson was a decorated veteran of the Burma Rifles in World War II who became well regarded for his crime and thriller novels beginning with the publication of his first novel, *Honour the Shrine,* in 1953. He had been hailed a war hero for leading sixty soldiers on a heroic 109-day march through nine hundred miles of jungle and mountains into Allied lines in Burma, with little in the way of ammunition, food, and supplies.

The author's background impressed Sinatra, who had just been denied a coveted title role in *Harper* (1966) on a deal that Dexter had failed to put together for the star (the role was instead given to Paul Newman). Dexter purchased Clifford's *The Naked Runner* for Sinatra Enterprises when it was still in galleys in January 1966 (it was published one month later). Dexter advised Sinatra Enterprises to pick it up as a starring vehicle for the star, in lieu of *Harper.* It tells the John Le Carre–esque story of Sam Laker, a successful industrial designer living in London, who is unwittingly enlisted as a hitman by British intelligence just as he is about to travel to East Germany for a trade convention. Advantageously lacking an intelligence profile that would make him recognizable, but armed with a wartime past that suggests an ease and skill with the trigger, Laker is duped and then blackmailed into assassinating a defecting double agent. His twelve-year-old son is kidnapped and held hostage until he completes the job, while labyrinthine (and ultimately incomprehensible) mind games are used to keep him in line. He first travels to Leipzig, where he has a rendezvous with an old wartime flame, who is used to turn the tables on him. The reluctant reemergence of Laker's long-dormant skills as an assassin lies at the heart of the film's drama.

Sinatra had been impressed with *The Ipcress File* and hired Furie as director because he was confident in Furie's skill at rendering espionage-genre material. Considering that the lead character, Sam Laker, lives in London as an expatriate and that much of the film was to be shot there, both Dexter and Sinatra were also comforted in knowing that Furie had a feel for London from having lived there himself as a Canadian expatriate for a number of years. The source novel would require such a command; the Byzantine plot was dense and convoluted, almost requiring detailed program notes for the reader. A script was immediately commissioned from Stanley Mann, who had been Academy Award–nominated for his screenplay for William Wyler's *The Collector* (1965). The project would also ensure shooting time in London, where Furie could stay near his family's home, along with other locations in Leipzig and Copenhagen. "Brad trapped me into directing by saying that if I backed out, he was out of a picture," said Furie in a 1967 interview. "I knew before starting both *The Appaloosa* and *The Naked Runner* that they wouldn't work, but I couldn't quit on a relationship basis. I guess it was also my ego, thinking I was indispensable to them, because they would have simply gotten someone else to do them."[51] Furie filled out the rest of the cast with Brits like Peter Vaughan, Edward Fox, and Derren Nesbitt, a veteran of the 1961 stage production of Tom Murphy's *A Whistle in the Dark*, through which he also met old friend and collaborator Dudley Sutton (as well as Oliver McGreevy, who appeared in *The Leather Boys* and *The Ipcress File*).

Dexter undoubtedly foresaw a long-term relationship in the works between Furie and Sinatra Enterprises. Enthused about his director, Dexter announced in *Variety* on May 17, 1966, that Sinatra Enterprises had set a second-picture commitment with Furie, a Western set in post–Civil War Mexico, based on a treatment by Robert B. Mitchell titled *Jack Bo,* to be possibly shot the following year in Mexico with Sinatra in a starring role. Furie now sees this as the first of many such Dexter press gimmicks. "I don't remember the first thing about that project," says Furie. "Brad might have brought it up to me once, and I probably said something like, 'Yeah, Brad, that's nice.' He just wanted to center some attention around the production company and my new involvement with it, because I was hot after *The Ipcress File.*" Independent of Dexter, Furie was also offered the director's chair on *Pretty Polly,* a Universal adaptation of the Noël Coward story "Pretty Polly Barlow," which was to be produced by George W. George. Guy Green ultimately directed the film, released as *A Matter of Innocence* in 1967.

For *The Naked Runner*'s $2.5 million negative cost, Sinatra's fee was a hefty $1 million plus box-office participation, rather extravagant for the time. Furie was paid two hundred thousand dollars to direct, his largest salary up to that point. The film was produced under the Eady Plan, a British film-production initiative spearheaded to reinvigorate British film production after the war, under which tickets sold at movie theaters were levied for the benefit of a fund that would repay producers to make "British quota films," with an overwhelmingly predominant British cast and crew. The initiative was named for Sir Wilford Eady, the Board of Trade member who hatched the concept in the late 1940s, although it reached its height in the sixties as a boon for British film production outfits. Despite various advantages, the major disadvantage of the Eady Plan was that you could not use many international stars. In a given production, only two of the film's key personnel could be non-British, usually the director and the star (in this case, Furie and Sinatra as an extension of Brad Dexter). Dexter made clear that the ultimately unproduced *Jack Bo* would likewise be made under the Eady Plan.[52]

"My main regret about *The Naked Runner* is that we really should have worked more on the script," says Furie. "I still think that, visually, it's one of my more interesting pictures, but the plot really never made much sense. The novel read pretty well. It was hard to follow for most audiences and we didn't really touch it much once we started shooting. One of the best things about the whole experience, though, is that I got to work with Otto Heller and most of the *Ipcress* crew again." Heller, the cinematographer whose lighting on *The Ipcress File* had given the film a certain dynamism, had shot the first *Ipcress* sequel, *Funeral in Berlin,* and *Alfie* in the post-*Ipcress* interim. After difficulties working with cinematographer Russell Metty within the Hollywood system on *The Appaloosa,* Furie was grateful to reemerge in a system that encouraged visually proactive directors, with the trusted Heller at the helm. Once again, Furie chose to employ the same "wild-angle style" that had been deemed intriguing and well-conceived by critics of *Ipcress* and dismissed as infuriating and superfluous by critics of *The Appaloosa.* "I thought that maybe since because we were back in the espionage world and that that style created tension in *The Ipcress File,* it would be acceptable to them again, and amplify the paranoia that Sinatra's character feels," Furie rationalizes.

During preproduction, Sinatra started wooing Mia Farrow, the twenty-one-year-old star of *Peyton Place,* who was twenty-eight years his junior. She clandestinely became his wife on July 19, 1966, almost two weeks before the first day of shooting. They eloped in Las Vegas in a veil of utmost secrecy, so much so that even Sinatra's daughters and Farrow's mother, Maureen O'Sullivan, were completely unaware of their marriage plans until after it was over. As far as the production crew of *The Naked Runner* knew, Sinatra just suddenly took off to take care of pressing "personal business," telling no one where he was going but guaranteeing his return in time for the first day of shooting. Furie, meanwhile, found himself invited to a dinner with Stanley Kubrick, actor Keir Dullea, and Roman Polanski. Polanski had just finished shooting the Martin Ransohoff production *The Fearless Vampire Killers, or Pardon Me but Your Teeth Are in My Neck* in northern Italy, where he met and fell in love with the film's star Sharon Tate, who became his wife on January 20, 1968. Tate had also been cast early on for a role in *Eye of the Devil* (aka *13*), the Ransohoff production from which Furie had departed in frustration. While in prep for *Eye of the Devil* at MGM's Borehamwood Studios, Furie had previously chanced to meet and spend time with Kubrick, who was there working on *2001: A Space Odyssey* (1968). "Irving Shapiro, the guy who bought *A Dangerous Age* from me in New York, had also bought Stanley's first feature film *Fear and Desire* before mine, so I always knew of him, even way back when."

At the Kubrick home that night, the male company discussed how the ailing Paramount had recently been bought by Gulf+Western head Charles Bluhdorn to diversify the corporation's subholdings. Bluhdorn's assets also included Madison Square Garden, Simon & Schuster Publishing, and a profitable zinc-mining company. In 1967, when Bluhdorn spotted an article about Robert Evans in the Sunday *New York Times,* written by Peter Bart, Bluhdorn hired Evans as Paramount's head of production. Bart followed his article's subject (and newest friend) to work at the studio, where he set up as an executive and rose to become vice president in charge of production. "It was a very memorable evening with Stanley, Roman and Keir Dullea, not necessarily because of the company, which was great, but because I would spend the next eight years of my career at Paramount," says Furie.

On Monday, August 1, 1966, shooting of *The Naked Runner* commenced in North London. Furie, Dexter, and their crew were lining up their first shot when Sinatra arrived, with Farrow beamingly flanking their business-as-usual star, wearing an impressive wedding bauble. She continued to haunt the set for most of the rest of the production. Incidentally, *The Naked Runner* made its U.S. premiere on the couple's first wedding anniversary exactly one year later. Sinatra tried in vain to combine his honeymoon with the production of the film in London, much to the annoyance of Furie and Dexter, the latter of whom was growing increasingly impatient with his employer's capricious, half-hearted attitude revolving around his work. "I can say, though, without a doubt that he was always punctual and on-time when he was called to the set," Furie says.

"We needed a World War II Quonset hut for the final scene in the movie," recalls Furie. "And they don't have Quonset huts in Central London, so you had to go out to the suburbs to find them. The one we used was in Surrey. We all drove out there, but Sinatra got to the location on a helicopter. When he got there, he was pissed. He said, 'I came all the way out here to shoot in this?! Why couldn't we do this in London?' I just said, 'Frank, they don't have Quonset huts in London.' He gave me daggers and said, 'Well, I don't care.'" Furie then proceeded to explain to Sinatra that he had read that on the set of *The Devil at 4 O'Clock,* a film in which Sinatra had costarred with Spencer Tracy in 1961, he had made them move the set because he did not want to go to the proper location.

"Let me tell you something, Frank," Furie launched into his rebuke, "We're not moving this Quonset hut. We can't. And in any case, this is your company's movie. And you know what? I've had it! I've got my new Jaguar here that I drove out here. I'm going back to London. I'm not going to put up with your Hollywood bullshit."

Dexter looked at his employer with disdain: "I'm backing the director on this, Frank," turning his back coldly and following Furie. Sinatra, for his part, gave the man to whom he had given a producing career a look of resentment.

Having reached his Jaguar, the director heard Sinatra bellow from behind him, "Okay, Furie, you win! Get the hell back here!"

"Frank had to listen to reason and know that we weren't going to move the Quonset hut to central London," says Furie. "He had a completion bond on the picture from his company and we would have been throwing time and money out the window if he refused to shoot, or if I actually had left that day."

Unsubstantiated behind-the-scenes stories precipitated during the production of *The Naked Runner* and its aftermath and were falsely reported as fact. The weightiest one involved Sinatra leaving the film before it was finished shooting. "Frank was there every day we needed him," Furie claims. "All that stuff about him leaving and sending his lawyer to Copenhagen to request that we finish shooting in L.A. is total nonsense." Another such story had Sinatra putting a bitter end to his relationship with Dexter both because of Dexter's criticism of his marriage to Farrow and because he had chosen to finish the film with a Sinatra double after Sinatra had fled the production. "I don't buy that. Brad Dexter's death warrant with continuing to work for Sinatra was signed and sealed when he sided with me on the Quonset hut incident," Furie claims. "He was just dead meat with Sinatra from that point on. We did go back to shoot more when we were editing the film with [editor] Barrie Vince, using a double for Frank, but he did finish the principal shooting with us. The script on that film was a lot of trouble, and we never got it right, so we went back in editing to try to fix some of those problems. We couldn't avoid it being confusing."

Indeed, by the time Furie and Vince were putting *The Naked Runner* together and were having difficulty making it cohere, Sinatra had already taken the leading role in 20th Century Fox's *The Detective,* the adaptation of a Richard Thorpe novel and a primary pet project of his before *The Naked Runner* was launched. He was unavailable for the reshoots. George Jacobs, Sinatra's longtime valet, claims that Sinatra "hated London being taken over by the Carnaby Street Mod atmosphere so much that he basically dumped the picture, went back to L.A. and let the producers worry about putting together what footage they had."[53] That Sinatra disliked location shooting in any form just made things worse.

Ultimately, Furie's fondest memory of Sinatra involves a dinner he shared with a former high school teacher of his, who was coming to visit London. Farrow had just begun shooting *A Dandy in Aspic* with director Anthony Mann in London, and was occupied.

> Frank asked me if I wanted to join him for dinner. I just said thanks but no thanks, because I was going to be having dinner with my teacher. Next thing I know, Frank is asking, "Can I tag along with you two?" And I just laughed and said, "Tag along with us? She'd have a heart attack!" Frank was with us at that dinner and could not have been more charming, and he couldn't have been more of a gentleman. He gave my teacher a real night to remember. That's the kind of guy he could be, and he gave her the Frankie Boy she knew him to be.

Furie's apprehensions concerning the film's convoluted story were significant even by the time production moved to Copenhagen on August 30, 1966. Later, in editing, the third act appeared even harder to penetrate, rendering the potential for a satisfying or even acceptable ending elusive if not impossible. In a later 1970 interview, Furie recalled that he had gone through the "worst period" of his life trying for ten desperate months to pull *The Naked Runner* together in some fashion. "I was running out and shooting bits and pieces of additional footage, trying things in editing to salvage it," Furie recalls. "The story was just incomprehensible when it approached the third act, and I knew I needed to do something to save it."[54]

The film opened in the United States that summer to dismal reviews but good business, particularly considering the failures of Sinatra's previous two pictures. It was the first Sinatra film to make a profit for Sinatra Enterprises. The *New Yorker*'s Pauline Kael, who was fast becoming Furie's chief nemesis within the critical establishment, wrote of the film, "The director, Sidney J. Furie, provides enormous vistas for small bits of dialogue, close-ups of cups of creamy brown coffee, fancy simulations of Magritte. What on earth for? Done straightforwardly, this movie still would have been nothing, but it would be half the length." She branded the story "implausible," "unconvincing" and "without a single witty idea." Charles Champlin of the *Los Angeles Times* wrote favorably of Sinatra's acting, stating, "It must be said that even in this undemonstrative rendition of undistinguished material, he commands the screen. Given the plot, there must have been a temptation to shout, moan, and chew the scenery. He puts the temptation down, way down, and understands the histrionics. The result is a sense of power held in check, of power wasted."

In relation to both *The Appaloosa* and especially *The Ipcress File, The Naked Runner* is the least successful of Furie's unofficial "Wild Angles Trilogy" and exhibits the most evidence of Furie's growing pains, though it also effectively wraps up this trio of paranoid studies of "lone wolves," men operating alone and cut down to size by circumstances beyond their control. It stands as his first unqualified failure, one in which it is all too easy to perceive the filmmaker struggling to fine-tune his aesthetic in a way that fits the specific film as a whole. Frustration then sets in. Overtly making stylistically risky pictures with established box-office stars has always been a difficult feat, and it was much more so at the time Furie was attempting it.

Although the film, as he feared, literally falls to pieces in its third act, there are effective sequences that function well individually. For instance, the scene in the Kromadeker watch and clock shop in Leipzig, in which Sinatra's character Sam Laker is reunited with an old World War II flame, builds deftly and skillfully. A "straight" shot-reverse-shot method would have rendered the scene lifeless or at least derivative, whereas Furie's decoupage magnifies the way the actors play the scene with bated breath and fragile gazes. Here, he hides the actors behind turning clock wheels and plays with planes of focus, obscuring each of them as they slowly learn each other's identity. The forest sequence in which Laker comes dangerously close to being executed frames Sinatra in extreme close-up as a fluctuating flood-light on his face fades in and out. The look of terror on Sinatra's face is real and palpable, and the transition to the next shot, a graphic match, juggles visual efficacy with emotional resonance, even if it still also strikes one as self-conscious. Dramatically, the scene in which Laker reluctantly owns up to being the sharpshooter that the blackmailing officials have reputed him to be comes off the best. Even tongue-in-cheek visual jokes, like framing Laker through the strings of a marionette, strain to alleviate the many scripting issues and succeed only in meager strides.

The film, however sleek and stylistically audacious, is a glorious mess narratively, but even without Furie's style, the movie is dense and difficult to follow. The picaresque use of camera sadly becomes the film's only anchor, although this aspect does feel affected in a way that it did not in the two previous films. In *50 ans de cinéma américain,* Bertrand Tavernier and

Jean-Pierre Coursodon observe that "these baroque artifices are not reprehensible in a film like *The Ipcress File,* in which a more traditional approach was condemned, but they do nothing for a talky, arbitrary and boring scenario like the detestable *The Naked Runner.* Furie's best film of the time seems to be *The Appaloosa.* The decorative frames harmonize well with the slow unfolding of a story reminiscent of *One-Eyed Jacks.*"[55]

The scene in the warehouse, in which Derren Nesbitt's icy character Colonel Hartmann first turns the tables on Laker, plays with screen space in intriguing ways, and the cutting between these strategically plotted counterimages is unnerving. An effective score, pulled from veteran composer Harry Sukman's "Nightfalls into Starlight" symphony piece, provides the film with an operaticism. As Robert Murphy, who had previously praised Furie's identical style in *The Ipcress File* in his book *Sixties British Cinema,* writes, "Furie's increasingly extravagant style—out-of-focus chairs block half the screen, disembodied voices intervene unexpectedly, giant close-ups of coffee cups loom threateningly—makes it a very disconcerting film and it is easy to lose patience with it. But once one ceases to worry about realism and begins to see the film as the nightmare of its central character, it begins to make satisfying sense."[56]

The finale, which blows over the story's rickety house of cards with a whimper, simply to terminate any pretense it might have had toward coherency or structure, is framed by Furie almost as a practical joke. On the ending, Murphy continues, "Laker, after shooting his victim, throws away his gun and rushes through a dark tunnel to confront the man he thought he had killed (the hated East German security officer) and the man who had sent him on the disastrous mission. This is ludicrous on a plot level but it makes a satisfying end to Laker's nightmare."[57] Furie, for his part, says of the film after seeing it forty years later, "It feels like a work-in-progress to me." In a 1970 issue of Andy Warhol's *inter/VIEW* magazine, Furie spoke quite dismissively of *The Naked Runner,* feeling that it was "really nothing."[58]

Furie received many other studio offers after *The Naked Runner* flopped, and its negative press and reviews did little to impede the director's new A-list reputation. "[Producer] Arthur Jacobs offered me to direct *Planet of the Apes* after *The Naked Runner,*" says Furie. "I turned it down because I thought the idea was stupid." Ironically, around that time, *Apes* star Charlton Heston invited Furie to lunch and tried to lure him into adapting Harry Harrison's 1966 science fiction novel *Make Room! Make*

Room!, another postapocalyptic tale of a world gone mad. In 1973, MGM released this project as *Soylent Green,* under Richard Fleischer's direction.

Meanwhile, *The Ipcress File* was landing plum jobs for other directors. To explain: When attempting to sell Lee Marvin on the merits of director John Boorman for the job of helming *Point Blank* (1967), producer Judd Bernard screened *The Ipcress File* for Marvin and fooled him into thinking Boorman had actually directed it. At that point, Boorman's only previous feature-film credit was *Having a Wild Weekend* (aka *Catch Us If You Can*) (1965), starring The Dave Clark Five. Marvin, who had director approval but was evidently not well viewed or informed in terms of new releases, would have never approved Boorman for the job on the basis of a pop musical. The ruse worked, and Bernard confessed his deception to Furie only a year later when they met on the set of Furie's longtime friend Silvio Narizzano's first Hollywood film *Blue* (1968), which Bernard produced.

With Brad Dexter, for his trouble, promptly dismissed from Sinatra Enterprises on bitter terms, the husky dynamo joined forces with Furie to create Furie Productions. Dexter himself weighed in on why he was dismissed: "I realize now that my rescue efforts probably severed the friendship then and there. Frank didn't like feeling indebted to anyone. He never thanked me for having done it, then or later."[59] He was given word of his firing while Sinatra was in Los Angeles campaigning for California governor Edmund Brown, who was running in a political race against Ronald Reagan. Robert Evans had offered Roman Polanski a chance to direct *Downhill Racer* for the financially embarrassed Paramount. The studio was looking for directors to helm a new slate of pictures. Remembers Furie, "I hired an agent in Los Angeles named Joe Schoenfeld, and he got me invited to a special meeting for directors at Paramount. There I was in a room with Roman [Polanski], Charlie Bluhdorn, Bob Evans, Peter Bart and a bunch of other guys, so I started mouthing off about the kind of movies they should make, and the ones I wanted to make, and Charlie Bluhdorn turned to Bob Evans and said 'Evans! Hire this kid! Hire this kid!'" Furie was to enjoy a fruitful eight-year tenure at Paramount Pictures. Polanski and Furie were among the first directors hired by the new Paramount regime.

Chapter 6

Professional Winners and Professional Losers

Winners make ordinary people feel . . . a little uncomfortable.
—Eric Scott (Harold Gould) in The Lawyer

Thanks in large part to the stellar performance of attorney (and press hound) F. Lee Bailey in the role of murder-trial lawyer, Cleveland osteopath Sam Sheppard, the "wife-killing doctor" who had himself become a newspaper and tabloid "star," was acquitted of the crime of second-degree murder on November 16, 1966, more than a decade after the original verdict on December 21, 1954. Sheppard relocated to Germany shortly after his acquittal.

The story of Sam Sheppard, which had been adapted for television in the series *The Fugitive,* was one of the projects Robert Evans shopped around to 20th Century Fox at the time Charles Bluhdorn hired him at Paramount, having given a $10,000 option against a final $125,000 for Sheppard's book. Prior to Evans's involvement, producers Norman Baer and Phil D'Antoni, who went on to helm *Bullitt* and *The French Connection,* optioned the material in the summer of 1966. The Baer-D'Antoni option expired. Costs finally incurred by Paramount for the full rights to the screen story totaled $175,000, with the studio purchasing the tapes onto which Sheppard dictated his book *Endure and Conquer: My 12-Year Fight for Vindication,* as well as journalist Paul Holmes's *The Sheppard Murder Case* (for the Holmes book the studio paid $40,000, with an additional $10,000 going to Holmes as script consultant) and Sheppard's brother's *My Brother's Keeper.*

At the time Bailey won Sheppard's acquittal at his appeal trial, Furie and Dexter had moved the production of *The Naked Runner* to its final leg in Copenhagen. Brad Dexter, Furie's new partner, promptly started developing *The Sheppard Murder Trial* as their follow-up, particularly when it was becoming apparent that Dexter soon would no longer be employed with Sinatra Enterprises following picture-wrap. He told the *Los Angeles Times* in an October 1966 interview that he was "tired of acting" and wanted to do more producing.[1]

On March 2, 1967, Dexter issued a press release announcing the project, stating, "I think Bailey has already proven himself as an actor. Certainly he's the right man to play himself in our picture. Mr. Bailey has my formal offer to appear in the film when it starts this summer if he isn't otherwise engaged playing himself in some courtroom."[2] The move was one made in fine Premingerian tradition. Otto Preminger, who was in a five-picture contract with Paramount when Furie and Dexter arrived for work at the financially crippled studio, had hired Judge Joseph N. Welch, the real-life hero of the McCarthy Trials, to play the judge in *Anatomy of a Murder*. Preminger had also invited Martin Luther King Jr. to play a key role in *Advise & Consent* (King wisely, but gracefully, declined). F. Lee Bailey, however, accepted the offer to play the role himself, justifying his decision by famously exclaiming, "After all, I created the role!"[3]

On March 23, 1967, Robert Evans and Bernard Donnenfeld convened a forty-five-minute Paramount press conference to announce their extravagant casting decision; Evans opened it with a showman's bravado akin to Bailey's, making a case that the Sheppard story was the type that "had never been told before on film."[4] Dexter then assured the roughly 120 reporters in attendance that the film would "certainly not be an exploitation picture" and would have neither a "Horatio Alger touch" nor a "Perry Mason ending."[5] Bailey, who was also probed about his involvement in the recent 20th Century Fox film adaptation of *The Boston Strangler*, then warned Dexter and Furie, "I'm no actor, and never will be, and if I forget my lines in the script, I'll probably start ad-libbing," additionally stating that he took the role with "some trepidation." Furie was absent for this press conference.

"It was really a publicity stunt designed and engineered by Dexter and Bob Evans," Furie claims. "Anything to get a mention in the columns and to get a buzz around the picture! But I loved Bob Evans, and Bob Evans loved talent. He had the greatest respect for directors." Barry Newman, the actor who eventually played the F. Lee Bailey–based role, had been completely unaware of this publicity stunt at the time, but he commented,

"Bailey was never going to play himself, and worked in no advisory capacity whatsoever with the film. In the end, I wasn't really so much playing Bailey at all."[6]

Furie, who had freshly joined the Director's Guild of America and signed a five-picture deal at Paramount on February 8, 1967, immediately started developing his own ideas for the story. He emigrated to the United States from England on April 30, 1967. In the search for a screenwriter with whom he could collaborate on a script, Furie initially returned to Norman Bogner, the British novelist with whom he had joined forces on *13* just two years earlier. The two soon ventured to San Quentin with Brad Dexter for discussions with Warden Laurence Wilson. When their months of work together proved unsatisfactory, Furie junked what he deemed an "uncinematic" script, Bogner left the project, and the Paramount talent pool was probed.

Harry Korshak, the youngest son of high-powered "Paramount consigliere" Sidney Korshak, had been haunting Paramount at the time while considering making his foray into movie producing, with the help of his father's influence. Sidney Korshak had famously represented Jimmy Hoffa, Al Capone, and MCA-Universal chiefs Lew Wasserman and Jules Stein, among others, and had become the major figure at the top of the Paramount food chain. Harry, who promptly befriended Furie, was married to Ginger Buchman, the daughter of screenwriter Harold Buchman, whose last completed script was for the 1961 British film *Operation Snafu*, starring a pre-Bond Sean Connery.

Buchman, who had been blacklisted in the 1950s and emigrated to England for work, was eager to break back into screenwriting after an eight-year absence. Furie appreciated that Buchman had been a fellow émigré from North America to England, and he wanted to base the film's structure on his earlier British film *The Boys* (1962), which used variable flashbacks from multiple perspectives of the events in question to frame the drama inside the courtroom. Buchman read a draft Furie had written solo after Bogner's departure and deemed it "a disaster," signing on for rewrites around the time Furie and Dexter set up their offices on the Paramount lot. There, they received a project development fund and small but functional quarters. Marlene Pivnick, an old friend of Furie's from his early Toronto days, had also recently set up house in Los Angeles and took the job of Furie and Dexter's secretary and assistant. Silvio Narizzano, Furie's Canadian filmmaker comrade from his Toronto days, had just scored an unexpected key success with *Georgy Girl* (1966); he was editing the Western film *Blue* (1968) for Paramount while the newly established Furie Productions labored to ready *The Sheppard Murder Case* for its January 1968 start date. Furie saw Narizzano intermittently during this period, after having lost touch for a number of years. Roman Polanski had, at this point, forsaken *Downhill Racer* for a special Robert Evans project, the Ira Levin property *Rosemary's Baby*.

In April 1967, Furie, Buchman, and Dexter ventured together to a Naples, Florida, courthouse to watch F. Lee Bailey "perform" at the trial of Carl Coppolino, yet another case concerning a "wife-killing doctor." Furie remembers of watching Bailey at that trial, "It was like watching an actor. He was very performative, very showy. Our version of Bailey in the final film is, believe it or not, as close as anyone would want." After watching Bailey give his tour-de-force, Furie, Buchman, and Dexter spent time with Bailey aboard the lawyer's private jet, studying him intently in an effort to fully absorb the most telling idiosyncrasies of such a character. Bailey had already been aptly nicknamed "Clarence Darrow in a Lear jet" by many of the era's leading periodicals. In these moments of observation, the screen-writing team decided to center their film around a Bailey-esque attorney, after previously intending to focus their story on the accused doctor. The title was changed from *The Sheppard Murder Case* to *The Lawyer* to suit these new ambitions. After five months, they resurfaced with a script that rectified the insoluble bits of plotting in the earlier draft. "I pretty much wrote the whole script," Furie remembers. "Buchman was really just a sce-narist and a bouncing board during my writing process. We would talk through everything."

Their lawyer hero was hence renamed Anthony Petrocelli, a brash big-city attorney living in a small "hick town" who is struggling to win a mur-der case involving a rich local doctor. When the court inquest becomes a "three-ring" spectacle held at the town's fairgrounds—to the whistles, cat-calls, hoots, and hollers of the crowd of townies that has gathered to lis-ten—he realizes that the odds are stacked against him in the defense of his client. The community at large, along with the local law enforcement, has already independently found the doctor guilty.

Because of impending legal troubles involving Bailey's taking the role himself, and with the film now restructured to suit the needs of a character piece, the celebrity attorney backed out of making his screen acting debut. Dexter's Premingerian flourish was gone with the wind. Furie, for his part, told the press, "Suppose I am making a film and in it there is the role of a butcher. I can go out and get a real butcher, but all I've got is a real butcher, and a bad actor. On the other hand, if I get a good actor, I've got a butcher."[7] In a Valentine's Day 1968 press release, Dexter stated that the film would be cast with unknown actors. "We still have all the rights. The story will be fictionalized. We're looking for a young actor to play F. Lee Bailey in real life."[8] Furie's conscious choice to cast an unknown offered him a welcome vacation from the type of temperamental box-office stars that had taxed the production teams of his two previous pictures. Even Herbert G. Luft, then president of the Hollywood Foreign Press Association, noted in an interview with Furie that he had "come to the conclusion that he just cannot work with stars, at least not with stars who remain stars on the screen."[9] Furie and Dexter also thought it would be more exciting to fish a newcomer from obscurity. "We wanted to try and match Lee Bailey," says Furie, "And no established star at the time had that swagger. We found the idea of a hunt for fresh talent exciting. We wanted someone biding their time in New York waiting to be discovered."

In the spring of 1968, while visiting New York looking at stage plays from which he could pluck the unknown New York stage actor to play Anthony Petrocelli, Furie caught an off-Broadway double-bill production of two one-act plays at the Astor Place Theatre, the second of which was Israel Horowitz's *The Indian Wants the Bronx*. The cast of that play included Al Pacino and John Cazale. "The first of the plays was so bad that I left the theater before I could see the second one," says Furie. "If I had stayed for the second, I might have cast Al Pacino in the role." Through New York casting sessions, the Furie and Dexter team first met an Actors Studio–trained stage and television supporting player named Barry Newman, an "always broke, but always working" actor who, when shows closed, worked as a waiter and as a hatcheck boy at the upscale speakeasy "21."

"I got back from riding my bike in Central Park and I got a call from my agent telling me to go to an audition at the Paramount Building at 1501 Broadway," Newman remembers. "I met Sid, who was there with Brad Dexter, and he didn't make me read anything. We just talked. I had lunch with the guy, then I had three dinners with the guy. We got to know each other." One of the dinner meetings with Newman was attended by Furie's wife, Sheila. At the time, the couple was on the verge of divorce, but it was here that Newman was given a pass-or-fail "sex appeal" test. Newman recalls, "Sid told Sheila, 'From a woman's perspective, just tell me if you think this guy has sex appeal or not. I'm thinking of casting him.'"

At the end of the week, Furie recorded Newman on tape in a television-studio session, having the actor improvise dialogue based on the character sketch Furie had only offhandedly provided over the course of the lunch and dinner meetings. At that point, Newman still had not seen a script. By the end of the improvised taping session, he was straightforward with Newman, locking eyes with him as he told him, "You are what I wrote. You are this character. The problem is that Paramount still wants me to go with a star." Shooting had already been pushed back from January 1968 to the following summer owing to the belabored casting of the lead, with Furie stating that "no star at that time could really pull off that role." He remembered in a later interview how, in actuality, he decided early on in the vetting process that Newman was the one and only, when the actor entered the audition space with pitch-perfect braggadocio and sprezzatura, sounding off, "I'm your man, so don't waste your time looking any further."[10]

With that, Newman quickly considered how his odds for landing the lead role in *The Lawyer* had, in his mind, so swiftly become nil. The actor had, at that point, appeared only in supporting roles in two low-budget films, *Pretty Boy Floyd* and *The Moving Finger*, three off-Broadway plays, including the musical version of Budd Schulberg's *What Makes Sammy Run?*, as well as occasional bit parts on the television shows *Get Smart*, *The Naked City*, and *The Edge of Night*. In 1967, he was as far from being a bankable star as could be expected, let alone the type of performer Paramount would have desired. Furie told Newman that if he could not find a star to match the character he had written on the page, he would give him, the "perfect" unknown, the role. Continues Newman, "I just remember thinking, 'Well, there that one goes!'" A week later, as Newman was painting the bathroom of his New York apartment, he received the surprising news that Furie had indeed finally cast him as Petrocelli. Newman had impressed the director with his assertiveness and his air of daredevil confidence. "I looked at a lot of actors. As far as I was concerned," says Furie, "there was just no one else for the role except for Barry. We just had to go with him." Once hired, Newman spent a month observing trials in Manhattan criminal courts.

Most of the film's other talent was likewise scored from the New York casting sessions, including veteran Harold Gould, who took the role of

Eric Scott, Petrocelli's courtroom nemesis on the side of the prosecution. Rounding out the cast were Robert Colbert, Kathleen Crowley, Warren Kemmerling, Ken Swofford, and William Sylvester. Television and stage actress Diana Muldaur was cast out of Los Angeles, after coming off a plum role in Frank Perry's *The Swimmer* and a stint on *Star Trek*; Muldaur, in the role of Petrocelli's wife, Ruth, replaced another actress who had suddenly developed a curious case of facial pimples requiring surgery. In short, not a single "bankable name actor" had been recruited to quell Paramount's quiet discomfort, which was no doubt growing as Paramount continued on a steady path toward bankruptcy. Furie and Dexter, however, received no direct flack from their risky casting decisions.

"Brad Dexter started taking me around the Hollywood scene," says Newman. "After working twenty hours a day, we'd go off to the Beverly Hills Polo Lounge. He knew everybody in town, it was that kind of thing. He'd introduce me as 'his star.'" Newman developed a close friendship with the gregarious producer, and Newman recognized him as the man who seemed to know everyone, big and small, mighty and meager. "Brad lived with his mother out in Pasadena," recalls Newman. "She was this little Serbian lady, about 4'8" and I'd go out there for dinner and she would run him down for whatever reason, and I'd see this huge, physically imposing guy all of a sudden become this little puppy when this little old Serbian lady screamed at him. It was really hilarious." When Diana Muldaur was reminded of Dexter, one of the first things she remembered about him was his mother.

Newman's stock immediately began to rise in other ways, as well. Once he had been cast as Petrocelli, he received a call from producer and future Paramount executive Stanley Jaffe, who enlisted him for two sessions to read opposite Ali MacGraw for *Goodbye, Columbus* tests. Meanwhile, Furie and Newman started sketching the Petrocelli character more intimately. "For instance," begins Newman, "we worked out that the character only owned three suits and that was it. He would keep a pattern of wearing each one. The film is very much a character piece, with a true-crime dimension." As per Furie's previous four pictures, there was no period of rehearsal prior to shooting.

Furie separated from his wife, Sheila, in February 1968 after ten and a half years of marriage, with four kids between them. By the time interior shooting on *The Lawyer* commenced on July 8, 1968, Furie had been served with the official divorce papers. Furie, meditating on that period, remembers, "During the editing of *The Appaloosa*, I met John Cassavetes and spent an evening with him, and it was so obvious how much in love he was with Gena. It was a beautiful thing to see. When you realize that you don't have that in your own marriage, in your own life, it is a wake-up call. There is no way Sheila and I were soul mates, so we parted." Furie is quick to point out that his life with Sheila Furie was "another life" from the one he lives today, and the one he started living after marrying his second wife. "I remember on *The Young Ones* how hung over I was the day I shot the concert stuff with Cliff at Finsbury Park Empire theater toward the end of the film. I had been out the whole night before, then to wake up and have the loud music and the young girls screaming at Cliff, that was one of my first wake-up calls. There is no other way to say it . . . it was another life."

Furie's "new life" arrived when he met Linda Ruskin, a recent divorcee and the daughter of a prominent Chicago doctor, through a mutual friend. Linda had grown up in Los Angeles and had spent her whole life there, graduating high school next to the children of many celebrities. Although there was instant electricity, Furie first tried to set her up with Brad Dexter, who had been divorced from singer Peggy Lee for fifteen years and treasured independence so as to be able to care for his mother. He then tried to match her up with Barry Newman. Newman recalls, "Linda was a knockout, but for one reason or another, I forget why, I declined his attempt at matchmaking. I just remember he looked at me and said, 'Maybe I'll take her out.' I had seen him through this whole process, because I had met and become familiar with his first wife, and then I was watching him falling head over heels for the woman who became his second." Before long, Furie moved in with Linda, in a house near Century City, after she had become a regular presence on the set of *The Lawyer*. The two married in October 1968, shortly after *The Lawyer* wrapped shooting. "It was a whirlwind romance because we knew we were perfect for each other," says Furie, referring to a marriage that has, to date, lasted more than forty-seven years. "It couldn't have been better. Everything that didn't work with Sheila worked with Linda, and more. We were on exactly the same page." Linda Furie concedes that "it was love at first sight. I think if you put it in a movie, no one would believe it, because it happened so fast and we just knew it. To be honest, I never thought I'd marry someone in show business."

One month after their marriage, the new Furies were expecting their first child. Around that time, Furie had purchased a home for his parents in Palm Springs, where he retired them. He put his father officially on salary at Furie Productions as a script reader. "When my company paid him to critique the scripts I was working on, his comments were always some of the best, and some of the most valuable. It was all my way to repay him after he helped me make those first two films."

In the summer of 1968, shortly before he headed off to location for *The Lawyer,* 20th Century Fox sent Furie the script for *M*A*S*H.* He was one of about fifteen directors who famously turned it down. In his words, "The *M*A*S*H* script was the biggest mess I had ever seen. I could not find the movie in it. Hell, no one could find any movie in it!" As with *A Hard Day's Night,* Furie acknowledges that, on the extremely unlikely chance he had taken that job, it would not have become, in his hands, what audiences know it to be. "Projects often choose directors, and there is a reason that certain films wind up in the hands of certain directors. I could never have done the Altman thing on that picture, and his style is what brought that shitty, disastrous first script to life. It turns out, I guess, that he didn't use it much at all, so there you go."

Relative to the tumultuous production histories of his previous three pictures, *The Lawyer* was exactly the kind of movie set Furie had craved: one unburdened by actors with heavy egos. "After Brando and Sinatra, any director would want an actor they could push around and mold a bit more," Furie says. To help dispel the rumors that had served to build his reputation as a director who went to war with his stars, Furie told *Interview Magazine,* "My humility only grows with success. It's with Brando and Sinatra that I'm impossible."[11] Furie also confided in Barry Newman early on that he was not going to lace the film with trick shots and baroque, elaborate visuals, as he had with his three previous pictures. To help ensure his vacation from heavy photographic style, Paramount mandated the use of "Academy aspect ratio," which limited Furie's usually panoramic "Cinemascope" palette. "People attacked the style of *The Naked Runner* so much that I thought maybe it was time to move on from it, at least temporarily," says Furie. "Like painters paint in periods, and artists change, and people change, I thought it was time for a different way of directing."

Although Furie had hung up his cloak of heavy style, it did not stop actress Diana Muldaur from thinking of her director as a rather particular sort. "Well, there was a special attention paid towards what I would call visual minutiae," says Muldaur. "More than any director I'd worked with up to that time, Sidney invested a special interest in the shooting of the picture."

In terms of reportable incidents, there was little on the set of *The Lawyer,* according to both Furie and Newman. "We really just worked on it, and that's all," Furie says. "It was one of the easiest shoots I can remember." For Newman's part, he says simply, "It was one of the easiest shoots of my life." Diana Muldaur corroborates her collaborators' account of the production. "Everybody got along. I attribute that to a lack of clashing egos. We were all actors, not stars."

The film's only drama concerned its delayed release. "I had heard that it was a tax write-off picture," says Newman. "I never knew such things existed, but I guess Paramount was threatening to close throughout 1969 and I heard they needed to delay the distribution of pictures scheduled for release that year." Editor Argyle Nelson Jr., the son of Desilu Television editor Argyle Nelson Sr., inaugurated his tenure with Furie that eventually spanned six films and eight years. The Furie-Dexter crew watched and waited while Paramount feared the worst. Writing about the position of the studio in August 1969, Paramount head Robert Evans remembers, "The success of *Rosemary's Baby* hadn't been enough to turn Paramount around. Charlie Bluhdorn was flying out that night for weekend meetings. This time the threats sounded real: the studio would have to be closed down."[12]

"I did a whole other movie, *Number One* with Charlton Heston as the professional football player, right after *The Lawyer,* and *Number One* was released first," Diana Muldaur recalls. "I just assumed that *The Lawyer* would come out eventually, but I think we all wondered what was going on with it."

Bearing a conspicuous 1969 copyright, *The Lawyer* premiered in Boston's Saxon Theatre with an audience of mostly Harvard law students on February 9, 1970. Amid frequent bursts of laughter, applause, and strange hisses (apparently signifying a delighted recognition of legal maneuvers and procedures) throughout the film's running time, the erudite audience then dissected the film's judicial proceedings for legal accuracy during its question-and-answer session. It was at this event that Barry Newman first met F. Lee Bailey, the man upon whom his character in the script was modeled.

When confronted about the film's occasional minor errors in legal procedure and its violence and nudity, F. Lee Bailey jumped to the film's defense on both matters, attributing the courtroom violations to human character error and stating, "In a law trial, we call a spade a spade. If there's violence, we show it. If there's nudity, we show it." Barry Newman, for his part, remarked that "a movie is essentially for entertainment, not a study in jurisprudence."[13] Furie left this session when a "black militant" in the audience challenged the film's questionable relevance within the current times, dismissing the film as bourgeois and behind-the-times, since it concentrated on a rich doctor while people were dying in Vietnam. It was at this exact moment that audience member Andrea Maletz, writing for *Boston after Dark,* noted in her review of the event, "Sidney J. Furie, a sensitive recluse of a filmmaker who dislikes both publicity and critical attack, left the stage in the early part of the discussion." Furie told his comrades simply, "I'm a very sensitive person. I've got humility. I've got to leave."[14] According to another, Furie huffed and puffed, stating that he did not have to accept such an insult and that he was "just making a movie, not trying to fix the world." According to an anonymous attendee, "It got heated. Furie said more than once that he didn't have to put up with that sort of attitude, then stormed off the stage."[15] In the *Harvard Crimson,* critic Clifford Terry panned the film, calling the cast "generally undistinguished" and observing, "Barry Newman seems a better candidate for the Borsht Belt than circuit court."

An unnamed top New York theater booker pronounced that, in his estimation, *The Lawyer* was "not an East Side picture"[16] and, as a result, would not see the expected New York opening that films with any level of prestige received. As the studio instead started favoring national multiple bookings, an appeal was presented to Stanley Jaffe, Paramount's new executive vice president in charge of liaison. Jaffe acted as a "communication bridge" between studio executives and the studio's new flock of independent producers and directors, of which Furie was one. Suited up with an ad campaign that the New York booker found appealing, *The Lawyer* did open in New York on March 10, 1970, then went into wide release on May 15.

The Lawyer met with mostly middling reviews. Vincent Canby, whose lengthy review was conspicuously lacking in words of pointed opinion, wrote in the *New York Times,* "*The Lawyer* looks bleak, but it's not especially tough," remarking that the courtroom performances were "nicely if conventionally acted." *Time* magazine noted that despite the film's limited ambition, it possessed "magnificent pretensions," ultimately branding it an overbaked exercise from which "few emerge unscathed." *Life* magazine stated that Furie made a familiar movie plot seem "fresher and more entertaining than one would have thought possible." Also jumping to the film's defense were its Los Angeles critics. In defense of the film, Charles Champlin of the *Los Angeles Times* wrote that *The Lawyer* "is the kind of picture you come out of feeling very pleased and satisfied, and you say to yourself, 'Hey, that was a damned good little picture.' And if you go to the movies a lot, you probably think to yourself how seldom it is these days that you are able to say something is a good little movie." Bridget Byrne of the *Los Angeles Herald-Examiner* labeled the film "a sharp-eyed view of a sharp young man," also opining that "it is a movie good for Newman and Furie's careers." Michael Schau of the *Motion Picture Herald* wrote that "Furie is to be commended, for he manages to get the most out of his actors by giving them the most in the way of zesty dialogue and effective, if unconventional, camerawork." The rest of the reviews were respectful if not necessarily plaudits. This particular film somehow missed Pauline Kael's cross-hairs.

Although cultivated as a "major league" studio property, *The Lawyer* never belies its true B-movie origins with its classic ripped-from-the-headlines approach. After some delay, it finally arrived in theaters complete with a lurid ad campaign: "Wilma Harrison had it all. A wealthy doctor for a husband. A big playboy for a lover. A beautiful home. And a horrible death." Barry Newman's Anthony Petrocelli appears in precious little of the film's promotional materials; instead, the film's primary poster design exploits the image of a wildly laughing socialite, based on the murdered Marilyn Sheppard, who is decked out as a "lady of scandal." This tawdry campaign recalls a 1950s Monograph Pictures true-crime noir poster. All that said, although the film succeeds on these terms, it does not especially distinguish itself among Furie's other work. Furie, early on in the writing process, wisely chose to counterbalance an overweight of substance by spotlighting story versus plot. The film's formal plot, as adapted from the real Sam Sheppard case, becomes secondary to its real intent as a study of a plucky defense attorney's travails as a "professional winner" in defending a man against evidence that paints him as indefensible. If the film had been adapted "straight from the headlines," it would have arrived to movie screens anesthetized.

The film tracks Petrocelli, one of Furie's lone male characters driven by an stubborn sense of commitment and personal duty, who must wade through a sea of moral ambiguity and make a central identity-defining choice, just as Harry Palmer, Matt Fletcher, and Sam Laker had done in the precariously composed spaces of the previous three films. Although it lacks an overt style, *The Lawyer* eventually succeeds in becoming another of the director's personal statements about the nature of such duty and personal commitment and the questioning of it. As Harry Palmer's allegiance is put to the test in the final sequence of *The Ipcress File*, Anthony Petrocelli's mettle is tested in a similar way in terms of his commitment in defending Dr. Harrison, the fictionalized Sam Sheppard figure. All this is compounded with the "subjective flashbacks" around which Furie built his earlier British New Wave courtroom drama *The Boys* (1962). In these sequences and in the one involving the rowdy, jeer-infested legal inquest held at the fairgrounds, the film becomes the most discernibly stylish. Because of the decision to render a character piece built around the Bailey-based defense lawyer, as opposed to a straight, parochial docudrama profiling the real-life court case, Furie is given more latitude to construct his character; the artistic license invigorated him and gave him a thankfully free rein as a writer and director. Barry Newman's central performance as Petrocelli, a charismatic depiction of a man at odds with standing victor without the spoils, also carries the film.

With the director feeling he had been cut down to size by the critical lambasting of *The Naked Runner,* another thing that certainly limits Furie's auteurism in *The Lawyer* is Paramount's mandate of the 1.85:1 aspect ratio. Although the film maintains a fairly brisk pace, one gets a sense that Furie, who was by now so predisposed to painting on a wide canvas, felt constricted by this mandate. While the film certainly was not an outright failure, Furie deftly observes that "it always felt more like a made-for-television film to me. I do think, though, that Barry's performance was the best thing about it. And the screenwriting in it is all me, one hundred percent. The dialogue and the observations and Petrocelli's speeches is me at my very center." He especially names a Petrocelli speech that was reused in the specially filmed trailer of the film, in which the character says the following: "I don't keep a cat or dog because they eat too much. Little kids bore the pants off me. And when I go to a ballgame, I root for the visitors. I never cried at a wedding or a funeral. I never sent a Christmas card. And I cheat on my wife, if I have the time. But I've got one soft-spot: 'A man is innocent until proven guilty.'"

In 1974, television writer E. Jack Neuman, along with Paramount television producers Edward K. Milkis and Thomas L. Miller, adapted *The Lawyer* into the television series *Petrocelli*, in which Newman reprised his role as the bellicose lawyer. Furie, who had no involvement in the series, received a "Created by" credit along with Harold Buchman. The setting and shooting location was transplanted from Colorado Springs to the blisteringly hot Tucson, Arizona, where Newman suffered the woolen agony of wearing a three-piece suit in one-hundred-degree weather. "Originally the first few scripts were like Perry Mason with these melodramatic scenes of people confessing on the stand and everything," says Newman. "I didn't want to do that kind of thing, so they changed that aspect. And Tucson with the heat, I remember that the cameraman could not hold on to the metal handle of the camera. I changed my shirt at least three times a day. It made you miss Colorado Springs on *The Lawyer*." *Petrocelli* played for forty-four episodes ranging from 1974 through 1976.

"I really owe my career to Sid Furie," Newman claims. "Because of *The Lawyer*, I was given *Vanishing Point* and starring roles in a few other studio pictures like *The Saltzberg Connection*, and then I continued the role of Petrocelli on television. I turned down a major role in *M*A*S*H* and Mike Nichols offered me *Catch-22* when I was on the set of *The Lawyer*, because he was lining that film up at Paramount. I became an actor who worked regularly, which is always a wonderful thing." On the chase picture *Vanishing Point*, a 1971 drive-in classic and one of the most successful cult movies of its day, 20th Century Fox insisted Newman be cast in the role in lieu of Gene Hackman, who was director Richard C. Sarafian's first choice. Screenwriter-turned-director Ernest Lehman also courted Newman for the title role of *Portnoy's Complaint*, but that part went instead to Richard Benjamin.

The March 1970 release of *The Lawyer* closely coincided with another famous case involving an allegedly murderous physician. Dr. Jeffrey MacDonald, a Green Beret doctor convicted of killing his wife and two young daughters in cold blood, pleaded innocent and blamed the crimes on Mansonesque hippies breaking into his house in Fort Bragg, North Carolina, on February 17, 1970. Years later, in a bit of highly ironic typecasting, Barry Newman played MacDonald's lawyer Bernie Siegel in *Fatal Vision*, the 1984 made-for-television movie version of those events, which also starred longtime Brad Dexter chum Karl Malden. "It was a real casting coup for them. You can't help but think they saw this real-life blustery defense attorney for MacDonald and thought of Petrocelli, a movie and TV character who happened to have been born within a month of the McDonald case first taking shape," Newman muses.

For Furie's next film, the director found himself in the comfortable middle ground between the bold, overt cinematics of *The Naked Runner* and the semianonymity of *The Lawyer*. He also kept Brad Dexter, cinematographer Ralph Woolsey, and, especially, editor Argyle Nelson in his arsenal of personnel. "Up till now, pictures have picked me. From now on, I'm picking my own pictures,"[17] Furie said in his 1968 interview with Herbert Luft. In another interview, he expressed interest in "a contemporary subject that could contain the philosophical, psychological and social commentary encompassed in work like Fellini's *La Dolce Vita*."[18]

In *The American Cinema: Directors and Directions, 1929–1968,* the seminal text by Andrew Sarris in which Sidney J. Furie is listed and appraised as an auteur under the "Strained Seriousness" classification, Sarris makes an unusual but intriguing claim. "From the black leather jackets of *The Leather Boys* to Marlon Brando's Indian blanket in *The Appaloosa,* Furie seems to elevate fabric fetishism into a personal style."[19] If there is any credence to this curious observation, then *Little Fauss and Big Halsy* is undoubtedly the denim crest in Furie's fabric fetishist quilt. And, in the same way that *The Leather Boys* infiltrates the motorcycle café milieu to use it as the backdrop for a character-driven study of loneliness and male bonding, *Little Fauss and Big Halsy* infiltrates the similarly contemporary motocross racing milieu of the American Southwest. There is no getting around the fact that *Little Fauss and Big Halsy* is a crossroads of Furie's career in terms of both thematic common threads and stylization. It is the knot in these threads.

While *The Lawyer* profiled a professional winner, *Little Fauss and Big Halsy* profiles two professional losers, one a handsome, self-mythologizing, skirt-chasing opportunist named Halsy Knox and the other a mumbling, unsuspecting simpleton mechanic named Little Fauss. As they romp through the motorbike racing circuit, they pick up a flighty, coquettish female drifter named Rita Nebraska after she runs completely naked into their pickup truck while escaping a band of Hell's Angels. When Fauss breaks his leg in a racing accident, Halsy hatches a plan to race under his name. Leaving his redneck parents behind, Fauss takes to the road with Halsy, only to be ensnared in a jealousy trap with Rita, who soon becomes impregnated. When Fauss and Halsy part ways out of spite, the former begins to emulate the latter in his careless approach to living.

Throughout development and preproduction, this narratively parsimonious tale seemed to fit quite snugly into the pantheon of New Hollywood films that celebrated outcasts of both the deliberate and accidental variety who fester on society's fringes and ultimately realize the tragedy of their own inconsequence. The mismatched antiheroes Little Fauss and Halsy Knox spoke with certain command to the disenfranchised 1960s American film audience's need for edgy alternatives to classical, larger-than-life Hollywood storytelling. Screenwriter Charles Eastman's original draft of *Little Fauss and Big Halsy* closes with the following dirge: "Somewhere is Halsy, somewhere is Little, but they are lost in the crowd for they are not winners but rather among those who make no significant mark and leave no permanent trace."

The iconoclastic Eastman was known throughout the film world as Hollywood's favorite script-doctor, having done uncredited writing work on *The Americanization of Emily, The Loved One, The Cincinnati Kid,* and *This Property Is Condemned,* starring Robert Redford. His sister Carole Eastman had written *Five Easy Pieces,* which director Bob Rafelson was shooting simultaneously in 1969. *Honeybear, I Think I Love You,* a spec script by Charles Eastman, gained a reputation throughout the 1960s and 1970s as being the best unproduced screenplay in Hollywood.

"Charles was sensitive and friendly, but not terribly open with many people, which is interesting considering I worked with him on a fair number of projects, none of which have so far been made,"[20] says filmmaker Monte Hellman, who early in his career had cast Eastman in small roles in the low-budget Westerns *Ride in the Whirlwind* and *The Shooting.*

Hogan's Heroes producer Albert S. Ruddy, a neophyte in feature-film production, with only one previous movie credit to his name, handed off Eastman's script to Brad Dexter, who in turn handed it off to his directing partner. Furie, Ruddy, and star Robert Redford (who plays Big Halsy) recall equally that there was a certain reverence originally paid toward Eastman's *Little Fauss and Big Halsy* script. Furie found himself in Eastman's company only once, when visiting Albert Ruddy's Paramount office; he found the screenwriter standing beside two bull mastiff dogs. "It was kind of a hello and goodbye, but those two big dogs made it most memorable," says Furie. "I never got to know him; that was because we never really asked him for any rewrites. But I never had that much reverence for a script before or since." Albert Ruddy recalls of Eastman, "He was much sought after at the time, but a very reserved kind of guy."

Of Eastman's screenplay, Redford remembers it vividly for being the best screenplay of any film he has ever done. "It was without a doubt the most interesting, the funniest, the saddest, the most real and original. It was the great writing that got me. Plus it did exactly what we tried to do with *Downhill Racer,* which was deflate false myths."[21] Eastman's colorful, folksy-deluxe dialogue in *Little Fauss and Big Halsy* provided, in equal degree, potential challenges and delights for performers. A consummate example is offered up in one of Halsy Knox's lines: "No Scott Roddy Rick Nifty Van Deusen Jim Dandy Sinclair's going to lift his leg on me and get away with it."

By 1969, Redford had developed a reputation for being a "problem child" at Paramount, and Ruddy was well aware that Redford needed a Paramount film to run out his contract with them, following a tenure that included the hit *Barefoot in the Park* (1967). When the star left the production of Silvio Narizzano's *Blue* in 1968, it resulted in a vitriolic feud with the studio's legal department over his alleged breach of contact. Terence Stamp replaced Redford in that film. He had taken a loss on his salary for *Downhill Racer* and rejected many of the other scripts Paramount offered him over the course of two years. "To my surprise," recalls Peter Bart, Paramount's vice president in charge of production, "Redford liked the lowlife role and the colorful setting [in *Little Fauss and Big Halsy*], and felt Furie had an original take on the material."[22]

Redford explains, "I had an idea of wanting to do a trilogy of low budget films around the subject of winning. I grew up in America hearing 'It's not whether you win or lose; it's how you play the game.' I gradually discovered that that was a lie. In this country, everything mattered. You got to behave however you wanted. It didn't matter your behavior, your morality . . . as long as you could win, you were okay. And people like Halsy do their thing and vanish. Their lives have no consequence."[23] Redford had not been familiar with Furie's other films at that point, and it took agent Richard Gregson, then Natalie Wood's new husband and Redford's business partner, to introduce the star to *The Ipcress File* and *The Naked Runner,* both of which Redford liked.

Furie had been unsuccessfully developing his pet project at Paramount, the ultimately unrealized *As Pretty Does,* a sensitive love story between two women. He accepted the role of director on *Little Fauss and Big Halsy* while trying to resolve the trouble on the other project. Though Eastman's script was truly more in line with Furie's own thematic fascinations, the job offered him temporary respite from directing television commercials, a task that was then highly uncommon among American motion picture directors (though British directors often did it). In a 1970 interview, Furie expressed the allure of working for advertisers: "It gives me the opportunity to experiment with new equipment and working with Madison Avenue's whiz kids."[24] Beyond this, working in advertising and commercials ensured easy paychecks when *As Pretty Does* continued to fail to come together.

Ruddy ventured to Guadalajara, Mexico, to score Redford for the role of Halsy Knox. "Redford was down there shooting *Butch Cassidy and the Sundance Kid*," says Ruddy, "and I went to the hotel where everyone on that film was staying there. I rang up and asked for Señor Redford, I gave him the script, told him that Sidney as the director was the fait accompli, and he agreed to do it within twenty-four hours." A truly effective performance in the role of Halsy Knox would involve a healthy dose of devil-may-care swagger, not dissimilar to Barry Newman's Petrocelli character in *The Lawyer* (but now overdosed to the point of apogee). Halsy Knox was a womanizing, carefree hustler and a brilliant sociopath lacking in any scruples about conning anyone targeted for his all-smiles deceptions. Little Fauss and Halsy Knox were barnstormers who made an incredibly unlikely team, so for the part of Little Fauss, Furie and Ruddy were tickled by the prospect of offsetting those qualities in Redford's Halsy with the diminutive Michael J. Pollard, whose generally offbeat mien would result in singular and exciting on-screen chemistry.

Furie and Ruddy announced their official Pollard casting decision in February 1969. Pollard had just shared his first above-title star billing with Oliver Reed the previous year in Michael Winner's *Hannibal Brooks,* after having established himself as an actor on the rise with his Oscar-nominated role as professional criminal C. W. Moss in *Bonnie and Clyde.* Pollard, a remarkably short-statured, 120-pound self-professed hippie (in a 1969 interview with Roger Ebert, he referred to the film as the story of "two guys and a chick" and professed that he and his wife had been "up until 7 this morning rapping about things")[25] who claimed he learned to drive a motorcycle on *The Wild Angels,* was not traditional movie-star material by any stretch of the imagination. The Actors Studio–trained Pollard, represented by agent Stark Hesseltine, had built a résumé partly around an inadvertent habit of playing children on television well into his adulthood, owing to his short stature and boyish affectation. In a 1967 *Star Trek* episode, the twenty-seven-year-old Pollard played a boy of fourteen, and he had done much the same thing in episodes of *Lost in Space* and *Gunsmoke.* Redford referred to his costar as "a self-absorbed Actors Studio anarchist"[26] and gradually developed a total aversion to what he perceived as a woeful unprofessional streak.

For the female lead of Rita Nebraska, the woman who tags along with the two antiheroes down their road to nowhere, Lauren Hutton, a top Revlon model who had broken into movie acting the year before in *Paper Lion,* was cast. Karen Black auditioned for this role and had an hour-long meeting with Furie. Ruddy, however, did not want to dismiss Hutton, whose similarly offbeat quality and gapped-tooth smile augmented her movie-star beauty with a vital dose of idiosyncratic character flourish. Furie acquiesced to his producer. Rounding out the cast were veteran character actors Lucille Benson and Noah Beery Jr., cast as Ma and Pa Fauss, and Ray Ballard, an actor with whom Furie attended Carnegie Tech in the early fifties.

"The first time I met Sidney, he and Brad Dexter pulled up together in a convertible for the first pre-production meeting," associate producer Gray Frederickson recalls. "In those days, you rarely got one without the other. He was Sidney's sounding board, always. On a daily basis, we would all retire to Al's office every night for a glass of scotch. There was a general spirit and a general sense among pretty much everyone that we were about to embark on a really great movie. Everyone was wild for that script."

Ruddy traveled to Paris to persuade Pierre Cardin to design the characters' motor racing leathers, because Ruddy wanted the personalities of the characters to be reflected in the uniforms they wore while in action. Meanwhile, Furie and cinematographer Ralph Woolsey oversaw the design of special camera mounts attached to the front of the practical motorcycles to capture the racing action from new vantage points. "The goal was to give the audience the firsthand sensation of the race, even more than [John] Frankenheimer's movie *Grand Prix* did," says Furie. The financially ailing Paramount set the film's budget at $2.5 million, out of which Redford was paid $90,000, a relatively scant $30,000 raise from his salary on *Downhill Racer,* which had become Redford's labor of love. Al Ruddy soon discovered, however, that business matters were far from squared away.

Ruddy, who had scheduled the film for shooting throughout the summer of 1969, remembers a run-in with Paramount's head of business affairs Bernard Donnenfeld. Recalls Ruddy, "One day, I'm sitting in my office and I get a call from Donnenfeld, 'Can I come up and see you?' I immediately knew something was going on. He comes up and says, 'You know, Al, I'm in real trouble. We're all in trouble. Everyone in New York has gone over-budget. I want Paul Monash to produce *Little Fauss and Big Halsy* in your place." Paul Monash was an experienced producer who had just completed *Butch Cassidy and the Sundance Kid* with Redford for Fox, while *Little Fauss and Big Halsy* was to be Ruddy's first studio project. Donnenfeld's concern, however, stemmed from the fact that Paramount had indeed been in increasingly dire straits following a string of box-office disasters that included *Paint Your Wagon* and *Skidoo*. Blake Edwards's *Darling Lili,* the film reported as an extravagant wedding gift from a lovesick director to his film's raison d'être Julie Andrews, was also spiraling wildly out of control in London. In between bouts of picking up the pieces on failed and failing releases, the Paramount bank was rapidly depleting, with little to bail it out. Around that time, Bob Evans even decided to move Paramount's production offices off the lot to a building he had rented in Beverly Hills. Ruddy, nonetheless offended and upset by such a proposition, protested Donnenfeld's directive. Ruddy continues, "I just told him, 'Bernie, you can't fucking do that! It was my idea, I developed the script down in Mexico. But I'll tell you what I'll do for you, Bernie. You get Paul Monash in my office. If he knows anything about my own fucking movie that I don't, I will make your job easy. Give me my money, let him produce the movie and I'll get the fuck off the lot.' He looked me, walked out, and I never heard from him again." Ruddy's and the studio's concerns were mollified by Furie's commitment to fiscal responsibility and his respect for the ticking clock throughout the thirteen-week shooting schedule.

At the first table-reading of the script, much to the puzzlement of Redford, Ruddy, and Frederickson, Furie had the actors switch characters, so that Redford read Hutton's part, Pollard read Redford's part, and Hutton read Pollard's part. Although vivid for Frederickson, Furie does not remember this incident. However, occasional eccentricities like this were treated kindly and with little or no protestation, particularly when the production team realized Furie's level of skill in making the days and getting things done. On this count, Al Ruddy speaks to his impression that, "In all my years in the business, I've never seen a director as turned-on when working. Any other director would have taken six hours on a set-up he tackled in forty-five minutes . . . and better!" His often impulsive method of shooting meshed with a brand of military precision heightened the crew's ability to meet the demands of the rigorous schedule.

For one scene involving an extended discussion at the back of a broken-down pickup truck, Gray Frederickson remembers that Furie randomly chose the location for the scene as they were driving. "We were driving through Pearblossom, California, and suddenly, he just said, 'Stop! We'll do the pickup truck breakdown scene right here.'" Ruddy, who was known for saying later in his career "Show me a relaxed producer and I'll show you a failure," corroborates Furie's startling adeptness and efficacy. "He got Redford walking through the crowd at the motorcycle races, and he was often grabbing a handheld camera to shoot some of the stuff himself, as one of the camera operators. He has what I call 'big attacks,' meaning unbounding energy at key moments, and he's very quick on the uptake. All the shots in the film had movement, they were dynamic, and he knew how to stage them to make them both artistically effective and economically effective. He was always ahead of the curve. He also always had quick answers, because he innately trusts his instincts." For the first time since his earliest independent films, Furie opted to not use the studio for photographing his interiors. "The locations, both interior and exterior, all had to be real from top to bottom," says Furie.

Supervising the action sequences was Roxy Rockwood, a retired motorcycle policeman and public-relations director for Yamaha International. Rockwood also acted as radio announcer and commentator at racing events around the country. Furie had previous experience shooting such racing material, as the motorcycle relay in *The Leather Boys* had proved logistically ambitious for such a low-budget endeavor. *Little Fauss and Big Halsy* was the director's opportunity to heighten the same type of action in a more fiscally privileged production scenario. Also, for the first time in his career, Furie resorted to using multiple cameras to shoot his dramatic sequences, at a time when this was not yet common practice. Setups that would have taken additional hours were cut literally in half, allowing for the breakneck pace the crew maintained to yield the best results. "From *Little Fauss and Big Halsy* onward, Sidney's biggest contribution to the movie industry as a whole is his use of multiple cameras," posits Gray Frederickson. "He was the first director to really pioneer that." Al Ruddy says, "When Sidney moved at such a brisk pace because of the multiple camera approach, it never threatened to short-change the actors or their scenes."

In terms of visual style, Furie nestled his aesthetics in between the bold, overt cinematics of *The Naked Runner* and the semi-anonymity of *The Lawyer*. The film's heavy reliance on cranes and fluid shot-to-shot camera movement finds him situated in a comfortable middle ground as a visual stylist. With *Little Fauss and Big Halsy,* Furie establishes a comfort zone as an artist that he hones in his successive work.

Although Furie and Redford's on-set relationship was amicable, there were evidently veiled resentments on Redford's part. Furie remembers, "I called Redford and Pollard in for a meeting together. And afterward, Redford told me, 'You should call us separately. Please don't call us together again.' I guess he thought that he was a star then and that Pollard was only a character actor." However, others have spoken of a rumor that Pollard and Harry Korshak, a production assistant on the picture, would resort to the area behind the prop truck to indulge in illicit substances. "Michael and Harry were like two peas in a pod," recalls Gray Frederickson. "They were often together, and I think Redford and Sidney, who were consummate professionals, resented that Michael might not have been taking his job all that seriously." The rumors quickly circulated around the set that Pollard and Korshak were snorting coke together behind that prop truck. No one on the set can recall Redford and Pollard coming to blows, but a cold war did develop, with the result that the two stars did not socialize in any way outside of the scenes they shared together when the cameras rolled. "A lot of people felt that Pollard was kind of a screw-up," Gray Frederickson claims, "And I don't think people were very happy with him on that set." When Pollard once missed a half a day's shooting because of such extracurricular activities, it certainly made it harder for him to relate to Redford in any way outside his character.

Furie once described Redford as being like a young executive: personable, matter-of-fact, no small talk. The star's parsimonious approach to dealing with people matched that of the story in which he was a performer, but sometimes he crossed over to more definitive displays of exasperation. Once, while lining up a long-lens shot, Furie had difficulty keeping Redford in the frame. Confronting Redford about this difficulty, the star responded with bluster: "Too bad." Furie casually pulled the star aside, telling him, "You're right, it is too bad, because if you ever do that again, I'm leaving. I don't need to stay here and hear that and be embarrassed in front of people. I'm trying to make this picture. If you don't think the shot's working, then let's talk about it. I don't treat you that way." Looking back on the incident, Furie says, "I don't think he meant it quite the way it sounded, but I know he respected that I put my feelings on the line and didn't harbor it."[27]

For his part, Redford admitted, "I was so involved with *Downhill Racer* when I made *Little Fauss and Big Halsy,* it was like doing something in your sleep almost. I didn't shortchange the performance. I mean, I gave, but I have very little memory of the experience. And I was also very detached on that picture. I didn't have any hostilities or anything so much. It's just that I was so preoccupied with these other things. And I was also beat."[28]

As the cast and crew continued migrating from raceway to raceway in 110-degree weather, showcasing tracks ranging from Manzanita Raceway in Arizona's Sonoran Desert, to Willow Springs Raceway near Los Angeles, to Lancaster Raceway in New York, Furie received word on July 21, 1969, that his new wife, Linda, had given birth to their first son, Chris, at Culver City Hospital. Ruddy was known to have quipped to his director, "You setting up another basketball franchise?" (in reference to Furie having five sons and at the time being part owner of the Phoenix pro basketball team). A new branch of the Furie family was thus spawned. Only weeks later, they moved into a house in Benedict Canyon, just off Cielo Drive, where Roman Polanski and Sharon Tate lived. The Furies became their new neighbors less than a week before the Manson Family murders. "I remember that morning very well because there was a helicopter hovering right above our house and the police cars were swarming the area," says Furie.

Picture wrapped for *Little Fauss and Big Halsy* a full eight days ahead of schedule, at Sears Point Raceway, north of San Francisco. A far-cry result from Bernard Donnenfeld's original concerns, Ruddy remembers, "I've never seen the likes of it since. On the off chance we ever fell behind, Sidney could condense many shots into a single and come up with something better than what we originally intended. The shots were incredibly dynamic. Either that, or he'd yell, 'Give me the C camera!' and shoot the shit himself. And his handheld work was great."

Paramount was both astounded and delighted at the early completion of principal photography. Redford, as a token of goodwill to his director, let Furie use his house at Sundance for rest and relaxation. "I needed to get the sound of motorbikes out of my ear," Furie said. "*Little Fauss and Big Halsy* is probably the main culprit behind the hearing loss I have today. That taught me more about Redford than I had learned during all of the filming. There was nothing pretentious or phony about the place. It was easy living—the place he escapes to."

Upon his short-lived return to Hollywood, Furie pleaded to a journalist who attempted to erroneously categorize the film: "Yes, the picture is about motorcycle racing, but please—it's not about the Hell's Angels."[29] Furie, Ruddy, and Dexter then flew to Nashville to work with Johnny Cash on an original song score. The idea of a Cash score was a Ruddy concept intended for the film from its very outset. Furie, attempting to direct Cash's performance of his songs as he would a film actor, found the country superstar entrenched, informing his director, "I can only do it this one way." Cash ultimately provided four songs, including "The Ballad of Little Fauss and Big Halsy," "Movin'," and a cover of the Bob Dylan tune "Wanted Man," as well as additional instrumentals. Just a few weeks later, Cash recorded the song score for John Frankenheimer's *I Walk the Line,* starring Gregory Peck and Tuesday Weld.

"Paramount thought *Fauss and Halsy* was going to be the biggest picture of the year," Barry Newman, star of *The Lawyer,* remembers. "The word of mouth on it was just sensational." While piecing the film together with editor Argyle Nelson, Furie marveled at Redford's commitment to the slippery aura of Halsy Knox. "The cute smiling prep boy wasn't there. He was really acting," opines Furie. According to Furie, Ruddy, and Frederickson, Redford mostly enjoyed his time shooting *Little Fauss and Big Halsy* and got on well with his director. However, in the years that followed, Redford griped and aired his grievances about the film every chance he got, later describing the end product as a "fucked movie"[30] to *Rolling Stone.* In response to the star's adverse reaction, Ruddy observes, "Actors have different yardsticks for what is a success and for what is a good director. Redford's always been slightly anti-septic, and Halsy is Bob stepping out of his comfort zone. I thought for a long time he was going to be the first actor to become president. I can assure you that the final movie measured up for me, it measured up for Sidney, and I believe it measured up for the other actors." Around the time the film was first broadcast on network television, Redford was shooting *All the President's Men* with director Alan J. Pakula. Much to Redford's surprise, when he confided in Pakula his dislike for the film, Pakula revealed his high regard for it, later citing it as "the last unself-conscious revelation of the actor's real-life edge."[31] Redford's son Jamie also considers *Little Fauss and Big Halsy* his favorite of all his father's films.

"Furie was one of the dictatorial, do-it-my-way-and-don't-ask-questions brigade," says Redford in his biography, "and that works with a lot of actors; in fact, they crave it. But it wasn't for me. The trouble was, I knew this Halsy character. He was the kind of self-serving bum I'd known in my younger days, and that was an interesting psychology in the context of where America was going in the early seventies. But Furie wasn't up for that."[32]

The film premiered on October 21, 1970, after having tested dismally in August 1970 for an unenthused Upper East Side audience. In his review, Vincent Canby became one of the first critics to cite a thread and an auteurist sense of thematics in Furie's work: "It is not so much a bike movie, or a movie about contemporary life styles, as you might believe from the ads; rather, it is another in a continuing series of betrayed male relationships that seems central to the screen career of Sidney J. Furie." Pauline Kael, ever petulant about Furie's films, writes in her catty review, "The picture is truly terrible," observing that the script had aspirations toward "trying to tell us about people's quests for something or other—it isn't clear what." Echoing Kael's enmity toward the film was Molly Haskell of the *Village Voice*, who called the film "rotten to the core." Charles Champlin, who had defended Furie's previous film in a sea of apathetic and antipathetic reviews, did not do so for *Little Fauss and Big Halsy*. He wrote, "It is a deliberate concocting of fashionable ingredients, in which the ingredients never meld to produce a viable whole. You taste the flour and the shortening, not the baked cake." Amid taking issue with most everything else, including Eastman's "mannered" script, Champlin did single out Redford's "vivid" performance for accolades. Larry Cohen of the *Hollywood Reporter* gave the film one of its few raves, calling it "an important portrayal of faces which have up to now been lost in the crowd" and opining that it was Furie's "best directed picture to date" because the drama had "an emotional logic and depth of characterization." Hollis Alpert weighed the good with the not-so-good in his judicious *Saturday Review* piece, citing a "surprising maturity for its genre" but writing, "Good as it is, it might have been better." Alpert's observation that the script had "some of the keenest, sharpest dialogue yet heard in movies" proved true for *Esquire* when the magazine awarded the film its Best Screenplay prize in its annual roundup. The *Esquire* award was shared with Bernardo Bertolucci's *The Spider's Stratagem*. The script was one of the few works published as part of Farrar, Strauss & Giroux's Noonday Original Script series, coinciding with the film's release.

When Paramount sensed that *Little Fauss and Big Halsy* was not catching on with audiences, they double-featured the film with an ill-performing Western called *The Deserter*. It then vanished from theaters.

Looking at the film in today's light, and within the context of Furie's larger output, *Little Fauss and Big Halsy* is one of the filmmaker's most fascinating pieces of work because it is his most obvious contribution to the era's New American Cinema, exploring themes both important and native to the emerging talents of this movement. The tagline on the film's promotional materials ("Little Fauss and Big Halsy are not your father's heroes") reflects this as well. It is also Furie's most plotless film, an attribute that many mistook for aimlessness. There is no central quest, no real objective, and no real driving force. These are rootless riffraff characters, losers who cling to the only arena in life where they can be winners, if only fleetingly. Furie peppers much of Eastman's snapshot of the lostness felt by an unlikely threesome of misfits with baroque crane shots and fluid camera movement in consecutive setups. However, Furie's ever-dynamic framing is decidedly more covert in *Little Fauss and Big Halsy* than it was in his "wild angles" trilogy, appearing less imposed but just as audacious. In this much, it is one of the turning points of the director's career. Gone was the overt visual style, because the time had come to meet himself in a comfortable (but no less identifiable) stylistic middle ground.

Furie uses spatial configuration motifs from film to film. In photographing the Fauss-Halsy-Rita threesome, Furie rarely allows the characters to be seen in the same shot together (it should be noted that he later favored the use of the three-shot in *Sheila Levine Is Dead and Living in New York*). Instead, he chooses to foreground one and background the two others, or vice versa.

He also favors "stacked" profile shots. Seventeenth-century Spanish baroque painter Diego Velázquez is a parallel to Furie in another medium, because Velázquez attested to composing for the spaces between the figures in his paintings, driven more by that space than the figures themselves. By doing so, Furie expresses more about the interdependent characters' internal struggles from a strictly visual, cinematic level than he would have by shooting the scenes more traditionally. When the drama boils down to just Halsy and Little, Furie stages the two men so that they often literally do not see eye to eye. A few of these instances openly reference the final tracking shot in Furie's other "male bonding" story, *The Leather Boys,* as when Halsy returns to lure back a stubborn and wounded Little as his mechanic, after having ensnared him in a jealousy trap involving the Hutton character, trailing him down a dirt road. The shot situates Halsy as the background to Little's foreground, just as Pete was the background to Reggie's foreground at the finale of *The Leather Boys*. These two shots echo each other. All of these visual citations are particularly striking when viewed properly on a wide-screen print.

Admittedly, this talk of screen-space dynamics is cerebral, particularly for what seems to be a simple quasi-buddy movie, but this needs to be considered when discussing the film explicitly as a piece of cinema. Furie also deserves commendation for having provided the best direction of the three films produced from Eastman's idiosyncratic original screenplays. Three years after *Little Fauss and Big Halsy*, Eastman himself made his directorial debut with *The All-American Boy* (1973). In 1981 Hal Ashby directed Eastman's *Second-Hand Hearts* (aka *The Hamster of Happiness*). Both films also overfocus on the actors' self-conscious fine-tuning of Eastman's dialogue to fit their own speech patterns. Whereas Eastman's direction of his own material proved muddled, humorless, and even pretentious, Ashby's proved twee and dubiously whimsical. All three pictures, including Furie's, failed critically and commercially. However, Furie succeeds where the other directors of Eastman's original scripts fail, because he gives proper space to Eastman's story construction and his homegrown, rough-hewn "poetic wisdom," to the point where *Little Fauss and Big Halsy* becomes a work that is well balanced between the extremes of Eastman's and Ashby's directorial approaches. Furie's film is also distinguished as being the most fleshed-out on a stylistic level, complete with performance-centered long takes, exemplified most in the scene in which Little and Halsy shoot the breeze at the back of a broken-down pickup truck. In filmmaker Bertrand Tavernier's and Jean-Pierre Coursodon's *50 ans de cinéma américain*, first published as *30 ans de cinéma américain* on the heels of *Little Fauss and Big Halsy*'s release, they write that the Redford-Pollard-Hutton trio is "remembered well, and fondly."[33]

Moments such as Little's emotionless announcement that he has been drafted for service in Vietnam, the revelation of Rita's pregnancy, Halsy's pathetic indifference to Rita's labor pains, with the ambulance arriving at the racetrack as he completes a lap, are endemic to the film's environment. It is a so-what world that Eastman writes and Furie realizes. The camera might be the only conscience the audience has to lock onto, yet the film paradoxically never judges. In many ways, the film could be considered a close cousin to Monte Hellman's *Two-Lane Blacktop* (released one year later) and Bob Rafelson's *Five Easy Pieces* (released later in 1970). Like Furie's film, *Two-Lane Blacktop* is an on-the-road story about two rootless, aimless race-hounds and the trampy girl who flounders between the two. Lauren Hutton's Rita Nebraska character closely parallels the Nicholson character in *Five Easy Pieces,* in that both characters shed their privileged backgrounds to "slum it" in a somewhat less than cultured and less than enlightened middle-American subculture. All three films are key existential American "journey films" of their time.

Little Fauss and Big Halsy is ripe for rediscovery. This excavation, however, might prove difficult, because the film has never been released in any home-video format, owing to copyright disputes with the Johnny Cash estate. Mostly butchered pan-and-scan copies, sourced from 1980s television, are available. "*Little Fauss and Big Halsy* was a little bit of poetry. I still love that film after all these years," says Furie. "It's one of the ones I still feel closest to."

Hit or failure mattered not to Paramount in this particular case. Whether or not the film lived up to expectation was ultimately secondary to bringing in a picture under budget and eight days under schedule, particularly in their stressful 1970 season. The Ruddy team was about to reap its reward.

Chapter 7

Idol Worship in Jazz

Lady Sings the Blues and Hit!

My first successes with *The Leather Boys* and *The Ipcress File* were instinctive, but I'd never analyzed how they worked. It took the two failures that came after to learn for myself why you need a beginning, middle and end, a central character you can root for, in a conflict you can understand and care about, and to have a sense of humor. It seems so obvious, but I know that next time, I may miss again, but now I know how to come back to it.
—*Sidney J. Furie,* Interview Magazine, *1970*

As Furie settled into a whole new life with second wife Linda and his newborn son Chris at their new Benedict Canyon home in Beverly Hills, *Variety* reported on December 30, 1969, that, while in postproduction of *Little Fauss and Big Halsy,* Furie was suing Paramount in Superior Court over *As Pretty Does,* alleging studio breach of contract over financing and distribution of the intended project. Not long after this misbegotten legal showdown, settled out of court, producer Al Ruddy brought Furie on to direct the pilot for a Paramount Television series called *Thunder Guys,* an hour-long pre-*CHiPS* action drama following the exploits of a pair of motorcycle cops. The pilot, which started shooting on November 16, 1970, brought Furie and his cast and crew to California's Redwood Forest.

This pilot definitively returned Furie to the heavy visual style of his "Wild Angles trilogy," *The Ipcress File, The Appaloosa,* and *The Naked Runner.* "He really went to town with the camerawork on *Thunder Guys,*" says Ruddy. "On that show, he put the camera in places that I never thought it was possible to put a camera." Gray Frederickson reprised his role as associate producer from *Little Fauss and Big Halsy* on the ill-fated television pilot, saying of the experience, "We went to New York to show ABC the pilot and they were absolutely wild about it at the time. We thought we were onto something, but then they never aired it and called it too avant-garde for television. Then years later, they came out with *CHiPS,* which was just a big rip-off of our show without the style to sell it." Shortly thereafter, Robert Evans and Paramount Pictures gifted Ruddy with *The Godfather* to produce. Names like Arthur Penn, Costa-Gavras, Elia Kazan, and Richard Brooks were immediately floated as possible directors.

"I got the movie because at a certain point a lot of the people at Paramount didn't even want to make it at all," claims Al Ruddy. "And the only reason they did make it was because the book never went off the best-seller list. So, when they were cornered into making it, they wanted it to be low budget, and they knew based on *Fauss and Halsy* coming in under budget and under schedule that I, more than anyone, could do it as a quality low-budget movie. In other words, they weren't going to have some crazy runaway budget on their hands with me as the producer." Ruddy recounts how "the gang was threatening to shoot Bob Evans" and how there was such an enormous effort made to stop the movie. "I was fired and then I was hired again. There was so much pressure put on New York for the Italian thing. But I told them that I really badly wanted to sign it with Sidney Furie. I told Bob Evans, 'You kidding? Sidney Furie and I would knock the shit out of this thing!' So Sidney was absolutely my first choice to direct, no question."

Following the success of *Love Story,* the Robert Evans blockbuster that put Paramount back in the black, no property was dearer to Evans's heart than *The Godfather,* which was entitled *Mafia* in its early drafts, having optioned it as a studio property for $12,500. The studio shepherded the project early on by partly subsidizing the writing of Mario Puzo's novel. Puzo later wrote that he agreed to work on the novel because "it was really time to grow up and sell out, as Lenny Bruce once advised."[1] But despite Evans's enthusiasm for the property, corporate head Charles Bluhdorn and the Gulf+Western shareholders' cold feet about the project partly stemmed from the critical and commercial failure of another Sicilian Mafia picture, *The Brotherhood* (1968), directed by Martin Ritt and starring Kirk Douglas. "They didn't want a bunch of Jews doing any more movies about the Sicilian Mafia," says Ruddy. Writes Evans in his book *The Kid Stays in the Picture,* "'Sicilian mobster films don't play' was distribution's bottom line. When you bat zero, don't make another sucker bet. *The Brotherhood,* a perfect example . . . Kirk Douglas, an all-star cast, terrific reviews, no biz, not even a good first weekend."[2]

Apprehension existed because Furie, like Martin Ritt, came from Jewish stock. Another unsettling conflict of interest explained Paramount's reticence about producing the novel as a film. Notorious Sicilian financier Michele Sindona, a known money-launderer and trusted adviser to the Gambino crime family, had purchased substantial interest in the Paramount lot in 1972 through the Vatican front corporation Immobilare, eventually claiming ownership of over half of the backlot. "Reduced to simplest terms, the Mafia bought the lot," claims Peter Bart in *Easy Riders, Raging Bulls.* Of the "unsavory" Sindona, Bart correctly notes that he ended up being murdered with cyanide in a Sicilian prison. "But at this moment in time, he was a banker, and immediately started shooting porn movies on the lot."[3] Needless to say, the last thing these new interests in Paramount Pictures wanted was a film about a Sicilian Mafia family, in whatever degree of detail and no matter how far removed from reality.

"Sindona had deplored Paramount's decision to make *The Godfather,* which he felt betrayed the inner workings of the Mafia,"[4] says author Bernard Dick in his book *Engulfed: The Death of Paramount Pictures and the Birth of Corporate Hollywood.* Sindona, who would often visit corporate head Charles Bluhdorn, had much in common with the gregarious, crusty entrepreneur who was celebrated for having built the formidable Gulf+Western from the ground up. Like Bluhdorn, Sindona's business interests were eclectic: pharmaceuticals, textiles, publishing, metals, real estate, and, latently, motion pictures. Bluhdorn's dealings with reputed Mafia lawyer Sidney Korshak, another "hot potato" relationship, also threatened *The Godfather*'s big-screen adaptation's seeing the light of day. Yet another *Godfather* detractor proved ironically to be Frank Sinatra, who is depicted as "Johnny Fontane" in Puzo's book and in the final film. Sinatra, who long harbored bitterness toward Brad Dexter for having "defected" to Furie on the set of *The Naked Runner,* angrily confronted Puzo in Elaine's Restaurant on New York's Upper East Side when the indignant star had been pressured to meet the author, who just happened to be dining there that night. Puzo later wrote, "I do remember him saying that if it wasn't that I was so much older than he, he would beat the hell out of me. What hurt was that there he was, a northern Italian, threatening me, a southern Italian, with physical violence. This was roughly equivalent to Einstein pulling a knife on Al Capone. It just wasn't done."[5]

Barry Newman, who played Anthony Petrocelli in *The Lawyer*, remembers, "When I was shooting *Vanishing Point* with Richard Zanuck and Richard Sarafian, Sid called me and told me to read Puzo's novel of *The Godfather*, and he asked me to tell him which character I wanted to play, either Sonny or Michael." With Ruddy continuing to push Furie as his director of choice for the increasingly besieged project, Francis Ford Coppola, who at that point had only directed a string of financial failures that included *You're a Big Boy Now*, *The Rain People*, and *Finian's Rainbow*, and was struggling to sustain his crippled production company American Zoetrope after the failure of George Lucas's *THX 1138* (1971), was soon recruited by Robert Evans and Peter Bart to direct *The Godfather*. It was thought that his Italian heritage would subdue the concerns and calm the increasingly virulent unrest in the Italian American community, who despaired that the film might cast its constituents in a negative light (Coppola first declined the offer for this very reason, only agreeing to do the film as "a family chronicle" and "a metaphor for capitalism in America"). Robert Evans, who was famously quoted as saying, "I want to smell the pasta in Coppola's *The Godfather*!" writes in his book, "That's what brought the magic to the novel—it was written by an Italian. The film's going to be the same."[6]

Thus, with few strokes of the pen, Sidney J. Furie was out and Francis Ford Coppola was in. "Ruddy was really disappointed when he couldn't get Sidney to direct because he wanted him badly," remembers *Godfather* associate producer Gray Frederickson. "Al lobbied for him hard, but once he got working with Francis on the picture, everything turned out for the best." Ruddy says, "The core of the movie had to be Italian, and hiring an Italian director diffused the attacks on us. And Coppola deeply understood Puzo." Incidentally, Michele Sindona's dealings with Paramount Pictures and the Vatican bank later partly formed the basis of his film *The Godfather Part III*, as Coppola regularly spied Sindona in an elevator going up to visit Bluhdorn throughout the production of the series original.

Sidney Furie's future in the movie business was destined for a completely different project, but nonetheless another prestige-type film that underwent similarly intense scrutiny.

The Billie Holiday story had been discussed as a movie property as early as August 1957, when Lester Cowan optioned William Dufty's 1956 oral history *The Lady Sings the Blues* (published three years before Holiday's passing) as a United Artists project for Dorothy Dandridge and director

Anthony Mann. This deal fizzled and, in 1960, producer Albert Zugsmith bought the option, ultimately failing to take it beyond the development stage. After Ossie Davis announced plans to produce the story in 1965, the project was mined again in 1968, this time as a prospective project for Diana Sands, at a time when the film world saw a preponderance of successful musical biopics produced by major studios in America and Great Britain. That year alone, Ray Stark produced William Wyler's Fanny Brice musical biopic *Funny Girl* for Columbia Pictures, 20th Century Fox produced Robert Wise's Gertrude Lawrence musical biopic *Star!*, and producers Robert and Raymond Hakim produced Karel Reisz's Isadora Duncan biopic *Isadora* for Universal United Kingdom. All three films, particularly the first two, heavily pulpified the movie lives of the real-life figures they depicted, suffusing the biographical elements with an assured degree of melodrama. All three films, however, earned Academy Award recognition, even when *Star!* and *Isadora* failed to prove financially advantageous. The demand for the Billie Holiday story logically increased. In November 1968, it was reported in various news outlets that producer David Susskind was engaged in a haggling match over rights to the Billie Holiday story with Joe Glaser's Associated Book Corp, which repped the Holiday estate. Still, nothing materialized.

Lady Day's biography came replete with dramatic potential, between her harrowing childhood spent in brothels, her crushing drug addiction, her often turbulent love life, her relationship to other jazz legends of the time (including Count Basie and Duke Ellington), and her own emergence as a unique vocal talent. That no party could reach a conclusive deal and produce at least a functional screenplay, especially in light of its obvious appeal and the industry trends, proved unfortunate.

Enter Jay Weston, restaurateur and publicity agent for Paul Anka, Cinerama, and the Newport Jazz Festival. Weston had ascended to become the production story executive for the newly formed Palomar Pictures International in 1967, after having produced the Broadway play *Does a Tiger Wear a Necktie?*, which ran for only thirty-nine performances but nonetheless garnered unknown future *Godfather* star Al Pacino a Tony Award for his performance. Weston was well covered in the trades in 1965 when he sold his own script *The War Horses* to Joseph E. Levine at Embassy Pictures for the sum of fifty thousand dollars. The Billie Holiday story appeared on Weston's radar as early as 1964, at which time he kept his eyes firmly on the various hands into which his brass ring had fallen and passed.

Sometime in the mid-1960s, Weston announced his intentions to produce a story covering the American Revolution.

Approximately four weeks later, a script by Terence McCloy appeared on his desk. McCloy, who up to that point had written innumerable film scripts on his own but had long remained a rookie without a single produced script to his name, made a habit of checking items in *Variety* and other periodicals, investigating material that various producers were developing. "Sometimes I'd hear a producer had bought a certain book, and then I'd write a script of that book and send it off,"[7] McCloy claimed in a 1973 *Montreal Gazette* profile piece (his only known interview; he relocated to Montreal after the successful release of *Lady Sings the Blues,* seeking privacy). "I met this young Canadian," remembers Jay Weston. "I showed him Dufty's book on Billie Holiday and he produced a draft of the screenplay. He wrote draft after draft for years until I thought he got it right, or at least close to right."[8]

"Jay was delighted with my script," McCloy said.[9] Following Weston's success with producing the Sidney Poitier vehicle *For Love of Ivy* (1968), Weston budgeted the majority of his time to developing the Billie Holiday story, setting up a deal for the picture at the newly formed Cinema Center Films in 1969 and intending the coveted lead role for Abbey Lincoln, the star of *For Love of Ivy.* Cinema Center Films turned the offer on the film down flat. When he felt McCloy's script was ready, he sent it along to Furie and Brad Dexter. Weston knew Dexter personally but had not yet met his partner. Said Weston, "Linda Furie told me that when Sidney first read the script by Terry that I had given him, he threw it across the room. She picked it up and read it and told him he was crazy and should do it."[10] Furie, for his part, doubts the particulars of this Weston story, but he corroborates that he did not think McCloy's screenplay was much good. "I think Jay might be conflating me with another director in terms of throwing the script across the room. Terry was a good writer and a gentleman, and should be respected most of all for filling the blank paper and getting the whole process started," says Furie, noting that he mandated extensive rewrites as a condition of taking the reins as director, and he worked with McCloy on the rewrites before taking the project to Paramount. Clearly another of Furie's departures, the world of this project was significantly more genteel and sophisticated than the one delivered in the rough-and-tumble realm of *Little Fauss and Big Halsy.* Furie thus continued the practice of reinventing himself from film to film through chronic genre-jumping.

Early on in preproduction, on January 27, 1971, Brad Dexter married Star-Kist Tuna heiress Mary Bogdonovich. "This tuna heiress took Brad out of show business," Furie says. "The excuse was 'Too many girls in show business' and she was definitely the jealous type." Although the henpecked Dexter was still ultimately credited as one of the producers of *Lady Sings the Blues,* his involvement took a decided backseat relative to the prominent status he enjoyed on the previous two Furie-directed pictures. Nevertheless, Furie, Dexter, and Weston soon met up for a "jam session" to discuss possibilities for the project. Weston first suggested Diahann Carol and Diana Sands for the role of Billie Holiday. Having just seen "Diana!," Diana Ross's television special broadcast on April 18, 1971, Furie had convinced himself that Ross could play the role best. "I remember saying 'You've got the wrong Dianas! We need Diana Ross.' In Diana's TV special, she improvised comedy, and it was totally ad-libbed, in the moment, and I knew that if you could do comedy well and be that loosey-goosey, you could act." Weston, at first uncertain about the idea of a nonactor like Ross, suggested both Cicely Tyson and Lola Falana before realizing that Furie was adamant. Ross had only previously appeared on-screen in television, specifically in guest roles in *Make Room for Granddaddy* and *Tarzan,* in which she played one of a trio of nuns.

In January 1970, the Motown star had just done a farewell performance at the Las Vegas Frontier Hotel, leaving the Supremes to forge ahead on a solo career inaugurated by the release of a self-titled studio album. "I was taking a big leap, a leap of faith. I was afraid, because I didn't know what was going to happen in my life," Diana Ross recalls.[11] In these uncertain times, Berry Gordy Jr., the self-made Motown mogul, had become sole guardian of Ross's future, more than ever before. Diana Ross was his most cherished property at Motown, and the last thing he wanted was for her to take part in a fiasco that would tarnish or completely ruin her career. Taking such a chance had every possibility of proving a fatal faux pas. "It was a gamble, but I really knew she could do it because she was magic," Furie said. Even with Furie's faith in her abilities, most others were concerned that the role would be much too demanding for her.

Berry Gordy recorded most of the meetings and conversations held in his office at Motown Records on Sunset Boulevard, mostly, he claimed "for posterity." The first meeting between Furie, Gordy, Weston, and Furie's agent Joe Schoenfeld, who also happened to represent Motown, was so recorded in May 1971. Furie and Weston were fairly point-blank in explaining their agenda. Over a game of billiards, Gordy opened with a glib pronouncement: "The only problem is that Diana's not an actress." Furie, startled by the quickness of Gordy's dismissal, to whatever degree coy, and immediately pressured to defend his admittedly tall proposition, countered with a rather grand and eyebrow-raising guarantee: "She'll be nominated for an Oscar." Gordy, intrigued by the audacious confidence of his guests, particularly Furie's, then explained that he had long considered facilitating Motown's breakout onto the moviemaking scene, provided the right debut project.[12] Gordy was suddenly envisioning himself in the whole new guise of both high-powered record executive and movie mogul, and he soon found himself eager to prove Ross as the movie star who had been skillfully reinvented from pop singer. As far as his interests were concerned, they had a deal. Everything now boiled down to Gordy meeting with his longtime lady-luck to approach her with their suggestion. Flustered and riddled with self-doubt about her own acting abilities, as well as her frightfully limited experience, Ross first demurred and then outright inveighed against the notion of being cast as the woman whose talent she worshipped. Indeed, the very thought was originally almost blasphemous to her. Appealing to her known admiration for Barbra Streisand, Gordy assured her that it would all come together, encouraging her that she had what it took to make it work. Diana Ross had never even laid eyes on a film script before being offered the role in *Lady Sings the Blues*.

Furie first met Ross in the company of Gordy at Le St. Germaine restaurant, close to the Paramount backlot, and fell in love with her immediately. "She had this magical presence about her from the getgo," Furie recalled. Still worried, Ross then asked Gordy and her director, "How am I supposed to remember the lines? Why can't the movie just be five scenes?" Furie and Gordy, smiling at her disarming naïveté, echoed each other's sentiments in assuring her, "You're in every scene and you're going to be spectacular in every single one of them!" Eventually, she acquiesced.

Ross was announced for the role in July 1971, to much backlash. It did not take long for Ross's insecurity to reemerge amid cruel press that heavily scrutinized the controversial casting decision. Most everyone's initial reaction to the announcement was one of doubt, if not pure trepidation. "We got a lot of 'Can she act? She's just a singer not an actress,'" Furie recalls. "I guess in retrospect it was a logical concern for a lot of people and it turned a lot of heads. All kinds of people asked me if I really thought

Diana could plumb the depths in that kind of role." In his later review of the film, critic Roger Ebert admitted his own early prejudice, writing, "My first reaction when I learned that Diana Ross had been cast to play Billie Holiday was a quick and simple one: I didn't think she could do it."[13] Other reactions were decidedly more vehement, including that of Louis McKay, one of Billie Holiday's husbands. McKay was the only husband depicted in the final movie, but in June 1971, he fired a warning shot, stating, "You guys better not make a movie about my wife using that singer girlfriend of Berry Gordy's."[14] Leonard Feather, a jazz pianist who befriended Holiday in her cabaret days, likewise blasted the news. In many ways, this casting selection seemed even more controversial than the eventually overturned "stunt casting" of F. Lee Bailey for Furie's *The Lawyer* just two and a half years before.

Ross was crushed at the public's lack of faith in her potential as a movie actress, and it was often Gordy's job to boost her morale. "Berry told her not to pay any attention to what people were saying about her," Furie recalls. "I helped as little as I could because Berry had a way with her just from having known her for so long." Ross fought back against her detractors the only way she knew how—with total immersion into the role. She delved into Holiday's memoirs, spoke in depth with drug-clinic doctors, interviewed those who knew her personally, listened to her records and performances nonstop, even falling asleep to them, almost as if she were absorbing Billie Holiday's essence through osmosis.

Furie and Weston had to occasionally hold Gordy's and Ross's hands throughout the process. Gordy's cursory concerns that the film might prove too earnest for Motown were easily overcome with Furie assuring him the film would be a smash hit. "Berry was a hit-maker, a showman, a master of presentation, which was definitely an advantage, but he didn't know the rules in the film world, which was actually a good thing," says Furie. "He didn't know the first thing about making movies. I remember him bringing in a woman and introducing her, saying 'Here's the script supervisor.' And I said, 'Berry, do you know what a script supervisor does?' and he said, 'It's the person who supervises the writing of the script.' I had to explain to him that a script supervisor keeps the notes of what we shot. It was that kind of lack of education."

Gordy launched into his role in the project by immediately bankrolling script rewrites, assigning his creative assistant, future president of Motown Productions Suzanne De Passe, and trusted confidant blues diva

Chris Clark to the task of first polishing then completely making over a script that none of the principals felt was working. "Almost the entire script was rewritten and reshaped by Suzanne and Chris," says Jay Weston. "I don't know that there were more than a couple lines left from Terry McCloy's original."[15] Furie rewrote a lot of the screenplay himself. At Gordy's request, the writers combined Billie Holiday's three great romances into one central romance, specifically her marriage with Louis McKay, and conflated other real-life figures into single characters. "But that's not the way it all happened," Ross posited, in protest over such egregious violations of biographical facts. Gordy fired back, "White people certainly don't worry about changing the facts to make better movies. Why should black people worry about it?" Vis-à-vis the dramatic license that was being taken, Furie stated to the press, "My film is as much a product of imagination as it is of the reference book."[16] Gordy likewise told the same reporters, "The picture is honest, but it's not necessarily true."

"I started going to Sidney Furie's office every day for three or four hours to work through the screenplay," says Suzanne De Passe. "We discussed how we found it very difficult with a biopic of a real human being, much less with music, to tell that life in anything that resembles totality of that life. I think there's a difference between a blatant taking of liberties and a well thought out plan to try to hit the milestones in the approximate order in which they happened."[17]

Frank Yablans received the *Lady Sings the Blues* script on the first day of his new job as president of Paramount Pictures, May 10, 1971, and he instantly made a deal for Paramount to finance $2 million, with Gordy bound to investing additional personal finances beyond the principal sum in the event there were any overages. Paramount also saddled the burden of overcoming the various hostilities generated by the so-called stunt casting of Ross as Holiday; the studio's publicity department assumed a proactive role in deflecting any such ridicule and scrutiny. Yablans brought the discontented Louis McKay into the *Lady Sings the Blues* deal, paid him off, and got him billed as the film's technical consultant. However, other powers at Paramount were concerned about what seemed like the film's limited box-office appeal, chief among these voices being Charles Bluhdorn, who, overlooking the standard set by Lena Horne many decades previously, stated categorically, "White people don't go to see movies about blacks, unless it's Sidney Poitier." The rationale for this in 1971 was cold and shortsighted but logical in historical context: films with predominantly black characters were automatically tainted with the then-dubious "black film" shibboleth (i.e., most of the "black films" of the day were "fast and cheap" exploitation and genre products with a limited audience). *Lady Sings the Blues,* a "straight" black picture that the studio executives felt would never play beyond the major cities, was an anomaly, above all else. It is fair to deduce that Bluhdorn's cold feet about *Lady Sings the Blues* might have mildly alarmed Yablans from the getgo, as will be illustrated later.

"Berry was fond of telling such detractors that the only color was green," Furie says, laughing. Furie, a Canadian by birth and by nature, who grew up under the influence of parents who found the racial tensions in the United States barbaric and backward, was confident that a mainstream Hollywood film would have a distinct black voice for the first time ever, because of the talent and personnel involved. "I'd be in meetings in which everyone in the room was black, and I was the only white person there," Furie remembers. "And you'd totally forget about it, and then a white person would walk in and you'd think, 'God, they look pale!'" Paramount, to mitigate their tremendous doubts, had Gordy pay the completion guarantee because of their uncertainty about the casting of Ross in the role.

Auditions were held for the role of Louis McKay in early June 1971. Gordy's first choice for the role, Motown star Levi Stubbs, was on tour in Europe with The Four Tops at the time, thus was ruled out early on. Because three romantic figures in the life of Billie Holiday had been effectively conflated and whittled down to a single character in the writing process, Gordy felt a need to cast an actor with a matinee idol persona, so he dedicated his search to finding an actor with this attribute above all others. "Sidney went to New York and tested a bunch of actors at the Paramount building, and we looked at all the tests and we hated all of them," remembers Shelly Berger, Diana Ross's manager. "So Berry told Sidney that we had to go and get more actors. The next day, it was a Friday, and two actors came in to read: Paul Winfield and Billy Dee Williams. Winfield's reading was magnificent. Billy Dee walked in and said that he didn't know he was supposed to read, and he was horrible. We did some screen tests with Winfield and Billy Dee on Monday, and Winfield's test was better than his reading. Billy Dee's was worse than his reading."[18]

While Furie argued that there was no question about casting Winfield, Gordy, who noticed the chemistry between Williams and Ross before and after his audition, was not the least bit convinced. "Billy and Diana were having fun, and he was flirting with her. And with the two of them, I saw magic,"[19] Gordy says. A battle of wills ensued, resulting in the first of two times that Furie quit the production in protest. Jay Weston, for his part, was confident in Williams's abilities, having seen him perform in the 1964 premiere production of William Hanley's play *Slow Dance on the Killing Ground* on Broadway. "There was a real battle among different factions to get Billy to play Louis McKay," Suzanne De Passe recalls.[20] During the time Furie was out of the project, Gordy called him on the phone and asked, "If these guys were white, who would you pick? Wouldn't you pick the handsome one? Wouldn't you pick Clark Gable?"

"I vividly remember the moment he mentioned Gable," says Furie. "He asked me why I couldn't give little black girls a sexy black guy at the movies. From when that decision was made to cast Billy in the role, I was crazy about him, but it caused the first of many heated arguments between Berry and myself."

Cast in what was originally a bit part, stand-up comic Richard Pryor was, at that point in his career, known almost exclusively among black audiences for his pioneering comedic use of the word "nigger" in his routines. "I had never ever heard of Richard before Berry played me a recording of one of his stand-up routines on tape," Furie says. Richard Pryor writes in his autobiography, "Given the word on the street, I wasn't surprised Berry Gordy and director Sidney Furie assumed a lot of shit about me when I auditioned for *Lady Sings the Blues*. From the questions they asked, I realized they thought I was a junkie. They thought I shot up heroin. I never had. But if it was going to get me the job, I didn't mind, you know." Pryor told them that he had grown up around people like Billie Holiday. "I knew that if I was her friend and caught her doing drugs, I wouldn't be surprised. I wouldn't get angry. I might not like it, but I'd understand, I'd be sympathetic to her need. So I pretended to fix up some shit as I talked to her. They gave me the role of Piano Man right there."[21]

Modeling himself after a piano player named Jimmy Brinkley he had known growing up in Peoria, Illinois, Pryor saw his role expanded from the one scene written in the script for the Piano Man character. As the shooting progressed and Furie and Gordy realized the depth of the comic's prodigious gift for dramatic improvisation, Pryor's role grew more and more prominent, until he was ultimately the third actor billed. Rounding out the predominantly African American cast were character actors Virginia Capers, Isabel Sanford, Yvonne Fair, Benjamin "Scatman" Crothers, and Harry Caesar. Desilu Television actor Sid Melton, a veteran of the *Danny Thomas Show* whom Ross had met during her guest appearance on *Make Room for Granddaddy,* was cast in the key role of a nightclub owner who first discovers Holiday.

During the casting period, Ross recorded the double-album soundtrack for the film. Gil Askey, the man who was widely considered to be the architect of the Motown sound, was summoned from Las Vegas, where he was conductor for the New Supremes, to supervise the recording of the soundtrack. Ross, who very early on rejected the idea of lip-synching to the real Holiday recordings, considering even the suggestion insulting, meditated intently as to whether she would mimic Holiday's patented vocal style, hybridize elements of her own style with the Holiday style, or branch out in a completely individual vocal direction and completely redefine the Holiday sound for the movie. "Diana could do a perfect, absolutely flawless Billie Holiday impersonation, but we all agreed that Diana doing a slightly modified version of her own voice would suit the film's vision best," Gordy says. "Who would have wanted to hear just an imitation? Most of the audience was really coming to hear Diana sing, not to listen to her do an impression."[22]

While Ross recorded seventeen Billie Holiday songs for the film's double-album soundtrack with Askey, Furie and Gordy continued to clash throughout preproduction, with the director quitting again soon after his first attempt at departure. Gordy, who was always somewhat insecure about his foray into movie producing, claimed that Furie's walking out "two and a half times" made him feel even more insecure. Furie's second resignation was a result of general frustration over Gordy's often overexerting his influence, second-guessing creative decisions Furie had made. "One day, he just walked out of a rehearsal, leaving me to run the whole show. I was lost, wracking my brain for who could take his place,"[23] Gordy says of Furie.

Standing up to Furie, Gordy exclaimed, "My people say I shouldn't submit to you." Furie recalls saying the same thing back to him, "even though 'my people' only meant Brad Dexter." Paramount had another film waiting in the wings for the stymied Furie and told him that they would find someone else to work with Gordy. This did not sit well with the director, who felt a certain degree of attachment to the project from the moment he and Weston scored the "magical" Ross for the role. So, once again, he returned with an even mix of trepidation and moxie. Furie told Gordy that he wanted his input but that the film had to have only "one boss on the set."

Says Gordy, "I agreed with that. I knew that was the right way. We made a pact. I told him that I would never interfere with anything he said or did on the floor. If I didn't like something, I would tell him personally and in private."[24] Corroborates Furie, "If we had another altercation, we'd discuss it constructively and I promised I wouldn't just walk off the picture again."

"Sidney was working with so many elements," says Suzanne De Passe, remarking on the occasional tensions between Furie and Gordy. "He had a brand new actress in her first movie, and he had Berry Gordy who thought he knew the best way that Diana should do things."

Two days after principal photography commenced on December 6, 1971, with cinematographer John A. Alonzo—an ex-actor who costarred with Brad Dexter in *The Magnificent Seven* and who shot Martin Ritt's *Sounder* later the same year—behind the camera, Ross emphatically aired her grievances against the dowdy wardrobe that had been selected for her Billie Holiday character. At that point, the painstakingly coordinated original wardrobe was one of the few things that had been meticulously based on factual life of the real Holiday, who famously wore gardenias in her hair but was never the glamorously wardrobed figure many might have been led to believe. The authentic 1940s gowns had been designed based on photos of Holiday taken in public as well as general period photographs. The tall and plump Holiday's wardrobe was often markedly more casual and "civilian-like" than the svelte Ross could have envisioned for herself in the role. The money was assembled to hire fashion icon Bob Mackey to redesign the wardrobe with his partner Ray Aghayan.

"We were often designing the clothes the day before they were to be shot," says Bob Mackey. "Diana Ross was just so far removed visually from the Billie Holiday pictures that you see. Billie Holiday was kind of a heavy-set woman who didn't look like she could move very fast. And Diana was this skinny, amazing-looking creature. We just really looked at the period and we took elements that Billie liked, like the gardenias in the hair, and matched that with certain kinds of clothes."[25]

The wardrobe setback was ultimately Ross's only tantrum throughout the production, and many of the principals could empathize, considering it her prerogative to be concerned with the particulars of her appearance in her debut movie role. "Diana Ross is an absolute dream to work with," Furie claims. "She is one of the most professional and one of the most gracious actors I've ever had the pleasure of directing in all my decades in the business." However, amid an atmosphere recalling the harried daily script rewrites of *The Ipcress File, The Appaloosa,* and *The Naked Runner,* all shooting environments in which the technical crew often awaited the arrival of new pages, Furie insisted on shooting the film in sequence so that he could work with Ross on improvising many of the scenes. "Because we shot in sequence, we were feeling the picture as we went along," Furie rationalized. The jittery Ross, ever beleaguered out of sheer insecurity, felt most comfortable ad-libbing her lines, with Furie providing the broad strokes of the scene, giving her the framework within which she could fill in the broad outline. From take to take, they would workshop the dialogue and the action, and Furie would capture each version of the scene with multiple cameras. From the project's outset, the multiple-camera method functioned as a form of insurance for getting the best out of a novice actress by whatever means possible. Following *Little Fauss and Big Halsy,* Furie had developed the use of multiple cameras almost down to an exact science. Billy Dee Williams says, "Everything was being rewritten all the time, which is par for the course, but they'd wake me up and give me new pages to memorize in the middle of the night, and then I'd get to the set and Sidney would tell me that we were going to improvise because Diana gave a much better performance that way. It took some getting used to, but it was one of the happiest sets I can recall."

Once, when Gordy offered his two cents about the improvisation in a scene, Williams told him, "I have an idea of my own I'd like to try. After all, I've had twenty years' experience and you've had none." Gordy responded in kind, "Right, but look at it this way: If I make a mistake, I pay for it. If you make a mistake, I pay for it. Get it?"

For Richard Pryor's part, he reveled in the improvisatory tone of the scenes, deftly ad-libbing his lines for both comedic effect and pathos. A scene late in the picture between Ross and Pryor, the "who's that knock-ing" scene, proved a telling example of how effective Furie's approach to directing newcomers appeared. Director Henry Jaglom, himself no stranger to heavily improvisatory filmmaking, remembers a phone call from Richard Pryor on the set of *Lady Sings the Blues.* Says Jaglom,

Richy reminded me that he first started using improvisation with me at The Improv when it first opened in New York in the sixties. On that phone call, I specifically remember Richy telling me that he never thought all that improv stuff we did back then would come in handy anywhere. That is, until making *Lady Sings the*

Blues, where it turned out to be, to use his word, a "goldmine to have the background we did," because he could dip into it for his character in the movie. He was surprised and delighted that Sidney Furie not only let him, but actually *encouraged* him to do it, whereas other directors had openly discouraged it up to that point.

Pryor once explained that the film put him "into another perspective." "I'd been working in clubs before groups of three hundred people doing my thing and was happy with it until that movie. At the end, I felt like I'd opened a new door. Suddenly, people wanted to meet me." In his autobiography, he adds, "I talked about becoming a movie star all the time, and I tried not to get high as we shot the movie. It seemed to let me hold my own."[26]

Thanks to Gordy's famously close and lengthy relationship with Ross, he provided a vital resource for Furie as a director, standing by to advise him whether she could do more in any given scene. Furie was known to bellow to Gordy after a take, "Can she get to more?" "One of the things I was allowed to do with this very first film with Sidney Furie," begins Ross, "was that he allowed me the freedom to do it over and over and over again if I felt I needed it. There was never the pressure."[27] Although Ross's comfort was of the essence, there were many moments when her discomfort over certain bits of material emerged. Ross, who was very body conscious, felt awkward and self-aware performing both the scene in which she disrobes down to her brassiere to shoot up heroin in a bathroom and the nightclub scene in which she hesitates over picking up dollar bills with her thighs. "One thing you could see was that when we got to actually shooting, it was such a high for her that she never seemed worried about all that nasty stuff people had written about her being cast in the role and all the stuff people were saying about her, at least on the surface," Furie recalls. "I was scared to yell cut. You never knew if Diana or Richard Pryor were going to pull aces out of their pockets." To reap the most rewards in the chemistry between Diana and both Williams and Pryor, Furie opted to keep the cameras rolling longer than he normally would for a given take, capturing the in-the-moment performance inventions often in long take.

Well before the cameras rolled, Furie, Gordy, and Jay Weston had visited Albuquerque, New Mexico, to investigate whether the film could be shot there, to qualify for filmmaking tax incentives that were then made available in the state. When this was ruled out, the *Lady Sings the Blues* team opted to shoot nearly all of the film's interiors on the Paramount backlot, with exteriors on the Universal backlot. The Warner Bros. backlot was used for a day, for shooting the scene involving a run-in with the Ku Klux Klan, but the company found that it looked too artificial as a substitute for a real location.

"*Lady Sings the Blues* had the longest gestation period of them all, just because there were so many moving parts, and there was so much we all wanted to do with the material," Furie says. "There were a lot of hands stirring the pot. But by the time all those big dramatic sequences were shot, we had arrived at those moments the way the characters had."

In the middle of shooting, the impetuous but enthusiastic Gordy started editing the film on his own accord, taking cassettes up to his house on a nightly basis in an effort to paste things together in test sequences. Furie allowed Gordy some leeway in directing performances firsthand on the few occasions that Gordy insisted. In these instances, Furie would tweak Gordy's direction. A specific example of Gordy's taking a more proactive creative stance during the production is found in the scene after Billie Holiday's welcome-home party, in which Billy Dee Williams had to passionately kiss Ross. There were definite reasons for his vested interest in this particular scene. "Berry would want them to rehearse, and at the end of the dialogue, they'd have to kiss, but he'd always stop them before they got to that point," Shelly Berger recalls. "This happened every time, and everyone started laughing, because he only wanted them to kiss the one time when the cameras were actually rolling."[28] While Gordy's feelings toward Ross, who was married to music executive Bob Ellis Silberstein, were transparent to most everyone working on the production team, it still raised questions as to the extent of his "hold" over his biggest star.

"Everything on the movie was crazy," Furie recalls. "It truly wasn't like anything I had been used to. I'm not used to things all over the place that I can't control. It was *zer dreyt,* as my father used to say . . . all mixed up."

Gordy often had a reckless but well-intentioned disregard for spending and would tell his director, "Forget about the money, Furie! We're making a classic!" For the first time in Furie's career, a picture of his went over budget. Halfway through the filming, they had used up 95 percent of the $2 million Paramount had given them. Gordy ventured to the office of Frank Yablans to get Paramount to invest more money in the project, believing that requesting a budget hike in Hollywood was a common thing. Yablans steadfastly refused, stating, "The most we've ever given a black film is $500,000. We're giving you $2 million, and you're over budget!" Gordy, adamant that it was not a "black film" but rather "a film with black stars," pleaded about the picture's potential and its high standard of quality to Yablans's deaf ears. When Gordy asked him what they should do to finish the film, Yablans coldly responded, "Just stop the film and put a title card that says E-N-D at the end." Gordy, insulted and bemused by Yablans's insolence, decided with all due haste to buy out Paramount's interest in the film and renegotiate with them. Gordy would then be forced to invest his own personal savings to fill in the film's widening money gap. Paramount, no longer the collaborating production company, was now reduced to distributor. Gordy would deliver the film to them upon completion. As Marvin Gaye famously exclaimed, "Berry's betting the bank on Diana!"

In January 1972, as Berry sat in his office holding the $2 million check in his hand, Shelly Berger and an anxious, scared Diana Ross were both present. Gordy was about to deliver the check to Yablans. Ross uttered nervously, "I am frightened now that I am making you put up all this money for me." Gordy responded, "If I am guessing so wrong on this film, then I deserve to lose this money."

"I have always thought that if you believed in me, I can do whatever you think I can do. Berry Gordy believed in me,"[29] Diana Ross said.

The final battle between Furie and Gordy during the shooting erupted as a result of the third act, with which Furie was disenchanted, thinking that the film had to explain why Holiday ultimately goes back on drugs. Gordy exclaimed, "You know nothing about drug addicts! You don't have to explain a goddamn thing! The real question is 'Why are they off drugs?'" Furie, who at the time failed to grasp this notion, arranged to have his name taken off the credits as one of the four script writers, with McCloy, De Passe, and Clark maintaining credit. "I of course now know after all these years that Berry was right. I was naive about that kind of thing back then."

When shooting wrapped in February 1972, both Furie's wife, Linda, and Diana Ross announced they were pregnant. Sidney and Linda Furie's son Chris was approaching two years of age at that time. The expectant father resigned himself to the daunting task of editing *Lady Sings the Blues* with Argyle Nelson. "*Lady* is the only picture where I felt that I needed an R&R during the editing process, just because I was so deep into the emotion of the thing," Furie recalls. "Argy and I worked nonstop on the film. He would take his lunches by working out at the Paramount gym. We would try to whip scenes into order, and with quite a few of the scenes, it took a lot of perseverance to get things right. It was trickier than any of the films we had cut before." Gordy organized close to a dozen test screenings in studio screening rooms. "We made so many changes as a result of those screenings that, after awhile, Argy and I kept saying, 'We hate this movie! We hate this movie! When are we ever going to be done with it?'" Furie laughs.

Gordy believed in previewing the film in various rough-cut stages. According to Furie, Gordy would recruit people he knew to be members of a test audience. Before the lights dimmed, he would tell everyone present, "Don't tell us what you like because we already know it's a classic. Tell us what you *don't* like." Furie recalls, "God, I used to cringe when he said things like that!"

During one of Furie's "editing breaks," title designer Lawrence Schiller persuaded Gordy to let him recut a version of the picture, with the help of editor Millie Moore. Schiller, the man behind the film's evocative still photo montages and a filmmaker in his own right, had designed similar such photo montages in *Butch Cassidy and the Sundance Kid*. This, however, was the only complete version ready when Frank Yablans requested that the film be brought to New York to screen for Paramount executives. When Gordy informed Yablans that the film was not ready to be shown, the Paramount president told Gordy not to worry because they were "used to seeing things that are rough." Toting Schiller's version of the film to New York to 1501 Broadway, Gordy remained confident and hopeful the studio executives would have enough of an open mind to see evidence of a great film under the morass of roughness that pervaded the Schiller edit. When the lights came up, Yablans entered grimly, intoning in the gravest of tenor, "We have real problems here. The film is a disaster and I'll have to get a film doctor."

Furie and Argyle Nelson quickly returned to work in the cutting room, when Gordy called his director imploring him to do so after the disastrous showing of the Schiller cut. The editing team promptly restored sequences Schiller had inexplicably cut from his version. Michel Legrand's score for *Brian's Song* was used as the musical temp track during the cutting stages; on that basis, Legrand himself was hired to score the picture. Gordy continued test screening the film, keeping the faith that the film was a classic and taking cues from what his selected viewers and confidants were saying. However, Furie's removing his name from the screenplay shook his confidence, just as Furie's early preproduction departures had.

Says Linda Furie, "Berry would call the house at 6 a.m. and he would ask me 'What did you think of such-and-such a scene?' because he knew I had been to the test screenings. I wasn't awake or cogent, so he would then say, 'Is Sid there?'"

When the final cut of the film was screened for Paramount in July 1972, Paramount executive Peter Bart, no doubt having absorbed the Yablans stigma, exited the screening room, telling Gordy, Furie, and Weston, "Congratulations, fellas, you just wrecked the career of Diana Ross." Shaken but still hopeful that the film could make its money back on the novelty casting of Ross alone, Paramount previewed the film in August 1971. By that point, Furie was in the thick of working with screenwriter Alan Trustman on the screenplay of his next film, *Hit!* Theater chains and studios at the time made it a practice to preview pictures as a "sneak" next to other pictures that were already officially in release. When *Lady Sings the Blues* previewed after the police drama *The New Centurions,* Peter Bart brought along his UCLA film-criticism class to demonstrate to them "how to wreck a career before it begins." Bart was met with the unexpected: not only did his class not understand what he was saying when he denigrated the film, but they loved the picture they saw. Certain he had a blockbuster on his hands, Berry Gordy ventured back to Paramount to purchase the foreign rights for the film.

Furie had his first run-in with the Coppola rendition of *The Godfather* as the sound on *Lady Sings the Blues* was being mixed. Furie remembers, "They were screening the reels completely out of order for postproduction technicians at this screening room at Paramount, so I saw reel eight, reel five, reel ten, reel one, etc. It was *famisht,* but the really amazing thing was that it still worked out of sequence. I called my wife afterwards and told her I had seen one of the greatest movies of all time. I was, at that moment, glad that I didn't do *The Godfather,* because I could have never done what Francis did. Same with *A Hard Day's Night.* I got the projects I got for a reason. I don't think Coppola or Dick Lester could have done *Lady Sings the Blues* like I did it."

During the postproduction of *Lady Sings the Blues,* Furie forged one of the lengthiest and closest friendships of his life. Paul Lynch, an aspiring filmmaker born in Liverpool but raised in Toronto, arrived in Hollywood with the intent of locating and meeting Sidney Furie, the man he referred to as his "filmmaking hero" and whose career he had been religiously following since *The Ipcress File*'s Canadian release. Lynch was about to embark on directing his debut feature, the Canadian independent film *The Hard Part Begins* (1973), and he sought the advice of Furie, a filmmaker then only vaguely known for having made two of the first dramatic feature films made in English Canada. He had written Furie a letter years prior, and Furie, who received a share of fan letters around that time, only answered Lynch's purely because of the Toronto connection.

"I was staying at this dump hotel on Sunset called the Sunset Doheny. I leave all these phone messages with Marlene, Sidney's secretary," remembers Lynch. "Marlene kept on assuring me he'd get back to me and that he was busy editing. I went to see Al Ruddy with this script I had written, because Al was also a fellow Canadian, from Montreal. He said that he wasn't interested, but thanked me for coming, 'Always nice to see a fellow Canadian.' Then, when I get down to the lobby, I see that Sidney Furie has an office in the same building, and think to myself, I'm not going to leave here without seeing Sidney." Lynch journeyed back up to Furie's office, where he met Marlene, at the front desk holding the fort. When he informed her of his identity, she exclaimed, "You're the guy who's been calling here endlessly!" She proceeded to dress him down, with Brad Dexter "magically appearing" and doing more of the same. Finally, Furie summoned the beleaguered wannabe filmmaker into his office. "After about five minutes of Sidney scolding me for harassing him or whatever, I tell him my story, tell him how much his work has meant to me, and say, 'If you don't have the time, I'll leave right now and never bother you again.' As I walk towards the door, he asks me where I'm staying and then says, 'I'll pick you up at seven for dinner,' and we've been friends ever since." Furie helped Lynch score his first Hollywood directing gig in 1976, with an episode of *Petrocelli,* the TV-series spin-off of *The Lawyer.*

Upon the release of the *Lady Sings the Blues* soundtrack, which coincided with the October 1972 movie release, the album climbed to number one on the Billboard charts, becoming the only one of Ross's solo albums to rise to that coveted top spot. It maintained its status as a best-seller throughout the following eighteen months. The NAACP sponsored the October 12, 1972, premiere, with Duke Ellington presiding as honorary chairman of the premiere committee. Paramount, and not Motown, ponied up to buy Furie and Weston's plane tickets to the premiere.

"Motown was doing its best to freeze us out so that Berry could claim the movie for his own," claims Jay Weston.[30] The pregnant Ross, stuck in Los Angeles under orders from her doctor not to attend the New York premiere, anxiously awaited the news of the film's reception, which arrived in the form of a late-night phone call from Berry Gordy. *Lady Sings the Blues* turned out to be such a critical triumph that even regular Furie opponent Pauline Kael had to admit that the film worked. Famously, she stopped taking notes midway through her screening of the film and simply exclaimed, "I love it!" In her *New Yorker* review, she writes, "Factually, it's a fraud, but emotionally it delivers," and asked, "How can you trash an artist's life and come up with a movie as effective as *Lady Sings the Blues?*" Of Diana Ross's movie-star-making performance, she continues, "Diana Ross, a tall, skinny goblin of a girl, intensely likable, always in motion, seemed an irrational choice for the sultry, still Billie Holiday, yet she's like a beautiful bonfire: there's nothing to question—you must react with everything you've got. You react in kind, because she has given herself to the role with an all-out physicality, not holding anything back."

Charles Champlin, writing for the *Los Angeles Times,* observed that the extensive use of improvisation in the scenes "explains their harrowing immediacy and the fact they play as drama rather than melodrama." Roger Ebert for the *Chicago Sun-Times* writes, "What brings the movie alive is the performance that Diana Ross and director Sidney J. Furie bring to the scenes." He continues, "This was one of the great performances of 1972. And there is no building up to it. The opening scene is one of total and unrelieved anguish. The high, lonely shriek which escapes from Ross in this scene is a call from the soul, and we know it isn't any 'screen debut' by a Top 40 star; this is acting." Dave Kehr of the *Chicago Reader* echoed his Chicago comrade Ebert's praise, saying, "The director Sidney J. Furie never seemed so adept or comfortable with genre material: this show-biz bio hits all of the high points of the formula with some measure of precision." One of the few dissenters was Vincent Canby, who wrote in his *New York Times* review, "Sidney J. Furie, the director, and the three people credited with the screenplay, cannot use the basic truth of their facts as a defense for the film, although the facts have been generalized to protect the innocent (and the people who wouldn't give releases to the producers). They've made trite and meaningless such things as the child rape, indentured servitude in a Harlem whorehouse and an addiction to drugs that eventually contributed to Lady Day's death at age 44." The rest of the reviews, however, were uniformly positive, and most all of them were raves for Ross's gripping performance.

Leonard Feather, a friend of the real Billie Holiday who had been one of the dissenters to first dismiss Ross's casting, said, "To my amazement, I confess it, this newcomer destroyed almost all of my reservations. Miss Ross brought to her portrayal a sense of total immersion in the character. Dramatically, it is a tour-de-force."[31] As far as Ross was concerned, she had been fully vindicated.

Two weeks after the New York premiere of the film, Linda Furie gave birth to Sara Elizabeth, on October 28, 1972, at Cedars Sinai Hospital. After fathering five sons, Furie finally was blessed with a daughter. Linda Furie remembers, "The doctor told me that out of all the babies he had delivered in his entire career, he had never seen anyone react the way Sid did. He was crying uncontrollably, and was so happy and thrilled because he had his first daughter." Because of a nurse's strike, the hospital consolidated by having patients normally consigned to private rooms share their rooms with each other. At one point, a nurse informed Linda that a "Mrs. Silberstein" wanted to visit her. "I told her, 'I don't know Mrs. Silberstein.' And she said, 'I think you do.' And I just said, 'No, I know I don't.'" The woman in question turned out to be Diana Ross, who had given birth to her second child, Tracee Ellis Ross Silberstein, at the same hospital less than twenty-four hours after Linda had. "We would visit each other while we were both in the maternity ward," Linda Furie continues. "For her first five years, she sent Sara a birthday card."

Lady Sings the Blues grossed nearly $20 million, staying number one at the box office for four straight weeks. The film returned to the number-one spot three weeks later, after having been temporarily dethroned by *1776*. Furie and Gordy's picture, made against great odds, had risen to become Paramount's second-biggest money-maker of 1972, behind only their all-time record-breaker *The Godfather*. Berry Gordy's having "bet the bank on Diana" had paid off handsomely, as Yablans, Bluhdorn, and Peter Bart (who later recanted his earlier statement about the filmmakers having ruined the career of Diana Ross) were forced to eat their words.

The film was nominated for five Academy Awards, including Best Actress (Diana Ross), Best Screenplay Based on Factual Material or Material Not Previously Published or Produced (Terence McCloy, Suzanne De Passe, Chris Clark), Best Music, Scoring, Original Song Score and/or Adaptation (Gil Askey, Michel Legrand), Best Art Direction (Carl

Anderson, Reg Allen) and Best Costume Design (Bob Mackey, Ray Aghayan). Everyone involved knew that Ross was a shoo-in for a nomination, and that the picture was a sure thing to score other nominations, but everyone feared that Ross's performance and Cicely Tyson's performance in *Sounder* would "cancel each other out," a sign of the times in a less-enlightened era when voters were keener to pigeonhole the rare black nominees.

Missing were nominations for Pryor as Best Supporting Actor, Furie as Director, and the film for Best Picture. "It was reward enough for me to see Diana be a frontrunner as Best Actress," says Furie. "I didn't need it, because knowing that I was the one who first suggested Diana for the role against all the nay-sayers and can'ts, it was enough just knowing that I directed her in that performance." Despite high hopes, no one on the team was rewarded on Oscar night, March 27, 1973. Furie, on location for his next picture, did not attend the ceremony and claims he would not have been present in any event, even if he had personally been nominated and was not working.

Liza Minnelli took home the Best Actress award for her work in *Cabaret.* Says Berry Gordy, "When Gene Hackman announced the Oscar for Best Actress and said Li- and not Di-, I wanted to die."[32] The confident Gordy had pumped hundreds of thousands of dollars into a controversially aggressive Oscar ad campaign for the film and faced severe criticism for what many considered an attempt to purchase the award for Ross.

"After all these years, I'm still convinced it was highway robbery, even though I know Liza Minnelli did a fine job in *Cabaret,*" says Furie. Ross won the Golden Globe for Most Promising Newcomer-Female. Even though the film won none of its five nominations, Furie was firmly back in the studios' winners circle again, for the first time since *The Ipcress File* seven years before. Paramount feted Coppola and Furie as the film ended its run at the closing-night screening at the 1973 Cannes Film Festival. Gordy was present, but neither Furie nor Weston attended the screening. Jay Weston says indignantly, "It was outrageous that Gordy forbade Sidney and myself from attending that showing of the film. But once he bought the co-executive producer title from me, he wanted to assume credit for the movie himself. In my opinion, it's typical of him."[33] Furie says on this matter, "Without Berry, there'd be no movie. He gambled everything he had to gamble on it. I know that it's also my film and that I was its director. That's all I need."

"Only in retrospect have I come to fully appreciate what a hero Sidney Furie was," claims Berry Gordy. "I learned so much from him. We had vowed early on not to let our egos get in the way of making a great film. We didn't."[34]

Lady Sings the Blues, like *The Ipcress File*, has lived a rich legacy, having been inducted into the Black Movie Awards Classic Cinema Hall of Fame in 2006. At the event, Furie chanced to meet filmmaker Spike Lee, who gratefully expressed to him how much *Lady Sings the Blues* had inspired him as "a black kid growing up in Brooklyn in the early 70s" and "how rarely if ever Hollywood got it that right." In 2008 *Time* magazine critic Richard Corliss named the film one of the "Top 25 Important Films about Race."

One of the significant achievements of *Lady Sings the Blues* proved to be its remarkable crossover success. Gary Storhoff writes in his 2002 piece in the *Journal of Popular Film and Television*, the first academic piece written about the film,

> Long neglected by film scholars because of its fundamental dishonesty, *Lady Sings the Blues* deserves close analysis for what it sets out to accomplish. The film has far more significance to the history of popular culture than it does as Diana Ross's career move after her departure from The Supremes or as Gordy's strategy to gain Motown's foothold in the movie business. *Lady* is a historical marker for African-Americans in Hollywood, for it ushers in the "crossover" film and defines the demise of the blaxploitation era of filmmaking. The film is the *locus classicus* of the crossover text, created to win the sympathies of both a white and an African-American audience. Supposedly based on Holiday's autobiography, *Lady* is representative of Hollywood's attempt to create America's mythic melting pot, supposedly eluding boundaries of race, gender, age, and class in favor of a "universal" romantic plot.[35]

As to the dishonesty and faux history that Storhoff broaches in his essay, Bertrand Tavernier and Jean-Pierre Coursodon censured Furie and his work in their *50 ans de cinéma américain*. Tavernier, who later proved his jazz-education mettle in earning plaudits for directing *'Round Midnight* (1986), echoed the voices that were offended by the liberties taken. "The music we hear in *Lady Sings the Blues* is so anachronistic, so foreign to the jazz of the period, that it serves to completely unravel the film. [Diana Ross's] singing style could not be more different from that of Billie Holiday. Even the strongest elements of the film, especially Diana Ross's superb performance (which sometimes borders on histrionics), are corrupted by ambient dishonesty."[36]

In response to Tavernier and Coursodon's critique, Furie says, "It just sounds to me like they missed the point. I'll leave it to them to make the historically accurate version of the Billie Holiday story, but that's certainly not the film I was making." Surely, when Tavernier calls the film "a wicked melodrama in the worst tradition of Hollywood biopics" and writes that the film "could have been the opportunity to pay tribute to one of the most important jazz singers and the prominent musicians that surrounded her, because no film at that time had been devoted to a major figure in black jazz,"[37] it does sound like another filmmaker projecting his own vision onto the work. In the final analysis, its central "dishonesty" had no effect on either its critical acceptance in the United States or its box-office returns.

Beyond the various social and racial lines that Furie and Gordy's film crossed, the film also succeeds in purely cinematic terms. There are really three films in *Lady Sings the Blues*. On the most basic level, there is the musical, the biography, and the classic Hollywood melodrama. But on a much deeper level, there is the film about the life of Billie Holiday, the film about the development of Holiday's art, and the film that Furie is ultimately making. The directorial strategy involves something like wrapping the film's subject in its obvious biopic cocoon, then watching it act outside the confines of that cocoon.

Lady Sings the Blues is a rare film: a Hollywood biopic about a jazz icon featuring dramatic stretches written in the metaphoric language of jazz. The film stretches the limited elasticity of the biopic genre to prodigious lengths, because the direction is most attuned to evocation and less concerned with mimicry and wholesale historical representation. This works on many levels. On the first, the filmmakers never permitted Diana Ross at any point to parrot the inimitable style of the iconic jazz chanteuse she portrays, although both Furie and Berry Gordy had noted Ross's uncanny ability to impersonate the trembling, dulcetly quivering voice of the real-life Holiday. That Ross's voice is her own means that her Billie functions more as interpretation and evocation of the real-life figure, wisely avoiding claims toward "gospelship" on Holiday's life and career. Therefore, accusations made against the film because of its blatant, unapologetic fictionalization are both knee-jerk and near-sighted. The release of *Lady Sings the Blues* did not mark the first time that historical purists and biographical scholars had bones to pick with Hollywood, and it was not the last. But this admittedly ultraliberal reading of recorded fact is part and parcel of the film's objective, and as a result, the film feels less constricted and more alive than most biopics, which are more often than not rigidly sober when claiming a gospelship—a gospelship that is still doubtful despite all efforts.

Diana Ross's characterization and Furie's direction of it strive for an impressionistic outline of Billie Holiday and of a life itself, as it is defined and then redefined by the era in which the film is made. It never seeks to encapsulate. What would have been a paint-by-the-numbers portrait of the subject becomes a deconstruction of the genre and a creation built from the ground up. To this end, and regarding this question of evocation versus wholesale representation when looking at the work on a more over-arching level, the injections of classical Hollywood melodrama can breathe and exist within a carefully constructed framework that revolves around an original kind of friction—a friction of classical form and something close to anarchy. In the "who's that knocking" scene late in the film, Diana Ross and Richard Pryor improvise a relatively lengthy and off-the-cuff dialogue as the harbingers of the more formally written scene knock impatiently at the door, ready to faithfully play something more inclined toward the dictates of the written page. Furie chooses to open with a pan and dolly from a candle just used to bake the contents within a fresh syringe, one that has just been injected into the characters' arms. After this setup, the film continues as a single take. A director less inspired would have started with the master shot and cut to close-up coverage. The film is formal in its way, but in scenes such as this, it is in no hurry to answer the door to its own formalism. Eventually, when our improvising actors do answer the door and the structured story, such as it may be, continues, the scene plays out with both components of the friction in a strange harmony.

In Scott Saul's biography of Richard Pryor, the author singles out the "who's that knocking" scene as an example of Furie's directorial signature:

Here and in other scenes, Richard's improvisations played into the hidden strengths of director Sidney Furie, who, before impressing Hollywood with his spy thriller *The Ipcress File,* helmed *The*

Leather Boys, a gritty treatment of England's gay biker subculture. Piano Man's last three scenes with Billie Holiday felt almost as if they belonged to a different film, something closer to *The Leather Boys* than a mainstream musical biopic like *Funny Girl:* the scenes were open to emotional confusions and seemed as if they might go in any number of directions as they played themselves out. They were intriguingly off-balance, like the character Richard improvised into existence.[38]

Furie's direction gives the work a certain dramatic latitude, dynamic range, and versatility. His sensitive, elegant camera placement also sets him apart from other directors working the same biopic material in more conventional ways. The stylistic choices and, by extension, the technical choices made for Hollywood biopics usually proved deadeningly objective in terms of staging and composition, even throughout the sixties and seventies. Directors like Otto Preminger would take this objective camera approach to artful levels so as to transcend it, but a directorial approach such as his was certainly the exception. Furie actively rethinks traditional camera voice in the biopic with *Lady Sings the Blues,* particularly in one scene featuring Billie Holiday confined in a padded cell during a period of drug detox, during which Louis McKay, accompanied by a doctor, tends to her restlessly gyrating body. When one considers that the audience's first entrance into this same space is at the very beginning of the film, with an obstructed aerial view of the cell that serves to objectify the action to the point where the camera effectively becomes an outsider's vantage point, the later scene in the same space assumes new possibilities and levels of meaning. The opening minutes serve simply to create the snapshot into which Furie will be taking the audience for closer examination. The opening aerial shots vaguely recall Furie's own obstructed frames in *The Ipcress File.* The first scene ends with a twisting zoom revealing Billie caught up in the memories that will result in the story's first act; it also is an overture to the scene much later in the picture. Only when the audience has fully entered the narrative does Furie finally return to the padded cell space, approximately 100 minutes into the film. He opens this second scene with a close eye-level view of Billie's tortured face strung out from narcotics withdrawal, from which the camera pulls out to reveal more of the surrounding space. When Louis McKay and the doctor enter, Furie's camera starts to return to its earlier closer position. The scene is played out in a single three-minute master. However, what would normally be an objective fourth-wall view of the scene's events becomes a much more proactive view as the perspective moves from subjective to objective and then returns to a subjective view that has been altered by time and change in perspective, all with the efficient use of blocking in conjunction with two camera moves.

Again, as in *The Leather Boys,* Furie conveys emotion almost on the merits of the camera orchestration alone. The final delicate movement back in toward the faces has a certain whisperedness. The camera is a proactive observer, and we become aware of it without a feeling that the proceedings are abrupt or self-conscious. Furie also allows space and respect to the performers in this single shot.

The picture ends with Billie Holiday at the height of her success, as superimposed newspaper clippings intimate her looming future troubles involving her failed attempts at obtaining a cabaret license, her addiction, and ultimately her death. The individual is placed in proportion to the popular illusion of the individual. The real-life headlines offset the fabricated drama that Furie uses to depict Holiday's life in the film.

Ross's movie-acting career never again reached the heights of *Lady Sings the Blues,* which turned out to be the professional turning point for which she and Gordy had been hoping. Berry Gordy himself directed her follow-up performance in the soapy *Mahogany* (1975) after firing director Tony Richardson, with whom he had irreconcilable creative differences. "I thankfully was never asked to do *Mahogany,* even though it would have been great to have worked with Diana again," says Furie. "Even if I had been interested, I think I was much too strong of a force at that time to be brought back in by Berry, because by then he got more of the creative bug and wanted to direct things himself, without anyone else putting their stamp on things. That's really why he drove away Tony Richardson. The whole time he had wanted to direct it himself." *Mahogany* tanked with critics and most audiences. The Motown production of *The Wiz* (1978), blandly helmed by "miscast director" Sidney Lumet, proved to be Ross's final movie role.

Lady Sings the Blues is also a key early success for Richard Pryor, as the film realized his potential as a dramatic actor years before his outstanding dramatic work in Paul Schrader's *Blue Collar* (1978). Furie's use of Pryor in *Lady Sings the Blues* and in the following year's *Hit!* showcases his multifarious performing talents, demonstrating a talent beyond that of just a stand-up comic who crossed over into movies. The aforementioned "moments of performance jazz" are strewn throughout both of Pryor's performances in Furie films. His success in *Lady Sings the Blues* brought *Blazing Saddles* his way; originally slated to star in that film next to Gene Wilder, he was signed on only as coscripter, with Cleavon Little instead assuming the role.

"Between Sara being born and the movie being a big success, it was probably the best time for us, in a marriage filled with best times," says Linda Furie. "There was definitely the feeling that Sid's career was taking off with *Lady Sings the Blues.*" Quite so. Furie now had earned the personal artistic freedom to branch out as an established and now highly successful Hollywood studio filmmaker. What he had exclaimed to the Hollywood Foreign Press Association four years before never seemed more within his reach—pictures no longer had to pick him; he could now pick his own pictures. For this, he harked back to something from his past, from his days as a movie-mad Canadian teenager.

In 1970, Furie professed in an interview that he was steadfastly "not part of the Hollywood scene" and was "not one of those guys who checks with New York" in fear of whether or not a given picture "works."[39] However, as the legions feted *Lady Sings the Blues,* the instinctively private director was advised to take action in the press. The message was repeated ad nauseam: "Get yourself a publicist." Having systemically ignored this counsel each time it was offered, Furie now reflects,

> I never cared about my public image. I wanted the privacy to make my movies and do it without the hassle of worrying what people thought of me as a personality or a public entity. I never wanted to face surrendering to the cult of the individual. In many ways, I always sort of wished I could direct movies by secret account. Directed by Person B-107 or whatever. I'd rather assume the name of one of the forms in *The Ipcress File* if it meant not worrying about having a publicist insure that I come off like a good boy or a great director or whatever.

An immediate follow-up movie allowed him to deflect further such propositions.

Hit! started as something like a whisper, officially having gone into preproduction during the postproduction of *Lady Sings the Blues.* The film, entitled *The Rogue's Team* and *The Hit* in early treatment drafts, marks the first original story property Furie spearheaded since *During One Night* in 1961. It likewise premiered with a whisper and then quietly disappeared from theaters. However, *Hit!* is one of Furie's richest films and certainly one of his best, particularly for this period in his career, perhaps because it is one of the most personal. It is also one of the least seen and most rarely discussed today.

After switching agents from Joe Schoenfeld to Creative Artists Agency's Jeff Berg in mid-1972, Furie became acquainted with Alan Trustman, a "name" screenwriter whom Berg likewise represented. Furie proposed the principal story idea to Trustman, who had previously received accolades for penning *Bullitt* and *The Thomas Crown Affair.* The disheartened Trustman had temporarily quit the business after fighting with Steve McQueen over the racing picture *Le Mans* when Columbia Pictures head David Begelman solicited Trustman to compose a series of original scripts. Furie, who extolled the domestic scenes Trustman had written for *They Call Me MISTER Tibbs!* (1970), involving the Poitier character with his wife and two children, went to work on a treatment with the disillusioned scribe. Based on this treatment, Trustman forged ahead solo on an original script, the first of Furie's films not to have been adapted from a novel or literary source since *Wonderful Life* in 1964. The director, fresh off a glossy, high-profile Hollywood biopic that had become a recent Oscar contender, wanted to tell a deceptively simple story, an action caper that was narratively a close cousin to Robert Aldrich's *The Dirty Dozen* and Howard Hawks's *Rio Bravo* in its portrayal of the growing camaraderie among an unlikely gang of misfits on a perilous mission.

The film is particularly Hawksian in its themes of order outside of law and group responsibility. The idea at its core originated mostly from the heroic fantasy that the proudly Jewish Furie harbored in his youth—a Walter Mitty–esque dream of joining the Royal Canadian Air Force and getting stationed in Europe so he could personally spirit away an aircraft to the newly established Israel, to protect the Jewish settlers in their struggle for survival. This narrative concept reached its apotheosis more than a decade later in Furie's considerably more commercial *Iron Eagle* (1986), which incidentally was filmed in Israel. *Hit!,* by far the more "arty" picture using this sensational setup as its foundation, tells the story of a G-man so adrift in mourning his teenage daughter's death by heroin overdose that he goes rogue and recruits an ad hoc motley crew of civilian avengers with the intent of executing a fat-cat group of Marseilles drug smugglers, with a "get 'em where they live" battle plan. The story featured the characters in the process of recruitment, training, and execution and then developed them collectively as something vaguely (and quite ironically) familial.

Furie's focus, however, was not on stringing together a series of action set pieces, as would normally be expected. Rather, the ingredients of *Hit!*'s "secret sauce" can be broken down as the film's deliberate, offbeat pacing (anomalous in an action genre picture), its emphasis on quirky character development, and Furie's continued extensive—but articulated—use of improvisation in the tried-and-true *Lady Sings the Blues* style. "The idea was 'Why don't they just take matters into their own hands, go over there and kill the bastards?' It was easy and even exhilarating to take it from there with the actors in the situations, using Alan Trustman's script as a base," says Furie. "I acted out the entire story for Alan and he took notes. He then put it together brilliantly. It was a first draft and I remember no rewrites." While Trustman, for his part, claims the original story concept as his own, remembering having written it as just one of a group of original spec scripts commissioned by David Begelman at Columbia Pictures, Furie's own adamant claim of originality would seem to make better sense; one must consider how this customized, high-concept vigilante-thriller formula reappears in a number of later Furie pictures, starting with *Iron Eagle* (1986) and culminating with *A Pride of Lions* (2012).

Says Alan Trustman, "I had my years of fame and glory, but was kind of on the outs with Hollywood at that point because the line producer Walter Mirisch hired for *They Call Me MISTER Tibbs!* butchered my script. I wrote *Hit!* very fast, probably in two weeks, and I was excited about it because I was in love with Sidney's work on *The Ipcress File* and *Lady Sings the Blues*. I told him that I thought *Hit!* would be a great picture for Charles Bronson. I'm still convinced to this day that *Death Wish* stole the concept from us, because both stories were fairly similar and both were Paramount pictures." Trustman received joint credit on the script with David M. Wolf, the unemployed husband of one of his wife's friends. "I was living in Boston by that time, and I had no one to talk to about the project while living there. David wanted to be in the movie business, so I brought him in and gave him a percentage."

The filmmakers quickly ruled Charles Bronson out when Billy Dee Williams, Richard Pryor, Paul Hampton, and Sid Melton were renewed as cast members after *Lady Sings the Blues*. "All of a sudden, with the casting of Billy Dee and Richard Pryor in *Hit!,* everyone at the studio started calling it a 'black action movie' or a 'blaxploitation' movie," remembers executive producer Gray Frederickson, a veteran of *Little Fauss and Big Halsy,* who had just served as associate producer on *The Godfather* with Al Ruddy. "And when we were putting *Hit!* together, we kept on being asked, 'How in the world do you think you guys can compete with *Shaft?*' They didn't want to think there was possibly more to it." This particular kind of scrutiny stemmed from the fact that the "blaxploitation" directors of the time, like Gordon Parks and Ossie Davis, had a special foothold as black directors in that recently inaugurated subgenre. Although Furie secretly resented the pigeonholing of his newest project as a blaxploitation enterprise, he used the boom of the "black action" film to his advantage, successfully eliciting other interest that proved useful.

Billy Dee Williams, the new anointed "Black Gable" who had been put under contract at Motown during the production of *Lady Sings the Blues,* had to request Berry Gordy's approval to star in Furie's film; this was easily granted. "It was all still very familial at that time between Sidney and Berry," Williams remembers. "I was having a lot of success at the time, and thought it was a departure for both me and for Sidney. It was an incredibly different kind of film from the types of things we'd been doing before. As an actor, it was a great part, particularly for a little brown-skin boy like me." Indeed, the Nick Allen character that Williams plays did provide a serious departure from the actor's previous roles, noble and sympathetic figures like Louis McKay and like Gayle Sayers in *Brian's Song.* The strangely likable antihero Nick Allen, a refined master of toothy brinksmanship and dogged resolve, proved an exciting challenge to a performer vying to break out of the type of painstakingly moral, empathetic character roles with which Williams had become synonymous. As an often stone-cold figure with Machiavellian morals, the Nick Allen character assumes the headship of his curiously idiosyncratic death squad with take-no-prisoners brio.

Of Richard Pryor's casting, Williams recalls his puzzlement at the outset.

> I expressed my reservations to Sidney and Harry Korshak. I knew Richard very well and thought it was the wrong kind of humor for that character. I first met him on a TV movie we did together in 1969 called *Carter's Army,* which later resurfaced on video as *Black Brigade.* I was surprised when I heard he was cast because

his humor was not what I had envisioned for *Hit!* when I read it. Sidney is this iconoclast, a wonderfully crazy director in the most creative of ways, so I knew I'd love working with him again. Alan Trustman's script was really in line with what I was always trying to do as a performer, and Richard's kind of so-called "ghetto humor" was never really something I had much interest in. I wanted the movie to be a totally brand new experience, devoid of stereotypes. There was never any tension between Pryor and myself, though.

Pryor, in his autobiography, writes, "Billy Dee's self-assurance in front of the camera made me jealous, though I thought he took himself way too seriously." Furie justifies Pryor's casting as not capricious but well thought out and necessary. "Richard wowed everybody with Piano Man in *Lady Sings the Blues.* I needed and wanted more of that for *Hit!,* simple as that."

The rest of the supporting actors were cast throughout November and December of 1972. John Alonzo extended his tenure as Furie's cinematographer, and a budget of $1.6 million was ensured by Paramount once they received and speedily approved Trustman's script. Basking in the long-withheld Paramount approbation, Furie reassembled his *Lady Sings the Blues* team as the studio was giving the film a "second wind" rerelease just before the Academy Awards. Gray Frederickson remembers that the studio suggested the idea of making the film into "*The French Connection* Part II," even ruminating on whether Gene Hackman should be offered the lead role. Of this notion, Furie says, "It was always my story from the getgo, and it was the most natural thing in the world to carry Billy Dee, Richard, and the rest of the cast and crew over to the new project. I was never at any point a party to discussions about casting Gene Hackman or making a sequel to *The French Connection.*" With Gene Hackman, director John Frankenheimer helmed *French Connection II* in Marseilles just two years later.

Amid a cast comprised of predominantly Furie alumni, there were two "new recruits": Gwen Welles and veteran character actress Janet Brandt, known for playing a wide variety of stereotypically Jewish roles in films like *Up the Sandbox* and *The Mad Adventures of Rabbi Jacob.* While Brandt renewed her previous matriarchal Jewish persona in the role of the unlikely hit-woman Ida, Gwen Welles, a relative newcomer who had debuted in the film *A Safe Place* just two years earlier, was a seventeen-year-old junkie wandering the Sunset Strip when that film's director, Henry Jaglom, discovered her. Welles had been in and out of institutions attempting to cage her addiction, and she was personally involved with Roger Vadim when Furie hired her for the role of Sherry Nielson, a heroin-addicted call girl who is recruited for her knowledge of French. Says Jaglom, "Gwen was one of my closest friends. After *A Safe Place,* I know there were many directors who couldn't figure out how to use her in movies. She kept failing all these auditions. The key was really to let her be herself within the framework of the story. Her best performances stemmed from directors just telling her what the overall scene was about, and maybe giving her the opening lines, but never working with exact dialogue. That's why she flourished in those Altman movies, because he did that with her too."

Furie remembers of Welles, "I was struck by Gwen's vulnerability. I knew nothing about her real past, but she just seemed to me like a real addict . . . not your conventional actress but someone unique, and an interesting counterpoint to Billy Dee."

Hit! launched Furie's partnership with the newest member of his creative entourage. Harry Korshak, a handsome twenty-eight-year-old with dark, kinky hair who introduced Furie to Harold Buchman, his screenwriter on *The Lawyer* and who had haunted the set of *Little Fauss and Big Halsy* as production assistant, became Furie's producer and his new bouncing-board, a la Brad Dexter. Sidney Korshak, who was Charlie Bluhdorn's lawyer, openly facilitated his son's movie-producing career. "Brad Dexter was out of my life and Harry came along, and was a very sensitive person, a painter and artist type, just a very thoughtful person," claims Furie. "I needed another guy to bounce things off, and during that period, Harry was that guy." Alan Trustman professes that Harry Korshak's involvement in producing the film was originally his suggestion ("After I made the suggestion, we had the deal by 10:30 that morning"), submitted in an effort to expedite the process of Paramount's giving the green light to the project. Beyond this, however, Korshak's involvement had been a foregone conclusion.

In Peter Bart's memoir *Infamous Players,* the Paramount exec recounts being somewhat nervous about what he personally perceived as a Sidney Korshak's over-presence at the studio, particularly when he became aware that Korshak's son Harry had been given his own projects to produce.[40] One might say that Peter Bart saw the Mafia in his soup at Paramount, but the executive was nonetheless asked by Sidney Korshak to keep a watchful eye on his son. "The films I did with Harry really had nothing to do with

Sidney Korshak," insists Furie. "I always get asked about the Korshaks. Sure, I knew about Sidney Korshak! Who didn't? But there was no subterfuge about it. It was what it was: a focused businesslike creative partnership. Yes, Harry's father got him the job and that is common knowledge by now, but I truly got a great deal out of our partnership from a totally creative standpoint. Harry always had useful and intelligent things to say, and I wouldn't have done three films with him if he didn't contribute anything." And neither was Robert Evans concerned about essentially what was by most accounts a nonissue. According to Bart's memoir, Evans dismissed Bart's questions and concerns about the arrangement. Evans, however, also labeled the Korshak-Furie pictures as low-budget projects relatively low on Paramount's overloaded list of concerns. "That's probably why we were able to get away with a 135-minute running time on the picture," Furie laughs. "No one ever asked us to change a thing in the editing. But Paramount in those days was like a twenty-four-hour party scene. People just came and went to the offices, with no guard at the front. Anyone could come by, and did!"

Relative to Furie's other films, *Hit!*'s use of locations proves most noteworthy. As on *Little Fauss and Big Halsy,* no studios or backlots were used for shooting. From the salons and yachts of Marseilles, to a prison yard in Chino in California, to the small coastal Pacific Northwest town of Gig Harbor, Washington, to ghetto neighborhoods in Los Angeles, Chicago, and Washington, DC, and many places in between, the film proved to be an epic venture, despite what were ostensibly limited ambitions. By all accounts, the production of *Hit!* was very run-and-gun and, relative to the sizes of Furie's other sets at the time, a rather more intimate affair. For an elaborate chase sequence in the center of the picture, one that normally would have required many filming units, two consolidated camera units wound up executing the complex action set piece. As on *Lady Sings the Blues,* improvisation and shooting everything mostly in sequence remained a vital element. For all intents and purposes, that intuitive process of in-the-moment invention was sustained. Even though Furie openly invited and encouraged his screenwriters to come to the set to observe the shooting (so he could "bounce" with them), Trustman begged off and blew town. "I never visited the set of any of the films I wrote, particularly after *Bullitt,* because by that point, I was firmly out of the movie business," says Trustman, who had become involved in other businesses in Boston by the time he was conscripted to write *Hit!*

Claims Furie, "The American leg of shooting *Hit!* really went off without too much of a hitch, and I say that with some confidence because, believe it or not, I remember very little about shooting the parts in the States. The locations were all real, everyone got along, and we just banged it out." Gray Frederickson, however, remembers one major incident that almost brought ruin to their guerrilla operation, an incident that further defined Sidney Korshak as a living and breathing deus ex machina. "We went to Washington, DC, to get guerrilla second-unit kind of shots just with the star walking around the city streets and stuff, just to steal stuff in this dark van. We were going to be there for one day because we were on our way to Marseilles. And we arrived at the hotel that night, and somehow or another, the Teamsters heard we were coming."

Awaiting the *Hit!* stealth crew in the hotel lobby, the Teamsters approached the Furie, Korshak, and Frederickson triad, stating with staunch certainty, "We heard you guys are shooting a movie."

Frederickson, thinking on his feet, prevaricated. "No, we're just going around looking, scouting locations and shooting some still photos."

The "arch-Teamster" in the crew, calling Frederickson's bluff, insisted, "No, we know you're shooting. We'll see you here at the hotel tomorrow morning."

Frederickson continues, "Sidney [Furie] just looked at me and said, 'We're screwed! We can't afford to pay drivers or anything. This is just a little guerrilla unit.' So we were trying to figure out what to do. Then, I just looked at Harry and said, 'Harry, call your dad and see what he can do,' because Sidney Korshak was the lawyer for the Teamsters. So, Harry called his dad, and he told us that he'd see what he could do to help us."

The next morning, the three men met up in hotel's lobby, gulping with some degree of trepidation when they saw the same Teamsters approaching. This time, however, they were singing a different tune.

"They came up to us and basically started groveling, saying, "Oh my God! We're so sorry! We had no idea who you guys were! Listen, you've got motorcycle police escort out here, you got as many drivers as you need, you've got an ambulance out here in case of emergency. It won't cost you a dime." Frederickson and Furie looked dumfounded toward Korshak, their minds blown. "Damn, Harry, no joke, your dad's really got some power!" Frederickson remarked., "Well," said Korshak, "Once in awhile it's good to have a powerful father." The conjuring of this magical arrangement pleased and conflicted the first-time producer in equal doses. The Korshak name may have carried with it such power and advantages, but it may have been the nepotistic stigma that made people second-guess Furie's new partner far more than he ever deserved.

When *Hit!*'s skeleton team arrived for shooting in France, they spent a full week of prepping and casting the French sequences before proceeding to Marseilles. "Wherever we went, we picked up new crews," recalls Furie. "We cast all the French actors in one single session, and I couldn't believe that this one French casting agent had more 'types' than any Hollywood casting agencies. It was the most soup-to-nuts casting, and I never had to ask her to bring me more of this type or that type. All one session! It was truly extraordinary."

When they informed the Parisians they were bound for Marseilles, Gray Frederickson remembers, "They expressed a kind of disgust, like 'Why would you want to go there?' It was like telling them you were off to the third world. It was considered the least desirable part of France when we were there." When they arrived in the south of France in January 1973, they discovered that local North African immigrants were demonstrating against the rising levels of poverty, low-quality public services, and escalating crime in the city, all owing to an economic downturn that stemmed from a national oil crisis. The rise in crime had given France's second-largest city a somewhat seedy reputation. "We learned a new French word, 'manifestations,' which we learned meant protest demonstration," remembers Furie. "We would arrive at a shooting location only to find riot police parked in buses blocking us from the location. Entire streets were often blocked off by marching picketers. I believe most of them were Algerians." This flurry of activity in the city often necessitated sudden changes in locations.

Most of the cast and crew stayed at the Grand Hotel Noailles on the Canebière, the main waterfront street in the city. In the true spirit of the project, the lobby of the hotel was often used as a shooting location for the scenes involving the French druglords. "We had heard that the Germans in World War II used it to house officers and we used to sit in there and have a drink and picture what it would have been like," says Furie. "It was all a bit morbid and creepy." Other members of the crew stayed at Hôtel la Résidence du Vieux-Port on the south bank of the old port; this was likewise used as a shooting location.

Hit! opens with a title card that states, "The producers gratefully acknowledge the cooperation afforded them by the City of Marseilles."

Although Furie and Korshak had the full cooperation of the local French government, Gray Frederickson remembers that the cast and crew "were in a lot of places in Marseilles we weren't supposed to be." Billy Dee Williams corroborates, "Yeah, there was a lot of stealing shots. More than I am used to." Of this practice, Furie rationalizes, "It was really the spirit of the thing. We needed a sense that we were moving with the characters from place to place, from location to location, and almost operating in a way that the characters were operating. And after all, I graduated with honors from the 'school of grabbing' in the early sixties with *The Leather Boys*."

Despite the potential dangers of this modus operandi, the amount of stress proved exceptionally low on the set of *Hit!* relative to Furie's previous and following films. Resulting from an equal combination of Furie's position at Paramount after the success of *Lady Sings the Blues*, the auspicious involvement of Harry Korshak, and the newly bankable star power of Billy Dee Williams, the demands of the shooting schedule were met with ease. Although Richard Pryor's star was likewise on the rise, he did not begin to enjoy the height of his stardom until at least five years later. Gray Frederickson remembers:

> Once we got to Marseilles, Richard Pryor wore me out. He was such a wild man. He'd just . . . erupt into where we were all gathered and say something like, "We are going *out tonight!* Come on!" And I'd say, "Richard, I've gotta get up at six o'clock tomorrow morning and you don't have to work until noon." He'd just look at me and say, "Come on, Gray baby! Tonight'll be dy-na-mite!" And then he'd take us out and keep us in stitches so badly all night that the French locals in these places would look at us like a bunch of crazy Americans.

Richard Pryor served in other capacities on the set of *Hit!* as well. Furie's son Noah, then fourteen years old, remembers how he killed time while his father and the crew worked around the clock at the film's Gig Harbor locations.

> It was a given that growing up with dad in the film business meant that most vacations were on the set of his current movie. Most of the time, all of the Furie boys invaded the set, so we found things

to do together. But on this particular trip, it was just me. After a few days, there was nothing to do but watch take after take after take. One of the guys on the set saw that I was getting bored, so he asked me if I wanted to play chess. I said sure, and we played every single day the entire week I was there. That guy turned out to be Richard Pryor, truly the nicest guy to me. He actually taught me how to play the game, and made the vacation worthwhile . . . more than it would have otherwise been.

Although working with another novice producer, Harry Korshak, directly after his experience with the impetuous but energetic novice Berry Gordy, Furie was nevertheless back on firm ground again. *Hit!* proved to be exactly the type of production experience any director would have wanted, to follow the irregularly developed and constructed *Lady Sings the Blues*. "Honestly, the only bit of contention I can remember on the set of *Hit!* is when I asked John Alonzo if I could borrow his hat for a scene, to put on a character when we shooting at Chino, and he wouldn't give it up," says Furie. "I never knew what that could have been about, and I was a little sore about it at the time, but who knows and who cares?"

According to Richard Pryor's biographer Scott Saul, the real inmates at Chino stopped pitching hay to watch Furie and his team work. In between takes there, Pryor opened up to a Paramount publicist who haunted the set that day. "I want to do something to show that I have depth," he expressed. "It's time to branch out, time to stretch my talents as far as they will go. The happy-go-lucky comic—that's an act. I like to do parts. But I don't want to be one-dimensional, to lock myself in."[41] The Chino-set scene turned out to be one of Pryor's big emotional moments in the film, the one in which his character is unwittingly reunited with the man who raped and murdered his wife; the man then acts out on him in a fit of vengeful rage. Says Henry Jaglom, "I remember Richy saying how Sidney Furie was constantly challenging him, and taught him to expect greatness in himself as a dramatic performer."

When the company landed in Marseilles, which was then the heroin capital of the world, they found that there was no shortage of drugs in the general vicinity, although drugs were not at all pervasive on the set. "If Richard or Gwen or anyone did use anything drugwise while shooting the movie, they kept it well hidden," says Gray Frederickson. "There was no incident or concern about drugs, even though we were in a hotbed of it."

Furie says, "I honestly don't know how many on the film smoked dope, but they must have had no problem finding grass in Marseilles. I don't remember hearing any complaints."

A rather conspicuous, joyously sick inside joke arrives in one of *Hit!*'s later scenes. The alter kocker vigilante played by Sid Melton stews nervously while awaiting the precise moment to dispatch the unsuspecting French drug smuggler he has tailed into a Marseilles cinematheque. Melton's character Herman declares, "This is for Joey!" before brutally blowing his man away in cold blood. While he escapes the horrified crowd seated captive in the dark of the theater, prominently superimposed onto the cinema's movie screen is the main title text for the film *Le parrain de Mario Puzo,* known in English as *The Godfather.* Adding to this inside-joke irony is that the diegetic score we hear during the movie-within-the-movie's title sequence is Lalo Schifrin's Main Title cue for *Hit!* One can imagine Furie in the editing room grinning while putting this sequence together. What Furie directly tells the audience in this brief shot is that he has constructed his very own "crime family," to whatever degree of success or similarity, totally independent of his previous involvement with the Puzo property. Billy Dee Williams's assembled team of rogues, a kind of ragtag mafia, has become Furie's Corleone family by proxy and by default, stripped of its dynastic elements and operatic aspirations. The filmmaker's decision to center the film around a critically weighty second act, in which the interrelational dynamics between the members of the hit squad are established, ensures this. Furie explains, "It took so long to get *Hit!* right in the editing. Argy and I were on that picture for seven or eight months, versus my normal five or six months. I'm happy it didn't get swallowed up by studio guys saying 'Speed it up! Speed it up!' because it could have been butchered if they didn't allow it to breathe." Michael Atkinson writes in the June 2012 issue of *Sight & Sound* that *Hit!* culminates "with an echo of the ending movement of *The Godfather*" in that it revolves around various "assassination scenarios" that are intercut.

Screenwriter Alan Trustman thought the third-act killings were "a lot more imaginative" in his script. "I was originally disappointed, and I tried to convince Sidney to reshoot the ending." That said, he also remarks, "When I saw the movie again not too long ago, I discovered that it wasn't half-bad. I think it has aged well, at least for me."

From its oblique opening sequence to its unresolved denouement, the confounding *Hit!* successfully establishes itself as an uncompromising antidote to its era's most puerile action-thriller conventions, defying outright the knee-jerk blaxploitation categorization that the filmmakers initially feared would stigmatize it. The action set pieces are background rather than the film's raison d'être. For instance, when Janet Brandt's character Ida slices the throat of a female target in a powder room, Furie's camera is placed at considerable distance from the two women, coldly objective and efficient when everything that has come before it, that is, the character development, has been rendered for spatial and emotional proximity. When the film is digressive, Furie makes his deep affection for these characters (what Canadian film scholar Clive Denton referred to as the "trademark" of Furie's exceptional "respect and caring for his characters") always perceptible. All this is enough not just to carry the work through its surprising detours, but to also allow those detours to render the film thankfully idiosyncratic. The violence is orchestrated without the Grand Guignol excess that audiences had come to expect with such enterprises and is reserved for only the final fifteen minutes of what essentially becomes an epic film in both length and vision.

The film also avoids easy typification in a very immediate sense, from the way the opening sequence is edited. From its first frame, it seeks to establish rather than build, which is unusual for a thriller. Lalo Schifrin's metronomic percussion-only main title theme acts as an apropos prelude to a form of elliptical crosscutting that sets up a larger theme of class division. This opening provides a coy, deceptively simple snapshot of the cross-continental hierarchy that exists when it comes to the masters, servants, and victims in the narcotics trade. Beginning in Marseilles, tracking an affluent French couple from behind as they deliver two bottles of champagne to be opened aboard their yacht, the opening sequence is skillfully protracted, setting up a deliberate pace very early on, as no other reportable incident occurs in these opening minutes. The opening edits choose to linger on these figures, however, as the camera observes the yacht crew getting ready to set sail in what feels like real time, while the rich prepare for expensive leisure.

When the film then cuts suddenly to a ghetto neighborhood in Washington, DC, Furie sure-handedly illustrates the obvious abruptness of the parallelism he constructs. It is here that he also sets up an effective expositional trope that carries the narrative from location to location for the rest of the film: shots that focus on license plates denoting the current locale. The "run-and-gun" nature of the production is part of *Hit!*'s effectiveness as a genre exercise, albeit a subversive one. For one, the license-plate trope allows for a conspicuous lack of titles and opticals, which in turn speaks to a larger and general sense of efficiency and economy, despite glib pronouncements later on about the film's 135-minute "overlength." One must also consider the logic of the intercutting. It is daytime in both Marseilles and Washington in these brief divertissements. Simultaneity and temporal parallel therefore become less likely and less acceptable. Chronology becomes skewed. Furie's and Argyle Nelson's cutting of the film thus assumes a bolder ambition. While crosscutting in Hollywood productions by its very nature assumes some manner of simultaneous action, the crosscutting here is freer to be more allusive, provocative, theoretical. Furie highlights the rigid dichotomy he intends to turn upside down in the telling of his story, calling into question how viewers choose to connote places and spaces. Can and will these worlds touch each other? This construction is overstated, but deliberately so.

Other moments, such as when Gwen Welles poisons her target's wine in a French bistro, focus steadily on faces in extended shots that deliberately foreground characters relative to background action. In one key shot from this sequence, Furie focuses on Welles's anxious expression as activity stirs behind her. Also, Furie's propensity for spatial-configuration compositional motifs is again manifested as the film tends to favor "ensemble shots" in which groups of people fill the wide-screen space. From the obstructed perspectives of the Wild Angles trilogy to the stacked two-to-one/one-to-two spatial arrangements in *Little Fauss and Big Halsy*, Furie carries the torch with *Hit!'s* ensemble compositions. In *Hit!*, whether the villains are framed together in an opulent French salon, or the heroes are framed together in the isolated Gig Harbor "militia training hacienda" while reviewing their targets, the Hawksian theme of group responsibility that Furie probes is given firm visual grounding.

The use of improvisation in *Hit!* also liberates the film from its more dubious origins, as Furie continues to write his scenes in performance jazz. The film might have originally appeared to prospective audiences as yet another confection in the Samuel Arkoff/Roger Corman mill of low-budget black action films. To exacerbate this image, John Alonzo's lighting in the film is more slapdash than it was in *Lady Sings the Blues,* and the camerawork itself is more rugged and prone to handheld. This functions more as evocation than negligence. It's a ragtag movie about a ragtag team. The camerawork, however, is duly packaged together with the jazz performance aspects. Pryor is given the most license for improvisation in scenes, whether it is composing an X-rated jingle in the freezing cold or affecting caricatured voices to entertain Gwen Welles's character in the backseat of a van. Furie again not only retains these moments but lets them dictate a sustained off-the-cuff tonality that permeates the entire movie. When he allows Pryor to ad lib a comedy routine as Williams's character parks a car and boards a ferry, an otherwise perfunctory moment that was no doubt written in the script as "Nick exits the car" is pushed well beyond the ordinary.

On August 9, 1973, 20th Century Fox released Ossie Davis's movie *Gordon's War,* a tale of returning Vietnam veterans on a vendetta to kill the drug dealers that have turned their neighborhood into a hell on earth, starring Paul Winfield. With *Hit!* forced to compete with another similarly plotted film, *New York* magazine critic Judith Crist stood alone in her defense of Furie's film when she saluted it as "a bunch of pros providing us with top-rank entertainment marked by topicality and talent, and doing so with complete and smashing success." The other notices were nowhere nearly as reassuring. Vincent Canby in the *New York Times* accused the director of "turning out movies as if they were yard goods," griping that "by the time it enters its third hour you may well think you've been trapped." The *L.A. Herald Examiner* faulted a "sagging middle" but conceded that it "opens and closes with verve and suspense." The *Hollywood Reporter* complained that the film had "no texture, no truth and no debut from a great new star to hold it together." Although ambivalent about its top-heavy exposition, *Variety* felt that "*Hit!* really scores with a number of sharp-edged secondary roles, a charismatic dimension to Williams' leading performance, some tautly edited and dramatically photographed action set pieces and some nifty comic business deftly handled by Furie." *Box Office* magazine most exemplified the perplexity of most critics when it tersely called the film "an oddity." Charles Champlin, writing in the *Los Angeles Times,* felt that Furie told his story with "energy and dash"; he gave the film its best review, for Champlin was also among the few reviewers to approach the fact that the onus was upon the audience to prove it as a work independent of the blaxploitation genre, even while Paramount amplified this categorization for commercial purposes.

"We got swept under the rug with *Hit!,*" recalls Furie. "It just opened and closed. It wasn't even abused, just dismissed, nothing you could do."

Despite the fact that *Hit!* was definitely not a "hit" in its original release, the film was justly reappraised upon its 2012 DVD release. With the fresh reviews came a resurgence of interest. *Sight & Sound* acclaimed the film's editing as "meticulous" and commented, "There's enough character quirk to pack two movies, and a startlingly nasty car chase on the northwestern suburban roadways that's shot with low-tech textbook precision (Furie's backseat swivel panic is still underutilised in such sequences)." The magazine also noted Richard Pryor's able participation, declaring that "the film provides us with another badly needed portrait of him as a young comic/actor, effortlessly stealing every scene with simply the disbelieving steadiness of his gaze."[42] *Combustible Celluloid* wrote that "it tries so many things we're not used to seeing, as well as relying on some old comfortable staples," remarking that the humor is "the kind of stuff that any director today would have cut in order to move the plot forward. In *Hit!,* it provides the film with its true personality."[43] Many others followed suit in appraising the film as a hidden gem. David and Joe Henry, authors of the 2013 book *Furious Cool: Richard Pryor and the World That Made Him,* wrote, "*Hit!* confounded the [blaxploitation] genre with its ensemble cast of multiracial and cross-generational heroes. For audiences expecting a blaxploitation thrill ride, Furie's art-house pacing, often disorienting camerawork and general attention to character and detail made for slow going. It has yet to find the audience it deserves."[44]

When seeing the film again forty years later, Furie found himself in disbelief over just how much he had gone out on a limb to experiment. "I can only assume Paramount had their hands full with other bigger projects and we were just a blip on the radar. I used to think it was an embarrassment, because I just made it as a genre exercise and then it disappeared. Looking at it now, I can't believe that it is probably, in my opinion, one of the best films I've ever done. I'm very proud of it." He also commented during the taping sessions for this book, "If I get nothing else out of working on this biography, I will have gotten *Hit!* back again. To have a film you thought was a failure and to see it again to learn it's something you're really proud of . . . that's a gift."

Hit! ranks deservedly high on a list of Furie's best work, along with *The Leather Boys, The Ipcress File, Lady Sings the Blues, The Boys in Company C,* and *The Entity.* In an Internet-fueled revisionist culture that applauds marginalized directors and *films maudit* (literally "cursed films," but really meaning "unjustly overlooked and neglected films") more than ever before, *Hit!* is perhaps the most deserving of Furie's work of being named a *film maudit*. The root of the critical antipathy toward Furie's work in 1973 most likely lies in the perennial critical impulse to lump film work into easily definable and digestible niches. *Hit!* defies any and all easy categorizations, posing a challenge to genre classification. To label it is indeed to negate it. The film's promotional materials mismarketed the film and set up its projected niche audience for disappointment.

While in postproduction on *Hit!*, Furie announced his next project with Harry Korshak, the man he had unofficially christened the heir to the throne of Brad Dexter. On July 23, 1973, Paramount announced that it had slated Gail Parent's best-selling novel *Sheila Levine Is Dead and Living in New York* for production and 1974 release, with the novelist adapting her own book, Harry Korshak producing, and Furie directing. Again, the filmmaker found himself about to take another sharp left turn, cementing his chameleon reputation after five consecutive genre jumps.

Sidney Furie's pious grandfather, Yitzhak Furie, in the Polish town of Krinick.

Parents Samuel and Ann Furie having a night on the town, ca. 1935.

Sidney Furie at age 6, dressed for the Jewish High Holy Days. Furie grew up as an only child.

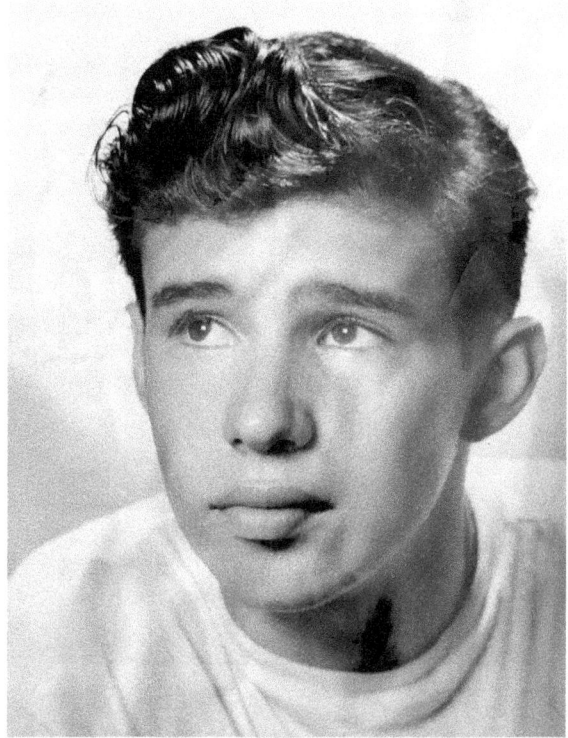

Portrait of the "angles-worker" as a young man—Sidney J. Furie at fifteen.

The pledge photo for the Beta Sigma Rho fraternity upon Furie's entrance to Carnegie Institute of Technology in 1950. He is in the back row, third from the right. (Courtesy of Carnegie Mellon University Archives)

Sid at the CBC. Occasionally, he took acting roles in live drama, though he later avoided performing when the time came to make his own features.

Ben Piazza and Anne Pearson as young lovers on the run in *A Dangerous Age* (1957), Furie's first feature film, a pioneer effort that was one of the earliest features made in English Canada.

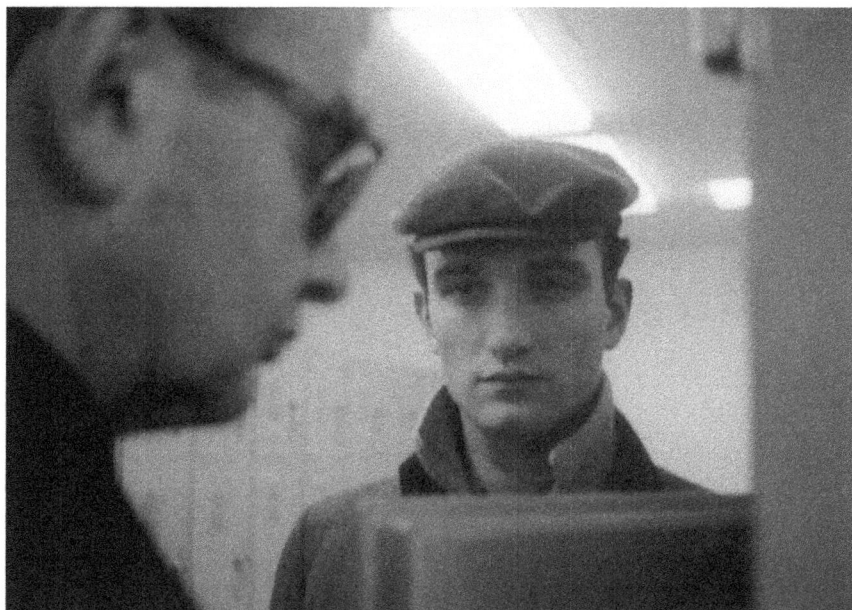

As a young actor in 1958, Tony Ray (son of director Nicholas) shuttled between Furie's *A Cool Sound from Hell* in Toronto and John Cassavetes's *Shadows* in New York City.

Upon Furie's move to London in 1960, his first job was to direct the horror movie "quickie" *Doctor Blood's Coffin* (1961), shot in Cornwall in the south of England.

Pleased with the results, the producers gave Furie another horror film, *The Snake Woman* (1961), shot in six days.

Juggling fatherhood with filmmaking. Furie had fathered two sons by the time he arrived in London, and more children came later. Here, he is pictured with the eldest two, Dan and Noah.

Furie swiftly rose as one of the new "young lads" of British cinema.

Here, Furie is unusually eager to speak with the press. He was not so forthcoming with journalists as his career progressed. (Courtesy of Paul Lynch)

Furie's first box-office and critical hit was *The Young Ones* (1961). Next to him is the film's star, rock idol Cliff Richard. (Courtesy of the Everett Collection)

Furie directs veteran British thesps Robert Morley and Richard Todd in *The Boys* (1962), while the young cast members loom above them. (Courtesy of the Everett Collection)

Furie with Socialist screenwriter Stuart Douglass, who penned the original script for *The Boys*. (Courtesy of the Everett Collection)

As ever, he is on the hunt for angles, and for a different way of shooting a scene. (Courtesy of the Everett Collection)

Left to right: script girl Helen Whitson, Furie, operator Chic Waterson, and camera assistant Robin Vidgeon on the set of *Wonderful Life* (1964), on a shoot in the Canary Islands that was somewhat less than wonderful.

Producer vs. director: Furie and Harry Saltzman duked it out throughout the shooting of *The Ipcress File* (1965).

Lining up an *Ipcress File* shot overlooking London's Grosvenor Square. Furie's camera stylings drove Harry Saltzman to madness. (Courtesy of the Everett Collection)

The Furie family at their first Hollywood residence, the Soupy Sales house.

The Furie boys Dan, Noah, Jon, and Simon, with their grandparents Samuel and Ann and their nanny, Anne Baynes.

"You'll never hear me badmouth Brando," Furie says. (Courtesy of PhotoFest)

Sidney Furie and Marlon Brando on *The Appaloosa* (1966): "The question everyone asked is 'Who will throw the first punch,'" wrote Peter Bart in the *New York
Times*. (Courtesy of the Everett Collection)

"I do it my way," Furie told Sinatra, yet another temperamental star, on the set of
Furie's *The Naked Runner* (1967).

Furie works the angles on *The Lawyer* (1970) in Colorado Springs. (Courtesy of Paul Lynch)

Furie finds his shot with cinematographer Ralph Woolsey, who photographed two of Furie's Hollywood productions.

The boys in Company F: Furie with his four sons from his first marriage on the set of *Little Fauss and Big Halsy* (1970): Dan, Noah, Simon, Jon (*left to right*).

Furie with his second wife, Linda, whom he married during the production of *The Lawyer*.

Furie directs Robert Redford and Michael J. Pollard, a mismatch onscreen and offscreen.

Son Dan at his bar mitzvah, pictured here with Samuel and Ann. Furie had set up his parents in Palm Springs shortly before this photo was taken.

Furie directed Diana Ross in an Oscar-nominated performance for *Lady Sings the Blues* (1972).

The multicamera man on a hilltop shooting a scene from *Hit!* (1973). Furie was among the first directors to use multiple cameras to shoot a film.

Jeannie Berlin gave her collaborators on *Sheila Levine Is Dead and Living in New York* (1975) more than they bargained for. Behind her is cinematographer Don Morgan. (Courtesy of Don Morgan)

Furie, cinematographer Don Morgan, and producer Harry Korshak (*left to right*) confer about how to shoot around their rebellious star Jeannie Berlin on *Sheila Levine Is Dead and Living in New York*. (Courtesy of Don Morgan)

Left to right: cinematographer Don Morgan, producer Harry Korshak, still photographer William Gillohm, and Furie. (Courtesy of Don Morgan)

James Brolin and Jill Clayburgh step into the shoes of screen legends in *Gable and Lombard* (1976) (Courtesy of the Everett Collection)

Furie had difficulty with the then-obscure Clayburgh throughout the shooting. It was her first lead role in a theatrically released feature. (Courtesy of the Everett Collection)

On the set of *Purple Hearts* (1984) in the Philippines. "The boys in company C would have thrown beer bottles at the screen," wrote one critic. (Courtesy of Eric Vasilik, an extra in the film)

High-flying, hard-fighting, red-blooded, all-American heroes in Furie's blockbuster *Iron Eagle* (1986). (Courtesy of the Everett Collection)

Above and below: Shooting *Superman IV: The Quest for Peace*, (1987), with no peace in sight behind the scenes. (Courtesy of the Everett Collection)

Furie (*left*) reunited with producer Albert S. Ruddy to direct the Rodney Dangerfield vehicle *Ladybugs* (1992). (Courtesy of the Everett Collection)

The Furie family at the wedding of one of Furie's grandchildren in 2012.

Furie, Ruddy, and book author Daniel Kremer (*left to right*) in the summer of 2013.

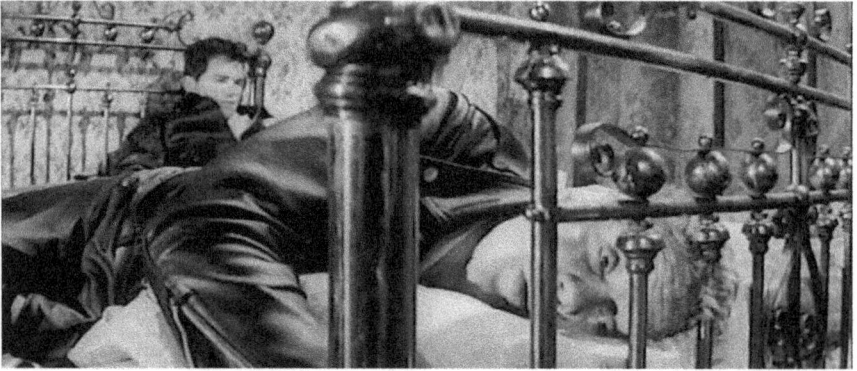

The wounded males in Furie's *The Leather Boys* (top two) and *Little Fauss and Big Halsy* (bottom) literally have difficulty seeing eye-to-eye.

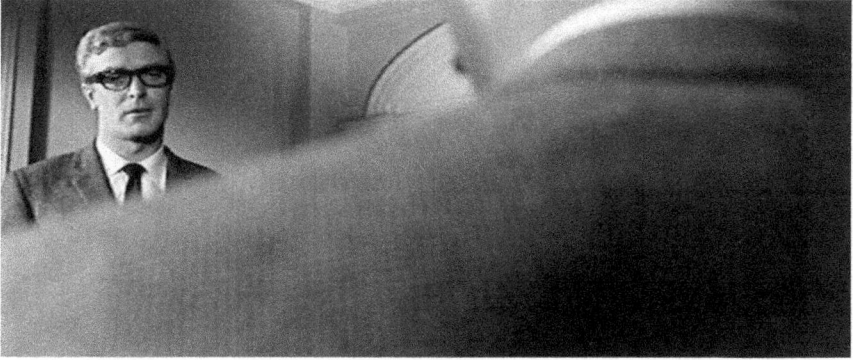

Hidden agendas: the camera itself is the spy in *The Ipcress File*.

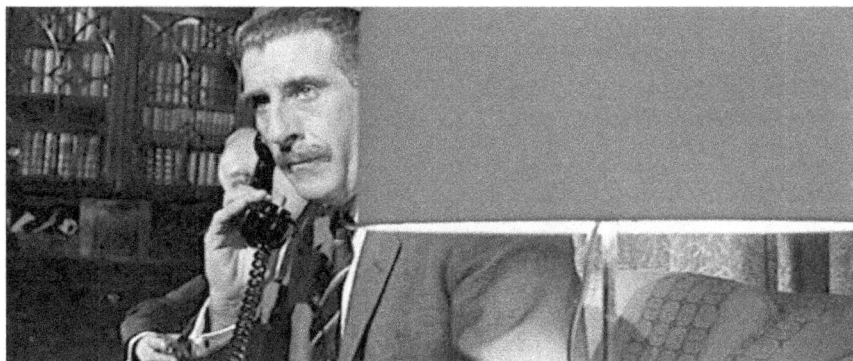

Film writer Gary McMahon writes of *The Ipcress File*, "Downbeat details are stretched to the anamorphic proportions of magic realism," finding "abstract expressionism in a lampshade."

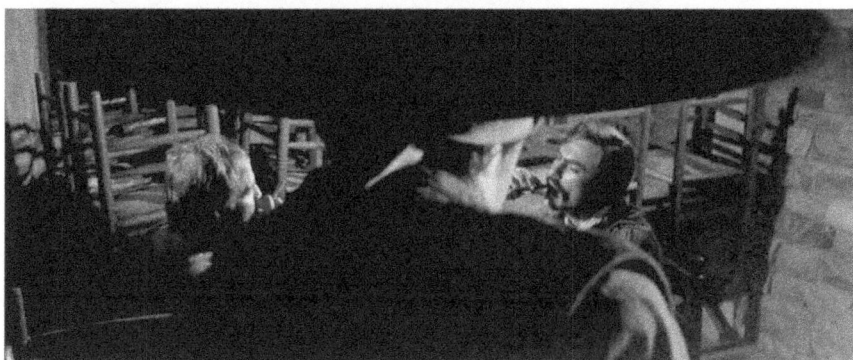

The camera hides again, this time to escape the dangers of Cocatlan in *The Appaloosa*.

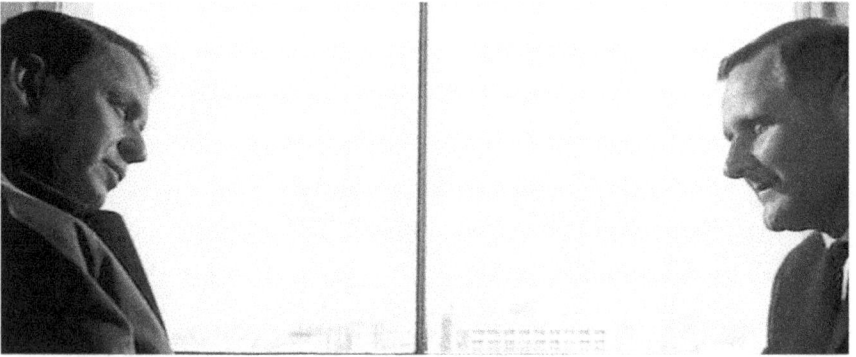

Trapped by geometry: wild angles to the nth degree in *The Naked Runner*.

The two-to-one arrangements of *Little Fauss and Big Halsy* (1970).

Three of the many ensemble compositions of *Hit!* (1973).

In *Sheila Levine Is Dead and Living in New York,* everything is oh-so-close or oh-so-far-away, with fearsome threesomes or hidden Sheilas.

A focus on peripheral action, with "crammed" foreground placements pushed to extremes in *The Boys in Company C.*

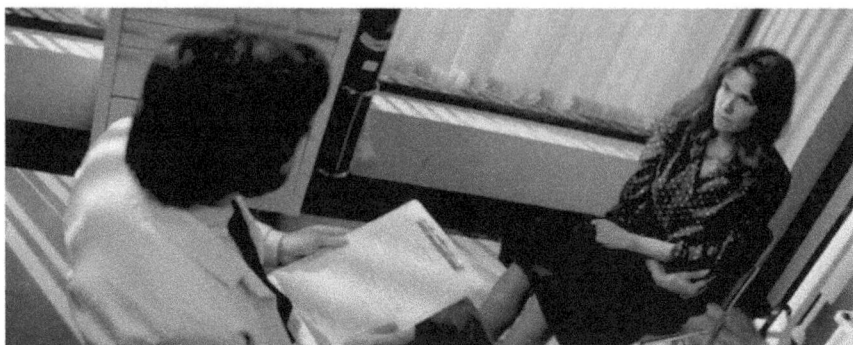

"We'll technique the shit out of it," Furie told cinematographer Stephen Burum when prepping *The Entity*.

Chapter 8

Sid & Carole
& Clark & Sheila

The Romantic Fantasies

Fact: Sheila Levine ain't never going to get married. She never had a chance.
> —*Gail Parent's novel* Sheila Levine Is Dead and Living in New York

The Nielsen ratings for *The Mary Tyler Moore Show* were at an all-time-high by the time *Sheila Levine Is Dead and Living in New York* started pre-production in August 1973. The sitcom's first spin-off, *Rhoda,* starring Valerie Harper as Rhoda Moganstern, was to broadcast its first episode on September 9, 1974, while Furie's film was unsteadily sputtering toward picture wrap, marking the end of its tumultuous (and many-times-disrupted) shooting schedule.

By the time Paramount first announced the project in the trades, there had already been a cycle of mainstream American films building stories around the "urbanized independent woman," including Fred Coe's *Me, Natalie* (1969), Herbert Ross's *T.R. Baskin* (1971), Alan J. Pakula's *Klute* (1971), and Otto Preminger's *Such Good Friends* (1971). Paramount Pictures released all but one of these films, capitalizing the most on the budding feminism of the era. The decade culminated with the ultimate expressions of this theme, on notes of tragedy, as in Richard Brooks's *Looking for Mr. Goodbar* (1977), and of triumph, as in Paul Mazursky's *An Unmarried Woman* (1978). *Sheila Levine Is Dead and Living in New York* seemed the next logical contribution to this cycle of films after the publication of the novel in January 1972, when it quickly became a *New York Times* best-seller.

Gail Parent had first intended *Sheila Levine Is Dead and Living in New York* as an original screenplay, to be cowritten with her partner Kenny Solms, whom she had known since their days together at New York University. Together, they penned television sketch comedy and variety shows, developing a track record with episodes of *The Bill Cosby Show, The Mary Tyler Moore Show,* and later *Rhoda.* Solms failed to express enthusiasm about Parent's first pitch of the literary venture. "Kenny just said, 'It sounds like that Joan Crawford movie *The Best of Everything* and I'm not interested in that,'" Parent remembers. "So I did it as a novel out of spite."[1] Parent's resulting manuscript, titled as a parody of the popular revue album *Jacques Brel Is Alive and Well and Living in Paris* and written over a year and a half during which she also wrote with Solms for *The Carol Burnett Show,* was the extended interior monologue (and suicide note) of the eponymous Jewish girl with a poor self-image. The book, filled with trenchant modern humor, fit effortlessly within the spirit of the times. The plump Sheila, upon arriving single in New York, restlessly quests for a sense of self-reliance and self-worth, pining for the vague promises of the feminist movement but still fearing she will be carelessly left out in the proverbial cold with only her doting caricature of a mother to "save" her, unsuccessfully.

While there had been a plethora of Jewish "heroines" among the decade's intelligentsia, within the literati and the political sphere, the 1970s was somewhat less than the best of times for the Jewish female as a film character, other than Barbra Streisand, whose outwardly Jewish femininity was either treated as novelty or glossed over completely. In an era when Elliott Gould's mug occupied the cover of *Time* magazine, a characteristically Jewish male ironically reigned king of box-office returns and the Jewish heroine all but provided the proverbial role of sideshow freak. The most flagrant and telling incarnation of this state of affairs can be seen in Elaine May's *The Heartbreak Kid* (1972), in which newlywed Charles Grodin dumps the "nice Jewish girl" Jeannie Berlin on their honeymoon, in favor of blond "super-shiksa" Cybill Shepherd. That film highlighted and basically set the tone for what seventies Jewish women had come to expect in their singles-saturated cities, as a shafted and unceremoniously passed-over species miserably drowning in the "romantic ideal" department. The zeitgeist was ripe for it. How auspicious it was, then, that the actress who played the jilted Jewish girl in May's comedy ultimately landed the role of Sheila Levine in the inevitable movie adaptation of Parent's book.

"Shiksappeal," a Jewish male's natural gravitation to the charms of non-Jewish women, reached new heights in the 1970s. In *Portnoy's Complaint,* a novel that had quickly risen to become a cultural landmark, shiksappeal provided the dramatic and comedic preoccupation, in both its literary and its cinematic incarnations. Parent expresses this phenomenon in her own novel: "Many Jewish boys, a la Portnoy, grew up hating-loving their Jewish mamas and vowing to marry a non-Jewish girl. So I'm ethnically undesirable. Flat-chested blondes are in—Jewish girls, Polish girls, Italian girls are out. Fact: Many non-Jewish girls want to marry a Jewish boy. They are encouraged by their mothers because Jewish boys don't drink or run around and they make such nice husbands. Jewish girls want to marry Jewish boys for the same reasons and because Jewish husbands let their wives have maids."[2] In a sense, Parent's first-person novel was kind of a female *Portnoy's Complaint* without the bawdy, take-no-prisoners tales of sexual mischief that colored Phillip Roth's famous work. However, the movie adaptation of Parent's novel, whose screenplay was credited to both Parent and Solms, turned out to be a completely different story, in a very literal sense.

On February 18, 1974, the *Los Angeles Times* Sunday Calendar section published an interview between staff writer Wayne Warga and the Gail Parent–Kenny Solms team. In Sidney Furie's dressing room on the film's interior Paramount set, Solms explained to Warga that Sheila is "much more sympathetic in the movie." Parent seconded this notion, stating that in the film, the humor "is in the situation," then outright admitted that Sheila does not wisecrack in the film as she had in the book. "Actually, she doesn't even try suicide, but there is a tiny little superficial death wish." Seemingly content with the alterations, Parent was perhaps under duress from the studio not to expose her personal reservations to the press. "It's the story of a triangle and this time Sheila gets the man—he doesn't run out on her."[3] When Warga suspiciously inquired if this was more than a little divergent from Parent's source novel, both writers responded in kind. "Yes, very different," said Solms. "A little bit," Parent said, smiling.

Their placidness in the presence of Warga could have scarcely been further from reality. When reminded of the interview, Solms incisively asks, "Were we just deluded or under gag order at that point?" Solms's cynical joke has a wounded edge because, by the end of the film's production, the two writers were horrified at what had become of their material during the adaptation process. "We eventually quit coming to watch the filming," says Parent. "We'd just stand around the set and listen to dialogue we didn't recognize. Sidney would walk over to the two of us and say something like, 'What do you guys think?' and we were always speechless."

During the casting process, five actresses were selected, by varying factions, as likely candidates to play Sheila. Barbra Streisand naturally headed Parent and Solms's list. So smitten were they with the idea of Streisand's casting that they composed an admiring personal letter to her "in classic Dear Mr. Gable fashion," appealing for her involvement. Streisand never responded to their offer, but Parent later wrote the screenplay for *The Main Event* (1979), a Streisand comedy vehicle. Another actress entirely topped the director's list. "I took Bernadette Peters up to Bob Evans's house so he could get to know her and consider her for the role," Furie recalls. At one point, Harry Korshak intimated to the press that Bette Midler, a new Billboard Top 10 megastar from her platinum 1972 debut album *The Divine Miss M,* was on the threshold of scoring the role. Interestingly, it would have been Midler's debut performance in a dramatic film, not counting background parts in scattered films. Others floated the idea of casting Liza Minnelli.

Eventually, however, Furie and Korshak turned to Jeannie Berlin, the daughter of Elaine May, in whose movie she scored an Oscar nomination for Best Supporting Actress. Bob Evans had originally suggested her, with Paramount's approval. Berlin, who had been snubbed both in her previous film's story (in which Charles Grodin as her new husband divorces her on their honeymoon) and at the 1973 Oscars, where she lost the award to Eileen Heckart, who won for her role in *Butterflies Are Free,* would perhaps have her day, like every perceived "dog." On August 17, 1973, she was officially cast and announced to the press as the film's star, as Harry Korshak proclaimed in the press release that the film would be the coronation of a new movie star. Indeed, it was her first-ever leading role in any film, large or small.

The widening gulf between the Parent and Solms script and the pages the actors and director ultimately followed stemmed from the fact that Jeannie Berlin had been granted license to rewrite everything from scratch. Owing to Berlin's contributions, Parent's literary heroine lost her pudge and her death wish. The film became the story of an ambitious wannabe-career woman from Harrisburg who falls in love with the doctor that her scattershot-minded actress roommate is dating. Furie posits,

> Jeannie was more than an actress. She was a full creative person. She's the daughter of a brilliantly funny woman, so some of those same genes are there. But the film was fraught with all kind of problems, and Gail and Kenny were bitter about how it was turning out, how Jeannie was rewriting everything. They were most angry at me for letting it happen. But in the end, Gail wrote a very unique novel, with these Nora Ephron–like vignettes, but it had to become a film and it was very difficult to translate it to the screen. I valued Jeannie's contributions at the time. I felt that, in a movie, you need more than just clever observations and savvy opinions on the modern world, no matter how witty it all is. You need a story you can hang on to, you need incident, you need crisis, a problem of some kind.

On the surface, a big-screen adaptation of Parent's novel may not exactly have had Sidney Furie's name written all over it. Paramount's case for Furie to helm the Parent property really rested in his sensitive direction of Diana Ross as the equally vulnerable Billie Holiday in *Lady Sings the Blues,* at that point in time a still lucrative film for Paramount and, especially, Berry Gordy. *Sheila Levine* was nurtured at Paramount, a virtual bastion for best-selling literary properties, and delivered to Furie by Harry Korshak, whose producing of projects at Paramount continued to elicit cynicism among the more skeptical. "We sold the novel to Paramount through our agent Ron Mardigian with the understanding that we would be handed the task of adapting it ourselves," remembers Kenny Solms. "So it was a real classic Hollywood story of how they sneakily lawyered that right away from us." Paramount was looking to bankroll the film inexpensively, cutting corners by shooting New York exteriors on the backlot.

After the project was first announced in August 1973, it was re-announced in October. "We weren't going to move ahead with it at all at one point, and then . . . we did," Furie recalls. Kenny Solms explained in Wayne Warga's *L.A. Times* piece, "The project no sooner started than it stopped. Everybody got different ideas about how *Sheila* should be done."[4]

Berlin was set up at the Beverly Wilshire Hotel, at Paramount's considerable expense, to rework the script. "She took all the mirrors and framed pictures off the wall of her hotel room," remembers Gail Parent. "She blotted out everything in that hotel room and went to work. One of the first things she did was put oak-tag all over the walls, where she had mapped out her version of the storyline. We were kind of incredulous about the whole thing. Who was she, the actress or the writer?" Furie remembers that the shafting of Parent and Solms "was not done in a gentlemanly way" and that much happened "in the heat of the moment trying to just get the picture ready to be made." Solms and Parent agree that they "felt bullied" by both Jeannie Berlin and Furie, who were, in turn, at odds with each other.

For a period of time early on, however, Furie, Parent, Solms, and Berlin would work together on the script at Solms's house, mostly in an atmosphere of civility. "We met at my place because Gail had little kids, and that wasn't conducive to getting work done," Solms remembers and Furie corroborates. Solms, however, intimates that friction between director and star started percolating early on. "It later got to the point that Gail tried to become the mediator between Sidney and Jeannie," says Solms. "By the time that was happening, I was already trying to wash my hands of the whole thing." A dialogue exchange between two characters in which abortion is called out as a barbaric act particularly repelled both of the writers. "We couldn't believe what we were hearing with that bit of dialogue," recalls a still incredulous Solms, with Parent tersely backing up his disdain. "We didn't understand why it was in there, or where it really came from, but there it was."

Myths and misconceptions centered around the people assembled for the production spurred rumors, to which the production crew either were oblivious or paid no mind. If the continuing Korshak intrigues were not enough, yet another nepotistic predicament invented itself out of whole cloth to twist and sully the reputation of *Sheila Levine Is Dead and Living in New York* during preproduction. Although Elaine May's complicated history with Paramount (involving the final cut of May's troubled film *A New Leaf* in 1970 and the surrounding legal contretemps) played into affairs in no direct or even indirect way, misleading and hollow gossip spread that Berlin was being given complete license and certain authority to rewrite the *Sheila Levine* script to expiate the studio's guilt over their feuds with May. Although that clearly could not have been further from the truth, this canard stigmatized and stifled the project in certain circles. The incessant stopping and starting of preproduction work on the project compounded the skepticism. Furie debunked these rumors while Parent and Solms pleaded ignorance on the matter. Says Furie, "Jeannie was hired because she had an Oscar nomination under her belt, and the other candidates did not. She was hired because she felt to us like the best person to fill the shoes of that character. Any devious studio intrigue or background action never played into casting the film, nor did it affect our rewrites. The rewrites would have happened in any event, with or without Jeannie. And I personally liked what Jeannie was doing."

Elaine May, while feuding with Paramount after infamously belaboring the directing tasks on her newest film, her equally troubled sophomore feature *Mikey and Nicky* (1976), accepted two dinner invitations to the Furies' house before production commenced on *Sheila Levine*. Linda Furie recalls, "She was a fun, eccentric guest. I think I offended her at one point with a joke I made that compared 'falling in love with your psychiatrist' to something unfavorable. When she left, Sid told me that she did fall in love with her psychiatrist. I was completely unaware, so I've always felt that comment might have unsettled her." Indeed, May had married Dr. David L. Rubinfine in 1963; the marriage lasted until the latter's death in 1982.

Furie and Korshak soon began auditioning actors to play the film's newly created ad hoc male lead character Sam Stoneman. Roy Scheider at that point had not developed a bankable name as a male lead, having mainly been cast as a key supporting player in *The French Connection*, in which he complemented Gene Hackman's hard-boiled "Popeye" Doyle, playing second fiddle and sidekick. *French Connection* producer Phil D'Antoni had given Scheider his first starring role in his own directorial debut *The Seven-Ups* (1973), which received raves for its daring car chase, but little else. Scheider was Furie's first and only choice for the role of Sam Stoneman, although Richard Dreyfuss auditioned for the role before flying to Montreal to begin work on Ted Kotcheff's *The Apprenticeship of Duddy Kravitz*. "Richard gave a great reading, but he would have been too young for the role," Furie explains.

In an interview with Rex Reed, published in the critic's book *Valentines & Vitriol,* Scheider explained that, after *The Seven-Ups,* he "immediately tried to get out of the cop mold." He liked *Sheila Levine* because it reinforced his position as a leading man: "I played a doctor, I didn't shoot anybody, I didn't muscle anybody. It was a light romantic comedy." A New Yorker himself, Scheider claimed that he had "a strong feeling for the Sams and Sheilas of Manhattan" because he had "come in contact with these people every day." He also joked with Furie, and later Reed, that he would now "rather be chased by girls than by automobiles."[5] Furie, who found the star immediately likable, also deeply appreciated how Scheider had internalized the film's New York milieu from having lived there. Because the Paramount lot in Hollywood was to double for most of the New York locations, the director believed that any input that could heighten the illusion of New York was welcomed and needed.

Jeannie Berlin personally recommended her close friend Rebecca Dianna Smith, a newcomer whose only previous movie role had been in a low-budget horror film, for the role of Kate Christianson, Sheila's flighty actress roommate and romantic rival (who came complete with an ever-appropriate shiksa surname). "Jeannie brought in Rebecca and I immediately thought she was right for it," remembers Furie. "There was never any casting pressure. It was just Jeannie's suggestion and it happened to be a good one. She did a wonderful job in the role." Once again rounding out the cast were Sid Melton and Janet Brandt, effectively reprising their roles from *Hit!* as almost the same aging Jewish couple—in this context, as Sheila's meddling parents. Another *Hit!* alumnus, Noble Willingham, was given a small part as a flustered elementary school principal. The rest of the cast were unknowns and film novices recruited from either stage or television.

The tenuous nature of the project during the development phase risked and finally ensured the loss of cinematographer John Alonzo, who had lensed Furie's previous two pictures. Alonzo, a cameraman Furie admired for his quickness and adaptability, became unavailable because Paramount and Roman Polanski had conscripted him to replace veteran cinematographer Stanley Cortez on *Chinatown*. Furie turned to the fledgling Donald M. Morgan, not yet the popular Hollywood cinematographer he later became, to fill the vacant position. In 1973 Morgan's only theatrically released feature as cinematographer was a B-movie Western called *Santee*, starring Glenn Ford. However, Morgan by that time had established a reputable name doing aerial photography on productions like *Skyjacked* and *Ace Eli and Rodger of the Skies*. "When I got the call from Sid Furie's secretary, Marlene, I was then doing aerial work on a Peter Fonda picture called *Dirty Mary, Crazy Larry*," says Donald Morgan. "Marlene left a phone message at my motel, which was somewhere in California in the middle of nowhere. Not too long before that, I had done the aerial work for a commercial that Sid was directing and he rode around in a helicopter to shoot with me."

The untried Morgan doubted that he could realistically be in the running for a full cinematographer's position, deducing that he was simply being tapped for more aerial work. When asked his availability to shoot *Sheila Levine Is Dead and Living in New York* over a more extended period than what was normal for a specialty shooter, he quickly realized the scope of the offer. "What I later found out is that Sid had seen *Santee* on an airplane," says Morgan. "He asked the producer to find out who shot it, and that's how he tracked me down. He didn't even remember me from the commercial. It was only from seeing *Santee,* so that was funny and rather ironic. He took a tremendous chance hiring me, but he gave me my start as a Hollywood cinematographer." Morgan, who was officially hired on November 9, 1973, remembers that in early meetings, Furie would often playfully remind him that he had "hit the big-time now." "*Sheila Levine Is Dead and Living in New York* was probably the most exciting picture I've ever been on in my life," remembers Morgan. "Gordon Willis was shooting *Godfather II* on the stage next door; the pilot for 'Happy Days' was shooting on another stage, and Conrad Hall was shooting *The Day of the Locust* throughout the lot."[6]

No sooner did the project finally go before the cameras in January 1974 than tensions started mounting between the quarrelsome Jeannie Berlin and most everyone on set. Gray Frederickson, a past member of the Furie retinue who was then working with Francis Ford Coppola on the neighboring Paramount stage, shooting *The Godfather Part II,* visited Furie's set. "I remember clearly Sidney and Harry Korshak both saying that Jeannie Berlin was a pain in the ass," Frederickson comments, laughing.

"On the first day of shooting, we couldn't get anything done," Donald Morgan recalls. "Jeannie argued about everything all the damn time. Sidney told me to go and light for a shot in this elevator because he told me that we had to put something on the camera report that we shot something, anything at all, that day." Berlin's incessant combativeness with Furie, Harry Korshak, and the writers took a toll on crew morale as well. Morgan continues, "We could never get an early start. My camera and lighting crew would be waiting so long while we tried to get a shot in. I was worried about the crew disappearing and visiting the other sets at Paramount. If the arguing and waiting around stopped, we had to make sure they were around on a moment's notice in case we were finally ready to shoot. We actually had to run some wire with a red light attached to a room where the crew would be gathered playing cards and stuff. When the light went off in that room, they'd come back. This was highly irregular even for a low-budget production. Usually on a movie set, you're working steadily until the end of your day."

Nowhere else were the tensions thicker than between Scheider and Berlin. Scheider later told Rex Reed that "the hardest thing about the film was working with Jeannie Berlin. You don't do a picture with that one unless you've got a personal stake in it. She's very disturbed, and it was hard for the director."[7] Furie remembers that Berlin would "totally recoil from Roy" in the romantic scenes. Parent and Solms, who had been announced to the press on January 9, 1974, as having bit parts in the film's party sequence, were often present to witness the burgeoning brouhahas.

Scheider, who seemed to be growing weary and restless from continuing to vent his angry frustrations at Berlin, soon aimed his outbursts at Furie, using his director as an emotional punching bag.

> He was pissed off at her and would snap at me. One day, when he blew up at me, I just said, "Come on outside, let's fight!" I think it shocked him, but he followed me out the door. We got outside the sound stage at the studio and I said, "Okay, let's fight!" He just looked at me and said, "Sid, this is stupid" and I said "Of course it's stupid." He apologized to me for his behavior and for taking it out on me, and I apologized for not having control over my own emotions and, for the rest of the shoot, everything was great between the two of us. We had a great time together, particularly when Jeannie finally left the movie.

Donald Morgan remembers another incident with Berlin on the warpath. "There was a scene in which Rebecca Dianna Smith is required to cry, and Sid expected her to cry on command at an appointed time during the scene, which is not unusual at all in my experience. Actors can work themselves into that headspace fairly easily in my experience. Jeannie Berlin just attacked Sid, saying stuff like, 'How can you direct any actor to cry on command like that?! You know nothing about people's emotions! You think people can just turn off and on! Let's see you cry on command!'" It was then, with a sudden thud, that Furie dropped whatever materials he was holding in his hands and started weeping, appearing all so suddenly inconsolable. Morgan was astonished. "The tears were real, dripping off his chin. He was really crying! The crew and everyone who was present started applauding him. It was really something . . . quite a scene." After about a minute, Furie gave his bawling and blubbering a proper coda and told her, with tears still streaming down his face, "This is what you're all paid to do as actors. If you want to argue about that, we can waste even more time. Whaddaya say?" Morgan confesses, "I remember thinking in that moment that the guy had such guts. To my mind, it was unforgettable."

Furie's best friend, director Paul Lynch, remembers, "Jeannie Berlin would take these long lunches with her friends, including Rebecca Dianna Smith. I guess her other friends would visit the lot to see her. And when she got back, for one reason or another, she couldn't do anything else for the rest of the day."

The pressures of the *Sheila Levine* set were proving tremendous, and it was rubbing off on Furie in adverse ways. The script was, as ever, constantly in a state of flux, with the credited screenwriters disheartened and openly angered by material they no longer recognized, and a loose cannon of a leading lady caused daily strife among the cast and crew. In fine tradition and in step with his previous work, Furie found the most solace in plotting, staging, and lighting the film's moody visuals. Furie had conspired with Otto Heller on a perceptible sense of visual style for *The Ipcress File* ten years prior, and he proceeded to do the same in a new genre, this time with a cinematographer eager to prove himself on his first studio picture. Morgan recalls, "When we first started shooting, all the suits came down from their offices and asked Furie, 'Does this guy know that he's shooting a comedy? It's too dark' and Sid just went completely nuts. He said, 'Have you guys ever laughed at radio? You don't see anybody's eyes on radio!' The next day, I kind of brightened things up a bit. We went to dailies and Sid started yelling, 'They've ruined you! They've ruined you! Go back to the way you were working before. Don't let those guys talk you into lighting brighter.'"[8]

Furie's artistic statement about the film is fairly definitive: "The movie is a noir. There is no question about it. I wanted Don to give it a shadowy, burnished look, an 'urban' look, and we discussed this in great detail. We were both in love with Gordon Willis and his work on *The Godfather*, and Don became aware that I had an ongoing love affair with dark, moody, high-ratio lighting, and that was it. It's film noir . . . that's just how I saw it."

With sixteen days left of shooting, the temperamental Jeannie Berlin walked off the movie after a row with Furie, never to return. "She left in a real huff-and-puff, very angrily," remembers Morgan. Paramount head Frank Yablans threatened to sue the actress if she did not return to finish shooting. Furie appealed to Yablans, and then pleaded with him, not to move on his threat, claiming that he could finish the picture without her. "I had had it with her by that point," Furie recalls. "I knew it would be easier to finish it without her." But still the question remained: how could the picture really finish shooting without a lead actress whose character appears in every scene?

"What are we going to do now?" asked a beleaguered Morgan, justifiably concerned that his first big opportunity to shoot a major studio movie was about to get scuttled. "Well," Furie began, revving up the tone of his voice to inflect a hardened military general attempting to lift the morale of his battle-weary troops, "I'll tell you what we're *not* going to do. We're not going to let some twenty-four-year-old pain-in-the-ass run us out of the business!"

Needless to say, the production had turned into a first-class mess. Furie, however, requested that Yablans not slap Berlin with a lawsuit. Donald Morgan remembers, "I got a call from Sid telling me to find plain, inconspicuous, black cases with no Panavision insignias or markings, to house the most necessary camera equipment we would need to take to New York. He told me, 'We're going to finish this fucking movie without her, and we're going to do it on the sly . . . and don't breathe a word about this to anyone, because if Paramount finds out what we're doing, they're going to shut us down for good.'" Furie's master plan for cutting his Gordian knot involved shanghaiing Roy Scheider, Jeannie Berlin's double, and a small skeleton crew to New York to shoot footage he could edit against shots of Berlin carefully lifted from other scenes. He also ordered Morgan to not even tell his camera operator what they were doing; Morgan would do his own operating for what remained to be shot, baggage-checking the equipment and taking along only his camera assistant (Jack N. Green, the future Oscar-nominated cinematographer of *Unforgiven*). Morgan's most important job would be to effectively copy the lighting to seamlessly match these earlier shots. As Furie had done on *The Appaloosa* with Brando and his stand-in Paul Baxley, he shot Berlin's double mostly from behind. For the unshot ending, he juxtaposed terse line readings from Berlin in another scene with new "emergency dialogue" to match, written by Furie for Scheider.

"I knew it could be done and that, for all intents and purposes, it would work," says Furie. "At that point, I just wanted the shooting to be over with. It was a very stressful scenario." Furie and Morgan had to resort to shooting a dark-haired stand-in from behind, lighting her frontal shots darkly enough so viewers would not notice. These shots appear mostly in the film's third act. Morgan remembers, "Sid and my crew would be in a New York elevator. When the door would open, Sid would peek his head out to see if the coast was clear. If it was, we'd grab these shots with Roy and Jeannie's double . . . no permits, nothing. It was like we were committing a crime. He was a live wire on that shoot. Wonderfully unpredictable."

Scheider was scheduled to start production on *Jaws* with Steven Spielberg on May 2, 1974. *Jaws* wrapped its own tumultuous production on October 6, 1974, after which Scheider returned to finish small pickup shots for *Sheila Levine* in November, tying up the few loose ends that had been left from the provisional "rescue-the-film shoot" in New York the previous April. Scheider wrapped Furie's film on November 17, 1974, according to *Variety.* Furie recalls that in the summer of 1974, "the film was coming together very well in the editing, considering the circumstances."

For the first and only time in his entire career, a Sidney J. Furie film had gone over schedule, wrapping a full five weeks late. "I thought we were all going to get fired," recalls Don Morgan. "I just knew that we couldn't be this far over schedule and not get into trouble with the higher-ups. The suits would come down and try to get things moving, but on most days, it just wasn't going to happen. It was out of control. I don't know how Sidney kept sane."

While waiting to complete *Sheila Levine Is Dead and Living in New York,* Furie missed out on other offers that would have proved lucrative. Producer Ed Feldman met Furie while developing *The Other Side of the Mountain* (1975), a project that unexpectedly became a sleeper hit under the direction of Larry Peerce. Feldman groomed the project as an inspirational romantic drama about a paralyzed female downhill racing ski champion who finds the strength to recover, thanks to the love of an extraordinary man. David Seltzer's script, adapted from E. G. Valens's book *A Long Way Up,* was based on the true story of Jill Kinmont. This was a logical fit for Furie after the not-dissimilar *Lady Sings the Blues.* Feldman had pitched the project to Furie one night at a dinner. Furie, intrigued, showed up unannounced at Feldman's house one morning to offer his services as director. Feldman recalls, "I glanced out my second-storey window at home and see this Talmudic-looking person walking up the driveway. Dark clothing, head bowed. He could have been mistaken for a rabbi on his way to Saturday morning services. It was Sidney Furie. It turned out that he read the script and wanted to direct the movie. And most important, he will direct it for $75,000. Furie normally earned several hundred thousand a film. You know, it's easy for people to say I'm in your corner. Well, Furie was in my corner."[9] Universal, it turns out, had been eager to do a picture with Furie after the financial and critical success of *Lady Sings the Blues*. So, with Furie in Feldman's camp, Universal green-lit the project. "But one day, I got a call from Ned Tanen asking me to come over," says Feldman. "He told me that Furie's current picture with Paramount was going over-schedule in New York, and Tanen thought it would be long enough to miss the snow season."[10]

Composer Michel Legrand, who had previously scored *Lady Sings the Blues* with Furie, was signed on to write *Sheila*'s velvety romantic score. With a wispy, almost diaphanous, stand-alone string section, the score consists of a lush central love theme that reinforced the cautious pas de deux between the Berlin and Scheider characters. Countering this is a funky, brassy party tune featured prominently throughout. Though Furie and editor Argyle Nelson were both pleased with how the film was shaping up, they were shaken when it was booed off the screen during a sneak preview at the Sutton Theatre on Manhattan's Upper East Side. Gail Parent and Kenny Solms were present to hear the Bronx cheers. Parent remembers, cringing, "I asked this woman in her thirties what she thought of the film as she was walking out. She looked at me and with this air of sarcasm, just said 'Didn't Gail Parent read her own novel?' It was also the shock that my novel had been transformed from a sardonic dark comedy into a kind of romantic melodrama. And it was so darkly lit that sometimes you couldn't see anything!" Kenny Solms quips, "It was like that scene in *Singin' in the Rain* where they preview the movie and it goes badly." About the traumatic preview screening, Furie conjectures, "You couldn't have come to a hipper crowd than the East Side of New York in that period. You were going to be dead if a movie didn't work in synch with their politics."

Furie, still not completely discouraged, took the film back to the editing room to work with Argyle Nelson on making a few changes to better their odds of pulling out a hat-trick. "Sidney was so sure the film would wind up being a hit that he offered to exchange our percentage points on the film's profits for his financial interest in a professional basketball team,"

Kenny Solms recalls. "We should have taken the basketball points." Furie, who for the first time in his career saw "A Sidney J. Furie Film" placed above the title in the opening credits, sat through the final cut of the film in the Paramount theater six or seven times in a row before release, checking the show-prints for exhibition. "I remember being moved sitting alone in that theater," says Furie. "I remember being proud of the way it turned out, thinking it was a good movie that would get through to audiences and be a hit. And after all these years, I still like the final product."

When he became aware that Paramount was just going to let the film quietly "escape" without promoting it in much of any way, he aimed straight for the top and called Charles Bluhdorn's office. Attempting to get the "big cheese" to intervene on his behalf was no small feat; Bluhdorn was embroiled in various corporate disputes at Gulf+Western and never returned the call. Furie's sturdy confidence was, most decidedly, to no avail.

Audiences mostly stayed away and critics widely massacred *Sheila Levine Is Dead and Living in New York* at its New York premiere on May 16, 1975. Vincent Canby of the *New York Times* was perhaps the most vicious and unsparing, bludgeoning it with labels like "grade-A mess" and "mere exploitation," adding insult to injury in calling Berlin's central character "a tired Jewish joke." He writes, "Miss Berlin, who was so good in her mother's *The Heartbreak Kid,* plays Sheila with bovine gracelessness that, I suspect, is what was required by the script and by the director, Sidney J. Furie." Pauline Kael's excoriating review stung no less. "Not only is this picture full of scenes that were clichés the first time they were done," she wrote in her *New Yorker* review, "but Sidney Furie brings worse than nothing to them."

Somewhat kinder was Charles Champlin of the *Los Angeles Times,* who, in wisecracking that "a New York book has become a Hollywood movie" also managed to praise it as a "well-made escapist fling in a time which could use more of them." Many singled out Scheider's performance as the film's primary strength. Molly Haskell of *New York* magazine wrote in her review, titled "A Terminal Case of Singles," "We shouldn't blame Roy Scheider for being a spectacularly compelling leading man. He exudes a quiet, sexy, old-fashioned, Shetland-sweater 50's kind of charm and makes the transition from semi-cad to committed lover with grace." Charles Champlin wrote that the "perfectly cast" Scheider is "a terrific discovery" and "the welcome surprise of the movie," singling out "the remarkable soliloquy near the end," which he ruled "a consummate piece of romantic acting." Rex Reed likewise recognized an upshot, deeming the film "a disaster for everyone but Scheider, who came out of it with a deluge of fan mail, a new leading man reputation and an elevated salary."

In what was both the most quoted critical rebuke against the film and the most sweeping political coup de grace in the eyes of the seething feminist movement, Judith Crist proclaimed in *New York Magazine* that the screenwriters and the director had "set the cause of women back some forty years." Furie, laughing about it decades later, quips, "Luckily, it only set the women's movement back an evening."

Amid the wreckage and embarrassment, the film was not without positive notices. Art Murphy of *Variety* called it "a very sweet movie" with "principals that are interesting and likeable," calling attention to the fact that "Furie's direction is totally free of the prop gimmicks that used to be a trademark of the happily dead 60's directing style; herein he often lets the characters do the work in long master shots." He also singled out Jeannie Berlin's performance as "outstanding" and Roy Scheider's as a "major career milestone." John Dorr for the *Hollywood Reporter* proclaimed that "a new major actress-comedienne is born on the screen, complete with her own mythology." Dorr also cited the master shots, calling them "Ozu-like," while complimenting the cinematographer and art director on the darkly shadowed interiors and stating that they "define the feminine point-of-view of a true woman's picture." The dialogue was acclaimed as "compassionate and personal," and Furie was given plaudits because he "dares to hold long static two shots if the scene can play that way." Eminent film historian William Everson, a critic and preservationist, writing for *Films in Review,* observed, "If the players are, in real life, reasonably intelligent and wide-awake, then the performances are masterly exhibitions of the 'method' technique." However, it was Gene Siskel, reviewing the film for the *Chicago Tribune* back-to-back with *Alice Doesn't Live Here Anymore,* who gave its most glowing notice:

> Two films about women opened in Chicago over the weekend: One screamed into town laden with Academy Award nominations and chorusing critical praise; the other tip-toed in silently for what looks like the old two-weeks-and-out routine. If anything, it should be the other way around. . . . Right away we know we are dealing with a movie female who is someone special. Most movie women, and most movie men for that matter, know exactly

what they want to do or what they feel at any given moment in the film. The source of their knowledge is that their lives have been scripted and that the actors involved can't breathe unpredictability into predictable responses. In the final analysis, it is the unpredictability of its lead characters that makes *Sheila Levine* intriguing. . . . More lasting than the script's considerable humor are the extended shots of Jeannie Berlin's face. When the camera lingers after she says sentences containing more than one emotion, we're given the chance to study the face of a woman with depth. That doesn't happen very often in today's movies. In tomorrow's review, we'll look at *Alice Doesn't Live Here Anymore*, a film that is less successful trying to do the very same thing—balance humor and emotional depth.

The film made back its paltry $1 million cost but made no profit before hastily disappearing as a critical and commercial flop that ironically echoed the failure of Ernest Lehman's adaptation of *Portnoy's Complaint* (1972). That said, *Sheila Levine* was a stillborn picture that was perhaps damned by its own title. Audiences who knew the book were understandably expecting a more faithful adaptation of the film's professed source, only to be appalled and disappointed with something that freely departed from what they had been led to believe. Had the film been retitled, repackaged, and distanced from any explicit connection to the book, it might have fared better. The segment of the maddened crowd spoiled by their allegiance to Gail Parent's novel could see the film as nothing other than a travesty. That Jeannie Berlin and the team of Parent and Solms refused to do any sort of promotion for the film, and that Scheider had already alluded to a troubled shoot in the press, made the critics smell trouble in advance, although Paramount's public-relations department diligently prevented news of Berlin's early departure from leaking to the public. It is fair to assume that the critics were sharpening their spears well before the picture ever hit movie screens because of these "telltale signs" alone.

Berlin's walk-off irrevocably tarnished her film acting career; she did not land another movie role until 1990. Film director Larry Cohen, who directed Berlin in his debut feature *Bone* (1972), says,

The rumors about her bad behavior on the *Sheila Levine* set were all over Hollywood and they single-handedly ruined her career.

No one would dare go anywhere near her after that. On *Bone,* she was still an unknown; she could be fussy and hard-headed, but she never got out of hand with me. On *Sheila Levine,* I guess she thought she was a big movie star and put on the whole prima donna act. I ran into her a few times over the years, including one time when she was on her way to an audition with Martin Scorsese for *The King of Comedy.* The *Sheila Levine* stigma had to still be hanging over her at that point, and Sandra Bernhard got that part. The moral of the story, I guess, is that you don't just walk off a film thinking that people won't remember.

Claims Furie, "After the movie bombed, I started receiving clippings of all the bad reviews in my home mailbox. No stamps or anything. These were personally delivered. I don't have one suspect. There are a few people I suspect. We never knew about whatever good reviews there were, nor would have paid as much attention to them if we did." Clive Denton, in a *Cinema Canada* magazine piece called "Furie Then and Now," which traced the director's career trajectory up to that point, remarked that while the director's other recent Hollywood films "showed a clear regression from the freshness and compassion" in the earlier films, "a commercial failure, *Sheila Levine,* seemed perversely encouraging, being closer to an artistic success." Denton noted that "a Furie trademark—respect and caring for his characters—reasserted itself strongly" in that film.[11]

To this day, the film has never been released in a tangible home video format. Beyond that, the original elements are allegedly either in jeopardy or lost. When critic and ex-programmer Scott Foundas attempted to schedule the film for Lincoln Center's "Hollywood Jew Wave" series in November 2011, a Paramount archivist informed him that there were no viewable film materials fit to be shown. "I really wanted to screen that particular film because it featured Jeannie Berlin in a rare leading role, which is something we would never . . . really get to see again,"[12] says Foundas. Recently, however, *Sheila Levine Is Dead and Living in New York* resurfaced on certain Internet streaming video sites and as a downloadable file in iTunes, in a complete anamorphic transfer from a negative scan. A micro-cult exists for this film as well as for his previous film *Hit!,* as evidenced by a healthy surge of positive online reviews written by fans of the film, on both IMDb and the Turner Classic Movies page.

In *Sheila Levine Is Dead and Living in New York,* Sheila and Sam's "square" relationship is founded in their "meet cute" scene, in which Sam attempts a curious pickup line ("I killed somebody today"). This segues into the awkward discussion between Sheila and Sam involving the ethics of abortion, which offended Gail Parent and Kenny Solms. The film was, in all likelihood, doomed with progressive audiences from that early moment onward. Following the Supreme Court's 1973 *Roe vs. Wade* decision, which was still fresh on the collective public's mind, feminists and ideologues of the day were not about to sit idly through a movie in which the male romantic lead soapboxed about expropriating their abortion rights. Supplement this sequence with another in which Sheila consoles a female friend weeping in a bedroom after flippantly offering herself to a man as a sex object at a singles party held at Sheila's apartment, and one realizes that *Sheila Levine Is Dead and Living in New York* had no chance of engaging with a 1975 target audience. However, had another director approached the film with a clear and tidy epochal feminist agenda, feminist or otherwise, the film would have dated more readily. Nonetheless, all of these factors also unfortunately helped to kill the film before it could be born.

The maltreated film remains a markedly rare seventies film, unusual for depicting the Jewish female as victor, in whatever degree triumphantly. In this much, it becomes a romantic fantasy, the direct inverse of and complement to the working-class "romantic reality" that Furie depicted in *The Leather Boys* (1963) twelve years previously. Furie plucks Berlin's victimized character from *The Heartbreak Kid* and transplants it into a dark urban world, far away from the blazing white sunlight of Miami that *Heartbreak* cinematographer Owen Roizman captures with measured, tasteful overexposure in May's earlier film. Jeannie Berlin's Sheila Levine is a self-sufficient, self-determining "career woman" who scores the ideal man—a Jewish one at that—and the film does not consider her final triumph as a novelty, an inside joke, or a piece of wink-wink irony. In this respect, it was quietly and inconspicuously revolutionary, for one brief moment in time breaking an ever-popular, ever-revolving trend that capitalized on the popular romantic screen pairing of "Jewish male and shiksa," for which the seventies had been a gilded age. Woody Allen, the foremost Jewish-American presence in American comedy of the time, had teamed with the "goyishe" Diane Keaton to become a movie odd couple beginning with *Play It Again, Sam* (1972). Elliott Gould had been cast opposite prominent Gentile actresses like Candice Bergen, Brenda Vaccaro, Dyan

Cannon, and Jennifer O'Neill, and Dustin Hoffman had been cast opposite Mia Farrow, Katharine Ross, Susan George, and Valerie Perrine.

Furie's themes of questioning duty and personal commitment emerge once again, this time with a feminine redefinition, as seen through the lens of the New York singles world. Sheila is committed to her pursuit of an idyllic life in which she is married to Mr. Right and has a "creative job." When she finds the latter, she becomes duty-bound to her job at a children's records company, assumedly in an effort to forget how gypped she feels about the former. Scheider's Sam Stoneman, first professing a commitment to bachelorhood and satyrdom, soon finds himself unwillingly committed to Sheila's roommate when he believes he has gotten her pregnant. However, Sam's heart is turned when he discovers that he is emotionally committed to Sheila. The seeming left turn Furie took to make this film after *Hit!* still reveals the same "author" at work. As throughout most of Furie's prime body of work, at least one character is driven to make a central identity-defining choice.

The film in occasional stretches feels as if it has crossed over into skitty sitcom territory, as in the section where Sheila desperately "dolls herself up like Messalina"[13] to woo back Sam. The latter scene becomes something like a grotesque burlesque on the absurd desperation of seventies New York singles. These comedic attempts can be very boldly stated, if not extravagant, making the shifts into Delmer Daves–style melodrama jarring, but no less intriguing.

One of the elements that keeps the picture from becoming a featherweight exercise is Furie and cinematographer Donald M. Morgan's decision to use a dark lighting and a color palette. The film's texture is earthy, burnished, sometimes even dingy. Across the board, Morgan starkly lights Fernando Carrere's sets to the point where the specter of Gordon Willis certainly feels palpable. It essentially feels like a Rhoda Morganstern story dressed up in film noir trappings. Characters often emerge from dark corners into strategically placed eye-lights and "kickers" (backlights), and facial features emerge often carefully obscured in the recesses of explicitly urban spaces. With *Sheila Levine Is Dead and Living in New York*'s bold visual style, Furie clearly experiments in exploring the elasticity of the romantic comedy. Furie and Morgan also effectively take full advantage of the anamorphic screen size they have chosen, often as assuredly as Furie and Heller had in *The Ipcress File*.

Sheila Levine Is Dead and Living in New York also showcases more scenes and sequences played out in handsomely mounted and impressively sustained long takes, a tendency that started with *A Dangerous Age* and became decidedly more frequent beginning in the director's Paramount period. Early in the film, an unbroken master shot clocks in at five minutes and eleven seconds. British critic and historian Leslie Halliwell's 1967 description of Furie as "the Canadian with the restless camera" sees its rebuttal here.[14] This shot, encompassing a whole scene in which Scheider attempts to bed a nervous Berlin with the help of shallow reasoning, is an effort to distance us from Berlin, also magnifying the initial distance between Berlin and Scheider's characters. Furie places them on totally opposite and extreme ends of the wide 2.35:1-sized frame. This is no new concept or visual schema where anamorphic wide screen is concerned. The effect is of course lost in the 1980s network TV version of the film, which turns this single shot into a series of cuts between two fragmented and cropped "faux medium shots." The more precise division of screen space is especially striking. Scheider assumes nearly two-thirds of the frame (counting feet on a coffee table), with Berlin ensconced uneasily and uncomfortably in the last of the thirds, at a discernible distance. From Scheider's point of view in the scene, she is a specimen to him—yet another go at a potential conquest. Coming early in the film, this scene's single camera placement, and the way it is sustained, heightens our consideration of Berlin's vulnerability as a new arrival to New York City. Her visual presence in the scene feels relatively microscopic (with a composition that almost suggests a microscope) compared to male lead Roy Scheider's foregrounded placement.

The camera often spatially distances us from Sheila. Furie loses her in vast urban spaces, behind a mountainous pile of items on a cluttered office desk, burrowed far away in a tight kitchen corner, pocketed in a bedroom doorway in a far corner of the frame. Psychologically, Furie attempts to establish this distance in an effort to make the audience desire more proximity. Furie's camera also meditates on what it is that the city itself is doing to our Harrisburg heroine, that is, making her a smaller entity relative to her new environment. For instance, the first long-take encounter with Scheider mentioned earlier is followed immediately after by a three-minute long-take in which Sheila is returned to prominence in the frame. Furie continues to strategically play with this unusual visual pacing throughout the film.

Another later scene, between Sheila and her nagging parents at a family breakfast table, approximates Furie's earlier "Wild Angle" style. As Mother and Father Levine meddle in their daughter's life, they are framed on either side of the back of the irritated Sheila's head, which assumes a large, voided middle aspect of the frame. Furie is also able to amplify emotion through camera movement, in almost exactly the same way he did in *The Leather Boys,* mainly through dolly shots that push in to close-ups of Berlin in the middle section of the film, most notably during the wedding sequence, in which a humiliated Sheila watches her younger sister tie the knot before she does.

The New York of the film is clearly a kind of simulacrum, a strangely enchanted "dream New York" that, to anyone who knows the real New York intimately, seems charmingly artificial, in almost the same way Stanley Kubrick's "mock New York" in *Eyes Wide Shut* (1999) appears. As Kubrick's New York reimagining heightens the dreamlike qualities of his story, Furie re-creates New York to accentuate the almost fairytale proportions of his ugly-duckling story. It also augments the sense of the film as a romantic fantasy and complements the tonal shifts from soap opera to broad comedy and, occasionally, to musical (in the scenes involving the Singing Squirrels recording group). Furie recounts how, when he visited New York with production designer Fernando Carrere, he "kept on noticing the smoke pipes coming out of the sewers." Having seen them on many street corners, Carrere adopted them into the cityscape he created on the studio backlot, along with the equally ubiquitous building scaffolding. Even in scenes lacking in incident, like one toward the end in which a lovesick, confused Scheider exits a bar in the daytime and strolls down a street littered with background "local color" extras, the film's misty-eyed New York always feels just out of reach from direct reality. This is a key aspect of the film's larger design; this is a storybook Manhattan.

Roy Scheider's stock in the film industry rose astronomically following the releases of *Sheila Levine* and *Jaws*. Although Jeannie Berlin's personification of the title heroine, who is front and center in every scene throughout the film, does resonate, Scheider's performance is perhaps the most purely compelling, and even more so because it manages to chart a gradual transformation in the Sam Stoneman character, from goodtime Charlie to henpecked he-man afflicted with quivering puppy love, without ever upstaging Berlin or any of the other actors. That Sam Stoneman was a pronounced departure for Scheider facilitated the actor's rise out of genre acting and into the mainstream, since he was only four years away from his career peak in Bob Fosse's *All That Jazz* (1979), for which he was Oscar-nominated. The sequence that critic Charles Champlin identified as the standout, Scheider's finale speech in the recording studio, in which he recounts his most humiliating memory from childhood, reflects a sensitivity in Sam's character that is brilliantly handled. It is paced slowly and designed to achieve a more engrossed, sustained emotional impact.

This is offset well by the implicit battle of wills and wiles between the superficially pretty, helter-skelter shiksa and our Jewish girl from Harrisburg. The characters' assorted rivalries feel civil, almost fragile, never stated so explicitly in direct drama as to disturb a kind of equilibrium (since Sheila's low self-esteem would never permit an outright altercation). Much more, therefore, hinges on the kind of close-ups Furie uses in quantity, in which we can perceive things happening nonverbally. Considering the implicit love triangle at the center of the drama, here, Furie works again with spatial configuration motifs, this time expressing this fragility through three-shots and triangular compositions. As the triangle complicates the pas de deux at the film's core, the quietness of the drama is thus visually never stale, dormant, or unconflicted.

"I was heartbroken when it flopped and part of me still hopes that it is finding some audience somewhere," Furie recalls.

> The Jeannie Berlin problems might have caused a lot of uproar at the time, but when all is said and done, I think she gave an excellent performance in the film and it is still a film of my own that I love. Bad reviews bother me for a day or two after the release, but I am usually able to move on quickly. Again, you do what you can do and keep movin' movin' movin' right along, just like the Johnny Cash tune in *Little Fauss and Big Halsy*. Before the movie even premiered, I was already working on my next film, *Gable and Lombard.*

However, friend Paul Lynch remembers, "I've never seen Sidney more withdrawn after a movie's failure. It really had an effect on him with *Sheila,* probably more than it did on any of the others that didn't do well, because he really thought it worked. But he's by far the most resilient guy that I know and just went right back to work." Linda Furie sums it all up by stating that making *Sheila Levine* "was definitely not the happiest experience in Sid's career."

Screenwriter Barry Sandler, who scribed for Furie on his follow-up *Gable and Lombard* (1976), has known *Sheila Levine* screenwriters Gail Parent and Kenny Solms personally for years. He remembers,

> In the early stages of working with Sidney on *Gable and Lombard,* he showed me *Sheila Levine.* This was before it was released, alone in a screening room at Paramount. I told him I had read Gail's book, so he was testing out the movie on me knowing that. I honestly loved it, and was really moved by it. The film was certainly a completely different interpretation of Gail's novel, but a really beautiful one as far as I was concerned. Gail and Kenny still think I'm a little weird for praising it. I believe deep down that if it had been called *The Girl from Harrisburg,* it would have fared better.

Such an even-tempered outlook on the film's nature as a literary adaptation aligns with film director Richard Brooks's conviction: "If you're going to make a book just as a book, then there's no need to make it a film at all."

The failure or success of *Sheila Levine Is Dead and Living in New York* aside, Furie's real cinematic Waterloo was directly ahead of him, with his next project.

Current sentiments about *Gable and Lombard* are fairly clear-cut, much as they were when the film first hit theaters in February 1976. "That film ignited such a shit-storm against me," says Furie, cringing even today from the memory of its stormy release. Furie was not in any way exaggerating this "shit-storm." Whereas there had been some redeeming reviews for *Sheila Levine Is Dead and Living in New York* to stand up against a strong tide of critical hostility, there was little such comfort for *Gable and Lombard,* a veritable fiasco that was so universally lambasted and reviled by critics that hardly a single reviewer of any stature opposed the tide. "Looking back, it was probably a bad choice and a bad idea," says Furie. "Nowadays, when I've seen biopics of people who I know what they look like, I've always been very uncomfortable. It's unnerving to me, and you really can't ever do it well. It should have been loosely based on the story of Gable and Lombard and titled something like *Him & Her,* so people would have asked, 'Is the story kind of based on Gable and Lombard?' But by actually naming it *Gable and Lombard,* we all had too much to live up to, and people went into the theater with these great expectations." This is not to say, however, that he truly regrets anything.

In a 1975 interview with journalist Clifford Terry, now writing for the *Chicago Tribune,* Furie expressed a kind of unbounding enthusiasm for the project, the inverse of his present feelings about the final outcome: "I feel like a missionary about this picture!," he proclaimed on the set in between takes.[15] Even if Furie felt any trepidation at the time, he understandably avoided torpedoing the project with bad publicity. By the end of the whole *Gable and Lombard* ordeal, Furie sang a different tune, as he wound up, at least for a short time, a virtual outcast from the studio system, ignominiously cut loose to direct one of the most important films of his career, *The Boys in Company C* (1978), for an independent off-shore production company in Hong Kong.

After Furie's original Universal deal on *The Other Side of the Mountain* with producer Ed Feldman fell through because of the schedule overruns on *Sheila Levine,* the studio eagerly extended a standing invitation to Furie to develop another project there. He accepted the offer, taking Harry Korshak with him, when the failure of *Sheila Levine* effectively completed his tenure at Paramount after a five-picture run.

Gable and Lombard, which, like *Hit!,* started as a pet project for Furie, tells the story of the fiery affair between Clark Gable and Carole Lombard and how the two matinee idols were forced to conduct themselves in secret to protect their careers from damaging scandal. Having grown up in Toronto at the height of their fame, Furie frames the story of their off-screen romance to mirror both the zany and the operatic on-screen romances upon which they had individually founded their careers during their studio salad days. Throw into the cocktail a pastiche of embellished thirties screwball comedy, high-gloss soap opera, and a considerable amount of sexual innuendo, and *Gable and Lombard* becomes the type of exaggerated romantic fantasy built around fictionalized fact that had become germane to Furie after the success of *Lady Sings the Blues.*

Jay Weston, the man who first brought *Lady Sings the Blues* to Furie, was simultaneously producing *W.C. Fields and Me,* another Universal biopic of classic Hollywood, directed by Arthur Hiller and starring Rod Steiger in the title role. Furie was not offered the directing reins on that picture, ironic considering how both projects coincided at the studio with respective *Lady Sings the Blues* alumni, but Weston reappeared in Furie's life just a few years later. *W.C. Fields and Me,* which takes as much liberty with W.C. Fields's biography as *Gable and Lombard* does with its biographical elements (and as *Lady Sings the Blues* had with Billie Holiday's biography), was released more than a month after Furie's film. Jay Weston remembers, "After *Gable and Lombard* bombed, they just dumped our film as a result, even though they had been high on it beforehand."[16] Later in 1976, Universal appropriately double-billed the two pictures in an attempt to recoup its losses on the lackluster individual releases.

The search for a screenwriter for *Gable and Lombard* proved fast and simple when agent Jeff Berg made Furie aware of a young scribe named Barry Sandler. Furie was sent another Sandler script as a sample. Another in a line of relative rookies to whom Furie gave opportunities, Sandler had previously written only two produced features: *The Loners* (1972), starring Dean Stockwell, and *Kansas City Bomber* (1972), starring Raquel Welch. The latter had been his UCLA master's thesis script. Neither film was well reviewed, nor did they do much business. "When Sidney told me that he wanted to do the Gable and Lombard story," recalls Sandler, "my initial reaction was, 'How are you going to get an actor to be a believable Clark Gable?' And Sidney said, 'Don't worry about that right now. I made the world believe that Diana Ross was Billie Holiday.'"

Renting an office near the corner of Roxbury and Santa Monica in Beverly Hills, the two plowed through research materials, mapping out the parts of the story on which they wanted to focus. Although many of the factual materials had been changed and rearranged for the sake of drama, and although Furie noted that "it was still tons of source," Barry Sandler admitted in a 1975 interview that "you have to invent the conflict, the drama," because "if you actually filmed a documentary about Gable and Lombard, it would be pretty dull."[17] Furie delivered the spec script to Universal late on Friday afternoon, and by Monday morning, they had a deal.

During preproduction, an author named Warren G. Harris, who had just published a book called *Gable and Lombard,* sued Universal alleging that Furie and Sandler were using his book as a prime resource. "It turns out that he had used the same sources that we did to put his book together," Furie recalls. To avert a lawsuit, however, the studio begrudgingly changed the title to *Lombard and Gable.* Furie fielded the notion of calling it *The Love Story of Clark Gable and Carole Lombard* because he "loved seeing the whole thing spelled out."[18] Months later, the title was reversed again when Universal bought the rights to the book and settled the dispute.

The title was not the only bump in the road in the preproduction phase. When the project was announced, in sure echoes of the development phase of *Lady Sings the Blues,* it was placed under the proverbial microscope, with columnists reminding audiences of what Hollywood had done vis-à-vis the two trashy incarnations of the Jean Harlow story, starring Carroll Baker in one version and Carol Lynley in another, released the same year and both titled *Harlow.* Rex Reed, who was somewhat more unequivocal in his disparagement of the prospective movie, appeared on the *Tonight Show* predicting to Johnny Carson that *Gable and Lombard* would be "an absolute disaster."[19] Lana Turner's reaction was just as virulent: "How dare they!"[20] Carole Lombard's onetime costar Fred MacMurray complained, "It's too recent to be done. It's okay to do a film about Disraeli—that's a long time ago. But this is too soon."[21] When the press asked the positions of directors Edward Dmytryk and Mervyn LeRoy, they both called the project "stupid," and Dmytryk added, "Gable was the king. He really had it. There was nobody like him. I don't know what kind of ego an actor has to think he can play Gable."[22] Dmytryk's point was harsh but well taken, as the deal-making or deal-breaking question for the filmmakers, above all, was who the Furie-Korshak team selected to play the title roles. Even for the best performers, successfully playing such legends would prove a mighty tall order.

Burt Reynolds was the first to turn down the role of Gable, and he ultimately wound up doing so three times. Warren Beatty and Julie Christie expressed interest in signing onto the picture, but they both preferred that it be a fictionalized couple based loosely on a real Hollywood couple of the time. It was Beatty who suggested the title *Him & Her,* but Furie's specific vision to tell the Gable and Lombard story was at odds with this notion. Of the Beatty-Christie proposition, Barry Sandler remembers that Universal tried to convince Furie. "They said, 'Hey, you've got Warren Beatty wanting to do this movie; give it some thought.' I also think Sidney heard that Beatty could be temperamental, difficult and controlling with directors. He wanted to maintain control of the film, and didn't want to hand it over to Beatty." Steve McQueen and Ali MacGraw expressed a similar interest on the same conditions.

"Looking back on it, I probably should have gone that route," Furie regrets. "It cannot be understated that virtually everybody except the studio people challenged the idea, because it was Gable and Lombard as opposed to Joe Smith and Mary Jones or something like that." James Brolin, who had become famous for playing Dr. Kiley on the television drama *Marcus Welby, M.D.,* had first been spotted by Furie while appearing on the *Sonny Comedy Hour.* Sticking to his claim that "If you can do comedy, you can act," which had proved true at least for Diana Ross's casting in *Lady Sings the Blues* after Furie had seen her improvise comedy on her 1971 television special, Brolin was tested wearing plastic protuberances to make his ears stick out like Gable's, then was handed the role with little resistance. "I couldn't believe it was the same Jim Brolin who was on *Marcus Welby,*" says Furie. "He did about four sketches with Sonny, using different voices and my wife said 'There's your Gable.' We spent five months testing and looking at films of 108 actors and actresses, but I never really considered anyone else except Jim."[23] Brolin's Universal contract was renegotiated to accommodate both Gable and his continued tenure as Dr. Kiley on *Marcus Welby, M.D.* Centering his performance around the intent study of Gable's films, Brolin explained that he also based much of his interpretation on the advice of one man who knew Gable personally. "[He] simply told me, 'Just remember: the guy loved to smile.'"[24]

Sally Kellerman was the first actress considered for the role of Lombard, but Furie, after screening her work, felt she was more in line to play someone more urbane, like Tallulah Bankhead. Barry Sandler remembers, "Sidney and I took Valerie Perrine to lunch. Universal urged us to, since she was hot off Bob Fosse's *Lenny.* She wasn't right for us, but wound up starring in *W.C. Fields and Me.* We talked about Susan Sarandon and Candice Bergen. I tried to push Natalie Wood, because I'd always been a huge Natalie Wood fan." One after the other, actresses were named, then either second-guessed or dismissed outright, among them Lesley Ann Warren, Andra Akers, Victoria Principal, Cher, Faye Dunaway, Joanna Cassidy, and Raquel Welch. They were even in touch with agent Sue Mengers about courting Barbra Streisand, who had just starred in the failed *Funny Lady,* for the part. With Sandler, Furie would take long, four-hour drives down the California coastline, consumed by their discussions of casting the female component of the famous twosome.

On the night of February 22, 1975, a primetime made-for-television movie called *Hustling,* based on an incendiary nonfiction book by Gail Sheehy, aired on ABC. In *Hustling,* Lee Remick plays a journalist writing a magazine piece on the prostitution racket in New York City. Barry Sandler, that night attending a Hollywood party where the television had been left on, promptly called Furie on the phone and instructed him to "turn on channel 2," calling his attention not to Remick or any other name actor, but rather to a complete unknown. "Jill Clayburgh played this New York floozy hooker, very far removed from Lombard, but she was brilliant," says Furie. Friend Paul Lynch ventured with Furie and Sandler to see Clayburgh in the newly released *The Terminal Man* (1974) during a period when Furie was running all of her other work, including a small role in *Portnoy's Complaint* (1972), to get a sense of her range as a performer. By the end of his vetting, the director became convinced that he had found his lady. Furie was delighted that the "simultaneously ballsy and feminine" Clayburgh could "say a rough word or a rough line and make it sound beautiful. Even though she didn't look right in *Hustling,* we recognized a great actress."

Clayburgh, a native New Yorker who graduated from Sarah Lawrence College with the benefit of a trust fund to get her started, had been vaguely known for having dated Al Pacino in the early seventies. Her mother was the production secretary to David Merrick, and her father, Albert H. Clayburgh, was a high-powered Manhattan executive. She possessed only a scant knowledge of Carole Lombard when approached to play the role, and had never seen any of her films. "She was my girlfriend's favorite actress; that's how I heard about her,"[25] Clayburgh later told the *Los Angeles Times.* Furie promptly flew her out to Los Angeles, where an uphill battle lay ahead in convincing the studio that she was the best choice.

When *Sheila Levine*'s cinematographer Donald Morgan was occupied shooting *Let's Do It Again* (1975) for Sidney Poitier, Furie hired Robert Surtees to shoot five screen tests with five actresses dolled up as Lombard: Sally Kellerman, Joanna Cassidy, Leslie Ann Warren, Gretchen Corbett, and, finally, Clayburgh. When the tests were projected at Universal's "black tower," the studio's executive office building, Furie and Sandler heartily believed it was obvious that Clayburgh had given the best of the five tests. The executives begged to differ, with one smarmily observing that she resembled "a young Maureen Stapleton."[26] Although Furie conceded to skeptical Universal execs that the brunette Clayburgh was not a "glamour type" and that "by many standards, she's no great beauty," he would not deign to reconsider in a shallow effort to allay corporate fears. The studio execs, struck and galvanized by the filmmaker's adamancy, gave him a fifty-thousand-dollar makeover fund to have her teeth fixed (by Furie's own family dentist), her hair done, and her face otherwise beautified.

Linda Furie remembers, "Sid stormed into the house one day and asked 'Who's your hairdresser? Call our dentist. We've got a take Jill to both of them.' It was a complete makeover."

With the kind of obstinacy that became typical of Clayburgh, she refused to dye her hair blond for the first screen test, protesting that she "didn't want to be stuck with a blond mop"[27] in the event she did not get the role—the first instance in a steady wave of Clayburgh-spurred strife. They then shot a second screen test with Clayburgh when she agreed to go blond, after having been otherwise "glamorized" and properly gussied up. "She felt terrible doing the whole makeover thing, because she was humiliated," says Barry Sandler, "but she wanted the part and went along with it."

James Brolin, at Furie's request, obliged to shoot the new and final screen tests with Clayburgh, to demonstrate the chemistry between the two. Lew Wasserman, Sid Sheinberg, and others convened to weigh in on the result. As the lights came up, the reaction remained reticent.

"Who would want to fuck her?" asked an unnamed Universal executive. Furie, taken aback by the unbridled coarseness of the question, remembered that this executive's wife was also an actress. Offended at the insolence of the question, he nevertheless fired back calmly, but with no less chutzpah, "What kind of a way is that to talk? It's possible someone could say the same thing about your wife!"

Before the executive could utter a single angry word of his retort, Lew Wasserman rose up from the back of the screening room and abruptly intervened, "This meeting is over. Make it the way you want it and show it to us when you're over and done with it." With that, the august MCA-Universal corporate icon exited the room.

Says Barry Sandler, "The studio never thought she was attractive enough to play Lombard, and they didn't buy the efforts to make her 'fuckable,' but to Sidney's credit, he told them, 'If you don't go with her, I'm not doing the movie here. I'll take it somewhere else.' So they went with it." Clayburgh, then thirty years old, had been flanked in many of her *Hustling* scenes by another young unknown named Melanie Mayron. Furie, sensing a good rapport between the two actresses, hired Mayron to play Lombard's personal assistant Dixie. Ultimately, *Hustling* was nominated for two Primetime Emmy Awards; shooting on *Gable and Lombard* wrapped earlier than usual on May 19, 1975 so that Clayburgh could attend the awards ceremony, having herself been nominated for "Outstanding Lead Actress in a Special Program—Drama or Comedy." Although she was the only performer in the *Hustling* cast who was up for any of the awards, she lost to Katharine Hepburn for her performance in *Love among the Ruins*, in which Hepburn costars with Laurence Olivier.

Rounding out the cast were Red Buttons, as Gable's agent-manager Ivan Cooper, and Allen Garfield, who reveled in the role of Louis B. Mayer. Universal spared no expense in consigning Edith Head to design the film's lavish costumes. Edward C. Carfagno, following a distinguished career and a résumé filled with big-budget classic Hollywood productions of the 1940s and 1950s (*Ziegfeld Follies, The Barkleys of Broadway,* and *The Bad and the Beautiful* among them), was brought on as art director. On *Gable and Lombard,* Carfagno meticulously designed sets for locations like Track Gate No. 1 at MGM, constructed across the road from the Sheraton-Universal Hotel when MGM refused to permit shooting on their own territory.

Three days before shooting was to begin, Furie fired cinematographer Robert Surtees. Jordan Cronenweth quickly replaced him. Claims Furie, "Surtees didn't fit. I had great respect for him, but he was tired and didn't want to learn new tricks. He was a hot lighter and I wanted a more artistic look. Jordan was an artist." With Cronenweth, a then up-and-coming talent who had photographed Robert Altman's *Brewster McCloud* and Billy Wilder's *The Front Page,* Furie designed a less drastic form of his darkened visual style, with clearer definition in shadow relative to the total lighting fall-offs of *Sheila Levine Is Dead and Living in New York.*

Principal photography on *Gable and Lombard* kicked off on May 12, 1975. Clayburgh speedily revealed herself as a nuisance disliked by many of the cast and crew. Surely this was, sadly once again and so soon, shades of Jeannie Berlin on *Sheila Levine Is Dead and Living in New York.* When casting an unknown, the director no doubt believed that tantrums and flare-ups would be more infrequent or even nonexistent, just as *The Lawyer* (1970) had been produced with an easy and agreeable cast of unknowns. In Clifford Terry's on-set account of the production, printed in October 1975, an anonymous "observer" told the reporter after a row between Clayburgh and Furie, "We'll be awhile. She's a real pain in the ass. Really. You can't talk to her. This is her first picture and already she's a Star. It's like the old days. You'd walk up to Lana Turner or Loretta Young and it was like getting an audience with the queen. You'd practically have to say five Hail Marys."[28] In Terry's firsthand encounter with the "high-strung" new star, he found that "interviewing Jill Clayburgh is like trying to persuade J.D. Salinger to appear on Hollywood Squares" and that her terse answers ran the gamut from yes to no. In her only answer of substance, she explained to Terry that a primary source of her character research had been seeing

Lombard's pictures five and six times over and studying Garson Kanin's book *Hollywood,* because it "contains some salty Lombardian dialogue." She continued, "I'm working my ass off. I'm trying to capture the externals, but more than that, her spirit. She was mischievous, fun, honest. She wasn't a comedian. She did comedy but she also did tragedy. She was an actress. I have to get my hair washed."[29]

Perhaps the biggest confrontation between director and actress stemmed from a wardrobe mishap. Despite being dressed in an Edith Head chiffon gown, Clayburgh had no qualms about trudging through a muddy recess of land on the shooting location to rest on a block of wood in between setups. When Furie saw that the hem of the gown had been muddied, he became incensed. "Look at your dress! It's on the ground! It's dirty! How's that going to look?" Clayburgh broke down crying. Furie continued, "Maybe these other people aren't going to care if you look like shit, but I am, and you are!" Clayburgh furiously protested in between sobs, "I'm an actress! I have to think ahead to the next scene. I can't worry about my dress!"[30] She then stormed off the set, retreating to her dressing room, still in a flurry of tears and sobs. She was not easily consoled—it took more than an hour of cajoling her to return.

Furie, before following to coax her back, took his grievances up with the wardrobe department. "Why didn't someone take care of this? They must do something on the big pictures, right? Hoist the actress up on a crane and set her down in a chair or something, right?" He then justified his protestations: "It may seem like a small thing, but in tomorrow's scenes, when she's sitting on a couch, that dirt on her hem is going to show and people are going to notice."[31]

Furie later admitted to Terry that "she thought I was being personal about the dirt on the dress. I said, 'Are you kidding? I did it for the good of the picture.'"

Furie's eldest son, Dan, then entering his senior year of high school, worked on the film as a production assistant. "It was my first opportunity to actually work on one of dad's pictures. Mainly I watched him work day in and day out, and I never saw dad get crazy or scream at anybody. Even when an actor was not doing what he wanted, he would pull them aside privately and give them some suggestions on how to do it better. Clayburgh and Brolin were both very friendly to me."

The meticulousness and often fussy nature of Cronenweth's lighting proved often too time-consuming for Furie, who prided himself on technical efficiency and "making his day" without the incessant tweaking of his technicians to put him behind the clock. He had perhaps been spoiled by the economy of John Alonzo and Donald Morgan and was not quite used to someone so persnickety about such things. "He took what seemed like forever to light," Furie recalls. "He would also often come back late from lunch, and he loved to have a martini at lunch. I think he was a slow lighter because of commercials, but he was rarely back from lunch within the hour." Friend Paul Lynch says, "Sidney was very pleased with Cronenweth's camerawork, but was always frustrated with how long it took to get things ready to shoot." Furie's penchant for bringing in a film either on or under schedule nevertheless prevailed, as shooting wrapped on time, on July 3, 1975. Furie was still often given room to boast about the directorial efficiency of his operation: "Earlier in the day, we were screwing around on the other location, but I knew that if we got the right light I wanted over here, we'd grab it fast."[32]

At the end of shooting, Furie confidently told Clifford Terry, "I think the skeptics will be pleasantly surprised over this movie." About his stars, he explained, "Those two are so different. Jim Brolin's a pro. No problem. Jill is high-strung, but she's a beautiful person." Smiling, he added jokingly, "I did learn one lesson, though: You never yell at an actress before a close-up. The makeup runs. What you do is yell at her after."

The film wrapped production in the nick of time before a Director's Guild of America strike would have forced Furie to picket his own picture. After work with editor Argyle Nelson over his somewhat usual six-month period, Furie flew to Paris to sit beside now-regular collaborator Michel Legrand's piano to have a first listen to the score he composed for Clark and Carole, one that surrounded a central love theme of unabashed sentimentality. When back Stateside, his paeans to the film flowed forth unabated and with alacrity: "Everyone's first impression is, 'Oh, it's another *Harlow!*' I love it when people go in and expect nothing. Especially the critics. That is beautiful. Their first question to the studio rep is usually, 'How long is it?' You're always aware that a picture may not work. They're all your babies, and when they don't work, it's sad. But this one . . . I don't know, it feels right."

The first test screening of *Gable and Lombard* was arranged for October 1975. Given the choice of testing in either Anchorage, Alaska, or Honolulu, Hawaii, Furie selected the latter, where the film previewed next to the John Wayne vehicle *Rooster Cogburn*. Says Barry Sandler, "It was the first time the studio had ever had a preview in Hawaii. They wanted to get as far away from Hollywood as possible, and it was a packed house in Honolulu—like, a thousand people. The reaction to that screening was the second-best reaction in the history of the studio. *Jaws* was first."

Furie corroborates this: "The cards from that Honolulu preview screening were absolutely unbelievable. I never saw such cards. I mean, the movie scored in the nineties! Those were some of the best preview cards in the studio's history at that time." They previewed the film again a few weeks later, this time in Denver, Colorado. Again, the film scored second only to *Jaws* with its ecstatic audience reaction. Furie pushed the studio to release at the end of the year to give it the awards season push, but they were deaf to these requests while hawking Robert Wise's *The Hindenburg* as their major Oscar contender. Instead, Universal booked *Gable and Lombard* as its Valentine's Day movie. "They were so in love with Sidney after those preview screenings that they really would have given him almost anything in exchange for the hit they thought they were getting." Universal also tried to buy out Furie's interest on the film by purchasing his profit points. The overall impression was that Universal had a *Lady Sings the Blues*–caliber hit on their hands and that Furie had worked the same biopic magic, this time under the Universal banner.

Clayburgh, then dating playwright David Rabe, whom she married in 1979, was beckoned to appear on talk shows to promote the film but found herself unable to reconcile her choice of profession with the spectacle that often surrounded it. She recounted later in a news article "bursting into tears—off-camera, thank God" and walking off talk shows before she got the chance to appear. She canceled a guest spot on the *Dinah Shore Show,* stating "I want to be an actress, not a 'personality.'"[33] Clayburgh's reluctance for promotion could not have boded well for the film that was the subject of the promotion. For decades after, she continued avoiding discussion of her role in *Gable and Lombard.*

The studio originally decided to release *Gable and Lombard* in more than six hundred theaters nationwide. However, it changed the release pattern to open it smaller, just as it had *Jaws.* Lew Wasserman wanted to let word-of-mouth and lines around the block sell the film; the studio, in turn, was quite confident the word-of-mouth would be sensational. Truly, Wasserman's hope that *Gable and Lombard*'s looming financial success would, to whatever extent, echo that of *Jaws* was very precious to the MCA/Universal head. *Jaws* producer David Brown remembers, "I believe that the only orgasm Lew Wasserman ever had was at the opening of *Jaws*. He would tell us what the movie was doing in every theater in the United States and Canada. He knew the theater, he knew how many seats there were, he knew what neighborhood it was in, he knew how it compared with other films. He was a human computer." Richard Zanuck remembers of the *Jaws* release, "The head of distribution proudly said, 'Lew, it's a record! We've booked 600 theaters and it's never been done before.' Lew looked at him and said, 'Lose half of them. Bring it down to 300. I don't want people to get into this. I want lines.' And he was right, because *Jaws* stayed number one all summer."[34]

Furie begs to differ: "In the case of *Gable and Lombard*, that was a big mistake, because I think the reviewers hurt the film before any audience word-of-mouth could do any good for it." As the studio failed in appealing to the MPAA to change its R rating to a PG, the marketing department saddled the campaign with a woeful tagline that many later lampooned: "They had more than love. They had fun."

Vincent Canby, writing mercilessly about the "fearfully bad" film in the *New York Times,* dismissed it as "a fan-magazine movie with the emotional zap of a long-lost Louella Parsons column," which featured "clichés culled from the worst movies of the period." Pauline Kael called the film "limply raunchy" and "meaningless" in the *New Yorker,* remarking that the hero and heroine "keep hopping on each other like deranged rabbits." Clayburgh took solace in the fact that Kael twice compared her to Jean Arthur, an actress who had inspired her from childhood. Judith Crist wrote in the *Saturday Review* that the film was "enough to set the stomach churning." Richard Schickel, in *Time,* called it out for being "vulgar, banal and finally repulsive." Roger Ebert, in the *Chicago Sun-Times,* branded the film a "mushy, old-fashioned extravaganza," commenting that "Brolin does indeed look a lot like Gable, but imitation here has nothing to do with flattery." Dave Kehr, writing in the *Chicago Reader,* called the film "a disaster on all counts." Jack Kroll was scathing in *Newsweek,* sealing his venom for the film by writing that "Sidney J. Furie apparently wants to become Hollywood's leading necrophiliac (he violated Billie Holiday in *Lady Sings the Blues*). As a necrophiliac, he's a lousy lay."

The rest of the reviews were equally dismal and merciless in their condemnation, with a lone positive review coming from *Variety,* in which Art Murphy called *Gable and Lombard* "a film with many major assets, not the least of which is the stunning and smashing performance of Jill Clayburgh."

Murphy also singled out Furie's direction for supplying "zest as well as romance" and said the film was "candid without being prurient, delightful without being superficially glossy, heart-warming without being corny." John Simon mustered up faint praise for Jill Clayburgh amid his own vitriolic dismissal, stating that "she has neither the looks nor the voice of the late star, but manages, except in a few totally reprehensible scenes, to remain a woman and an actress."

Says the director, "Once the reviews came in, we were toast. It was all very much 'Don't you dare even think about going to see this movie!'" Barry Sandler agrees: "It did huge business at the end of opening week, but then it went down. The reviews just killed it. It was a slaughter. I think if they had opened it in all the theaters at once, it would have done much better." Worse than that is that the reception of *Gable and Lombard* forced some reviewers to go as far as to reconsider their earlier positive reviews of *Lady Sings the Blues.*

Though the film was dead-on-arrival, it was further violated after its critical opponents had their way with it in print. Many of the real Gable and Lombard's contemporaries, friends, and acquaintances refused to see the film. Lombard's press agent at MGM, Eddie Lawrence, justified his disdain with "I hear it's a slop job. I just don't want to see it, that's all."[35] One of those who did see the film was Jean Garceau, Lombard's private secretary for years, including the years covered in the film. Garceau railed against the film, stating, "It is pretty unbelievable. I couldn't associate a single scene with anything that I'd lived through. Nothing, apparently, was checked. Nothing in it is right, not even the clothes. There was obviously no intensive investigating into the facts."[36] Fred MacMurray also chimed in, saying simply, "I don't think they should have made it. I wasn't too hot about the idea from the beginning."[37] Furie angrily shot back: "Our aim was to make it entertainment. Why should historical accuracy win out over drama? They're correct about Gable not being in uniform when Lombard died. But I loved the image of him in uniform, so I cheated for four months. And they're correct that she never went on the stand in court [in Gable's paternity suit]. But, without that, where do you get a third act?"[38]

Syndicated entertainment columnist Dick Kleiner, fresh from publishing his book *Hollywood's Greatest Love Stories,* went so far as to break down the specific errors of fact in the film one by one. Billie Holiday's old comrade Leonard Feather had overturned his position on *Lady Sings the*

Blues after seeing the final product, but no such commendation was afforded *Gable and Lombard*. Dramatic license in this case was treated as almost toxically spurious. Kleiner posited, "If you're going to make a fictional movie, make it about fictional people."[39]

"The critical reaction was tough," says Barry Sandler. "They could not grasp, or did not want to grasp, the screwball comedy stylization of the story, and I was criticized as the writer for taking certain liberties, which one has to do anyway with any biopic. You can't stick to every specific detail. You have to shape it into a dramatic narrative that's going to engage an audience even if you have to eliminate and consolidate and compress and rearrange. I also took a more fun, sexual kind of approach to the relationship, and the critics thought that was being sacrilegious."

The first phone call that Furie received after the reviews for *Gable and Lombard* was from Ned Tanen, who poured salt on the open wound: "I don't know how you get up in the morning." Furie's hopes to establish a continued working relationship at Universal were scuttled. The film also marked the end of his Harry Korshak period. Korshak gave up the movie industry to explore other fields, settling on architecture. Production designer Paul Sylbert, one of Korshak's closest friends from the time, observes:

> Harry never liked show business. When he was young and just getting into it, he was enthusiastic enough, but he got disenchanted. He was a guy who was always able to use objective judgment about what he was doing, and didn't like the fact that the movie business was taking him where he didn't want to go. So he took stock of himself. When I knew him, he was a big reader and he was the kind of kid who used drugs not just as recreation, but as an escape from the world as it was. He was always doing these drawings, these geometric drawings, and ultimately he went into business as an architect, and a reasonably successful one at that. He moved to London, then moved to Egypt after that and lived there for years.

Specifically, *Gable and Lombard* did yield one very fruitful after-the-fact creative marriage. Paul Mazursky, who had been coming up dry in the hunt for the leading lady in his self-written landmark drama *An Unmarried Woman* (1978), after Jane Fonda had turned him down, cast Jill Clayburgh after seeing *Gable and Lombard* during its theatrical run. Mazursky observes, "The movie was fair, but she was just wonderful. It's not easy to play Carole Lombard."[40] Clayburgh was nominated for the 1978 Best Actress Academy Award for her performance in that film, ironically losing to Jane Fonda for her performance in *Coming Home,* but quickly rose to became a first-tier film star as a result.

In 1964, Furie's characters towed the line between the real world and the "reel world" in *Wonderful Life.* In 1976, with *Gable and Lombard,* the real and the "reel" converge and become inseparable. The film presents a new "wonderful life" where the myths assume more absolute command. To be sure, *Gable and Lombard* is pure, unadulterated escapism and can best be categorized as a "bubble-gum biopic," much more readily so than *Lady Sings the Blues* could be. Its stylized revisionist history suggests a populist brand of mythmaking, selectively depicting Gable and Lombard's lives as idyllically similar if not totally identical to the pristine and charmed, but wholly artificial, worlds of their own 1930s films—two lovers in a mad-cap screwball comedy soap opera that mirrors the range of their own work, as well as the fan-magazine idolization of them at the time. It is gloss over grit. Everything is timed for the delivery of witty banter, and everything looks and sounds clearly movie-friendly. Furie, serving this popular illusion, gives moviegoers Gable and Lombard as they would like them to be and gives film scholars Gable and Lombard as they know they are not. Myths do not simply exist but completely take over, as Furie presents the central couple as beautifully untouchable, though he still attempts to maneuver the story for calculated emotional affect. It is escapism about the engineers of escapism.

Although it is one of Furie's most troubling films amid his prime sixties-through-eighties studio period, the film seemed to work best for those who were not educated about the real personalities it loosely depicted. This fact is well exemplified by the seventeen-year-old Mackenzie Phillips's spirited defense of the film; she is quoted in Dick Kleiner's dismissive column as calling it a "beautiful, funny love story."[41] In the same breath, she admitted that she knew nothing about the real Gable and Lombard. Additionally, pop star Aretha Franklin later named the film her favorite of all time.[42] When taken seriously, though, the film falters, and does so in a way that *Lady Sings the Blues,* which used the same conceits and ran the same risks, had not. The exaggerated conceptual element of it is overbaked, scattershot, and often becomes tonally shrill, because it is directed and performed without restraint or moderation, although Clayburgh fares best. James Brolin's take on Clark Gable does offer some amusement, but it is more impersonation than performance. He plays the screen idol as a lovably folksy, statuesque parvenu, with no qualms about calling a startled debutant "foxy" after showing up at a Hollywood soiree in a muddied tuxedo.

Gable and Lombard is the first of Furie's films since *The Lawyer* (1970) to be shot in standard 1.85:1 aspect ratio; as a direct result, it is one of Furie's least compositionally dynamic films, and certainly his most anonymous of the period in that department. Jordan Cronenweth's often beautiful lighting, however, does benefit the work as a whole. Consciously scaling down the frame size so as to more closely suggest the Academy aspect ratio of the motion pictures of the 1930s (mirroring Scorsese's use of older lenses for a 1.66:1 screen size in 1977's *New York, New York*), Furie limits himself by restraining one of the ways he expresses himself best as a film-maker, no matter how intriguing the reasons for the original choice. His special emphasis on the two-shot becomes somewhat stale as the film approaches its third act, whereas his use of spatial configuration motifs like this had elevated his previous work. Jordan Cronenweth's meticulous lighting, on the other hand, seems the most complex of any lighting in any of Furie's work and is the one thing that clearly does not evoke the movies of the 1930s. Robert Surtees was fired for the "hot" lighting that would have effectively resembled the "star lighting" prominent during Gable and Lombard's heyday. Cronenweth's lighting is Gordon Willis–influenced, a more chiaroscuro version of Donald Morgan's lighting in *Sheila Levine Is Dead and Living in New York*. This darkly muted, highlight-strewn style is the one thing that does give the film a visual edge, suggesting that the director had the perspicacity to realize that note-for-note mimicry would have nullified the entire exercise.

What also emerges to signify *Gable and Lombard* as a Furie film is, once again, the presence of his perennial theme of personal commitment. Clark and Carole are committed to their booming careers and the promise of continued material success to the extent that taking their love affair into the public sphere is forbidden. The joys of their privacy and personal commitment to each other are forsaken in favor of their public image, establishing a clear, if slightly more facile, conflict of love versus career.

Furie, trying as ever to deflect the momentary sting of negative reviews and bad press with forward-looking tunnel vision, started conceiving what he thought would become his next project. During the editing of *Gable and Lombard*, he had started developing a Western with Barry Sandler, provisionally titled *Victory*, a classic rip-roaring yarn about a woman who inherits a plot of land and builds it up, only to be met with local hostility (obviously not to be confused with the Joseph Conrad novel of the same name). Originally to have been a reteaming of Brolin and Clayburgh, Furie and Sandler began considering Barbra Streisand for the role when Clayburgh bowed out of the development deal. "If we would have actually done the film and that casting would have worked out, we would have teamed Brolin and Streisand decades before they first met and got married," says an amused Sandler, who moved on to write the not dissimilar *The Duchess and the Dirtwater Fox* (1976) for director Melvin Frank, while Furie turned his attentions elsewhere.

Sandler, who never again collaborated with Furie, concludes discussing his experience by stating, "Working with Sidney Furie was the best experience of my creative life. I couldn't wait to start work with him every day. The inverse of that was Mel Frank, who was a total control freak on *The Duchess and the Dirtwater Fox*. I got no warmth or feeling of creative synergy working with Mel. I always got that from Sidney, and I cherish the memory of working on *Gable and Lombard* every day, even if it didn't endear us to critics or whatever."

Journalist Clive Denton, in his 1976 *Cinema Canada* piece "Furie Then and Now" writes, "Another of his fruitful styles—people working—is oddly enough evident through the gloss of *Gable and Lombard*. And both these latest films of his remind us that love makes the world—and the movies—go round. I think that Sidney Furie may figuratively be coming home."[43]

Chapter 9

Cast Iron Jacket

You are doing a war picture. Shoot—Shoot—Shoot.
—*Joe Cohn, head of MGM's production office, in a telegram
to John Huston on the first day of shooting*
The Red Badge of Courage,
as recounted in Lillian Ross' Picture

"Hello?"

"Hello, is this Sidney Furie?"

"Yes."

"Hello, this is Andre Morgan, Golden Harvest Productions."

"Yes, hi."

"We're an off-shore production company working out of Hong Kong."

"Yeah, I know Golden Harvest, sure."

"We've done mostly kung fu and martial arts films up until now. We're looking for a director for a project we have in development. It's not a kung fu movie. We want to make it in Canada and need a Canadian director. It's called *Diamond Cut Diamond*. It's a jewel heist picture and . . ."

"Forget that, forget that. I've actually got a script here that I've been working on . . . a war movie. You'll love it."

Thus began the conversation that culminated in what perhaps is the most important film, personally, of Sidney J. Furie's career. After the vicissitudes of the critical drubbing that Furie's romantic fantasies weathered, he next directed what French cineastes would perhaps call his "testament film," a term meaning "a summation work that most expresses a director's artistic sensibility and philosophy of life." *The Boys in Company C* is "Furie's cinema" best defined. Released in the year of the Vietnam War's long-awaited incursion into Hollywood picture-making, a full ten years after the ignominy over John Wayne's pro–Vietnam War epic *The Green Berets* (1968), Furie's Vietnam film, the first work to be released in this new cycle,

235

soon went up against other films that likewise ended the moratorium on Vietnam-themed picture-making: Ted Post's *Go Tell the Spartans!*, Hal Ashby's *Coming Home,* and Michael Cimino's *The Deer Hunter.* Francis Ford Coppola's troubles in the Philippines on the set of *Apocalypse Now* (1979), the shooting of which commenced in 1976, were regularly being reported in the entertainment columns.

That the Hollywood moratorium on Vietnam ended with a sudden onslaught of pictures is a fascinating point to consider. As Peter McInerney observes in a *Film Quarterly* article written for the winter 1979–1980 issue, "How could films succeed which reminded audiences of military stalemate if not outright defeat, generated guilt about suffering inflicted on Vietnamese and Americans, or caused bandaged cultural wounds to bleed afresh?"[1] Indeed, lingering doubts about the war, compounded by the usual box-office worries, poisoned the whole notion in the years that followed John Wayne's infamous public-relations epic.

"Fathers shouldn't have favorites, but I'd have to say that the whole experience of making *The Boys in Company C* was the best in my life," Furie enthusiastically states, smiling. "Andre Morgan just let me make the movie I wanted to make with no pressure. And after all those years, it was time to give my obsession with the military some airtime."

By 1976, Furie, cast adrift in disappointment but never discouraged, had not scored a critically or financially successful film in the years since *Lady Sings the Blues.* After the horrific release of *Gable and Lombard,* he had been approached by Canadian producer Zev Braun to direct a project called *Jocasta!,* a modern-day retelling of Oedipus Rex, to be mounted in Montreal with Sophia Loren and Steve Railsback. The project, if Furie had remained with it, would have marked his return to the Canadian film industry after an eighteen-year self-imposed exile that was originally sparked by the country's formerly less-than-hospitable attitude toward its native filmmaking talent. When *The Boys in Company C* received funding and an official start date in November 1976, Furie left Montreal and Braun's project. Braun's curses followed, and the disgruntled producer took to the press. Furie, when confronted by entertainment reporters, responded, "He gambled and lost. My other picture came through and he didn't want to face that. He financed his picture independently and probably told the investors I was going to be the director. When I left, he was embarrassed. That's why he's talking like this. Braun knew when I got up there, I had another project and wasn't available to commit myself as a full-time director. I told him to get someone else. People who know me have never seen me walk out on anything."[2]

Jocasta! was eventually released in Canada with the title *Angela* in March 1978, under the direction of television veteran Boris Sagal. The film did not secure an American release until April 1984.

Prior to the Zev Braun controversy, to which most were apathetic, Furie had come into contact with Rick Natkin, the twenty-one-year-old son of Robert Natkin, an advertising executive for whom he had directed a handful of commercials. "I had written a three-hundred-page Western called *Borderlands,* about scalp-hunters in the Southwest," says Rick Natkin. "Sidney read it, or at least a healthy portion of it, and loved the writing, but was not so crazy about the story. I had just gotten out of college and was looking to get started in the business." Natkin, a Yale graduate, also happened to have written another script in college, based on the experiences of Vietnam veterans he had come to know as a student. He and Furie exchanged their individual work, as Furie had himself composed a full treatment, then titled *The Boys from Company C,* based largely on his reading of books on the subject, primarily Dr. Ronald Glasser's *365 Days,* a firsthand account of an Army doctor, and Tim O'Brien's *If I Die in a Combat Zone.* Says Natkin, "It turns out that my script and Sid's treatment were so similar that we could not wait to talk to each other again. We had the same kind of idea, and the same take on that idea." Beyond what he perceived as a mastery of storytelling, Furie found himself immediately infatuated with Natkin's style, which consisted of enthralling, page-turning bombast and crisp, character-driven dialogue. "The words just jumped off the page," Furie recalls. "He wrote with a lot of capitalization and enthusiastic punctuation, and you were really, vividly living the movie in your head as you were reading it." The two of them collaborated on a 350-page screenplay draft, then, customarily, thinned it out to a more appropriate length.

"Sidney was the first person to really treat me like an adult, which really meant something to me, because I barely was," says Natkin. Together, Furie and his young charge told the story of five draftees, all hailing from different backgrounds (an Italian American, a black, a southerner, a hippie, and a wannabe writer), who are inducted into the Marine Corps. For the first hour of the film, they undergo basic training under the command of a severe drill instructor, before being shipped off to the madness of Vietnam. The madness of war is further exemplified by the corruption of both the brass and the South Vietnamese, the near incompetence of their company commander, and a third-act soccer game on which their very future hinges. On the latter count, the battle-wearied group is given the chance to avoid further combat if they elect to play as the Marine Corps soccer team against the local South Vietnamese troops. When they take the assignment, they are told that they must throw the game to build the confidence of the South Vietnamese. Already disenchanted with their commanding officers, the boys turn the game into a farce, only to disobey orders and win in the end, just in time for a Viet Cong shelling of the playing field.

Furie and Natkin's script used the classic World War II ensemble drama as a proven formula for its examination of a band of brothers in a whole new American war. As in *Hit!* (1973), the Hawksian theme of group responsibility is also present. "It was turned down by every company in Hollywood more than once," claims Furie.

Following his success with *The Sting* (1973) and *Slap Shot* (1977), director George Roy Hill had just taken Universal up on an offer to spearhead his own production company under its auspices. Hill considered Furie and Natkin's script as a property that this new company could potentially support and bankroll. Furie, however, had specifically envisioned a "small picture" and, ultimately, Hill's company was not really set up for such an endeavor. "George was one of the most encouraging people when we were trying to sell the script around town, but it couldn't have really gone anywhere [with him] because I probably would have lost control of it," Furie continues. Prominent producer Walter Mirisch, whose Mirisch Company had decamped from United Artists to Universal the year before, turned the project down flat, finding the characters "too indistinguishable from each other," a criticism that Furie found maddening. Executive Bonnie Bird, also at Universal, recommended the script to her superiors, but the studio's recent money-losing experience with Furie on *Gable and Lombard* impeded whatever momentum it might have gained there. Roger Birnbaum, future MGM executive, at the time an independent producer and "respected hustler" around town, hocked the script, originally unbeknownst to the writers, and struck out.

By 1977, Golden Harvest had its sights on producing its first film independent of the Hollywood studio system. The firm had, after all, cofinanced pictures with Warner Bros. (such as the profitable Bruce Lee vehicle *Enter the Dragon*), worked with Fox on deals for its other product, and was eying to mount what was to be the first Hong Kong–Canadian coproduction. *Diamond Cut Diamond,* the misbegotten, never-produced genre project that Morgan originally offered Furie, had been "banged out" by self-styled British producer-screenwriter Harry Alan Towers, under the pen name Peter Welbeck, "in what was basically a week," according to Morgan. Looking for a Canadian director to helm the picture, to take advantage of the increasingly popular Canadian tax-shelter deals, Morgan, a longtime fan of Furie's, tracked him down through the Director's Guild. Furie, by that time, had left agent Jeff Berg and was using his lawyer as an ad hoc agent. At a meeting held in Morgan's hotel, Furie agreed to read the *Diamond Cut Diamond* script if Morgan would look at Furie and Natkin's script for *The Boys in Company C.*

Morgan and Golden Harvest impresario Raymond Chow discussed these new developments on the phone. The following Monday, Morgan met with his eager director. Furie immediately voiced his dislike for the *Diamond Cut Diamond* script, expressing no interest whatsoever in directing it. After working out a hypothetical budget for Furie and Natkin's script on the back of a placemat at the Beverly Hills Holiday Inn, Furie assured Morgan that he could bring the picture in for just under $1.6 million. Thailand and the Philippines were discussed as possible locations, although Furie's apprehensions about the latter possibility, resulting from news of Coppola's *Apocalypse Now* troubles there, were considerable. Coppola launched principal photography on what was slated as a five-month shoot on March 1, 1976. By May 1977, it had mushroomed to fourteen months.

Once Morgan spoke with the Golden Harvest partners in Hong Kong, the deal was sealed. Says Andre Morgan, "We knew *Gable and Lombard* was this big disaster for Universal, and that the fallout from that had more or less disgraced Sidney in many people's eyes. But Raymond and I both put a lot of faith in Sidney as an artist because we knew he was a powerhouse as a director. We knew he had a reputation for being emotional and occasionally difficult, but in our eyes, he was still the imaginative, passionate guy who gave us *The Ipcress File* and *Lady Sings the Blues.*"

Furie first flew to Hong Kong to consider it as the primary shooting location, only to be met with disappointment. There, however, Andre Morgan arranged meetings with his own Vietnam veteran acquaintances, all of whom had become expatriates. Many of these men, including the production's still photographer Hugh Van Es (who was famous for capturing many of the Vietnam War's most stirring photographic images), later came to work on the film, largely as technical advisers. After a brief stay in Golden Harvest's home city, Furie reluctantly flew to Manila to investigate the Philippines. This visit came just two weeks after Typhoon Olga pulverized the country, on May 26, 1976.

Morgan recalls, "As soon as we got off the plane in Manila, Sidney turns to me and says, 'It smells corrupt! We can leave tomorrow for Bangkok.'" Furie was confident that everything they needed would be in Thailand, but Morgan, who, with Golden Harvest, had made movies throughout Asia, knew the score. "Thailand in those days was far more corrupt than the Philippines on every count, so I appealed to him to have a closer look."

"We stayed in a crummy hotel with geckos running up and down the walls," Furie remembers. Much to his delight, though, everything seemed to resemble the Vietnam he had seen on the news, in photographs, and in documentary material. John Wayne's *The Green Berets,* after all, had been unconvincingly photographed in Georgia, Atlanta, and the Warner studio backlot, and other low-end, low-budget pictures centering on the Vietnam conflict had often strained visual credibility in presenting the specific landscape that American soldiers treaded on the nightly news. However pleased Furie was with the landscape of the Philippines in these terms, he wore his skepticism for what he perceived as local corruption like a suit of armor; he was convinced that this had some involvement with the sky-rocketing budget on Coppola's picture. By then, that film was six months into production with only a quarter of the final shooting completed.

After spending time with the government representative who was showing them around, the director's edge softened and his guard was lowered. He had been successfully charmed and persuaded to use the Philippines for the film's backdrop. Morgan recounts the words that did the convincing:

This guy looked at Sidney and said, "Mr. Furie, my observation is that when the producer and director are the same person, and they argue, the director always wins." It was a pretty fucking profound observation for a guy like this. Francis, basically, was in control of everything on *Apocalypse Now.* If the director is in control of the budget, he'll spend what he wants to spend when he wants to spend it. And that one thing did the convincing for Sidney. It was also spending the day with Francis and Gray on set, and seeing that we had the tanks and the helicopters and whatever else we needed, thanks just to doing the picture in the Philippines.

Furie remembers, "When Andre and I went up to visit Francis on his set, Francis recommended that I read Glasser's *365 Days*. It was one of the first things he told me. I of course told him that I had already read it and based a lot of my writing on it."

At this point in Furie's career, shooting an ambitious picture like *The Boys in Company C* on a relatively low budget proved a tremendous risk. For one, he agreed to a whopping pay cut, a scant salary of ten thousand dollars. "At that point, it was the closest I had ever come to a true passion project, and whatever I needed to do to get the thing made, I was ready and willing to do it," says Furie. When he was unable to keep his longtime secretary Marlene Pivnick on payroll during the production of the picture, Andre Morgan brought her on to run the Golden Harvest office, where she remained until her death in 1996.

In November 1976, when the Philippines officially approved Golden Harvest for its proposed shooting dates, Furie commenced casting *The Boys in Company C*. In much the manner as for *The Lawyer* eight years before, Furie wanted to shoot the film in sequence with a cast of unknowns, holding open auditions to find his talent. John Travolta, a fairly recent television sensation with *Welcome Back, Kotter,* stood among the hopefuls. Andre Morgan recalls, "Travolta really wanted the role badly, because the notion of a Vietnam War movie was fresh and exciting to people. Sidney just looked at him and said, 'I like you, but you're TV! You're sitcom! I cannot have sitcom going to Vietnam!'" With one future star passed over for the role of Private Vinnie Fazio, other fledgling actors like Andrew Stevens (son of actress Stella Stevens), James Whitmore Jr. (son of veteran actor James Whitmore), Stan Shaw, Michael Lembeck, and Craig Wasson were eventually cast as the central five young recruits, most of them with limited previous credits to their names. In the vital role of the Marine drill instructor, Santos Morales was cast. Ultimately, however, Morales's role was duly diminished.

R. Lee Ermey, a backup technical adviser on *Apocalypse Now,* had likewise been hired for *The Boys in Company C*. Ken Metcalfe, the only American casting agent in the Philippines, had made the introductions with Ermey in both the Coppola and the Furie cases. Before the arrival of both movie crews, Ermey, according to his own book, had set himself up in the Philippines fishing industry, owned his own bar, and had taken a Filipino wife. He had a retainer that bound him to complete his work on *Apocalypse Now*, but owing to various Coppola shutdowns, he had been given the privilege of living on the dole. This was his circumstance when Furie and Morgan breezed into town. As Ermey remembers, "Right away [Sid] asked me if I could call cadence. Was he kidding, or what? I asked him if he wanted to close the door, because this was going to be sort of loud. He said it wasn't necessary. I boomed out a couple of cadences, my voice shaking the walls. 'You're hired!' Furie said."[3]

On his second trip to the Philippines before production was to begin, Furie decided to return home by way of Tel Aviv, to visit a longtime friend. As he flew from Manila to Bangkok, then Bangkok to Tel Aviv, his luggage was still being held in Hong Kong. When he arrived in Israel, he was detained as a suspected terrorist, mostly because of his lack of baggage. "I was held for about eight hours incommunicado. I was also thumb-printed and IDed." During Furie's eight-hour detainment, people expecting him back in Los Angeles, from family to the *Company C* team, began to get concerned. A day later, he emerged. Morgan recalls, "It was all 'Would you believe this!' and so on." Years later, Furie struck a close relationship with the Israeli government when he brought *Iron Eagle* to them.

A mostly British crew was hired for the film. British camera operator Godfrey Godar, Otto Heller's camera operator on *The Naked Runner*, was brought on as the film's cinematographer, overseeing Furie's return to anamorphic wide screen after the experiment with diminished screen width on *Gable and Lombard*. It was Godar's first experience as a cinematographer after decades of working only under other cinematographers. Much of the cast and crew quickly got sense of the project's relatively low-budget status en route to the Philippines. Says cast member Andrew Stevens, who played Billy Ray Pike in the film, "Even though this was all under the Screen Actors Guild auspices and we were supposed to have flown first-class, the producers talked us into flying coach on China Airlines and we gladly accepted because we all wanted a job."[4] When Stan Shaw arrived on location, he found the conditions less than stellar: "The water was so foul that we got food poisoning, tomaine, jungle rot, you name it. I got bitten by spiders every night. I had these huge spider bites all over my face, and couldn't figure out where they were coming from. So I finally pulled my bed back, and there was a four-foot spider web back there with a whole family of spiders. And we had bat attacks every night—we had to wear helmets."[5] Linda Furie had her own critter incidents, namely with rats in their bungalow. Andre Morgan, who remembers Furie as a "lovable firecracker" while working on *The Boys in Company C*, remembers Linda calling her husband during a meeting. "She was crying uncontrollably about the rats in their bungalow," says Morgan, who laughed heartily recalling Furie's response to her: "I can't deal with this right now. I'm in a meeting about the movie! Don't you understand? I can't deal with rats today!"

Shooting commenced in February on the Philippine island of Luzon. Furie's base of operations was in and around Manila. Says Linda Furie,

My girlfriend's mother was married to the producer Pandro S. Berman. She used to always say, "You should be with your husband on location." I always felt such a strong connection that I feel that he's always with me. There was complete trust. I left Marseilles after only ten days when he was shooting *Hit!* When he was on the road for *Little Fauss and Big Halsy,* I was back home for most of that. On *The Boys in Company C,* I actually went to the set a lot, more than I usually do, because I was in the Philippines, and I had Chris and Sara with me. From being around and watching Sid make that movie, and the way he brought it home with him at night, I can say without a doubt that it was the best time Sid ever had making a movie.

Indeed, Furie was having quite the spree while shooting *The Boys in Company C*. He delighted in the fact that Morgan and Chow were mostly hands-off producers who did not interfere with any of the creative aspects of the production. Whenever Morgan was present, he was simply there to ensure the fluidity of the operation, never to step on Furie's toes.

When shooting commenced, the young actors approached Furie, imploring him to use R. Lee Ermey as a performer. This said, Furie found that he was not quite getting everything he needed out of Santos Morales as the boys' drill instructor, which unsettled him considering the role's importance. Recalling how effectively Ermey had called cadence in his office and taking into account what a dynamo he had proved to be in whipping the movie's sense of reality into shape as its technical adviser, Furie enlisted him to take over the role, effectively splitting one DI character into two. Says Andrew Stevens, "Sid clearly fell in love with [Ermey's] whole persona and demeanor. It really gave birth to R. Lee Ermey as a character actor."[6] From the very start of production, Furie customarily called upon all actors to improvise around the written dialogue, and Ermey certainly took advantage of this. "A lot of the best Ermey lines are his own," Furie attests.

After dabbling in many forms and genres over the years, Furie had finally found his cinematic calling with directing war. "I learned on that picture that there is no genre I have more fun doing," Furie confessed. "What attracts me to it is really the craftsmanship of the whole thing: planning the set pieces, orchestrating the action, placing your characters in this epic setting, with all the pyrotechnics at your disposal, like rigging the squibs and the explosions. I just loved it, and still do. And after the stresses and rigors of *Sheila Levine* and *Gable and Lombard,* the joys of doing that type of picture was exactly what I needed."

If first impressions of the locale did not bode well for Stan Shaw, the creative process offset the hardships of roughing it when the cameras were not rolling. Says Shaw, "We did a lot of improvising. We'd 86 the original because we got the same emotional value. When you film in sequence, like Sidney was doing, you know the character even more so than the writer knows him. And it was truly an ensemble effort."[7] Andrew Stevens remembers, "Sidney was known among the cast members as Sudden Sid, because he could change his mind on a dime, and you literally never knew what he was going to do next."[8]

As Andre Morgan attests, "With every day I was there on location shooting that picture, there is a great Sidney Furie story." A few weeks into production, Morgan adopted a laissez-faire approach to producing, managing the project from afar from his office in Hong Kong. In the event they needed him, the flight to Manila was just a short hour away. One day, he received a call that the cast and crew had been roadblocked from the day's planned location. Catching a flight within a moment's notice, Morgan soon found himself in the parking lot behind the El Grande Tropical Palace Resort Hotel, the cast and crew's rural accommodations, gazing at burning tires, army trucks in a circle with dozens of guns shooting, and Furie, enrapt, in the middle of a take. Noticing his producer in the wings, Furie sprinted over to Morgan to assure him that everything was under control, exclaiming "Don't worry! We didn't lose a minute! I'm shooting the scene right here! Watch the smoke! God, this is great! I love war movies!" With that, he ran back behind the camera to finish the take.

Sudden Sid's unflappability persisted. Nowhere else was this more on display than in the hillside scene, which required stark naked soldiers to cheer at the meaningless disposal of millions of dollars' worth of bombs and explosives. During rehearsal, the ammunition was set off and burned by accident. Without batting an eye, Furie repositioned his cameras so as not to reveal the scorched land, rejigged the explosives within the hour, and got the shot. "He took every challenge in stride," says Andre Morgan. "I've never worked with another director like him before or since. When we had to shut down for four days, for Easter, which is a big holiday in the Philippines, Sid went nuts. I remember him saying, 'How can we shut down the movie for this long? I'll take a camera out and shoot by myself!' And he was totally serious about it."

In spite of the cast's collective youth, off-hours shenanigans were kept to a minimum. With Ferdinand Marcos in office and martial law instituted in the country, occasional curfew violations were not uncommon. Andrew Stevens, James Whitmore Jr., and Rick Natkin were party to one particular incident. Says Natkin, "We lost track of time one night and we missed the curfew. We were what seemed like twenty miles away from our hotel, so we were forced to walk back the whole way after a night of beers and whatnot. We got picked up by the local Philippine constabulary and it was such that we weren't sure if they were going to take us back to the hotel, or take us into a field and shoot us." This encounter, needless to say, ended harmlessly, but it stood to remind everyone of the national climate.

Midway through production, word was received that Martin Sheen had suffered a massive heart attack and that Coppola's picture had been shut down as a result. Many of the *Company C* cast members visited Sheen in the hospital, when the prognosis initially appeared bleak. Up until that point, the Coppola and Furie teams would converge in Manila on weekends. Coppola's film had been predominantly staged out in the provinces, largely on the islands of Iba and Laguna. Gray Frederickson, a veteran member of the Furie retinue, was *Apocalypse Now*'s producer. "There was a lot of criss-cross going on," says Andre Morgan. "We were borrowing stuff from their sets, we were helping them out. There was a lot of horse-trading going on between Gray and myself." Coppola, after all, had struck a precarious deal with President Marcos: that his production would pay the Philippine military thousands per day (as well as overtime for the Philippine pilots) in return for Marcos's entire fleet of helicopters, as long as they were not needed to fight the Communist insurgency in the south. Much to Coppola's chagrin, the helicopters were often called away to do just that.[9]

The tanks, guns, and military hardware that Furie's set was supposed to receive from the government were often not available for this same reason. But another difference from *Apocalypse Now* was that the production was never crippled; Furie was fully able to shoot around this issue in most cases. Uniformly, *The Boys in Company C* proved to be the reverse mirror image of *Apocalypse Now*. While the latter endured every trial and tribulation, the former saw nothing but easy solutions to momentary interferences. As this "easy factor" seemed unusual in such an ambitious picture, cast and crew members took notice of the film's other unusual elements. "It was the only experience in my entire career as an actor, writer, director, producer or otherwise that I had ever been involved in that was shot in exact sequence," says Andrew Stevens.[10] This decision was made for practical reasons (largely because of the military haircuts and the growth thereafter), but also to give the actors the benefit of actively feeling the story's organic dramatic movement, a la *Lady Sings the Blues*.

Toward the end of production, the time had come to stage the film's soccer-game finale, for which the cast members had been practicing throughout the production. "We went out in South China Sea on this transport ship, baked in the sun, and we played a little soccer on board to practice for the movie sequence," says Andrew Stevens. The Panaglide, an experimental prototype for the Panavision version of the Steadicam, was used to give the sequence's fast movement a fluidity and grace. Approximately five hundred extras were packed into the scene, most of them local Filipinos. In the midst of shooting, a man stood up in the stands holding a .45 caliber gun, screaming, "Stop! Thief! Stop!" This man jumped the divider, tore out onto the playing field, and fired the gun. "It sounded like a fucking cannon, so everyone hit the deck," Andre Morgan recalls, laughing. "Sidney, because it wasn't in the script, just said, 'What's that?' When he saw the guy in the middle of the field, he pointed to him and yelled, 'You, with the gun, sit down!' As it turns out, it was a local cop trying to stop a pickpocket. No one was injured, but it was hilarious that Sidney hardly batted an eye."

Principal shooting wrapped on May 4, 1977. Raymond Chow, exceedingly pleased with the final product, and additionally pleased that a director in his employ, in classic Furie style, brought in a movie under budget and on time, wanted to reward Furie, especially after he had taken a pittance as a salary. According to Furie and Morgan, this is what transpired:

"Andre, I want to pay him some money. It's not fair he only got $10,000. I've never heard of this. Sidney, what would make you happy?"

"I don't know. I guess another 10 or 15,000."

"Another $50,000, huh?"

"No, 10 or 15."

"No, you said 50, didn't you?"

Chow wrote Furie the check for $50,000 right then and there. "That really tells you what kind of person Raymond Chow was," adds Furie. Adds Andre Morgan, "We knew after *The Boys in Company C* that we wanted to be in business with Sidney and we wanted to make him feel valued in that way."

At the start of editing at Goldwyn Studio, with a three-man team led by Frank Urioste (who was effectively ending a six-picture tenure with editor Argyle Nelson, who continued working on studio-funded pictures), Furie was adamant that the mixers complete the final sound mix before Golden Harvest started shopping the film around to studios for distribution, effectively asserting to prospective buyers that the film's final form was irrevocable. "We were in more of a position to say 'Cuts? Sorry, no can do. This is the movie, take it or leave it.'" Following a preview of the film in Westwood in Los Angeles, Barry Diller and Michael Eisner of Paramount liked the film but felt discomfited by the profanity, the "check your package" scene before the soccer game, and the 125-minute length. After some fencing with Diller and Eisner, Max Youngstein of United Artists and Ned Tanen of Universal (the executive fresh from the *Gable and Lombard* fallout) were approached; both also turned it down, appreciating the work but also expressing apprehension about the rough language.

Norman Levy of Columbia loved the picture as-is and picked it up immediately without requiring any cuts, ensuring what was in those days a wide release in nine hundred theaters. "It was known among Columbia Pictures executives, particularly the venerable head of marketing, as 'the motherfucker movie,'" says Andrew Stevens.[11] According to Stan Shaw, additional previews of the film went through the roof: "They cheered, they were screaming, they were talking back to the film. It was incredible. They went crazy, because they saw reality on the screen, and because they didn't think that anyone would film the things that actually happened."[12]

Opening to initially mixed reviews and an impressive $6 million weekend box office on February 2, 1978, while the East Coast buckled down, anticipating the biggest blizzard of the year, the film's two most encouraging notices originated from Kevin Thomas of the *Los Angeles Times* and Roger Ebert. In his glowing review for the *Chicago Sun-Times,* Ebert called *The Boys in Company C* "more than just exciting, or entertaining. I think the movie is, first and best, a thrilling entertainment that starts by being funny and ends up being very deeply moving." He singled out Stan Shaw's performance as "remarkably strong, and not least when he shows tenderness." The last paragraph of the review states, "Sidney J. Furie, the director, hasn't had a substantial hit since *Lady Sings the Blues.* But he retains the ability to make a picture move, grow on us and involve us. That's what happens during *The Boys in Company C.*" Kevin Thomas wrote that the film "pulls off the considerable feat of combining disenchanted contemporary awareness with traditional combat heroics and sentimentality in a thoroughly engaging way," also observing that "in most instances mainstream movies succeed to the degree to which they balance escapist fantasy elements with those of gritty reality. In a decidedly challenging context, *The Boys in Company C* strikes that balance with assurance."

Janet Maslin of the *New York Times* accused *The Boys in Company C* of naïveté in its adulation of "stereotypical" World War II movie models, calling it "as calculating as can be." She damned the work by stating, "As a film about heroism, it is chiefly remarkable for its gutlessness." She conceded, however, that the performances were strong, singling out two in particular. She writes of Stan Shaw, "As the black recruit, Mr. Shaw is handsome and more than competent, and the character he plays is wonderful in a way that only movie characters can be." Andrew Sarris, writing a noncommittal review for the *Village Voice,* observed, "Furie has not been a critic's director lately, and the whole project seems to have been financed with the international hard-core action market in the mind." *Variety* wrote, "Laden with barracks dialogue and played at the enlisted man's level, the Raymond Chow production, directed well by Sidney J. Furie, features strong performances by some very fine actors."

Commercially, the film made a healthy profit, although the ailing Columbia Pictures failed to support the film with television ads after its successful first two weeks in theaters, pulling it in favor of projected money-maker *Casey's Shadow,* starring Walter Matthau. Natkin posits, "I think the attitude was that 'This was a pickup. We didn't put anything into it, we got plenty out of it, and that's that.'" Profits continued pouring in when the fledgling Columbia Home Video distributed the film on cassette in the early 1980s. "It's really the only movie I ever worked on that had profits, and it was Sidney who originally insisted that I get profit participation," claims Rick Natkin, who has seen his collaborator's insistence on this front pay off. Corroborates Andre Morgan, "Raymond Chow made a bloody fortune on the film."

The Boys in Company C's legacy is somewhat more convoluted than that of any of Furie's other commercially successful films, mostly as a result of Stanley Kubrick's *Full Metal Jacket,* released nearly ten years later in June 1987 and based on Gustav Hasford's 1979 novel *The Short-Timers.* Casting R. Lee Ermey as the film's drill instructor character as well as specifically copying *The Boys in Company C*'s bifurcated structure, *Full Metal Jacket* often appears to have certain "Xeroxed" elements that are too close for comfort, both for fans of Furie's original and for Kubrick scholars who plead ignorance, beg to differ, or claim the picture as unassailable.

In the interim between *The Boys in Company C* and *Full Metal Jacket,* Ermey appeared in a second Vietnam-themed film directed by Furie, 1984's *Purple Hearts.* Nevertheless, in the summer of 1987, Furie received a phone call from Ermey:

"Listen, I've just landed in New York. I'm on a promo tour for *Full Metal Jacket,* and you're not going to like what I have to tell you. Stanley made me promise I would say this is my first film. He wants to be my discoverer."

"I don't care, Lee. That's fine. Good for you! I hope it helps you. *The Boys in Company C* is always going to be there and eventually people are going to know the truth."

Furie swears by this conversation. Eventually, magazine and newspaper articles surfaced, calling readers' attention to the fact that Ermey did have a history as an actor in a similar picture, accusing the Kubrick publicity team of strange territoriality and, in one case, even outright theft in the film's appropriation of certain *The Boys in Company C* conceits without any manner of acknowledgment, despite the fact that Kubrick, an acquaintance of Furie's from his London days, was an acknowledged fan. Furie, for his part, was not looking for that kind of credit but found Kubrick's desire to lay claim to his own discovery of Ermey as needless. "Stanley was one of the greatest filmmakers we've ever had! Why would he need that?" Unfortunately, Kubrick's startlingly similar (but not identical) picture has often overshadowed *The Boys in Company C,* indeed almost appearing to have canceled it out. In 1984, Roger Ebert reiterated his position that *The Boys in Company C,* a film he still "admired very much," was "lean and angry and filled with a bitter humor."[13] About *Full Metal Jacket,* Ebert was mostly apathetic, nearly dismissive, calling the film "shapeless," "cliché," and "too little and too late." In the rare discussion that seriously and soberly compares the two films, today's conventional wisdom does hold that *Full Metal Jacket* is the better and more sophisticated of the two pictures. At the risk of sounding willfully contrary, the allure of Kubrick's film lies not in its story (which many critics of its time found derivative and faulted structurally) but rather in its adornment with Kubrick's ultra-recognizable directorial signatures and remnants of his external legend (i.e., the graceful tracking shots, the deliberate mise-en-scène, the circulated production stories about the number of takes, the trademark performance tropes like the famous "upward glare," etc.). Added to this iconography is R. Lee Ermey's famous performance, amplified to operatic proportions from his previous on-screen incarnation as Furie's drill instructor, so as to become a novelty. That film has become almost "critic-proof," something of a sacred cow, and it becomes clear that a more stylistically subtle film like *The Boys in Company C* tends to disappear when put under the general public's comparative microscope.

Considering Kubrick's assistant Jan Harlan's claims that Kubrick "always wanted to make a stylized film about war, not necessarily the Vietnam War, but the phenomenon of war,"[14] Furie recognizes that the specific "phenomenon of war" in the case of Vietnam rests in identifying it as a whole new kind of war, in which (as stated in the closing voice-over of Furie's film) "living is more important than winning." For an antiwar film, this sentiment is more germane, but for an American war film proper, one that "criticizes a specific war while celebrating military values in general,"[15] this sentiment is uncommon, even subversive. Furie renders it without the intrusion of nondiegetic music or scoring (only the performance of actor Craig Wasson's original ballad "Here I Am" scores the film). Oldies-saturated soundtracks later became an easy trap into which filmmakers directing their cameras toward Southeast Asia fell when making more salient political points. Kubrick uses such music for the sake of snark and irony in *Full Metal Jacket,* while Furie altogether avoids it. In addition to this, *The Boys in Company C* is accented with an anarchic, biting, but far more subtle humor, which illustrates the *Boys*'s cynicism in a struggle against a vilified class of officers, the corrupt, obtuse men who sometimes frivolously use infantry soldiers as pawns.

It may be best to start by comparing Kubrick's film to Samuel Fuller's

The Steel Helmet (1951), then compare Furie's to William Wellman's *The Story of G.I. Joe* (1945). Both are landmark war pictures about combat soldiers mired in the soul-crushing grit of war, but the difference in respective approach here becomes appropriately analogous to the Kubrick-Furie analysis. There is a Kubrick mystique that effortlessly seduces audiences, but it is decidedly at its flimsiest in *Full Metal Jacket,* more than in any other film in the director's impressive career. This is certainly a controversial position to take, and perhaps it radiates with arrogance.

Kubrick's characters, essentially and by design, are "men from nowhere" with no previous personal history. Beyond that, they are puppets in a Nietzschian burlesque that has been fashioned as a mere intellectual exercise, diluted for popular consumption—war for the au courant consumer. The comfortably and carefully distanced Kubrick never expressed interest in sketching his characters outside the confines of their transformation into "born-to-kill" warriors, so they exist only in their present circumstances. This does speak to his theme of dehumanization. But Kubrick's intention to alienate grows shallow and tiresome, almost as if he expects that his beloved style and Ermey's colorful insults will provide his insurance. Luckily for the film's commercial fate, this was good enough insurance. The film is transparent and devoid of emotion even when Kubrick clearly aspires toward it during the finale's killing of a teenage girl sniper. Joker and Animal Mother's snark further obstructs them as people, with the droll, dry humor in the Vietnam section of the picture becoming a deliberate barrier. Billy Wilder, who claimed that "Kubrick never made a bad picture" demurred on the matter of *Full Metal Jacket,* ruling that the first half (i.e., the boot-camp section) of the film was "the best film he had ever seen."[16] Sam Fuller himself, however, was even less enthusiastic: "I got the first part in five minutes and if it wasn't Kubrick, I'd have left after ten. I think I wanted him to say something else: 'What are we doing here?' We're a country that can say anything we want. I made a film during Korea in which a character said, 'If this is a police action, why don't they send the police?' The military didn't like it but I said it anyway."[17]

Concerning Fuller's *The Steel Helmet,* critic Dennis Schwartz observes that Fuller "does not glorify the soldier as hero or try to explain the madness of war. He just lets things happen."[18] This objectivity is essentially Kubrick's method, but whereas he skillfully conceals the meanings and inner workings of his previous pictures, so as to enrich the subtext in his material, he makes a habit of "showing his cards" in *Full Metal Jacket,* occasionally making things dreadfully obvious. An example of this is a scene in which a colonel questions Matthew Modine's Joker as to why he wears a peace button and writes "Born to Kill" on his helmet. Kubrick scholar Jay Cocks rightly recognizes the Terry Southern influence in lines like "We've got to try to keep our heads while this peace craze blows over" and "Inside every gook is an American trying to get out."[19]

That Kubrick's film is more about war's cold confusion than about its madness is not of the essence. Objectivity in the depiction of an unpopular or ill-fated war (which *Dr. Strangelove* renders exceedingly well, often with broad satirical humor) is a tall task, because people cannot divorce themselves from their preexisting negative beliefs. Fuller's approach can function in a war with less heavy moral and political quandary, but not in a conflict that is mired in it. Those keen to make this observation are routinely accused of "not getting" Kubrick's message and/or method, so much so that the work almost becomes critic-proof. War's "cold confusion" is not depicted well from a directorial standpoint, and it makes the whole phenomenon of war feel oddly baggageless, even when Kubrick again shows his cards with nearly balletic Peckinpah-style slow-motion violence. Also, considering that Kubrick's best films are conversation pieces, serious discussions of *Full Metal Jacket* also often tend to appear superficial and mere projection. Martin Scorsese's description of the film, that it simply highlights "how important a drill sergeant is, and what the kids have got to go through,"[20] is such an example.

On the other hand, Furie first looks to establish easy empathy with stock characters (hippie, black, Brooklyn Italian, southern) because movie audiences had easily approached and embraced them so many times before, especially in classic World War II films like *Battleground, Bataan*, and Furie's favorite film, *They Were Expendable.* Amid the injustices of a newer, highly criticized war, he uses the resulting collective uncertainty to strip the stock types down to their barest humanity, depriving them of their free agency as individuals and reconstituting them as a single human unit. This element is what distinguishes it from a World War II "band of brothers film," or rather a picture set during a war that the American people largely believed in. As Douglas Kellner claims in his essay "Vietnam and the New Militarism," a "contiguous interconnection prevails" over a single point of view in *The Boys in Company C.*[21] The title itself reveals this. This is Furie's "third group of Boys," following both *The Boys* (1962) and *The Leather Boys* (1963). When one considers the male group dynamic in

Hit! (1973), *The Boys in Company C* is a whole new platform for Furie to meditate on male collective energy and the symbiosis and resulting feeling of group responsibility that naturally arises.

In William Wellman's *The Story of G.I. Joe,* war correspondent Ernie Pyle (Burgess Meredith) joins the 18th Infantry Unit, also called Company C, to acquire material for readers back on the home front. He witnesses much the same phenomenon, the "contiguous interconnection" established between these Company C soldiers, albeit in less fractured form because of a steadfast certainty about why the soldiers are fighting. They band together out of feeling united against a common enemy, not out of doubting the suspicious motives of their commanding officers amid an unjust war. It becomes no wonder that Furie and Natkin name their Company C in this film's honor, because the two scenarios complement each other so perfectly, presenting an apt contrast.

Neither *The Boys in Company C* nor *Full Metal Jacket* is much concerned with the geopolitical realities of Vietnam, even as the Tet Offensive marks the latter's midway point. Both use separate stylization in telling similar stories of soldiers shuttled from boot camp to the morass in Southeast Asia. The final soccer game in *The Boys in Company C,* when paralleled to the final football game in Robert Altman's *M*A*S*H* (1970), becomes a symbol for the real battles already seen and experienced in the film, which have been equally absurd. The battle scenes and the soccer game in Furie's film have a wild-card uncertainty. Furie prefers a chaotic perspective on war. Kubrick is too focused in his objectivity to acknowledge such necessary chaos in *Full Metal Jacket.*

Considering the incident at the prerelease screening of *The Lawyer* eight years earlier, when an audience member confronted Furie during the Q&A regarding making a film about "a rich, white doctor while people were being killed in Vietnam," it proved rather ironic that Furie officially became the first mainstream Hollywood filmmaker to deliver a Vietnam-themed film explicitly about soldiers putting their lives on the line in combat. The gravitas of the *American Graffiti*–style scrolling titles that conclude the film seems like an inadvertent direct answer to the earlier objection. As film scholar Brian J. Woodman writes in an essay, "The film took the World War II film formula and applied it to Vietnam, then shook it apart, making it into . . . 'an upside-down version of *The Green Berets.*' It entered unchartered territory in its portrayal of Vietnam as 'a breeding ground for imperialism, racism, corruption and death.'"[22] Additionally, Terry Christensen notes that "this platoon is like nothing seen before in a combat film. One soldier is addicted to heroin, while another steals drugs, and yet another destroys Army property for fun. Such nihilistic behaviors by stock characters are a tremendous deviation from the actions of characters in *The Green Berets*."[23]

Each frame is packed with visual information. If Furie does not refer back to the ensemble shots of *Hit!*, he "crams" the foreground to stage a shot for peripheral background action. For instance, he frames a shot predominantly to favor a bridge that the company is debating whether or not to cross, as three men, sectioned off to the far right of the frame, hash out their command and discuss what should be done. In another shot, actor Noble Willingham is pushed off to the far right of the foreground as he speaks before an assembled company of soldiers, while the rest of the frame favors the background, in which wounded are delivered and carried from a military ambulance. Thus, close-ups and singles have a weight they would not otherwise possess, as in the tight, silent pan across the five young Marines, stunned after Stan Shaw's Tyrone Washington fires a bazooka into two Vietnamese insurgents with no compunction. Such precision also exists in the orchestration of shots in the sequence in which Andrew Stevens's Billy Ray Pike defuses a rice-paddy landmine on which Tyrone Washington is stuck.

The film also bracingly tackles race the way it is rarely examined in American film, as a power struggle as well as a social struggle. A scene between Stan Shaw and R. Lee Ermey, in which Washington, the elected company leader, a black man, turns the tables on the gunnery sergeant and challenges him to measure up, exemplifies this notion. In moments of the scene, such as Washington's angry request that the sergeant remove his hat when speaking to him "man-to-man" (while also avoiding eye contact with him), the film assumes bolder ambitions than it lets on.

The Boys in Company C is the culmination of Furie's exploration of duty and personal commitment. In fact, the film may very well be the most direct manifestation of these themes, as the boys' foundering respect for their mission in Vietnam as Marines is finally toppled because they are made to feel wholly expendable, serving the comforts of the brass rather than defeating any threat or serving any ideology. Goldbricking is allowed to gleefully prevail, often in comic tone. The boys are seen in moments of outwardly shirking duty, defying a classic line spoken early in both *The Boys in Company C* and *Full Metal Jacket*: "Give your soul to God because your ass belongs to the Marines." Furie explores the ramifications of questioning one's commitment in an insane environment where individuality is forsaken in favor of a scared (and sacred) collective. For this and more, *The Boys in Company C* is one of Furie's masterpieces.

"Sidney was born to make *The Boys in Company C*. It was always his baby. For the time, I do think there was too much four-letter language, but it is a film that everyone involved can feel proud of," says Andre Morgan. Chow and Morgan offered Furie the chance to direct *The Shipkiller*, based on a best-selling novel by Justin Scott, which told the tale of a man who becomes a killer out to destroy the oil tanker that ran down his sailboat and killed his wife. In the end, as the numbers were added up, the project proved too expensive to warrant Golden Harvest's further considerations. Ultimately, Furie never directed another picture for Golden Harvest, although his relationship with them had been cemented and remained solid.

Shortly before the release of *The Boys in Company C*, Furie received a call from an old friend. Producer Jay Weston, the man who spearheaded *Lady Sings the Blues* and brought it to Furie and Brad Dexter in 1970, informed Furie that producer Arnold Kopelson was putting together a slate of pictures to be independently financed by Kopelson's Film Packages.

Jay Weston floated Furie's name for the ill-fated *Night of the Juggler*, an action thriller about an ex-cop who, quite literally, tears New York City apart to get his kidnapped daughter back safely. The deranged perpetrator, however, a disgruntled, viciously racist, disenfranchised New Yorker, has mistakenly kidnapped the wrong girl and hence asks the wrong father for a million-dollar ransom.

Night of the Juggler, a project Furie controversially quit in the middle of production, originated in 1975, under the title *Red Alert Central Park*, based on a book by crime novelist William P. McGivern, known for *The Big Heat* and *Odds against Tomorrow*. The 20th Century Fox–engineered script had been delivered by Bill Norton and *Serpico* writer Norman Wexler, with shooting scheduled to begin in April 1976. This first attempt at production was scuttled when Weston informed Fox studio head Alan Ladd Jr. that original director John Frankenheimer had been using Fox's money and resources to scout New York locations for another project he had up his sleeve, Paramount's *Black Sunday* (1977), when he actually had been sent to New York to scout locations for their own. *Night of the Juggler* was placed in turnaround until Kopelson's company picked it up and optioned it in early 1978.

When Furie agreed to direct the film, his first task was to have virtually everything rescripted. The plot was promptly stripped of some of its seamier aspects, including a subplot involving the kidnapper's annual serial raping and murdering of little girls on the anniversary of his mother's death. The villain transformed from a bloodthirsty "hulking, severely retarded"[24] homosexual into a disenfranchised malcontent with decidedly less pronounced psychosis. To help render the alterations, Furie brought Rick Natkin on board, not so much as a writer but as a glorified brainstormer. Says Natkin, "I basically went to New York with Sidney just to hang around with him. He brought me along as kind of like 'my pet goat' or a good luck charm or something." Furie, however, soon opened up to Natkin about his vision for *Night of the Juggler,* as "an extreme, hyperkinetic action caper" with constant movement and an incredible sense of urgency. The idea was to capture New York City's grittiest underbelly, sinking deeper into the morass of urban squalor and depravity than even Martin Scorsese had with *Taxi Driver.* Gradually, Natkin's contributions to the script were so substantial that he was granted full screenwriter credit.

For the lead role, a rugged "everyman" type, James Brolin, who had signed a four-picture contract with Ned Tanen at Universal during the filming of *Gable and Lombard,* was given special permission to accept the Furie project, and he grew a full beard for the physically demanding role. New York actors Cliff Gorman, Richard S. Castellano, and Dan Hedaya rounded out the cast. Victor J. Kemper, future president of the American Society of Cinematographers, signed on as cameraman in May 1978. With Kemper, Furie hatched an altogether new visual style for the picture, utilizing strictly long lenses in interior spaces. Long lenses, usually used for exteriors and crowd shots, compressed the film's interior scenes and heightened their sense of claustrophobia. This had not been done to such an extent before, but camera tests yielded the desired results.

Although Furie developed a stylistic specificity of purpose, neither Furie nor Natkin saw the project as anything beyond just a job. Says Natkin,

> I don't think Sidney found it a palatable experience. It was one of those movies that ends up getting made because someone made a deal to get it made. You've got a star, and a shooting date, and there are contracts, and you have everything but a movie. Neither of us were really passionate about it. The other writer, Bill Norton,

left before shooting and told me, "Listen, you and Sidney keep changing things. And that's fine, because this is not my baby and never was. Don't feel like you'll be stepping on my toes if you rewrite other stuff."

Furie's son Dan was given a spot on the film as apprentice editor. He commented, "I didn't spend a lot of time on the set because I was busy synching dailies, but I got a chance to see dad in action in the cutting room. He rented a place on Fire Island so that, on the weekends, we had a chance to escape the heat of the city."

Principal photography commenced on *Night of the Juggler* in New York on June 5, 1978. As much as possible, Furie once again attempted to shoot much of the film in sequence. This meant knocking off the film's extreme, no-holds-barred, ten-minute-plus chase sequence early on. "It was a gigantic chase. We really wanted to top them all, and start the picture off with a bang," says Furie. From the start, Furie and Weston often found themselves at odds with each other. Says Natkin, "I know that Jay Weston didn't get along with Sidney on that film, in many ways. I think that when Sidney ultimately quit, it presented an opportunity to distance himself from being second-guessed as a director."

On June 13, 1978, while shooting the foot-chase section of the big chase sequence, Brolin (ostensibly) broke a bone in his foot. With the actor's foot in a cast, the production faced imminent shutdown. Furie, however, continued to shoot around Brolin. Rick Natkin remembers, "I just kept making up scenes and we'd do them, and then, after awhile, we ran out of scenes to make up." Furie, determined to stick with the style and the ideas he had developed for the picture, was willing to wait for Brolin to heal. However, the producers and the insurance company, without first consulting their director, made the decision that they would write a fall into the picture, with Brolin left to play the whole movie on crutches. Says Furie, "That blew my whole concept for the movie. In the peak of anger for having a vision that they forced me to defer to, I quit." Natkin explained,

One Sunday afternoon, Sidney gave me an envelope and said, "Take this into Arnold Kopelson's office and just walk out." And that was when he told me, "Don't tell anybody, but I'm quitting. It's not going to screw up production and they have plenty of time to hire someone else, but this isn't my movie, especially not now." I told him, "Well, I'm leaving too!" And he said, "Don't you dare, because they have no idea what they're doing! You're the only person who has any idea what's going on." I was under the impression that they didn't want me around because I was Sidney's boy, his recruit.

On August 4, 1978, as Natkin left Kopelson's office, the beleaguered producer erupted as the door closed behind him, calling the young writer back to explain what he had just been given. "I don't know anything about it," Natkin told Kopelson, "Take it up with Sidney." According to Jay Weston, Furie called him from the airport to personally inform him. Says Weston, "He told me that because he could not make the film he envisioned, he didn't want to be a part of it. The whole thing was ridiculous to me, because he had been paid in full well in advance. The insurance company suggested we get another director, so we didn't waste any time trying to lure him back."[25]

Furie told *Variety* that he left *Night of the Juggler* because of "legal and artistic problems which culminated together," adding that "with the picture shut down, it seemed the proper time to terminate."[26] Soon after, a still surprised Weston fired back, "I don't know why Sidney decided to walk out. Sidney is an emotional, temperamental guy, but you ignore 90% of his mutterings. We had a problem with Brolin, but it was not insurmountable."[27] Weston revealed that he and Arnold Kopelson would certainly take legal action against Furie. According to Weston, "It took years to get back some of the money we paid him."[28] Furie and Weston have not spoken to each other since this ordeal.

Dan Furie remembers, "I learned that the circumstances of his departure, which were not good, dictated that I too would be departing, with six weeks supposed to be left of my summer gig." Television director Robert Butler was hired to complete the picture, on the heels of good news that Brolin's condition had been misdiagnosed. The actor had simply sprained and not broken a bone in his foot; he continued his work on the film unimpaired and entirely on foot.

"Something positive did come out of that picture, however," Furie says. "Bob Butler went on to direct *Hill Street Blues* and adopted that long lens style I had developed for *Night of the Juggler* for the show." Chiefly of note in the seedy, unpleasant *Night of the Juggler,* however, is the extended, unrelenting chase sequence that Furie did complete before resigning the picture. As an action set piece (featuring a young, unknown Mandy Patinkin as a high-strung Hispanic cab driver), it is one of the most volatile and energetic in memory and brims with a mixture of harried pace, "high-octane" brio, oddball flourishes, and a genuine feeling for how to best use the streets of New York. When finally released by Columbia in June 1980, the film as a whole tanked critically and commercially, dismissed for its hyperbole as well as its unforgivingly nasty depiction of the city.

Argyle Nelson, Furie's longtime Paramount editor, and the man who had been hired to put *Night of the Juggler* together, "defected" to Weston's camp when, in 1981, he edited Billy Wilder's *Buddy Buddy* (1981) under Weston's producership. Jay Weston, who was willing to discuss his involvement with Furie on *Lady Sings the Blues,* declined to discuss *Night of the Juggler* in depth, other than to say that it was a "horrible" experience.

The EMI-produced *The Jazz Singer,* another misbegotten Sidney J. Furie project, instantly trailed the *Night of the Juggler* debacle. Furie, fresh from the *Juggler* litigation but nevertheless still riding high following the successful release of *The Boys in Company C,* received a call from EMI head Barry Spikings's office about directing an updated version of the beloved 1927 Al Jolson property, the story of a pious Jewish cantor's son who pursues a dream of becoming a jazz singer. His father is heartbroken by his son's gravitation toward the limelight, yet the son succumbs to the sweet smell of success and faces a clash between family, tradition, and assimilation.

The idea of a pop-music remake had circulated from studio to studio in the years before Furie's involvement but never materialized. In the fall of 1977, after producer Jerry Leider wrestled the story rights away from United Artists and Warner Bros., the owners of the Jolson film, he joined forces with MGM to commission a full treatment of the updated story. MGM, deeming what screenwriter Stephen Foreman had given them "too Jewish,"[29] dropped out first. Leider then partnered his efforts with EMI, known mainly as a multinational record company. When Paramount likewise withdrew from negotiations, inexplicably, the project was placed in turnaround. However, that year, with *The Deer Hunter,* EMI hit Oscar gold with a coveted Best Picture win, convincing Spikings that a major independent production lay in the cards.

"I loved the Neil Diamond idea when they pitched it to me," says Furie, who signed on to the project in December 1978. "I also felt a personal connection to the material, because of my own background, and because I had

had a lot of fun doing *Lady Sings the Blues* with Diana, who was also a novice." Diamond, who would be making his movie debut, would compose all the film's original songs, compounding the film's marketability with soundtrack sales that appeared promising. "I was there when he performed 'America' for the first time, and it was very exciting. They were all great songs, and we were going to do the music in the film live, like the musicals of the old days." When EMI scored Laurence Olivier for the role of Diamond's stubbornly tradition-bound father, the thrill factor rose. The casting of Olivier, who had experienced a movie career resurgence after his Academy Award–nominated turn in *Marathon Man,* was perfectly in step with his previous casting in *The Boys from Brazil* (1978). Newly typecast as both Jews and Nazis, often back to back, he was to be paid a steep, stiff $1 million for just three weeks of work.

As on many of Furie's previous productions, there was constant rewriting. Stephen Foreman, delaying another opportunity of writing a movie based on the Eagles's album *Desperado,* took to the task of rewriting his old *Jazz Singer* script to suit Furie's needs, stating in a later article, "Originally Sidney told me there would be about a 10% rewrite. It became obvious after a short time that it was going to be more like 70%."[30] Well-regarded scribe Arthur Laurents was brought in to do "a polish" after the Furie-hired Herbert Baker delivered a draft that Diamond apparently disliked— one that reportedly "had the character becoming so rich and famous that he never returned home to make peace with his family at all."[31] However, Furie's claim regarding the matter begs to differ: "Contrary to what anyone says, my version of the script always had the Kol Nidre sequence at the end when Neil returns home to make peace with his father. We never did a version without it."

The April 1, 1979, start date was delayed when Diamond underwent back surgery. This was just the first of many such setbacks. In the heat of prep, Furie's mother, Ann, passed away from heart failure, on June 23, 1979. Because of her undocumented birth in Poland, her age at the time of death was officially unknown, estimated at around sixty-seven. Recalls Furie, who was profoundly impacted when he received this news, "I was even more upset when the producers didn't want me to take many days off to mourn, but I adopted the philosophy that the rigorous work would help dull the pain." As it turns out, this time, the work was not about to provide the best escape.

After a series of early delays, principal photography finally started on

January 17, 1980, in New York City. The picture went over budget quickly, largely as a result of Neil Diamond's jangled nerves. In his biography, Diamond is quoted as saying, "I'd come home at night exhausted, just mentally exhausted. After the first few weeks, I didn't think I could handle it anymore. Olivier would come home after a day's work on the set, swim laps in the hotel swimming pool and go out with friends for dinner. I came home and fell into bed exhausted knowing that I'd have to get up at four the next morning to study my lines for the day."[32]

One incident with the insecure star particularly miffed Furie.

We were shooting at a small club in New York, and we had no room for the extras to wait in the club, so they were all in buses with the motor running for heat. He was late and we kept on waiting for him to turn up. Then, he just didn't turn up at all. Same thing the second day, too. We had the extras in buses again and, again, he didn't turn up. I got angry and turned to Jerry Leider and said, "He'd better be here tomorrow!" He showed up on the third day and did the scene.

Throughout the shooting, Diamond often would not show up on set until two o'clock in the afternoon. The frustrated director, accustomed to "making the day" and executing all the planned shots, resorted to using upwards of five and six camera crews to cover everything that was needed within the limited time he was allotted. In a thwarted attempt to relax Diamond, Furie often used the type of freewheeling improvisation that echoed his approach to directing Diana Ross in *Lady Sings the Blues*. For Diamond, this instead had the opposite effect, confusing the uptight star.

Furie was later faulted by EMI and the producers for printing most of these improvised takes from the multiple cameras, even though it had been done to protect them in the cutting room. "The extra camera crew strategy worked fine, but it was not a good way to work, and I hated it because I could not function as a film director," Furie recalls. Furie's suggestion to the producers of scheduling the shooting day to start at 2:00 and wrap at 10 was shot down. Reaching his boiling point, he was now cornered, secretly asking himself "Who do I have to fuck to get off this picture?"

After two weeks in New York, production moved to Goldwyn Studios in Los Angeles. Although not cast in the film, actress Melanie Mayron, a veteran of Furie's *Gable and Lombard,* recalls visiting her friend Catlin Adams while she performed her scenes with Diamond. She was baffled and "amazed by what must have been six cameras in a semi-circle around the bed where Neil and Catlin were doing a scene together." Says Mayron, "I actually got up the courage to ask Sidney why he was doing it like that. He took the time to answer me and just said, 'I need to get everything I can. In the first place, Neil's not an actor. In the second place, we're way behind schedule and this is the only way to get through all the shots we have lined up.'"

At dailies, Diamond would visibly cringe and exclaim, "I look like a Jewish dentist from Brooklyn up there on that screen!"[33] Olivier was not making things any easier, exclaiming "This piss is shit!"[34] when reading the fresh rewrites in the morning. Most of all, Furie could no longer tolerate the internecine battles among the production team that resulted from the deadly cocktail of his star's fragility and ego. "I really think that Neil was just a regular guy scared to death to be acting in his first film,"[35] says Lucie Arnaz, who replaced Deborah Raffin as Diamond's manager–love interest, early on in production.

On February 29, 1980, Jerry Leider asked Furie to come in the next day, a Saturday, for the "umpteenth" script conference. Furie told Leider simply, "There's nothing to discuss. We have the final script." Leider continued to insist on the matter. Linda Furie remembers, "Sid told me, 'They said they're going to fire me if I don't go this meeting. I'm not going to the meeting. We're just going to take a drive to Malibu.'" They were true to their word. On the following Monday, March 3, 1980, Furie received his walking papers and the search for a "ringer" was mounted. With EMI's blessing, Leider first approached Michael Apted, whose *Coal Miner's Daughter* was due to open in theaters that Friday. However, when Apted promptly declined the offer, Richard Fleischer signed on. This made for a quick turnaround. On March 10, seven days after Furie's firing, shooting resumed. Fleischer, a journeyman who had also replaced Richard C. Sarafian on *Ashanti!* (1979) the previous year, had a history of conveniently stepping up to bat on other films when directors left under similar circumstances. (This happened in at least three other instances, with John Farrow on 1951's *His Kind of Woman,* John Huston on 1971's *The Last Run,* and Michael Campus on 1975's *Mandingo.*)

Furie, for his part, claims, "They had to fire me. They had to bring in a new director and issue a new edict to Neil, like 'Here it is! We're not standing for this shit anymore,'" says Furie. "I was relieved to be off that picture because I was not able to function as a film director. I didn't want to have to do six camera crews because this guy wouldn't show up. They paid me off and that was it." According to Fleischer's autobiography, Diamond's shenanigans did continue. He reported a particular instance when Jerry Leider had to resort to "some amusing Borscht Belt schtick"[36] with a crowd of extras to fill in the time needed for the star to built up the courage to come out of his dressing room.

Under Fleischer's direction, most of the final film was reshot, then released on December 17, 1980, to unanimously savage reviews but respectable box office. Roger Ebert famously quipped that the film "has so many things wrong with it that a review threatens to become a list." Olivier considered the film his bête noire, and his curses followed the film in subsequent years. "I've never had such a horrid time," he vented to Mark Amory, who taped over fifty hours of conversations with the actor. "The sickening, absolutely molasses-like Jewish sentimentality of it! It made me feel ill . . . it oozes sentiment like pus. I never saw anything, heard anything, read anything so absolutely awful."[37] *The Jazz Singer* did, however, outgross such hearty contenders as *Raging Bull, American Gigolo,* and *The Elephant Man.* Beyond that, Diamond's soundtrack album outperformed the actual film.

Variety reported on June 9, 1981, that approximately 10 percent of the final cut of *The Jazz Singer* was Furie's, most of that material existing early in the first act. Shortly after Furie's double trouble, Andre Morgan offered Furie the chance to direct *High Road to China* for Golden Harvest; they had exhausted other directors, namely John Huston and Brian G. Hutton (who actually went on to direct the film). Ultimately, schedules were not aligning and Furie declined when his next project eventually did come along.

Considering *The Jazz Singer*'s ultimate quality, its cliché-riddled script, its scornful critical reception, and the cold appraisal of Diamond's inauspicious acting debut, as experienced next to Olivier's camp interpretation of Jewish fatherdom, it was certainly to the benefit of Furie's overall oeuvre that he was fired. Fleischer, who topped off his career with other notorious flops like *Amityville 3-D* (1983) and *Red Sonja* (1985), never lived it down. The *Juggler* and *Singer* affairs caused great practical hardships for Furie at the time, though. When his next completed project did ultimately come down the pike over a year later, he made yet another quantum leap in genre.

Chapter 10

Cool Sounds from Hell

The Entity

Sid will very frankly tell you that his career was in jeopardy.
—*Harold Schneider, producer of* The Entity

By the time 1980 rolled around, the moviemaking climate had shifted dramatically in Hollywood, with the odds stacking stone cold against the auteur. Blockbusters like *Jaws* and *Star Wars* had redefined the paradigm overnight, while expensive and extravagant "personal films" like Peter Bogdanovich's *At Long Last Love* (1975), Martin Scorsese's *New York, New York* (1977), William Friedkin's *Sorcerer* (1977), and Michael Cimino's *Heaven's Gate* (1980) crippled and bankrupted studios.

In the eyes of Hollywood, the unwitting forty-seven-year-old Furie had fully reasserted his earlier enfant terrible reputation, as reflected in entertainment headlines that depicted him as temperamental and unmanageable. Furie, tireless, never truly let the traumas of *Night of the Juggler* and *The Jazz Singer* sink in or impede his forward thinking, especially when he stopped to consider how his exceptionally family-driven life had so dovetailed. His five sons and one daughter contrasted his only-child upbringing quite boldly. His son Chris had turned nine, his daughter, Sara, had turned seven, and his sons from his first marriage, to Sheila, were either in college or about to enter. Behind him at every moment, without fail, was wife, Linda. Added to the arsenal of support were Michael Caine and wife, Shakira, who had moved to Beverly Hills in the autumn of 1977. The Furies and the Caines quickly became social friends, and Furie still admits today, "I've never met another director who didn't say that Michael was the greatest guy they'd ever worked with, so having him as a friend and neighbor was such a blessing at that point."

Says Michael Caine, "We backed Sidney up all the way, because when you get into the situation he was in at that point, no one in town wants to have lunch with you, or dinner with you. That's Hollywood! But Sid and I saw a lot of each other then and he liked that he never had to talk about any of that stuff. It was just, 'Here I am having dinner with Sid.' And Linda and my wife, Shakira, were having their ladies lunches and became best friends. Our kids grew up with each other. It was all such a lovely time."

Days still provided their curiosities and adventures, spurring Furie's creative drive to direct a film to its completion after two years of creative miscarriages. He had started developing a personal project about a rough-and-tumble fraternity of cross-country truckers. "One might say it was a slightly artier version of [Sam Peckinpah's] *Convoy*," says Furie, who spent nearly a year struggling to assemble a script to his satisfaction. "It would have been a portrait of some of these men on the road, living by a code, banding together, pushing their limits, juggling it all with a home life that was far away somewhere. It was kind of a romantic view of that profession." Potential deals to fund the project's development fizzled, and the idea remains unrealized. "Maybe I would have called it *The Boys on the Road*," Furie jests, humorously acknowledging his proclivity for titles containing the word "boys." The film would have fit right in with Furie's other studies on male collective group dynamics.

One day, Furie received a call from Andre Morgan, who was on set in the Philippines with Roger Vadim. A distressed Morgan explained that Vadim was directing a spicy sex thriller entitled *Night Games* (1980) for Golden Harvest.

"The film is out of control, Vadim is giving me a lot of trouble, and he's essentially hijacking the production. I would like to shut the thing down, but I can't afford to shut anything down right now, let alone in the Philippines."

"So do you have any idea what you're gonna do?" asked Furie.

"Well, tell me what you think of this idea: If I give you a ticket, could you come to Manila and just hang out at the hotel with me for a few days?"

"Why?"

"Because Roger is very territorial, and if he sees that I've got another Hollywood director in the wings and thinks that I might fire and replace him, maybe he'll start to shape up."

"I see. Okay, you've got it! Send the ticket! I love the Philippines!"

The following day, Furie, happy to return to the country that midwifed *The Boys in Company C,* arrived in Manila. Vadim, believing that Furie was Sidney Lumet, complimented him on *Dog Day Afternoon.* When Furie's presence on set persisted, Vadim, sensing a shake-up, started behaving himself. After the three-day excursion, Furie returned home to an offer from Harold Schneider, producer of *Days of Heaven* and brother of *Easy Rider* producer Bert Schneider. He sent Furie a script that came ready-made: *The Entity,* an adaptation by Frank De Felitta from his own 1978 novel.

The whole concept aligned with a new trend toward supernatural subject matter and presented Furie with an opportunity to be visually audacious. Based on the real-life paranormal disturbances of Doris Bither, one of the most famous case studies in the history of parapsychology, De Felitta's novel and screenplay told the story of Carla Moran, a woman who finds herself repeatedly raped, assaulted, and otherwise violated by a raging poltergeist. The project warranted that special care be exercised in writing a rare female protagonist who fought back and bravely resisted, and also casting a strong, sympathetic female lead.

Furie, throughout all his genre-hopping since his earliest days in England, had not tackled horror after *Doctor Blood's Coffin* and *The Snake Woman,* both released in 1961. De Felitta had a solid horror pedigree, as the author of the smash best-seller *Audrey Rose,* adapted into a successful 1977 Robert Wise film. Upon reading the script for *The Entity,* Furie enthusiastically took the job. Says Furie, "Frank as a writer was such a pro, and we never had to touch the script. I loved it as soon as I read it, which was a good sign because I needed a happy picture after the chaotic two years I had just experienced."

Budgeted at $8.5 million and set up as a tax-shelter picture by Harold Schneider and Joe Wizan through the recently established American Cinema International (ACI) Productions, *The Entity* was first groomed as a project for Roman Polanski. There were two primary caveats for directors, though. Because of the tax-shelter deal, the film had to shoot for no less than ten weeks, double that of another film of this size (Furie later claimed that "it was the only picture where I was ever told to take my time every day"). The second red flag was ACI's "image problem," because it had a reputation for low-budget exploitation pictures, namely two early Chuck Norris vehicles. Considering the sensitive, potentially prurient subject matter, this would present a public-relations obstacle in hiring a director and, especially, an actress. For their part, Schneider and his colleagues always saw *The Entity* as the breakout picture that would elevate ACI's reputation.

Jane Fonda, Jill Clayburgh, Bette Midler, and Sally Field were considered, and all quickly declined. "There were even actresses who weren't so big who turned it down," says Frank De Felitta. "Two actresses told me they thought it would be a laughable movie."[1] Barbara Hershey, cast ten days before shooting started, off the strength of her performance in *The Stunt Man* (1980), first turned down the role herself because it required nudity. She only agreed when Furie told her they would use a stand-in and would construct a sixty-five-thousand-dollar mechanical mannequin for scenes that placed her in more compromising positions. "Barbara was like a gift from heaven to us," De Felitta claimed in a 1983 *Los Angeles Times* piece written on the heels of the film's eventual release.

Hershey was not without apprehensions. "When I was considering the role, I was frightened. I didn't know how it would be edited or marketed. But I knew that Sid saw potential in the film to approach the subject from a humanistic and psychiatric viewpoint, from a mother's viewpoint . . . and I felt it was a worthwhile risk." When later asked if she enjoyed working with Furie, she replied, "I loved it. I'm sure my performance was two hundred percent what I would have done otherwise."[2]

Certainly Furie's most stylish and dynamically formalist postseventies film, *The Entity* turned out to be an adventurous reeducation for cinematographer Stephen Burum, who remembers, "When I expressed my reservations about the script, the first thing that Sidney told me is that we were going to technique the hell out of it." This "techniquing" was going to involve extreme, canted "Dutch" angles, the use of split diopters (bringing two planes into focus simultaneously), carefully calculated mise-en-scène, and other devices.

After the second-billed Ron Silver was cast as Dr. Sniderman, the suspicious psychiatrist who reduces Carla's disturbances to degrading psychobabble, Furie got a taste of Harold Schneider's power-tripping distrust when Craig T. Nelson was tabled to play the role of the lead character's largely absent boyfriend, Jerry. "Harold Schneider was supportive in certain ways, but could also be vein-popping mad the way Harry Saltzman had been with me on *Ipcress,*" Furie recalls.

I told Harold that Craig was my first choice. He said he was adamantly against him and that I would have to recast. I had never been second-guessed on casting supporting roles like that. No matter how much I tried to plead with him, he wouldn't let me cast Craig. So, we had to go with Alex Rocco, who did a great job, but it troubled me that I felt I didn't have control over something I always had control over as a director. I think it was him just letting me know who was boss, perhaps because of the rumors that started after *Juggler* and *Jazz Singer*.

As with Diana Ross, Jill Clayburgh, James Brolin, and others, television once again informed one of Furie's casting decisions when New York–based David Labiosa, a handsome young Puerto Rican actor, was cast as Barbara Hershey's son, Billy. Having seen him on the television movie *Death Penalty*, starring Colleen Dewhurst, Furie had him flown out to Los Angeles when their other candidates for the role did not meet his liking. Labiosa remembers, "I didn't audition for Sidney. We just talked, because he seemed to think I had already auditioned for him, because I had been in *Death Penalty*. I actually met him at his house around midnight, and after we talked, he told me that he wanted me to meet Barbara Hershey, to get to know her. It was unusual, in my experience." Labiosa also confesses, laughing, "When I met Sidney and learned that he had been the guy who directed *Lady Sings the Blues*, which was one of my all-time favorite movies growing up in the Bronx, I went nuts. I told him how I felt about that film, and he probably thought it was just another actor desperate to get a role."

When a house in El Segundo was selected for exterior shooting, a studio set was built to match the interior. The accomplished Stan Winston, venerated for his work on *The Thing* (1982) and later *The Terminator* (1984), was brought on to render special makeup effects, including the infamous scene in which Hershey's breasts are fondled by invisible hands. With the cast filled out, the practical needs of production met, and the floor opened for Furie's "high style," things were looking up for the first time in years.

Shooting commenced on *The Entity* on March 30, 1981, and continued throughout late spring and early summer. Furie's experience shooting *The Entity* was mostly smooth sailing. Furie's son Dan, who worked on the film, remembers, "Dad was just happy to be working again. Just from looking at him, you could see it." In his own words, Sidney Furie delights in the experience of making *The Entity*: "There were no extras waiting in buses, no six camera crews, no bullshit. And at every point, we knew the film was working pretty well."

As in the director's earlier days, Furie's chutzpah seemed in fine form, especially when confronting a pair of technical advisers looking to score on the sidelines. Cinematographer Stephen Burum accounts how these technical advisers approached one of Hershey's young stand-ins, telling her that they detected she had a "spiritual problem." Soon they were asking to move their recording gear into her bedroom. "This stand-in went over to Sid and told him what was going on, and he told her not to worry. As soon as she stepped away, he told the assistant director, Tommy Thompson, 'Get Frick and Frack over here!' So these two guys came over and Sid laid into them. He said, 'Don't ever talk to our girls like that! If you're looking to get laid, just ask them and stop the bullshit. You know you've got a fifty percent chance. They'll either say yes or no.'"

Burum also recalls, "We would spend all day lighting the house, and this is after months of lighting the same parts of the house many times. You get tired of the monotony and, as a person working on a film every single day, you're looking to do things differently, to shake things up. When I told Sid, he just looked at me and, without batting an eye, said, 'Of course! We can do this scene anywhere. Where should we do it, do you think?'" For Burum, working with Furie was a joy. He explains, "Sid will take your idea and multiply it. And then you'll take his idea that builds on yours and multiply it, and then in the end, whose shot is it? He let me try anything I wanted to try. We used split diopters and played with the notion of anamorphic eyescan. It was like school, a real learning ground for everyone. Sid would always say things like, 'Between everyone present, we have 600 years of motion picture experience. We can figure this out!' You felt energized being around a director like that."

One of the few bumps in the road came as a result of yet another filming-incurred broken bone. This time, however, it was correctly diagnosed. In encounters with the invisible entity, actors were obliged to violently throw themselves back (that is, if they were not already attached to yanking wires that did the work for them). Labiosa injured himself during one such encounter and resurfaced wearing a cast on his arm. The script was rewritten in emergency time to accommodate this change, with Labiosa completely written out of other scenes that were planned with him. On top of this, Labiosa had originally agreed to have electrical charges planted on his body for when his character wrestles with the entity. At the appointed moment, electrical shocks would emanate from his hands and arms. When he refused, informing Furie and the crew that his doctor had warned him about a possible cancer risk, a silhouetted figure replaced Labiosa.

Perhaps the most controversial scene in the original script was one involving Hershey's character's seduction of her own son. In a steamy sexual-fantasy sequence, Hershey imagines deflowering Labiosa in Oedipal fashion. This scene was filmed but excised from the final cut of the film. "Everyone was very uncomfortable with the whole notion of incest," says Labiosa. "I think it was awkward for everyone to do, because of what the whole thing implied. I often wonder what the film would have been like if they had kept it in."

The extended duration of the shooting prompted many to jest, "What is this, *Gone with the Wind*?" Because of the film's tax deals, the cast and crew were forced to shoot for ten weeks, much longer than it normally would have taken. After finally wrapping in June 1981, 20th Century Fox president Sherry Lansing urged the studio to pick it up for distribution. Although the film enjoyed excellent previews ("The preview cards, like the ones for *Gable and Lombard,* were some of the best ever," Furie recalls), when ACI went bankrupt after the movie's completion, Fox unfortunately delayed and dumped the release of *The Entity* after an early-1980s corporate shake-up that inflicted other cinematic casualties like Martin Scorsese's *The King of Comedy* (1983), Robert Altman's *HealtH* (limited, scattered releases in both 1980 and 1982), and the Mike Hammer thriller *I, the Jury* (1982).

Released in the United States with a surprisingly tasteful ad campaign and little prepublicity on February 4, 1983, after a rocky British premiere the previous September that was met with protest demonstrations by women's groups, the film opened to good box office and mixed reviews. It had been a full five years since a Sidney Furie film had been released to American theaters, the longest period ever between two of his pictures. Richard F. Shepard of the *New York Times* remarked that Hershey carried off her role "convincingly" and observed that the film "offers thrills in short staccato bursts and dull science in long bursts." Kevin Thomas of the *Los Angeles Times,* outing himself as a fan, found it "more than just good." He continued, "*The Entity* is an intense and engrossing entertainment," and ended his review stating that it "stands alongside *The Leather Boys, The Ipcress File, The Lawyer, Lady Sings the Blues* and *The Boys in Company C* as one of [Furie's] best films." Dissenters included Susan King of the *L.A.*

Herald-Examiner, who found it "vile and exploitative" with "some of the most tasteless sex scenes depicted on screen." In one of the film's other more virulent detractions, *Variety* labeled Furie's direction "insipid" and Frank De Felitta's screenwriting "trite" and ruled that "none of the characters ring true."

On opening weekend, the film grossed $3.7 million; it ultimately grossed $13.3 million by the end of its run. Although there was no widespread outcry in the United States, woman's groups in England picketed the film. Dani Adams, a spokeswoman for the Canadian group Women against Violence against Women offered a statement about the film when interviewed by *Los Angeles Times* reporter John M. Wilson:

> As a woman, the movie made me nauseous. As a member of my organization, I found it very violent. I was impressed by how slick and well-made it was—but that makes it all the worse, because you get all the more involved in it. It makes certain feminist points very well—the things that often happen to a victimized woman happen to this woman. But the fact is, it is a woman being exploited again, with the rape scenes becoming progressively more graphic, showing more and more of her body, to keep the audience interested. The movie is clearly designed this way.

When asked about the muted outcry in the United States, Adams said, "It's usually the ads that tip us off first, although we have been getting complaints."[3]

Hershey, when confronted about these matters, responded firmly but without rancor, "I resent being put in the position of defending the film. We worked really hard not to make it exploitative. Rape is one of the ugliest if not the ugliest thing that can happen to someone. It's murder of a sort. I have no answer for those people who are offended. They're right, but I don't think our intention was to exploit the subject, or the result. Truly, I don't. I think we did well with it."[4] Schneider and De Felitta echoed her defense in their own words, with the latter pleading, "If I've done anything to hurt someone so terribly, I'm very sorry, but I would still write it and I would still see the picture made. Your being offended would not stop me."[5]

Subsequent appraisals of *The Entity,* however, seem to suggest acceptance and even some exuberant praise, and its successful video releases ensure a consistent stream of rediscovery and revenue. American critic Michael Atkinson writes, "There may not be, outside of David Cronenberg's wonder cabinet, a more nitro-powered horror-movie metaphor hell than that fueling this post-*Exorcist* remnant. . . . It's like the movie is writing its own library of fiery feminist theory. It remains unnerving and savage, arguably the most eloquent movie ever made in Hollywood about the struggle of the sexual underclass."[6] *Time Out* critic David Pirie writes, "The film's men are so uniformly creepy, and its heroine so strong and sympathetic, that apart from a couple of unpleasant moments the story often seems less like horror than feminist parable, especially when Hershey (giving a fine performance) is reduced to a laboratory object with her home recreated in the psychology department. It goes to show that commercial movies sometimes hit spots that more intentionally didactic efforts can't reach."[7]

In perhaps its most flattering plaudit, Martin Scorsese named the film as the fourth scariest horror film ever made, placing it above such works as *The Shining* and *Psycho.* In 1999, Austrian experimental filmmaker Peter Tscherkassky reedited shots from the film for his much-admired short film *Outer Space,* only to reappropriate that film for another short, *Dream Work* (2001). In 2009, Quentin Tarantino sampled Charles Bernstein's soundtrack from *The Entity* in *Inglourious Basterds.* Beyond these commendations and citations, the film lives on as a cult item that still sells out midnight film screenings. Visually, *The Entity* is Furie's most radical picture since his Wild Angles trilogy in the sixties. He is ever using the frame and its outer corners to suggest a menace that can enter from anywhere. Furie's evocative use of the split diopter, a favorite trope of Brian De Palma, with whom Stephen Burum later collaborated, allows the ability to maintain Hershey in focus with the others in the frame, no matter how near or far her position in relation to the lens. This suggests a rigidity in many of Hershey's encounters with the many suspicious figures in her life.

Kier-La Janisse, in her landmark feminist film theory book *House of Psychotic Women: An Autobiographical Topography of Female Neurosis in Horror and Exploitation Films,* devotes the first chapter to *The Entity.* Though Janisse's largely unfavorable assessment is sophisticated on the whole and well-reasoned in sections, her interpretations come off as alarmist and obtuse relative to other writings that place the work under the microscope of feminism, though they still open the floor for a potentially compelling debate. She writes, "Carla's response to the entity alternates between resignation and determination. Still, she doesn't seem especially hopeful; when Dr. Sniderman reaches out to her, and suggests that she needs to maintain contact with someone in the outside world who cares about her, she says, 'I don't want to make that contact.' Again, she exhibits the behavior of the masochistic woman who repeatedly returns to an abusive lover. In a sense, it's traumatic bonding—the abuse only strengthens the ties between the abused and the abuser."[8] Thus, Janisse refuses to interpret this scene as Carla taking another in a series of brave stands against other predators, the ones that are visible to the naked eye. Sniderman, arguably another "entity" in the film, a scoffer with a smarmy mastery of Freudspeak and Harris tweed couture, objectifies Carla (like other men in the film) after discrediting her.

Without question, Barbara Hershey, in the film's central role, plays one of the strongest, self-determining female characters of 1980s mainstream American genre cinema, a true anomaly in an era of helpless, one-dimensionally imbecilic damsels in distress.

Three key Furie films center around "women in trouble": *Lady Sings the Blues, Sheila Levine Is Dead and Living in New York,* and *The Entity.* These films represent disparate landscapes in consideration of feminism, and when seen together, they chart a progression of sexual politics in Furie's work over a ten-year period. In *Lady Sings the Blues,* Louis McKay motivates and sustains Billie Holiday amid a life-wrecking addiction. McKay is chivalrous, a "man behind the woman" upon whom the success of the Lady in question depends. The film nonetheless rightly succeeded with critics and audiences and was never beset by feminists, although the movement in this incarnation was in its infancy at the time of the film's release. In *Sheila Levine Is Dead and Living in New York,* Sheila Levine's station as a take-charge, independent career woman is easily shaken, temporary, and ill-fated when she throws herself, often in outright shamelessness, at the doctor who has captured her heart after a one-night-stand. Feminists took that film to the cleaners, and it bombed.

In *The Entity,* Carla Moran formidably goes head-to-head with a gaggle of men (including the "entity" itself). If the men of the film do not undermine her credibility or sanity, they objectify her, exploit her victimhood, belittle her ability to take control of her unfortunate circumstances, and ultimately give her the dignity of a glorified lab rat. The title becomes a double entendre as Carla herself risks becoming an entity, a specimen, a stake in a selfish, male-engineered power-play. She does have a boyfriend, played by Alex Rocco, who is always on business trips. His remiss, sporadic appearances and final abandonment do nothing to shake the heroine's courage and fortitude. One cannot help but think of *The Entity* as an influence and even a blueprint for Todd Haynes's *Safe* (1995), with its story of a woman besieged and victimized by that which she cannot see.

Early in his career, Furie made it his business to get to the heart of the wounded male consciousness, from the impotent fighter pilot in *During One Night* (1961) to the ne'er-do-wells in *Little Fauss and Big Halsy* (1970). Even *The Boys in Company C* featured various "cockfights" between members of the title group. Carla's invisible attacker is Furie's ultimate wounded male. Suggesting that the entity is Carla's sexually abusive Baptist minister father lashing out at her for wounding his sense of male dominance, Furie presents one of his favorite themes with a strong, indomitable female center, perhaps for the first time. No matter the skill of each respective actress playing the female roles in the Furie films previous to *The Entity*, characters like Anne Pearson's in *A Dangerous Age*, Carolyn Dannibale's in *A Cool Sound from Hell*, Susan Hampshire's in *During One Night*, Rita Tushingham's in *The Leather Boys*, and Lauren Hutton's in *Little Fauss and Big Halsy* were never quite afforded such admirable strength of character, to the extent that it easily eclipses that of the male characters. Men were mostly the center of the drama in Furie's stories, and through their eyes the director's point was realized. *The Entity*, in Furie's body of work, is sui generis, and ironically the summation of a career of thematic examination: a film about wounded masculinity that examines a hapless female victim of it. Complexity exists beyond this auteurist paradox, such as in the scene in which Carla experiences an orgasm when the entity gently rapes her as she sleeps. Despite the clear pleasure she experiences, she awakens to angry tears. The David Cronenberg–esque "body horror" eschews titillation and transcends being simply a showcase for the latest in special effects and movie prosthetics. Carla's privacy is violated and, by extension, her sense of self. She loses control over her own body as it, in this moment, refuses to align with her head. This sexual confusion in some way mirrors the male character's in Furie's *During One Night* (1961).

Carla stands alone, even when various surrounding men proclaim how they are "helping her." Tara Judah, in her essay "Attacked by Nothing: Barbara Hershey and *The Entity* in Peter Tscherkassky's *Outer Space* and *Dream Work*," observes that the film is about the feminine condition, in that "the harder she fights, the more she is disbelieved, ignored, or (as is so often the case with men questioning female subjectivity) written off as crazy."[9] On this matter, Kier-La Janisse writes, "[Sniderman's] interviews with her mirror the interrogation heaped upon abused women when they finally turn to someone for help: they are suspected of fabrication, provocation, even seduction."[10] If the rapist had been flesh and blood, one senses that the reaction to Carla would scarcely be different.

Several months into the editing of *The Entity*, Furie's father, Samuel, died of colon cancer, on September 6, 1981, just before his seventy-second birthday. Around the same time, Furie himself became afflicted with the same disease. Told by a doctor to get his affairs in order ("They were already well in order") and to hope for the best but expect the worst, Furie was reprieved by the tumor's considerable size. "It was so large that it didn't spread to anywhere else in the body," Furie says. "A friend of mine told me at the time that you worry about the little tumors, because they're harder to find and diagnose, and quicker to spread. It gave me and everyone a hell of a scare though." Nevertheless, as one generation of the Furie family passed into history, the next generation of Furies was about to make its entrance. Sidney Furie became a grandfather on April 25, 1985, with the birth of granddaughter Jess to his son Dan, who had scrapped dreams of becoming a film director himself and had instead entered law school.

The then-modest success of *The Entity*, perhaps the most thematically dense of Furie's films and, as a result, the most academically analyzed, ensured that if Furie's career had been down, it was, in actuality, far from over. He found himself once again in the position to pitch a personal project with confidence and without stigma. For this next project, Furie returned to custom-made material, after having exclusively tackled source material with *Night of the Juggler*, *The Jazz Singer*, and *The Entity*. The story of *Purple Hearts*, the second in the director's unofficial Vietnam trilogy, was hatched in a car ride Furie shared with his thirteen-year-old son Chris while on his way to pitch projects to Rick Natkin for presentation at the Ladd Company, a subsidiary of Warner Bros. spearheaded in 1979 by Alan Ladd Jr., Gareth Wigan, and Jay Kanter. The three founded the company following their departure from 20th Century Fox and produced hits and Oscar contenders like *Body Heat* (1981), *Blade Runner* (1982), and *The Right Stuff* (1983) under the new banner. One Ladd Company picture, *Chariots of Fire* (1981), took home the Academy Award for Best Picture.

If *The Boys in Company C* is Furie's rendition of *The Story of G.I. Joe* as set in Vietnam, then *Purple Hearts* is his take on World War II romances like *Waterloo Bridge* (1940) as set in Vietnam. Perhaps most fittingly, it is a near-remake of Richard Brooks's Korean War romance *Battle Circus* (1953), which starred Humphrey Bogart as an embittered-by-war surgeon who falls in love with a naive but lionhearted nurse, played by June Allyson. That said, *Purple Hearts* is the type of pulpy romantic melodrama that would have attracted moviegoers to the box office in the 1940s but left them cold in the 1980s. Furie and Natkin pitched the story of a Navy SEAL surgeon stationed on the front lines, who falls in love with a foxy, strong-willed nurse stationed near Saigon. Their turbulent romance is framed against the backdrop of America's most heavily criticized war, comprising a hybrid of romantic melodrama and combat action film. Complete with an ending that many critics deemed improbable (in which the lovers, each believing the other one to be dead, are tearfully reunited at a Stateside V.A. hospital), *Purple Hearts* unapologetically harked back to the days of American cinema when such operatic coincidence was regularly accepted, expected, and desired. The only thing different was the four-letter language and sex that was not just an intimated offscreen activity.

The notion of a Vietnam War love story appealed to the Ladd executives, and Furie and Natkin soon set up offices next to John Milius to work on the script and then preproduction. At the time, Milius was doing uncredited rewrites on Sergio Leone's *Once upon a Time in America* (1984), a Ladd Company production, and working on a project that later became *Red Dawn* (1984). Natkin, who then owned a camouflage Volkswagen bug, remembers, "John Milius was always wanting to borrow my car, and then one day, he offered to buy it from me."

When the Ladd Company greenlit and bankrolled *Purple Hearts* on March 16, 1983, at a relatively modest $2.8 million budget, casting got under way. The unknown Kevin Costner was Furie's first choice for the role of Dr. Don Jardian. Natkin remembers, "Sid seemed to like Kevin best, but I told him that he reminded me too much of the member of the *Boys in Company C* cast who cracked under the pressures of the Philippines." When Furie took Costner's screen test to the Ladd Company executives, Alan Ladd Jr. had two of his secretaries watch the tape. The verdict came in loud and clear. Both of the secretaries hated him. One of them called Costner a "sexless creep." Attentions shifted to another actor, one who was more emergent at the time. Ken Wahl had appeared opposite Paul Newman in *Fort Apache, the Bronx* (1981) and shared star billing in the Don Siegel–directed Bette Midler–starring *Jinxed!* (1982), a notorious behind-the-scenes "nightmare project" (exacerbated in the press by a well-covered war between Midler and Wahl), when Furie hired him for *Purple Hearts.*

For the female lead, the unknown and anxious Kim Basinger auditioned and was dismissed after a poor reading. "I had no idea at the time that she had a panic disorder," says Furie. "When I had the same type of situation with a dyslexic actor a year later, I refused to have auditioning actors read sides from the script from then on. It's cruel." Instead, Furie invented an audition technique in which actors improvise a phone scene in which they must make a series of emotional transitions. "I tell them to make the dialogue easy, not to get too complicated, and to show me a range of emotion from line to line, and from pause to pause. For any director, I think it's revealing and it certainly tells me a hell of a lot." With Basinger dispatched, television star Cheryl Ladd, fresh from her lucrative stint on *Charlie's Angels,* was cast in the female lead.

The director's return to the Philippines made for pleasant and mostly uneventful shooting. R. Lee Ermey, Furie's discovery from *The Boys in Company C,* appeared again, this time as a beleaguered Marine gunny in charge of commanding a rapidly dwindling platoon of men caught in the fusillade of a fiery quagmire. Completing the cast was the third-billed Stephen Lee, a television actor who later was singled out by many critics as having given the best performance in the film. Furie himself was slated to make a cameo appearance in the film as a general. "I was so embarrassed by my performance that I took the negative back to California and burned it," claims Furie. "I had never tried performing in any of my movies before, and I don't get how any director could look at him or herself and not be critical . . . and have it affect the editing process."

An important new figure made his way into Furie's creative retinue. The production supervisor Kevin Elders, affectionately knighted as "Conan the Accountant" by the crew, had been sent on behalf of the Ladd Company to keep the books on location. His real business, however, was in intriguing the director he was overseeing with creative discussion. "Kevin was a fully realized creative person," says Furie. "He was good at spitballing ideas, and he loved talking about movies. Boy, could he talk! It was incredibly unusual for an accountant, to say the least. They're always the quiet ones looking at the numbers and seething underneath."

The film opened the fourteenth USA Film Festival, which also premiered *Blood Simple, This Is Spinal Tap,* and Robert Altman's *Streamers. Variety* reported *Purple Hearts* as one of the worst-attended screenings, as it seemed few were interested enough to bother to show up. When the film went into general release, Kirk Ellis made a recommendation in his *Hollywood Reporter* review, not for audiences to see the film, but rather that veterans to whom the picture is dedicated "return this cinematic medal to sender." Roger Ebert trashed the film by harping on an earlier Furie success: "The boys in Company C would have thrown beer bottles at the screen." Janet Maslin wrote in the *New York Times* that the film, and by extension its director, "reveals a weakness for just the sort of Hollywood hokiness that can discredit any movie." She complained that "whenever the film's war scenes verge on becoming believable, which is often enough, the love story is allowed to take over." David Chute of the *L.A. Herald Examiner* found the film "dismal" but conceded for a moment that "Furie does display some pictorial skill in action sequences." Collectively, the rest of the reviews, including the one in *Variety* and the one by Kevin Thomas of the *Los Angeles Times,* could form an echo chamber in their impressions that the picture was better in the trenches than in the boudoir.

Much like the similar *Battle Circus, Purple Hearts* flopped. Grossing only $2 million, the film barely made back its scant investment, playing to mostly empty theaters. "Women loved it," Furie is quick to point out. "I got all kinds of letters from women telling me they loved the picture, and I kept getting them for years." *Purple Hearts* is anomalous as a Vietnam movie that takes no political stance on the war. In fact, the war is only present in the film for the purposes of staging action and providing an atypical backdrop for the romance at its center. It follows the lead of *The Boys in Company C* in celebrating military values and avoiding any gesture on the part of the director that could pass fast judgments. The film also represents Furie's definitive move toward an approach that reflected more populist, Hollywood-derived brands of storytelling. It is a love story with a willfully naive "give-the-audience-what-it-wants" mentality. But a film like this was out of line with the cynical 1980s movie audience, who were out to jeer endeavors that pandered to easy sentimentality, unless it came packaged with a lovable alien, a hot new box-office star, or unsubtle American exceptionalist attitudes (which Furie's next film unapologetically sported).

The film does have certain virtues, and it marks the last time in the director's work he truly experimented with anamorphic wide-screen composition. There is often the attempt to use every inch of the screen width. In many shots, he fragments the screen, composing for frames within the frame, just as he did during his "wild angles" period with *The Ipcress File.*

For instance, in one such shot early on in the film, Ken Wahl is covered from behind while in dialogue with actor Lane Smith. Wahl's head divides the screen in two, between Smith on one side and two working surgeons on the other side. Wahl's salute, which ends the scene, further divides the frame. Such stylism is not present in any form in Furie's next film, *Iron Eagle.* There are also many action set pieces that excite, such as when Wahl chases a VC guerrilla carrying a live grenade through the warrens of an underground passage. The above-ground component of the same sequence also stands out, both in its orchestration and in attention to visual detail.

When Furie returned from the Philippines, he started prepping a Lem Dobbs–scripted fantasy film entitled *Marvel of the Haunted Castle,* for which 20th Century Fox's Joe Wizan had hired him. "That one could have been interesting. It was an odd script set in a mythical land, and I worked on it with Lem Dobbs. It still would have been more of a hire-out position than a personal project, but I wanted to learn about the latest special effects and that would have been a way to do it." As the entire project was story-boarded (this was the first time a Furie project had ever been story-boarded), Fox printed a handsome brochure for the project in advance of its production in March 1984, declaring a projected summer 1985 release. When Furie departed the project in April of 1984, *Marvel of the Haunted Castle* fizzled. Dobbs was promptly put to work doing uncredited rewrites on Diane Johnson's script for *Romancing the Stone* (1984).

When Furie attended a screening of *The Last Starfighter,* Kevin "Conan the Accountant" Elders and Rick Natkin came along for the ride. Afterward, during a lunch conversation, the three of them discussed what they would have done differently had they written or directed the film. Collectively, they were unimpressed with the movie's flying effects. A week or so later, Furie ventured to Rick Natkin to pitch an idea. *Junior Eagle,* as Furie called it, told the story of a boy whose Air Force flyer father is shot down and imprisoned in a Middle Eastern country. With the help of the steely, experienced Air Force colonel who becomes his mentor, the boy commandeers a jet and hightails it to the Middle Eastern country with the intent of getting his father back safely. Natkin and Furie have separate conflicting memories of this pitch.

Says Furie, "Natkin didn't really like the idea when I told it to him, and he wanted to write something else with me. I was resolute in wanting to do it, so I looked for another writer." Furie eventually recruited Kevin Elders, a total novice, as his cowriter.

Says Natkin, "I would have loved nothing more than to work on another movie with Sid. The trouble was that I was involved with a CBS miniseries called *Alaska,* which unfortunately never got made. I thought the *Iron Eagle* story was just dandy. I actually knew it would be a hit."

Furie, disappointed that he would not be working with Natkin, his favorite writing partner, on a project that he prized, made his objective crystal clear to Elders, his new scriptwriting charge: "Let's make the kind of movie we used to sneak in to see on Saturday afternoons."[11]

Chapter 11

Matinee Buster

We knew we wanted to make a movie in which the audience could feel involved. And this seemed the right kind of story. I admit I consciously set out to make a mass-entertainment kind of picture; I did think, "Will millions go for this?" But there's no alternative these days. Nothing else works. And there's nothing sadder than an empty theater.

—*Sidney J. Furie, discussing* Iron Eagle

Because *Iron Eagle* managed to become his first major box-office hit since *Lady Sings the Blues*, Furie is all the prouder in admitting that his original *Junior Eagle* script was hawked around town and turned down by every major studio before finding its home at the newly formed Tri-Star Pictures. Says Furie, "If I'm honest, I have to admit that had I been in charge of a studio I might have said no too. There were no names attached to the script when it was going around. [Lou] Gossett came on board later. And you couldn't fault some executive for wondering whether the story could really work. Could an eighteen-year-old really fly an F-16?"[1]

Furie and Kevin Elders scripted the film during the 1984 Summer Olympics. Explains Furie, "That is part of what fueled us. We found it very inspiring, but that was before the second *Rambo* came out and encouraged all the kick-ass Americana feeling." Once the script was in working order, Joe Wizan sent *Junior Eagle* to independent producer Ron Samuels, who enthusiastically set up the project at Tri-Star Pictures. "It was just the kind of story I'd been looking for," Samuels later told *Los Angeles Times* reporter Roderick Mann. "It reminded me of the old John Wayne Westerns. It was a patriotic adventure about a boy setting out to rescue his father. I knew immediately I wanted to make it."[2] This ardor does not exactly conform to Furie's memory of things, though he admits that when he did the final bit of convincing on the project, Samuels backed him up on everything. "Samuels doubted whether it was plausible. I pleaded with him, 'It's a fantasy! No one believes Indiana Jones is real. No one believes any of these other commercial movies are real. What is this argument?'" In a frenzy over making a fresh commercial breakout, Furie kept lowering his budget estimations to Tri-Star studio executives: "I said something ridiculous, that I could do it for $2.5 million. When Ron Samuels finally committed, he said that was bullshit, and told me, 'You'll have $5 million and no less.'" The final budget turned out to be approximately $9 million.

Morgan Freeman auditioned for the lead role of the Air Force colonel who becomes a mentor to the young hero, before the part was given to Louis Gossett Jr., who had won the Oscar for Best Supporting Actor in 1983 for his work in *An Officer and a Gentleman*. Says Gossett, "I'm not exaggerating when I say that I was honored to get the part, for many reasons. It was a special movie on the level that a black character was mentor to a kid who wasn't black himself. I played someone who was dignified, someone that the other predominantly white characters in the movie looked up to, and it was perhaps the first time something like that was done, at least in a movie of that variety. And, on *Iron Eagle*, Sidney really had that instinct for what an audience would want." Gossett relates how Furie let him name the character Chappy Sinclair after Daniel "Chappy" James Jr., a Tuskegee Airman Red Tail fighter pilot during World War II.

After an open casting call exhausted candidates like Emilio Estevez and Jason Dillon, Jason Gedrick, star of the previous year's floundering comedy *The Heavenly Kid* (1985), was cast as the seventeen-year-old ace flyer Doug Masters. By the end of casting, Tri-Star executive Jeff Sagansky suggested a title change, from *Junior Eagle* to the more action-friendly *Iron Eagle*. Says Furie, "We didn't want to alienate the teenage audiences who would have thought *Junior Eagle* sounded like a movie for little kids."

Immediately, Furie knew that it was no use approaching the U.S. Air Force for help shooting the film, because it had an ironclad policy of not cooperating on any film involving the theft of a plane. Instead, the Israeli Air Force became the ringer. Jim Gavin, choreographer of the aerial action footage in *Blue Thunder*, was hired to act in the same capacity on *Iron Eagle*. When first approaching the Israeli Air Force, the filmmakers were met with resentment and indignation. Remembers Furie, "The pilots told us, 'We don't fly for Hollywood.' When we arranged for $700,000 to be given to the Air Force Museum in Be'er Sheva, the generals went back to the pilots and said, 'You're flying for the museum. These guys have given the museum a lot of money.'"[3] In the end, that money was not channeled to the museum, but rather to a general fund to subsidize the Israeli Air Force. Furie and the producers additionally agreed to pay part of the cost of getting the planes airborne.

Shooting for six weeks in Israel proved a breeze for the director and his cast and crew. With material that faintly echoed Furie's previous story work on *Hit!* (1973), the rate and ease of production matched. "The best part about the whole thing was being in Israel," says Furie, who had considered himself a patriot from the time of Israel's birth in 1948. He had only one gripe: "Pilots always complain. They're incredible. You think movie stars are complainers? No, it's pilots. They're a breed unto themselves."[4] Nevertheless, the relationships survived intact, enough so that the groundwork was laid for sequels to be mounted with the help of the Israeli Air Force.

With fond laughs, Lou Gossett relates a memorable story of flying in MiGs with the Israeli Air Force:

I was told the night before not to have breakfast the next morning, because we were going to be taken up in the air. I just assumed that there wouldn't be time to eat anything, because of the schedule or something. So, I abided, but it turns out that I was the only one they had instructed on the matter. Everyone else had their breakfast, which got me a bit cranky. But when they took us up in the air, everyone loses their breakfast, except me. I mean, these planes were flying like darts, faster than anything else in the world. We were breaking the sound barrier left and right. After shooting a lot of flying stuff, they take us down. Everyone got out of the planes looking really sickly. And right then and there, I didn't lose my breakfast . . . I lost my dinner.

Looking at the curious gestalt of Furie's career and its unlikely trajectory, *Los Angeles Times* writer Roderick Mann observes, "*The Ipcress File,* his first success, was a sophisticated, clever movie. *Iron Eagle,* on the other hand, goes straight for the stomach. That would seem to say a lot about how movie audiences have changed." Pumped with a soundtrack of songs performed by Queen, Twisted Sister, Helix, and King Cobra, the film was screened for an ecstatic, largely young preview crowd in Torrance, California, in November 1985. It confirmed Mann's statement about how audience's priorities had shifted. Says Furie, "The people who came to the preview at Torrance looked a pretty tough lot to us. But as soon as the planes appeared, they started cheering. The atmosphere was absolutely electric."[5]

Although intended as a summer 1986 release, *Iron Eagle* was rushed to theaters for a January 17, 1986, opening to prefigure the May 16 release of Ridley Scott's uncomfortably similar *Top Gun*. "I've made a lot of movies over the years, but this is the first time I've ever had a good review in the *New York Times*," Furie told the *Los Angeles Times*.[6] Right he was, when Janet Maslin wrote, "If we are indeed due for a rash of military-vigilante movies, and it appears we are, then they may as well be as skillfully done as this one." She observed that Furie "has certainly come a long way from *Lady Sings the Blues*" and noted that a large segment of the audience with which she saw the film was dressed in uniform or paramilitary fatigues. Two of Furie's most avid defenders parted with him because of his work on *Iron Eagle,* however. Kevin Thomas called the film "a total waste of time" with "a kind of perfection of awfulness" but noted Furie's direction as "energetic." Canadian critic Gerald Pratley, one of Furie's most notable critical defenders, writes that it "is ethically, politically and creatively disturbing, and not for a moment worth watching."[7]

Furie does not cave in when discussing *Iron Eagle.* "I stand by every frame of the movie. It is what we set out to make. That picture is me, in all my corniness." The vigilante conceit of Furie's *Hit!* (1973) is writ large in *Iron Eagle.* Indeed, when Furie originally set out to make a Saturday afternoon matinee–style movie reminiscent of the action-packed serials of his youth, he was true to his word on delivery; the final product comes complete with the American exceptionalist attitudes, jingoism, and propagandistic fervor of its cinematic antecedents. On these three accusations, *Iron Eagle* and its creator stand guilty as charged, but no more guilty than other films fostering the same nationalist slant, including *Red Dawn, Rocky IV,* the *Rambo* pictures, and *Iron Eagle*'s would-be counterpart *Top Gun*. Kevin Thomas remarked that the "dangerously preposterous" film's villains are irresponsible depictions "straight out of Victorian melodrama and silent movies." This is true, and a keen comparison. The film refuses to apologize for its overt stereotyping, and Furie certainly did not make the picture for critics. Looking strictly for a commercial success, he melded this popular nationalist fervor with the renewed Hollywood infatuation for material that catered to the teenage and general youth audience.

Getting beyond this for just a moment, *Iron Eagle*'s father fixation is worthy of consideration. Andrew Sarris once boiled down *The Ipcress File*'s final movement as one involving a "father fixation," discerning that the film ended "with its battered hero in the position of choosing which pater to perforate." The character of Doug Masters answers to two father figures, the biological one and an adopted one in the Lou Gossett character, just as Harry Palmer answers to Dalby and Ross in *The Ipcress File*. Although it is believed at one point that Gossett's Chappy, the young hero's spirit guide, sacrifices himself for the good of the mission, Masters still manages to have it both ways by the final fade-out and is triumphantly coronated for both father figures to witness. When nationalism prevails—lacking moderation, ambiguity, and self-doubt—so does a denouement lacking any kind of ambivalence. In *Iron Eagle*, Furie renders a happy ending for the eighties that earlier pictures like *The Leather Boys, The Ipcress File, Little Fauss and Big Halsy*, and *The Boys in Company C* could not afford. The man-machine fixation is also one to consider in this regard. Masters and his two father figures give themselves over to the aviation gear and the aircrafts they operate, and this is a fixation quite characteristic of its decade. Beyond that, the young Masters must trance himself into a sort of rock 'n' roll–enhanced zen state to properly operate the machinery. It is he, the "young gun" in the most literal sense, who especially communes with the hardware in some way that approaches the spiritual. If the "church" of the film is Americanism, the machinery on display is its most important "ritual vessel." As a result, Furie's sense of montage obliges this idea. He rejects the quicksilver jugular-aimed cutting style that would slice and dice other efforts in order to (often speciously) elicit thrills. Furie is concerned with letting the aerial photography breathe, to capture the machinery in action without the dubious enhancement of overblown novelty cutting.

In *50 ans de cinéma américain*, Bertrand Tavernier and Jean-Pierre Coursodon state, on the heels of *Iron Eagle*'s release into French cinemas, that "Furie's style has long since mellowed; it is no longer the most recognizable in his profession, as we stated earlier. All his newer movies are directed in a limited way, including the reactionary and bellicose *Iron Eagle*."[8] Furie even decided to forgo the use of the 2.35:1 screen size for the more standard 1.85:1, limiting the size of the canvas that had so readily identified his authorship in previous efforts. Barring *Superman IV: The Quest for Peace*, he never again composed for his treasured anamorphic wide screen until *Going Back* (2001), a war-film essay on Vietnam Marine veterans and the aftermath of battle. Furie had thus systemically started stowing away his stylistic signatures.

In an age when budget ceilings steadily rose and studios were more and more in fear of failure as a result, *Iron Eagle* put Furie's name on the list of newly bankable directors capable of making pictures that appealed to the new breed of audience. This privilege led Furie right to failure's doorstep on his next go-around.

"I never saw the final version of *Superman IV,* nor will I ever," says Furie, adamantly. "For many reasons, I never really felt part of it. I gave it my very best as I always do, but in the end, what was it?"

After Richard Lester's penchant for zany high comedy derailed *Superman III* (1983) from the more reverential vision of Richard Donner's original, much-admired 1978 blockbuster, Cannon Films impresarios (and cousins) Menahem Golan and Yoram Globus acquired the Superman movie rights from producers Ilya and Alexander Salkind. The Salkinds, despite solid box-office returns on *Superman III,* lost interest when the first series spin-off, *Supergirl* (1984), dramatically flopped. In approaching Christopher Reeve to respark the series for a fourth entry under the Cannon banner, they agreed to finance Reeve's pet project *Street Smart*, under the direction of Cannes Film Festival Palme d'Or winner Jerry Schatzberg, if he agreed to don the cape once more. Cannon Films's earlier success was based on cheap movies. As the eighties wore on, that changed, as Golan tried to improve Cannon's image with bigger budgeted "prestige" movies, with no shortage of problems. With sizable bank loans, the studio expanded its efforts, buying out cinema chains as well as setting up costly distribution.

Reeve haggled with the Israeli producers, whose names were synonymous with schlock, despite their recent ambitious attempts to create a branch of the company dedicated to art-house pictures, including films by Norman Mailer, John Cassavetes, Jean-Luc Godard, Andrei Konchalovsky, Robert Altman, Anthony Harvey, Ivan Passer, and Barbet Schroeder. Reeve, who had tired of the caped-wonder masquerade and the resulting ordeals in stepping out of the costume for more serious work, still aimed to restore respectability to the withering franchise, to give it a worthy last hurrah. He posed the idea of infusing the project with a sobering message about nuclear disarmament in the age of glasnost. The superhero would officially adopt Earth as his home and effectively save that new home from the threat of a nuclear arms race. Golan and Globus agreed to this notion and funded a screenplay that Reeve engineered. The star recruited Mark Rosenbaum and Laurence Konner, the screenwriting team behind *The Legend of Billie Jean* and *The Jewel of the Nile* (1986), and together, the three of them devised the ins and outs of the story.

In a meeting with Cannon and Warner executives, two names were floated as director: Sidney Furie and Wes Craven. According to Menahem Golan, Furie had recently come to the Cannon office to pitch a script of his own. Furie recalls neither the material he pitched nor ever venturing to the Cannon offices to pitch it. As *Iron Eagle* had just opened to solid box office, Furie won the director ballot hands down. When confronted with the offer, the director sounded off in the affirmative: "I had never done anything like it. I was like someone who doesn't know computers, but wants to learn computers. Having been a director all that time, I said, 'I've got to learn all this because it's something I don't know. It won't be boring.' . . . This was an opportunity to learn about effects and to run a very big picture."[9] Thus, for Furie's schooling on these matters, *Superman IV* effectively became a substitute for the abandoned earlier project *Marvel of the Haunted Castle.*

Having known Richard Lester quite well during his early days in London, Furie believed, like most everyone else, that he had botched the previous installment in the Superman series. When he confronted Warner Bros. executives with this sentiment, they haughtily countered with sarcasm, "Oh yeah, boy, was it bad! Fifty million dollars in film rentals. Give us half of that and we'll be happy."[10] Reeve was able to invigorate the original series stars to return for the fourth installment only when he promised that it would quash a Lester-like approach in favor of a Furie refocus that would live up to Richard Donner's vision.

Production would be mounted predominantly in London, because the previous films' work had been done there. The grand return of Sidney J. Furie to London was a long time coming . . . and a time of it he certainly made. Says Linda Furie, "Sid in London during that summer was like a tour guide. He had a memory associated with every part of town, a story for what seemed like every street corner, and he knew his way around like a taxi driver."

Remembers Dudley Sutton, star of *The Boys* (1962) and *The Leather Boys* (1963), "I pick up the phone one day in 1986 and I hear, 'Voice from your past.' I hadn't heard from Sid since he left London, so I drove him around to look for a place to stay while he planned his *Superman* movie. I just remember we argued about Margaret Thatcher, who he rather respected, and it pissed me off. To me, she is, was and always will be fucking murder! At the end of it, he offered me a role as an arms dealer in *Superman,* but I decided well before that that I'd never play gangsters again." (The prefame Jim Broadbent played the role instead.)

Furie also went backstage at a West End production of Dave Clark's *Time,* which starred Cliff Richard. "Cliff hadn't changed a bit. He was still that likable, clean-cut old British boy.

"I also had the chance to hang out with Roger Ebert at a rib joint. We talked about how much he loved *The Boys in Company C* and he never once mentioned *Purple Hearts,* which I know he didn't like. He was a perfect gentleman and a class act, and we had a wonderful evening together." Reflecting on his "old home week" tour of London, he stated, "I find it tough to go back to anywhere I've been, or at least to visit the people I knew there. I like returning to the city with just the ghosts of everyone and not actually them in person. Being in London in 1986 verified that feeling for me."

Renting a flat in Knightsbridge, the Furies later handed over their lease to Michael and Shakira Caine when they departed London at the end of production. The Caines had decided to move back to England after nearly ten years of living in Beverly Hills, and they used the Knightsbridge residence before buying a home in the country. Time with Michael in London comprehensively completed Furie's homecoming. His fondly remembered London of the early sixties had unalterably changed, rudely awakening him to that most obvious of lessons: that the past, no matter how gilded the memories, is ephemeral and just plain gone.

Before Furie exposed any of the negative of *Superman IV: The Quest for Peace,* Cannon Films exposed its own insolvency—and when the cameras did roll, corners were cut. "No director could have won the fight Sidney fought on *Superman IV,*" says friend Paul Lynch. With Cannon Films financially overextended, having put more films into production at the outset of the firm's 1986 season than it could handle, the budget of *Superman IV: The Quest for Peace* was sliced almost literally in half from $36 million to $17 million shortly before the actors went before the cameras in the winter of 1986 and 1987. Cannon was overextending itself with schlocky megaproductions like *Masters of the Universe* (1987) and Menahem Golan's own *Over the Top* (1987), for which Sylvester Stallone was paid a then-unprecedented $12 million to star (taking up almost half of that film's reported $25 million budget). (Rumors still exist that the budget of *Over the Top* was far more than what Cannon finally reported.) Just prior to budgeting these flops, Cannon had announced a loss of $90 million in the years 1985 and 1986. With this, the Cannon stock lost 75 percent of its value.

Former Universal Pictures chairman Tom Pollock, interviewed for *The Go-Go Boys*, a feature documentary about Cannon Films, offers perspective on the titanic financial troubles Cannon encountered in the late eighties: "Yoram [Globus] was great at finding money. Menahem [Golan] spent it faster than Yoram could raise it. Were it me, I would have tried to keep Menahem under check and have him not spend, but Yoram was not able or willing to do that." Pollock, as a Cannon outsider, sensed that Golan was somehow not then aware that "it isn't a volume business," but rather "a hits business." "You have to make hits in order to survive." On this point, Pollock explained that, whereas Universal produced around twenty films per year, Cannon wound up producing more than forty. He continues, "When they first got into money trouble, their solution was, 'Let's make more movies!' If we can make a million dollars a movie and we are running out of money making twenty movies, let's make thirty! Let's make forty! Let's make fifty!"[11]

Cannon Films attorney Sam Perlmutter offers that, "First, it was little money trouble with little movies. Then, it became big money trouble with bigger movies. You know like say, little kids, little problems. Big kids, big problems."[12]

Cannon Films thus proceeded to follow the prescription of their film's villain, Nuclear Man: "Destroy Superman now!" Special-effects wizards who had worked on the first three films and *Supergirl* left the team as a result of pay cuts, leaving the effects in the final product to be shortchanged and outright botched by lack of funds. In many cases, certain effects were never completed at all in time for the final cut. Visual-effects supervisor Harrison Ellenshaw, who had worked on *Star Wars* (1977) and many Disney titles, was initially excited to receive a personal phone call from the director of one of his all-time favorite films, *The Ipcress File*, but he soon found himself dismayed. Says Ellenshaw, "I very quickly found out that the budget was not even close to what the budget was on any of the first three *Superman* movies. I was up to the challenge. But as soon as I read the script, I realized that there were more effects on this film than there were on the first three combined. Eventually, the long version had 600 [effects] shots in it. Even when they cut out two reels, we still had about 400 shots. Yet we still spent only $3.2–3.5 million."[13] In addition to this, Christopher Reeve and Furie looked to save money by refusing to have their own private trailers while shooting on location.

The cast that was assembled proved to be the only asset, with series newcomers Mariel Hemingway brought on to play a new love interest for Clark Kent, and Sam Wanamaker corralled to play a slippery tycoon intent on making over the *Daily Planet* as a sleazy tabloid. The return of Gene Hackman as arch-villain Lex Luthor, which had justifiably excited the *Superman* film fan base, served the director with both joys and headaches.

Early on, Furie and Hackman built up a solid rapport: "He'd knock on my door wanting a Tylenol or something, I'd give him one and then we'd hang for a bit more and talk about things into the night. He was a mensch." Costar Jon Cryer, who shares many scenes with Hackman, remembers, "Gene Hackman was doing wonderful improvisational stuff—I loved working with him."[14] Midway into shooting, as the "strings" were starting to show and the problems were adding up, it was becoming more obvious to Hackman that he was trapped in a turkey. On one particular occasion, he acted out. Remembers Furie,

Gene showed up to set and I told him what to do, where to look and all that. He had to do this whole speech about the "primeval swamp" or something like that. So, he asked me where the primeval swamp was, and I told him that we'd have to shoot it later, but for now, he would just look offscreen. So he erupted, "You call yourself a director? How am I supposed to play this scene without seeing the primeval swamp?" And I just said, "Well, Gene, you're an actor. Isn't that what actors do? This is not Shakespeare. If anyone can fake it well, you can." And it wasn't quite the same after that, to be honest.

The scene in question never appeared in the final cut of the film, so there is no way to gauge the value of Hackman's spitefully feigned look.

Even though, to this day, the director avoids saying anything negative about his working relationship with Christopher Reeve, out of respect for his status as a symbol of hope and perseverance following the 1995 accident that left him paralyzed, to say it was strained would be putting it lightly. Costar Margot Kidder admits that she herself did not get along with Reeve during shooting and that his ego was inflated because of his involvement in the scripting of the film: "Chris was horribly rude and disrespectful to Sidney, but Sidney and I got on like a house on fire. At that point, Chris had a rather large streak of Narcissism, and it got embarrassing sometimes. Even on the first movie, he could be quite difficult with Dick Donner. So, by the time the fourth one came around, he thought he knew way more than Sidney about everything." Director Joe Zito, who was directing *Missing in Action* for Cannon in the Philippines at the time, recalls getting regular phone calls from Furie. "He would always ask me for advice about handling Chris Reeve. He was having all kinds of trouble with him and needed the friendly ear of another director. Meanwhile, my Filipino crew was really getting on my nerves because they were obsessed with Sidney Furie. He made *Purple Hearts* over there a few years earlier, so it was always, 'Sidney always did this, and Sidney always shot it like that.' While I was giving him advice about Chris Reeve, I also wanted to strangle him for what he did to my crew in the Philippines."

In his memoir, Christopher Reeve comes off as indignant on the matter of his director and the challenges that were faced: "Konner and Rosenthal wrote a scene in which Superman lands on 42nd Street and walks down the double yellow lines to the United Nations, where he gives a speech. If it had been a scene in *Superman I*, Dick Donner would have choreographed hundreds of pedestrians and vehicles and cut to people gawking out of office windows at the sight of Superman walking down the street like the Pied Piper." In lieu of actually shooting at or near the real United Nations, Furie and the crew were forced to stage the scene in Milton Keynes Industrial Park, "in the rain with about a hundred extras, not a car in sight, and a dozen pigeons thrown in for atmosphere."[15]

Collectively, the testimonies of what happened on set give one the sense of a very fractured production, where many lines were drawn in the sand when it came to who was loyal to whom. Screenwriter Mark Rosenthal, who was firmly in the "Reeve camp," explains, "Sidney would walk up to us all the time and brag about how many set-ups he fit into a day's work. It was never about doing what he thought was good work. It was always the number of shots and set-ups, like it was a race." Like Rosenthal, visual effects supervisor Harrison Ellenshaw felt that Furie might have been the wrong choice as a director, especially when he voiced his objective of "topping the action of the first Richard Donner–directed installment."[16]

Margot Kidder, however, begs to differ on these matters: "I think Sidney saw the weaknesses in the script and was always trying to fix them with humor. He has a delicious sense of humor, very Canadian, which I share with him. And Chris just didn't get it. I don't think he was as smart as Sidney in these matters, and he didn't get what he was trying to do. And I think part of the failure of the movie, apart from that dreadful script, was that Chris just refused to take any direction. It was awful." Kidder did demur for a moment in stating, "There was certainly a nice, sweet side to Chris too, but on a film set, he was not fun to be with. He was dictatorial about things he knew nothing about. He didn't act that way with Dick Lester because of the political implications behind the scenes of the first two films in the series, with Lester replacing Donner. I thought the way that was done was immoral, but Chris was worried about his career, so he played it nice with Dick Lester."

On Furie's end, the major issue during production was that he was never allowed to change anything in the script or make necessary adjustments. Reeve would not stand for it. Even though the villain role had been written as having Superman's same face, because Nuclear Man's DNA had been duplicated from Superman's, the director was obliged to hire unknown Mark Pillow to play the role, once again for the sake of the increasingly precious money. Rosenthal even admits that Furie "had his hands tied behind his back on a lot of stuff."[17] Behind-the-scenes footage of the moon-fight sequence would seem to reveal that the one giving orders and consulting video playback was Christopher Reeve himself.

In the midst of production, in October 1986, Cannon's accounting came under the scrutiny of the Securities and Exchange Commission. By 1989, this ongoing financial crisis had spiraled into the company being bought out by Giancarlo Parretti of Pathé Communications.

After Furie and his company wrapped, the exhausted and bedeviled director sat in on the edit of a 134-minute original cut of the film, which reused flying shots and effects many times over in an effort to cover up the errors on the part of the scaled-down effects team. Recalls Ellenshaw, "Sidney said, 'This is the way I want it to be' and he brought it back to Los Angeles and went to [Warner Bros. executive] Terry Semel's screening room in Beverly Hills." When that version tested poorly, the film was further butchered to a length of 89 minutes without Furie's consent, approval, or involvement. "We didn't have time to do a decent edit on the film, so basically, two reels in the middle came out," says Ellenshaw. "I regretted that we spent the time and the effort on the 600 [completed effects] shots when we could have spent the same amount of time on fewer shots. Fewer shots would have been better than spreading ourselves so thinly."[18] To quote Jon Cryer, "Cannon released an unfinished movie."[19]

Though Princess Diana, Prince Charles, Mariel Hemingway, and Margot Kidder were among those in attendance for the July 23, 1987, "Royal Premiere" of the film, Furie declined the invitation, as per his custom with photo ops and flashy promotional events. The event, however, mirrored the royal premieres that greeted his Cliff Richard pictures *The Young Ones* and *Wonderful Life* in the early sixties—events that Furie did attend. In the receiving line, Mark Pillow flanked Kidder while outrageously decked out in full Nuclear Man regalia.

Golan and Globus attested that they would later use the forty-five minutes of deleted footage for a fifth Superman film. This, of course, never materialized. The Reeve franchise retired with *Superman IV*. In a 1988 issue of *Drama-Logue,* Christopher Reeve was passive and polite: "I don't want to say a lot of negative things about a project that didn't work out. We just weren't given what we were promised. That often happens in a movie."[20]

Although the film is widely acknowledged as a fiasco of the first order, some rather outlandish analyses and arguments have surfaced over the years. On the Northstars.ca Canadian Film Database, the earnest Ralph Lucas professes that the film

> will occasionally trigger a debate that have some people saying [Furie] shot it as a satire of Hollywood. For example, it opens with a scene from *2001: A Space Odyssey* in which HAL's murder of the astronaut is corrected by Superman. Also, look for the "track-car gag" from [Michael Winner's] *The Mechanic* (1972) and [John Frankenheimer's] *52 Pick-Up* (1986) used by the villains, followed by the basic plot device from [Hall Bartlett's] *Zero Hour* (1957). Furie then plays with *Meet John Doe* and *Mr. Smith Goes to Washington,* moving quickly to *The Day the Earth Stood Still,* and then a cloning sequence right out of *Frankenstein.*[21]

Amusing as all this is, Furie will be the first to admit that he invested no such deep thought. Others on the Internet who make claims about Furie's overall auteurship have pointed out that Gene Hackman's homemade creation of his own superhero is proof of the director's burgeoning focus on masculinity and male inadequacy. Again, this is all mere projection, and rather laughable at that. "It was in the script! I didn't write the stuff!" Furie says in mid-guffaw.

What is key to note, however, is Furie's allegiance to Donner's original camera style. Whereas Richard Lester mostly preferred tracking with simple pans rather than camera moves, and approached his Superman movies with a flat visual style that specifically alluded to comic-book cells, Furie is intent on giving simple dramatic scenes slightly more visual dynamism. At one point, for instance, the camera dollies with a telephoto lens from a television news broadcast, up the whole of Kent's body, and finally to an intense close-up of the character in troubled repose. Other performance-oriented scenes prove faithful to Donner's original vision, such as the scene in which Margot Kidder's Lois Lane knowingly and tearfully opens her heart to a sick, dying Clark Kent. According to screenwriter Mark Rosenthal, the scene that comes off best is the "double-date sequence" in which "Sid's flair for French door-slamming comedy direction really pays off." Although most of the film's punches are telegraphed by clumsy editing, poor scripting, directorial gaffes, and often horrendous special effects, there is enough evidence in these small moments to suggest that, had the noble intent not been hijacked by other factors, the ill-fated film might have come together more seamlessly.

In 2014, in *The Go-Go Boys,* producer Yoram Globus admitted to his company Cannon's culpability in the *Superman IV* debacle: "Into *Superman* [IV], we should have put all of our efforts, to make from it a hit movie, a better movie than the first three. And because of so many productions [at Cannon], you don't have the time to devote to it. This is, for me, our biggest fiasco. It could have been our breakthrough into the top of Hollywood." In the same documentary, Menahem Golan refused to discuss the production, stating, "How do I benefit from talking about my failures in a documentary film about my life's work? I don't want to talk about negative things. If I had a failure, I erased it from my life. It never existed."[22] The film received only a single positive review in, of all places, the *New York Times.* Janet Maslin, who had curiously gone up to bat for *Iron Eagle* the previous year, wrote that "the Superman series hasn't lost its raison d'etre. There's life in the old boy yet." The rest are not worth quoting here, as they reiterate the same previously stated gripes in gleefully hyperbolic terms. When asked if he regrets not taking an Allan Smithee credit on the film, Furie says that he never believed in the practice of taking one's name off a picture. "You need to own up to having been part of the circus, no matter what."

He explains further his involvement in the production of *Superman IV: The Quest for Peace* with a metaphor:

> Usually, while waiting for a bus on a rainy, windy night, you jump on that warm, dry bus and you figure, "I'm going to change the direction of this bus! I'm going to make it an express! It's going to take me where I really want to go!" and you work like hell and sometimes it takes you all the way. *The Ipcress File* and *Lady Sings the Blues* are examples of that for me. A lot of times, though, you can't. Once you go with a story that isn't strong, it's very hard on rewrites because you're still stuck with that story.

Furie told *Starlog Magazine* before release, "To make a mainstream picture and make it well, no one ever knows what you did. They think it was churned out by a sequel machine. Not for one second would anyone know what a director goes through on any picture, let alone a movie like *Superman IV*."[23] As he learned revisiting his ghosts in London, the times (and the movie industry) had changed in a big way. In 2006, when Warner Home Video reissued the film in a special-edition DVD, featuring some of the lost scenes that were deleted after the disastrous preview of the 134-minute cut, Furie wanted no part of it. Shrugging, he murmurs, "Really, what is there to say about it that hasn't already been said? Can we move on and talk about the next movie now, please?"

It is the earnest and informed opinion of this author that, while the fiasco of *Superman IV: The Quest for Peace* can be attributed to many of the figures involved in its making, in concert with the discord that emerged because of poor choices these participants made, Furie as its director shares the least of the blame for its failure. He did what little could be done, considering the circumstances.

Chapter 12

Housemaster

I've told you a hundred times: I don't want to win awards! Give me
pictures that end with a kiss and black ink in the books.
—*Harry Pebbel (Walter Pidgeon) in Vincente Minnelli's*
The Bad and the Beautiful (1952)

Furie told *Starlog Magazine* in 1987 that his next picture would be "a
Holocaust story for Arnold Kopelson called *Day by Day*."[1] Kopelson had
forgiven Furie enough after the *Night of the Juggler* debacle to give him the
directing reins on a film whose story touched Furie at his deepest core. As
he is prone to telling people close to him, he was never able to personally
reconcile the horrors of the Holocaust from the time he was a child. "The
horror of the Holocaust sits with me every day," Furie confesses, "and I do
not exaggerate in any way. It has been known to interfere with the way I go
about my day sometimes." The film tells the true story of Salamo Arouch,
an Olympic boxer from Greece, who is deported and placed in Auschwitz.
There, his survival is ensured as long as he continues boxing for the entertainment of the Germans.

As a Jewish filmmaker with "deep spiritual and emotional ties to Israel
and the Jewish people," Furie felt inordinately close to the picture that was
eventually retitled *Triumph of the Spirit*. Unfortunately, Furie lost the job
to scheduling delays and his sensitivity to the practical demands of supporting a family. "I felt very badly that it didn't happen with me directing,"
says Furie. "It would have been a very special film for me to have made."
The project eventually went before the cameras in the fall of 1988, with
Robert M. Young as director and Willem Dafoe starring in the lead role. It
turned out to be the first major studio picture shot on location at Auschwitz,
and it opened to mixed reviews in December 1989. Furie, in the mean-
time, landed another sequel-directing job. "Kevin Elders called me one
day and told me that he wanted to do *Iron Eagle II* and that there was inter-

est and demand. So, that's what I did. I was never bitter about that. We had a good time, and the movie is what it is. I like it." Heralded as the first Canadian-Israeli coproduction, *Iron Eagle II* did mark Furie's first return to working in Canada, where he based most of his later productions. This time around, Tri-Star banned critics from its press screenings of the film, although *Los Angeles Times* critic Kevin Thomas, who panned the original film with rancor, found it "actually a far better film than the original."

On December 22, 1988, Furie's longtime assistant director Fred Slark passed away at age sixty-six. Slark had worked with Furie on every single one of his films since his second, *A Cool Sound from Hell,* in 1958. He was also a key figure for having secured him his first job as a director in England. "Fred's death hit me hard," says Furie. "I still miss him calling me 'governor' on my sets. Without him selling me to [producer] George Fowler, my life and my career would have taken a totally different path." It was the first death among Furie's closest collaborators.

The Taking of Beverly Hills, a genre product fraught with all manner of problems at literally every stage of development and production, followed *Iron Eagle II.* There were disagreements between writers (Furie contributed the original story concept, from which Rick Natkin and collaborators David Fuller and David Burke extrapolated the screenplay), shooting headaches, and postproduction and distribution peril. On the latter count, when the film's original production company, Orion Pictures, went bankrupt in the summer of 1991, Columbia's new Nelson Entertainment wing picked up the film to give it a short-lived theatrical run. When asked about *The Taking of Beverly Hills*'s behind-the-scenes troubles while on the set of his following film, Furie, who wished not to discuss it, told the reporter, "It'll be in my biography, along with Brando, Berry Gordy and Diana Ross."[2] Looking back on it now, Furie points out that "one of the best things about that picture was working again with Antony Gibbs." Gibbs had worked as editor on some of Furie's earliest British films, including *Doctor Blood's Coffin* and *During One Night* (both 1961).

Furie followed this up with the last picture he ever made for a major studio. Various talents who had thrived at Paramount in their 1970s heyday were invited back to helm a slate of new pictures for the studio in the 1990s. Often, these were directors and names that had somehow faltered or fallen out of favor in the 1980s. The results were often lackluster; William Friedkin directed *Blue Chips* (1994) and *Jade* (1995), ex-studio head Robert Evans produced *Jade* (1995) and *The Shadow* (1996), Peter

Bogdanovich directed *The Thing Called Love* (1993), and Herbert Ross directed *True Colors* (1991). For his part, Sidney J. Furie helmed *Ladybugs* (1992), a Rodney Dangerfield family comedy that starred the notoriously "disrespected" comic as the coach of a girl's soccer team.

"Why *Ladybugs?*" says Furie, repeating the question back. "Why not? It was something to do! One has to keep working, and believe me, it was one of the best paydays to come down the pike. I really needed it. And really, anything to get me on a set with a crew. To wake up early, go to the craft services table, get a doughnut and chat with the crew members . . . that's the good stuff!"

Spearheaded as an Albert S. Ruddy property and a variation on *The Bad News Bears, Ladybugs* also reignited a partnership with *Boys in Company C* producer Andre Morgan, who had partnered with Ruddy on a production company in 1984. Associate producer Gray Frederickson, who worked with Furie on *Little Fauss and Big Halsy* (1970) and *Hit!* (1973), remembers, "I ran into Sidney one day and he just said, 'You know what, let's head over to Al Ruddy's office to see if he's got anything for us to make. It was that simple. Once we started *Ladybugs,* he would take me and a few other people on long drives down the coast for those famous creative bouncing sessions. Sometimes, these were really long drives up the Pacific Coast Highway and it would take us hours to get home."

Casting the role of Matthew, the Dangerfield character's teenage soon-to-be-stepson, accounts for one of Furie's favorite career stories. For the role eventually given to Jonathan Brandis, the young Leonardo DiCaprio came in to audition. Keeping in mind that this character would have to dress up as a female soccer player and receive illicit laughs as a result, Furie remembers, smiling, "He was too beautiful. He dressed up like a girl, with a wig and everything, and he looked so convincing in it that it just killed the joke. Jonathan Brandis was cast because he looked funny in drag." Al Ruddy, on his own accord, related the same story like the most giddy of raconteurs. The following year, the critics applauded DiCaprio for his breakthrough role in *What's Eating Gilbert Grape?* (1993) and also for his lead performance in *This Boy's Life* (1993), opposite Robert De Niro.

Rodney Dangerfield had acquired an alarming reputation as a prima donna (and a formidable one at that), having not appeared in a film since *Back to School* in 1986. Says Furie, "I kept on hearing he was a film director's worst nightmare." According to Dangerfield's assistant Harry Basil, "Rodney walked off a couple movies in disgust. He left *Caddyshack II* and

The Scout. He also had a lawsuit with Caesar's Palace, and Warner refused to release his version of the animated movie *Rover Dangerfield*, and he had a bunch of other personal stuff going on. So he was in a bad mood when he started *Ladybugs* that summer in 1991."

Linda Furie remembers that Dangerfield arrived at the Colorado location with "suitcases full of spatulas and forks and knives" and that after lunch he would pack food from the craft services table in Tupperware containers. According to all involved, he threw tantrums in an effort to get specific people fired. When one of the young girls in the cast made an allegedly anti-Semitic crack, Dangerfield demanded that she be replaced. Another victim of such a campaign was Gray Frederickson, who incited the ire of the star for unknown reasons. Gray Frederickson recalls, "He didn't just throw me off the set. I was barred from Denver. Al Ruddy called me up one day and said, 'Gray, I think you should resume your work on the film back in L.A. Rodney doesn't want you around anymore.' So I went back to L.A. and managed things from there. It was a move to keep the peace." According to Basil, Frederickson was Dangerfield's "scapegoat."

One person whom Dangerfield loved, however, was Sidney Furie, who initiated what he called "the chill test." When Dangerfield wrote a joke, he would audition the joke for Furie for use in a given scene. According to Al Ruddy, "If it was good, Sidney would rub his forearm back and forth with two fingers and tell him, 'I got chills.' If it was bad, Sidney would gently tell him to work on it some more. Rodney walked over to me one time, looked at Sidney and said, 'He's always gettin' chills! I love that guy!'" According to Harry Basil, Dangerfield loved him most for how fast and efficiently he worked. In using at least three cameras for each setup, Furie was able to conserve the temperamental star's time, habitually allaying his impatience with the process. The star's placation was a gratifying by-product, as *Ladybugs* was delivered under budget and under schedule, with picture wrapping in July 1991. According to Basil, throughout shooting, Furie had been conferring with various parties over the phone about the building of a new house. Some months after completion of the film, he moved into this house.

Marketing a "dirty comic" in a family picture like *Ladybugs* was something that Paramount struggled to overcome; the studio considered changing the title to *The Coach* to soften the Dangerfield-family-comedy oxymoron. In February 1992, a month before the film's March release, Dangerfield let loose at Paramount's ShoWest banquet, delivering some bellicose jibes and one-liners: "Paramount is 100% behind *Ladybugs*. That's the great thing about Paramount, there's always someone behind you . . . they have to be behind you to do what they do."[3] Furie anticipated stories and rumors of his irascible star leaking from his set, so he beat one *Variety* reporter to the punch. "None of them are true." The reporter, responding to the director's proverbial circling of wagons, duly answered "What 'them'?"[4]

Ladybugs grossed below $15 million at the box office, a loss considering its $20 million budget. Reviews were dismal. Joe McBride of *Variety* attacked it as "a repulsive vehicle," while Michael Wilmington of the *Los Angeles Times* wrote, "Even though Sidney J. Furie is a better director than [Dangerfield] has had before, and though the producers are, amazingly, Al Ruddy and Gray Frederickson of *The Godfather*, the most of it has the stale, slick, worked-over look of standard studio product." Vincent Canby of the *New York Times*, stating that "Sidney Furie will not be remembered for his direction of this one," charged the film thus: "Curtis Burch, who wrote the screenplay, is given a one-sentence biography in the production notes, compared with the three pages devoted to the histories of the film's two producers, its executive producer, it's co-executive producer and its associate producer. The priorities are all wrong." The pressbook was indeed inadvertently revealing, announcing Furie's previous credits (in order) as *Iron Eagle, Iron Eagle II, The Taking of Beverly Hills, Superman IV: The Quest for Peace*, and a few others, with *Lady Sings the Blues* and *The Ipcress File* bringing up the rear as the last two mentioned.

The film made up the money it lost in theaters when it appeared on video and television, where it premiered on ABC as the network's "Family Movie" in 1994. According to Harry Basil, Oliver Stone, an inveterate Dangerfield fan, named *Ladybugs* his all-time favorite movie comedy while on the *Daily Show*. Although it baffles one to consider that the man behind *The Leather Boys, The Ipcress File,* and *Lady Sings the Blues* also directed *Ladybugs,* this curious little mainstream comedy fits into Furie's body of work quite snugly, especially on a thematic level. The story, after all, concerns an enervated Rodney Dangerfield, famous for his "I don't get no respect" catch line (which could be a battle cry for any defeated male), who is handed the task of relating to a team of young girls. He then attempts to get the coveted respect by dressing up his stepson-to-be as a girl to win their games. Dangerfield and Brandis are two more of Furie's wounded males, but it all ends happily, as Dangerfield, at long last, exclaims, "I finally got some respect!" As predicted, it is not a good film by any stretch of the imagination, but it deserves its place among Furie's oeuvre for its thematic constitution.

Although Furie had set his sights on developing other projects with Dangerfield, including a "Fellini-type" comedy called *Serenade Cafe,* a longtime Dangerfield pet project about a nightclub owner with opera-singing dreams,[5] the director left the studio system and happily closed the gates behind him (though he collaborated again with Dangerfield less than a decade later). For now, he was about to make a permanent return to Canada, a nation that, since his earliest days trying to actualize his film-director dreams to no avail, had made tremendous strides in nurturing a filmmaking community.

Work never ceased for Sidney Furie in the nineties, when he turned to directing a series of Canadian direct-to-video genre pictures, the most noteworthy of which are *In Her Defense* (1999) and *Hollow Point* (1996), which is by far the most successful entry in this cycle. *Hollow Point* has Furie hopping up his film on a cocktail of laughing gas and speed, to stage a ripping yarn that is so comically self-aware of its convolutions as to send up many of the less-than-wholesome hallmarks of direct-to-video movie-making. With its potboiler story of a money launderer plotting to merge Russian, Chinese, and Italian gangsters into a single organized-crime con-glomerate, the gleefully anarchic *Hollow Point* owns and then transcends its B-movie origins. It is his most joyously cockeyed film, and one that rev-els in in its tongue-in-cheek hyperbole with aplomb. In this and in its own way, *Hollow Point* is an unexpectedly brilliant piece of work and the Furie film of that decade with the most perceptibly customized directorial style.

Furie smirks when relating a memorable story from that set, concern-ing Donald Sutherland, who plays a cagey, oddball hitman in *Hollow Point:*

> They were preparing a set that was to be Sutherland's character's lair. But his character would never set foot on this set, but other characters would have stuff to do there. And he comes in upset one day and says to me, "Sidney, I've got to talk to you as soon as possible." I saw that he had tears in his eyes, real tears, and he told me that he couldn't have that set as his character's house. I told him that he didn't play any scenes in it and that he didn't work in it at all, and he said, "But it's my home. It reflects my character."

And we went into the set and he laid it all out: "I'd never have this, I'd never have that." And he asked me how he could act in the movie knowing that his house in the movie was wrong, even though he was never supposed to even see it. He told me what kind of place it would be, and I spent time getting his specifications. And so we built a whole new set. I think anyone's first impulse would have been, "You're getting paid! That's how you're supposed to do it, so just do it!" That was actually a first for me. On top of that, the budget was tight and the producer didn't like me very much anyway, but we still redid the entire set because Sutherland couldn't work knowing something like that was wrong. I believed it when he told me he would have left the movie.

Hollow Point played often in the late nineties on pay cable stations like HBO and became something of a minor cult film. *In Her Defense* riffs on *Body Heat* (somewhat intriguingly), telling the story of a lawyer defending his mistress in the murder trial of her husband, even though he himself killed the husband. Gerald Pratley, in his *A Century of Canadian Cinema*, praises *In Her Defense* as "an intriguing interplay of relationships and a thoughtful excursion into the law, with considerable tension and suspense." *Cord* (2000), which tells the story of a certifiably loony, childless couple who kidnaps and imprisons a pregnant woman in their basement, riffs on *Misery* (rather gratingly). Throughout this decade, Furie directed an array of talent that included Marlee Matlin, John Lithgow, Donald Sutherland, Dennis Hopper, Gary Busey, David Carradine, Tia Carrere, Peter Weller, Daryl Hannah, Vincent Gallo, Jennifer Tilly, Peter Coyote, Michael Dudikoff, Thomas Ian Griffith, Martin Kove, and countless others. He also reteamed with Rodney Dangerfield on *My 5 Wives* (2000) when the comic personally requested him to take the director's chair (Dangerfield had previously requested him for another of his comedy vehicles, *Meet Wally Sparks*).

The Rage, released in 1997, reunited Furie with Roy Scheider and cinematographer Donald M. Morgan, two members of the *Sheila Levine Is Dead and Living in New York* team. The project also introduced him to writer Greg Mellott, the newest key member of his creative retinue. Says Mellott, "I have no frame of reference for anyone like Sidney. I learned so much from him, perhaps more than anyone else, from both a personal and artistic standpoint. He is like a well-oiled machine on a set, always knows where to put the camera, and always knows how to talk to someone, whether it's an actor, a writer or a technician. And when I needed help the most when life got rough, he was there to provide it." Furie simply says of Mellott, "Oh, I love the guy."

Furie refers to these direct-to-video titles collectively as the "nonstudio pictures" and justifies his involvement with them as follows: "I had enough successful films to satisfy and, in the long run, the whole business of Hollywood studio moviemaking just got too crazy for me, so I left it. But really, the ego for me doesn't come from the pictures that worked. The ego comes from just being able to work. With the nonstudio pictures, there was no real chance that they would ever really be reviewed, so there was no pressure, no embarrassment. It was just a chance to work. And I've had tremendous fun on those pictures. Look at it this way: Most people work, right? So let's say they work at making deals. They don't get reviewed on every deal. 'Oh, he picked the wrong stock there!' Or a teacher. 'Boy, that student became a juvenile delinquent! The teacher bombed on that one.' But someone who supported their family, lived decently, they say, 'He's successful.' So why can't an artist have the same thing?"

Making these films in Canada also returned Furie to a treasured after-hours ritual. He explains,

> When you finished a day's shoot in England in the sixties, it was great to meet at the pub and discuss the day. When I got to Hollywood, I said, "Aren't you going out for a drink?" and they'd look at me like I was some drunk. It was a great shock that you didn't go out after and buy a guy a drink who you might've yelled at, to make up with him. There's something about breaking bread together that's important. In Canada, it's much more social. Big studios make for big tensions. In Toronto, in Canada in general, you don't have that. In Montreal, the crew members shake hands with you every morning, as a courtesy. Making movies is my golf. I enjoy it more than most seem to. Canada is the place to make it happen at this point in my life.

Furie kicked off the new millennium with two returns to form. The first of these was *Going Back* (2001), which capped off a trilogy of Vietnam films inaugurated by *The Boys in Company C* and *Purple Hearts*. The story, penned by Furie and Greg Mellott, covered a tour group of American war veterans, originally from the same platoon, returning to Vietnam decades later. During the trip, the group, still feeling embittered toward their company commander, attempt to get to the heart of a scandal involving the senseless death of men under his charge. The film is told in flashback, with a television camera crew, led by a pretty, plucky newswoman, shadowing them in the present day.

Coscreenwriter Greg Mellott remembers, "*Going Back,* like other things we wrote together, was born on long creative drives up the coast to Santa Barbara. Sid had seen a CBS television documentary in which they brought back a group of veterans to Vietnam, and they were also embittered towards their company commander. So, at the heart of *Going Back,* there is a true story. So I started doing my own research, and I gleaned a lot of other true stories that I started working into our script. On his birthday, I gave him the first fourteen pages of the script."

When a 182-page draft was completed in the fall of 2000, Furie attempted to involve Gray Frederickson, with whom he had just completed *My 5 Wives.* But a potential deal with producer Philippe Martinez dissolved, and the project was put on the back-burner. "I think that bugged the hell out of Sidney," Greg Mellott recalls. "Here was this script that he absolutely loved, and he had to put it on the shelf for a bit while he did these other pictures." After production wrapped on the Daryl Hannah–Vincent Gallo–starred thriller *Cord* (2000), that film's producer, Gary Howsam, was approached with the *Going Back* script. When Howsam was able to raise $4.5 million on the strength of the actor attached to the project, Casper Van Dien, who had just headlined Paul Verhoeven's hit science-fiction epic *Starship Troopers* (1997), Furie's latest dream project was off and running.

Going Back marked the director's return to shooting anamorphic wide screen. Although he was well known for his experimentation with anamorphic's extra screen width in *The Ipcress File* and had lensed the majority of his studio pictures in that format, he had not shot a film in anamorphic since *Purple Hearts* in 1984. "It was a big deal for him," says Greg Mellott. "There was an excitement that he would do the film in wide screen. He spoke all the time about what he wanted to do with framing and giving the images depth and clarity. I remember he says, 'There is only one way for me to shoot Vietnam, and that's in anamorphic.'" Using the multiple-camera process more and more over the years had trained Furie to be less fussy over composition and personal style. He claims that the need for efficiency on the later pictures had "hammered" this previous style out of him. Whereas with the use of a single camera, it was easier and logical to devote one's complete attention to considering such factors, with multiple cameras, the objective was to cut down on setup time and simply to capture as much of the action as possible on a scene-by-scene basis. *Going Back* was Furie's deliberate return to a personal style.

The location shoot was arduous, according to Gary Howsam. As *The Boys in Company C* and *Purple Hearts* had earlier taken Furie to the Philippines, so he returned there for *Going Back*, with additional locations in Saigon, which now stood as a teeming, more metropolitan, and no longer wartorn city. The cast and crew won the rare opportunity of shooting at Ho Chi Minh's Palace. Furie industriously staged some shots so that a simple cut would magically transport the actors from the streets of Manila to the streets of Saigon. When shooting wrapped, Furie worked with editor Saul Pincus on a 149-minute cut of the film. This was the version first shown at the Cannes Film Festival Market.

Says Gary Howsam, "We were hoping that Casper Van Dien's star was going to go in the other direction after *Starship Troopers,* but it didn't, and the movie became harder to sell because we didn't have much of a name. We also had some trouble with a special-effects house in Germany during postproduction, and that did not bode well for things either." Furie then pared the film down to 112 minutes, and the film premiered in Canada at this more marketable length. In the United States, a compromised DVD version was manufactured with the new title *Under Heavy Fire.* This version crops the anamorphic wide-screen frame, pan-and-scanning it to fit the size of a standard television screen. Along with conspicuously muddying the picture, it also destroys the film's detailed compositions.

Canadian writer Gerald Pratley called *Going Back* "a striking, powerful and penetrating war film set in Vietnam" and speculates that "this must have been a very difficult film to make, but the director pulls it off ably."[6] In ending his Vietnam film cycle, Furie examines a thematic aftermath: the tragic result when a character has questioned, or has outright shirked, his commitment. When this happens, he has to live with the memory that under his command men have lost their lives. The average shot is conspicuously longer than in most of Furie's post-*Entity* work. Photographed with meditative moves, prolonged close-ups, and the ensemble compositions that recall the packed frames of *Hit!* (1973) and *The Boys in Company C* (1978), *Going Back* feels very immediate and personal as a director's testament. Beyond the "band of brothers" sentiments that arch over the proceedings, the Hawksian echoes also present in these earlier titles are seen again.

"For years, people asked me whatever happened to that film and wanted to know why it never played much of anywhere," says Furie. "There was a special mention of that picture. After fifty years in the business, I just learned to bite the bullet on it. It's still a beloved 'son' of mine."

Global Heresy, a musical comedy farce, arguably marked Furie's second return to form. Swiss-born British writer Mark Mills wrote the script for it independently, then sold it to British producer Mark Shorrock, who had just broken into the business with *Ever After* (1998) and *Croupier* (1998). Shorrock corralled Gary Howsam into helping set up the project as a Canadian-British coproduction. By this time, Furie had firmly established himself as Howsam's go-to director. Remembers Furie, "Gary and I flew Mark Mills to Toronto to do just a few minor rewrites with me, but overall, the script seemed set to go by the time I first got hold of it." *Global Heresy* tells the story of what happens when quintessential British aristocrats Lord and Lady Foxley are forced to take in "corporate guests" to ease their dire financial situation. On the day their guests are due to arrive, the agency replacements for their butler and cook fail to show up. Determined that no one know of their hardships, they assume these menial roles themselves. To make matters worse, the "corporate guests" turn out to be Global Heresy, America's hottest young rock band, who intend to use the Foxley estate as the grounds for a rowdy artistic retreat before a worldwide concert tour. A culture clash ensues. Just as the band members adjust to a female replacement for a lead singer who has mysteriously disappeared, they find themselves under the threat of a contract that strips away their right of artistic freedom.

Because both Howsam and Shorrock were friendly with Peter O'Toole's agent, Steve Kenis, they proposed the venerated British stage and screen veteran for the role of Lord Foxley. When O'Toole immediately agreed, a London meeting was promptly arranged with Furie. Although this meeting was supposed to take fifteen minutes, they were still shooting the breeze four hours later. Furie remembers the meeting with a Cheshire cat smile: "We laughed a lot, talked about movies, theater, his career, my career, the thrill of working, life in general. We just hit it off right away." That Peter O'Toole had remained close friends with Furie's longtime ally Michael Caine, ever since Caine's days as O'Toole's understudy in the 1959 stage production *The Long and the Short,* also boded well for their future working relationship. In fact, O'Toole and Caine were "notorious" drinking buddies—just two members of a wild and woolly cabal that also included Richard Harris, Peter Finch, and Richard Burton.

American Alicia Silverstone, in the role of the band's female replacement Nat, and Joan Plowright, in the role of Lady Foxley, rounded out the cast. Plowright, though widowed after having been married to Laurence Olivier since 1961, had not met Furie during the short time he directed her husband in *The Jazz Singer* in 1980. With the prestige of the names involved came an appreciably higher budget of $12 million, besting the ones Furie had gotten used to during his poststudio period.

Shooting commenced in November of 2000. The most vivid memories on the set of *Global Heresy* are courtesy of O'Toole, who, by all accounts, appeared to be having the time of his life making the picture. On the first day of shooting, upon observing that the numerous young actors had only small trailers in which to park themselves between takes, O'Toole graciously announced, "Come to my motor home anytime you like! You are all most welcome!" Furie remembers hanging out there daily with his cast, whereupon O'Toole, a gifted raconteur, told his assembled company a variety of stories, both personal and otherwise. "All these times, he was absolutely sober and I had heard he was a complete drunk," says Furie. Indeed, O'Toole had built a reputation as a rabble-rousing lush on many film sets. Curiously, on Furie's set, he seemed to have conquered the problem. One day, however, when approaching O'Toole at the end of a Friday workday, Furie learned the secret of the actor's sobriety.

"Would you like have dinner this weekend?" Furie inquired.

The actor grinned and placed a hand kindly on his director's shoulder. "My dear boy, on Friday night, I proceed to get pissed. I will stay pissed until Sunday night. And on Monday morning, I'll be on the set and I won't take a drink again until the next Friday night." According to Furie, he confined himself all weekend to Toronto's Windsor Arms Hotel and drank. He learned in that moment that O'Toole had gained the ability to turn his alcoholism on and off, caging his addiction for the benefit of his collaborators.

After shooting wrapped, producer Gary Howsam had a revealing run-in with the Windsor Arms hotel manager on account of O'Toole's bar bill. "Mr. O'Toole's bar bill is his business," Howsam told the hotel manager. "That has nothing to do with our movie."

"Well, Mr. Howsam, the bar bill is rather steep, and we need to square it up somehow," the hotel manager meekly contested.

"How much is it?"

"Well, it's $15,000." Silence. Howsam made some attempt to digest what he had just heard, but he was simply floored by the figure. Could a single man drink $15,000 worth of liquor, he asked himself. The manager then explained that O'Toole made a nightly habit of buying drinks for the house and putting it all on his tab. "I guess he needed some other drinking buddies." No one can quite remember how the sum was eventually paid off, but it was. Be that as it may, Furie is abounding in praise for O'Toole. "Along with Michael Caine, Peter O'Toole is up there with the favorite actors I've directed in the whole of my career. I just loved that man. He was one of the most gracious people I have ever met, and treated everyone with equal respect." Howsam likewise uses the terms "gracious" and "generous" to describe the actor.

On the Furie-O'Toole alliance, Michael Caine muses, "Peter loved Sidney because Sidney is really the last of a certain breed of director, the type of director that Peter really understood and loved. There is just something very real about him. Sidney is forthright, says what he thinks and feels in the most direct way without puttering about, isn't out to please anyone just for the sake of making easy friends, loves what he does very dearly, and most of all, has a vision you're willing to get behind, no matter whether the script is good or bad in the final analysis."

When *Global Heresy* was completed, it was shopped around to major distributors, a practice contrary to the approach taken in circulating Furie's other nonstudio pictures. Because of its star power and a buoyant, easygoing charm that seemed to effortlessly appeal to audiences, two scouts from Miramax pursued the film and recommended it to the Weinsteins for pickup. Because of a number of factors, mostly involving the way the numbers were adding up (in comparison to a standard video release that appeared more financially advantageous to the original backers), the deal never materialized. The film received a theatrical release in Canada and a premiere in the UK, opening to respectable notices, most of which called it slight but charming. In the United States, it was retitled *Rock My World* and premiered direct-to-video. Canadian critic and film historian Gerald Pratley writes, "With knowing players, the games, romance and music make this an entertaining piece of make-believe."[7] Leonard Maltin, who in the early 2000s, owing to space issues in his doorstop *Movie Guide,* ceased covering direct-to-video and made-for-television titles (and relegated older and obscure titles to another volume dedicated to "classics"), curiously broke this new code by reviewing *Global Heresy* in the main publication, remarking that it is "far more engaging than its theatrical fate would indicate." Through frequent television showings, it has become something of a minor audience favorite.

Global Heresy is best seen as the late third entry in Furie's cycle of Cliff Richard musicals. Whereas those films pitted age against youth in a classic *Babes in Arms* struggle, *Global Heresy* has age and youth joining forces against a more general class of users and abusers. As opposed to the "let's put on a show" or "let's make a movie" proclamations of *The Young Ones* (1961) and *Wonderful Life* (1964), the young heroes in *Global Heresy* have settled for "Hey, let's have a jam session." This allegorical little comedy is also one of the director's most personal pictures in the wake of *The Entity* in 1982. The message is fairly loaded and the personal statement is there to be perceived.

Furie's flight and exile from major studio filmmaking are directly addressed in *Global Heresy*. As the title band risks losing their artistic freedom, thanks to a more corporatized music business bent solely on profits and trends, they escape civilization to regroup at a remote estate where they can work in peace without being relentlessly covered and judged by the press. This falls right in line with Furie's view of the Canadian nonstudio pictures as "just a chance to go to work," without the pressure of being seriously reviewed or put under any kind of spotlight. Gary Howsam attests to the fact that "Sid approaches every movie, good or bad, like it is going to win him the Oscar, and you're happy to follow that feeling blindly." Be that as it may, pictures like his Dolph Lundgren vehicles *Detention* (2003) and *Direct Action* (2004), which followed in *Global Heresy*'s wake, are "jam sessions" with the time having been happily spent.

Once the band arrives at the Foxley Estate, the servants maintaining the place are actually the masters in disguise. This is enough of a symbol already. Lord and Lady Foxley, who are themselves in danger of losing everything near and dear to them, lower the bar, keep under the radar, and do what needs to be done to keep afloat amid difficult financial times. Whereas the band's conflict speaks to Furie's artistic struggle, the Foxleys' struggle speaks to Furie's practical need to make a living. In the process, both they and he find that their bitter pills have gone down quite easily, as they respectively reassume the role of housemaster. Lord Foxley's legal expertise saves the day when he prevents the band from signing the suspect contract, and the band saves the day by employing Lord Foxley as their lawyer. As *Wonderful Life* ends with the song "Youth and Experience," which celebrates the two forces joining for the greater good, *Global Heresy*'s final image is of the two elderly stars dancing to the music of the young, struggling to maintain a rhythm that is harder for them to identify but feeling no less exhilarated. It is the perfect note on which to end, when one realizes that filmmaking, a demanding enterprise ostensibly fit only for the young, has kept the aging Furie full of vigor long after his A-list status burned out. He himself dances to the music of the young. Seen within the context of Furie's overall body of work, *Global Heresy* is a fulfilling and even beautiful film. When removed from the context of a career, it is a pleasant, airy farce that makes for, as Leonard Maltin quips, "a couple of harmless hours in front of the telly."

During the decade that followed, Furie's closest associate was producer Gary Howsam, who continued working with him over the course of fourteen productions. Furie spent the years helming a trio of military pictures, *American Soldiers* (2005), *The Four Horsemen* (2008), and *Conduct Unbecoming* (2010), all centering around Marines and America's involvement in Afghanistan and Iraq. "I'm in love with the Marines," claims Furie. "Why? I don't know. But I love making military-themed pictures. Deep down, I would have loved being a general."

Says Gary Howsam, "There wasn't particularly a huge cache for military pictures, let alone one that Sidney cultivated. I'm sure one does exist in some form. Sidney just wanted to do them, and he came up with the ideas for the script and worked with the writers." With *The Veteran* (2006), Furie lent his name to a film on which he worked sparingly. "That one is hardly even a movie," says Furie. "To be honest, I don't know what it is, but I don't see it as a feature movie. They used some war scenes, action shots and improvised bits that had been cut from *Going Back,* all stuff from the Philippines, and then shot five days of stuff around it in Canada. The producers wanted to make an extra buck, and they got it, and I told them I didn't want them messing with that stuff without me, even though I suppose it was their prerogative. As far as I was concerned, the best things in it are those improvised bits."

Meanwhile, over the years, Furie's family had flourished. In the overall analysis, his family of six children could be seen as an appropriate and proportionate response to having grown up as an only child in a family without nearby aunts, uncles, and cousins. From his first marriage to Sheila: his eldest son Dan studied law and became senior vice president of business affairs at Warner Bros.; Noah became the CEO and cofounder of a real-estate brokerage firm as well as the chairman of the Cultural Heritage Commission (dedicated to the preservation of historical landmarks in Beverly Hills); Simon became a financial adviser in the world of gaming and leisure. From his second marriage to Linda: his son Chris found great success in entering the real-estate brokerage and mortgage business; his daughter, Sara, cultivated a career as a costume designer, helping to put her husband through medical school, then abandoning it all to raise a son and two daughters. Furie's grandchildren currently number eleven, with a new generation of great-grandchildren on the horizon.

On July 18, 2009, however, perhaps the most momentous personal tragedy of Furie's life occurred, when his forty-eight-year-old son Jon took his own life by jumping from the top of the Pacific Design Center. In covering Jon's dramatic death, *Variety* reported that the ultimate tribute rested in the fact that between 700 and 1,000 people were present at his funeral. Jon headed up Montana Artists, a below-the-line agency for artisans and technicians in film and television. One of his clients, cinematographer Alan Caso, who had lensed his father's film *Top of the World* (1997), claims that in 2009, after the economy collapsed and the industry at large was affected, it "adversely affected not just his clients but many other people he knew . . . it ate away at him." Says Jon's close associate and business manager Howard Soroko, "Even though about 70% of our clients are working, Jon worried so much about the other 30% that he wasn't sleeping."[8]

In late 2009, while on the set of *Conduct Unbecoming*, a military courtroom drama with echoes of *A Few Good Men*, Furie was having as difficult a time as he has ever had directing a film. The specific pressures of the shoot, stemming from various sources, were compounded by the emotional fallout from Jon's passing. Furie was never keen to discuss this matter, even with those closest to him. In the midst of these hardships, however, he received word that the Director's Guild of Canada was to honor him with its Lifetime Achievement Award. At the ceremony on September 25, 2010, he delivered a seventeen-minute speech that wildly departed from the one he had written and printed beforehand, though he still managed, in winging it, to charm and touch his audience with a warmth and trademark vigor. Linda Furie remembers, "They loved Sid and everyone was affected by that speech and the way it was delivered. There were tears in my eyes, and they kept on coming."

Furie discussed how the main objective of a filmmaker—more than culture or fame or critical acclaim—should be to "affect people." He also took pause to ruminate on how the Canadian film industry had grown and flourished since his humble beginnings making *A Dangerous Age* in Toronto in 1956. "Today, to see a room this size full of people . . . and to think then [in 1957] we could have had this award dinner, if we had awards, in the men's room of this hotel, and that's the truth. So, to be here tonight and to see what an industry has evolved in Toronto! And how proud I am that I was a pioneer. . . . Canada has now arrived to where it should have been, and you should all be proud to be part of an industry here that is so, so respected." Because of a life of directing motion pictures, he claimed to still be a "seventeen-year-old inside" although his exterior suggested a man of seventy-seven. He ended by saying, "Let's have a lot more shooting always." The audience rose to their feet for a hearty applause. Overall, this was just the "medicine" his heart and head needed.

Before Furie, the Director's Guild of Canada had honored many other Canadian film luminaries: Norman Jewison (2002), Daryl Duke (2003), Arthur Hiller (2004), Daniel Petrie Sr. (2005), Allan King (2006), Paul Almond (2007), Eric Till (2008), and Carol Spier (2009). In the years after, the Lifetime Achievement Award was given to Ted Kotcheff (2011), Michael Anderson (2012), and John N. Smith (2013). In "Certain Tendencies in Canadian Cinema," Janice Laurie Kaye cited Furie as "an inspiration to Canadian moviemakers" who leaves "a career legacy of Canadian, British and American movies" that was "unmatched" in the time that he directed his earliest hits.[9] Not only did his *A Dangerous Age* stand as "probably the first Canadian feature to rate serious criticism" (to quote Penelope Houston's original 1957 review), but his masterpiece *The Ipcress File* was the first film by a director from English Canada to compete at the Cannes Film Festival for the Palme d'Or. (Had Michel Brault's and Pierre Perrault's excellent *Pour la suite du monde* not played in competition just two years earlier, it would have been the first film by a director from any part of Canada to play in competition.)

Reunited in 2012 with Margot Kidder and Lou Gossett, two alumni of his previous films, for the shooting of *A Pride of Lions* (aka *The Dependables*), Furie prides himself as ever on his undaunted perseverance, even though recent reviews have often given sufficient cause to be daunted. *A Pride of Lions* again reflected the *Hit!–Iron Eagle* formula, this time following a group of ex-military senior citizens who venture to Afghanistan to rescue their prisoner-of-war grandchildren. He added Seymour Cassel, Bo Svenson, and Cedric Smith to the long, impressive list of actors with whom he has worked. "A lot of people will look at such a film, or any direct-to-video work of mine, as just another unsophisticated little action thriller with the customary cheap thrills," says Furie, "but the work is of the utmost importance to me, and I always sit in with the color-timer and the sound mixer. These movies are what they are, but I always take a proactive role in every stage of production. I'm never on autopilot and I never take my leave from a project when the shooting stops."

Margot Kidder speaks of *A Pride of Lions* with warmth and undaunted affinity, as a satire on the follies of aging:

> Most people missed the joke. When we did that film, Lou Gossett had just gotten out of the hospital after cancer treatments, I had a knee replacement recently done, one of the other actors had some kind of open-heart or bypass operation, Seymour Cassel had memory and hearing problems. And Sidney is behind the camera, yelling to all of us, "Get up! Run! Drop! Shoot!" like he's in World War II. And I was just like, "Are you fucking kidding?! We're old! It'll take us a half-hour to do all that!" I haven't consistently laughed that hard on a movie set in years. We had such a good time.

Unexpected delights arose from the writing of this book, as Furie discovered many things that he would otherwise not have known, most of all about the present-day status of many old friends and collaborators—for instance, that Nicolas Roeg wound up marrying Harriet Harper, the daughter of Kenneth Harper, producer of *The Young Ones* (1961) and *Wonderful Life* (1964). Says Nicolas Roeg, "It's stranger than fiction, really. And when Harriet previously married the director Stuart Cooper, Sid gave them a set of Modigliani prints, which he'd had since university, as a wedding present. Her father Ken loved Sid, and he must have first met him around the same time I did." Furie's gleeful response to this was akin to experiencing a movie with a perfect ending: "Unbelievable! Harriet was such a great girl and I always wondered what happened to her. It's so fantastic that she wound up with Nic!"

Among other unexpected news flashes, Furie was also contented to hear that both Tony Ray, the star of *A Cool Sound from Hell* (1959), and ninety-one-year-old jazz artist Phil Nimmons, who composed the scores for both *A Dangerous Age* (1957) and *A Cool Sound from Hell,* are still around. In Nimmons's case, he still regularly performs music, quipping during his interview, "Sidney's only 81, he's still a young punk." In Ray's case, Furie always wondered what had become of him after his sudden departure from the movie industry in the late eighties; he was happy to recently hear that it was simply a retirement.

Furie is much like Nic Roeg in that, during taping sessions for this book, when Roeg was asked if he would like to be put back in touch with Furie, he responded with quiet dignity, "I much prefer the happy memories of people I haven't seen in decades. It's hard to cope with the passing of time, and you can only really know that when you're my age. But just knowing he's still out there and still working, and that I hear from you that the old fighting spirit is still there, I can smile and have that be enough."

In Furie's youth, before making even one of his fifty feature films, when he professed his filmmaking aspirations to his father, Samuel Furie answered, "If you make movies, you won't have to sit at a bench all day working without time for lunch. You'll be able to go out for lunch, and you'll have a better life." Furie remembers this as a kind of blessing his father gave him, one that signed and sealed the remainder of his life.

"Well, dear Dad, I've had a lot of lunches!"

Epilogue

Still Working the Angles

Lawyer, house-builder, rabbi: all of these were career paths Furie considered after he failed to set the world on fire with his first feature, *A Dangerous Age*. In many ways, these are splinters of the filmmaking profession and a breakdown of a movie director's job. A director fights for justice for his or her project, especially in the face of undue compromise, practical blunders, and distribution woes. A director constructs a project, building it from the ground up, often from its earliest stages. A director is the spiritual counselor to the actors and artisans working the various angles on a movie set. As a filmmaker, Sidney J. Furie remains a lawyer, a house-builder and a rabbi, especially as he prepares to make his last film, his swan song.

Drive Me to Vegas and Mars is a personal project, the first screenplay he has written completely solo since *During One Night* in the late 1950s. Furie will admit that the script was written to counteract the effects of being forced by a biographer to look into the past. He prides himself as a forward-thinker, one who does not even keep memorabilia. He once told me, "I save nothing from the past. If my house is burning down, I take my wife and my tax records." *Drive Me to Vegas and Mars* is a comedy-drama about aging, about regret, about final orders of business, about the joys and pains of staying in the game, about paving a path and keeping it clear for the next generation. Furie is past writing wounded males and having characters question their commitment. By now, his perennial "boys" are sure of themselves enough to know that their problems concern the proper ways of channeling that energy. And they are committed.

Sidney pitched me the project on his first trip to New York during our initial interview sessions for this book. He had intimated in earlier messages that he was hatching ideas for what he was calling "his last movie," telling me that it would be "a summation of what I think about this thing called life." At Central Park's boat pond, sitting on a bench on a sunny March day of heavy winds and cloudless skies, I looked up at him as he

319

stood over me acting out the story for *Drive Me to Vegas and Mars* as he then had it. We had been recording our conversations about the past for most of the day, so this was our little oasis, a long walk in the park where we could talk about our present and the future, particularly his. Bit by bit, character by character, situation by situation, he described everything in his classically animated, excitable manner. The first thing I noticed about his story was that it felt somewhat more scaled-down and personal than the type of genre work he had been geared toward making for the past twenty or thirty years. When I confronted him on this point, he started questioning me about how my regular "filmmaking posse" made our microbudget, do-it-yourself features. And as the two of us got to know each other more and more, he became ever more inquisitive about these methods, and this whetted his appetite to work in a similar way. "I've been making movies for so long where my assistants have their own assistants," he then told me. These conversations were so persistent that, after awhile, we could order preferred drinks for the other without even blinking. For me, an IPA. For him, a pepper vodka at lunch or a nice rosé at dinner.

When he arrived at a draft he was ready to share, he sent it to me in October 2013. I read it eagerly, returning to the Central Park boat pond, the spot of his first pitch. The writing, in both style and narrative, was the man himself, the writer and director himself, revealed—Sidney as I personally knew him to be. In sending him my impressions and then bouncing with him on them, I became officially adopted into the lengthy dynasty of "creative bouncing boards" that included Brad Dexter, Harry Korshak, Rick Natkin, Greg Mellott, and many others. He started phoning me more regularly, mostly musing on actors who could possibly play the lead role of Cowboy. Many names were mentioned, and he ping-ponged between them for the better part of a year. He eliminated characters, then revivified them in later drafts. Elements came and went, then returned, as he worked through literally hundreds of drafts. He took every opportunity to tell me how he had never enjoyed the writing process more, quipping that he would certainly have more fun writing it than actually shooting it. In our walks through a Sherman Oaks mall on my research trips out to Los Angeles, he would continue working through problems in the writing and production with me. We bounced back and forth and to and fro, in more ways than one, between Macy's on one side of the spacious mall and Bloomingdale's on the other.

As I prepped my own feature, *Raise Your Kids on Seltzer,* which was set to shoot in the San Francisco Bay Area, Sidney asked if he could observe the way I ran my set, knowing it to be a considerably more intimate affair. The cast, crew, and I enthusiastically welcomed the opportunity. On the night of May 8, 2014, Sidney showed up on location in Berkeley, amazed to find only three crew members and five actors present. My cinematographer acted as his own gaffer, and when our sound man stepped out for a quick break at one point, I operated my own sound while grabbing a quick shot. That Sidney was liberated was obvious. He even seized the downtime between takes to regale everyone present with his industry stories, the Brando and Neil Diamond tales being favorites. At one point in the evening, when no one else was around to operate the slate (i.e., clapboard), my cinematographer meekly asked Sidney to oblige. Smiling, Sidney replied, "I've done nearly fifty movies and I've never touched a slate. Do I get to rehearse?" He rose from his nearby chair and called the take and scene numbers, relishing the novelty of the whole enterprise.

Sidney repeatedly exclaimed, leaving the set with us that night, that he finally knew how to tackle *Drive Me to Vegas and Mars*. He hired my own cinematographer and started to think in practical terms about finally realizing what he insisted would be his last picture. To see this eighty-one-year-old veteran director in the company of young filmmakers working on the outermost fringes of the industry, it was nearly impossible to sense much of an age gap. In this sense, he walks in the footsteps of his mentor from the early television days, veteran cinematographer Eugen Schüfftan, whose surprising vigor at an advanced age inspired his younger crew.

At the time of this writing, he is still rewriting and prepping. On some days, he doubts whether he has what it takes to make it really well, in the way he wants to make it. I often try to pep-talk him out of these funks. Eventually, something will galvanize him, often a sentiment he realizes time and again: "Time is limited, and what am I really to do with the rest of it but do what I've been put on this earth to do, to make movies?" Whether or not he brings this last movie to fruition is not a question in my own mind. He must, and he knows it. To be in his presence, even briefly, is to sense this as truth. After all, this is a man who walks into a restaurant, evaluates its lighting, then muses on what it would take if one wanted to shoot something in it.

In conclusion, the matter of one's favorite filmmakers says a great deal about a cinephile as an individual. Next to Jacques Rivette, Claude Jutra, Andrei Tarkovsky, Jean Vigo, Nicolas Roeg, Ritwik Ghatak, John

Cassavetes, Robert Altman, George Cukor, and the Archers (Michael Powell and Emeric Pressburger), Sidney J. Furie is among my favorites. As I see it, he sits comfortably in the ostensibly more distinguished company and is in many ways my true favorite because his films require more effort for me to defend. One might equate this to an activist advocating an unpopular cause, but to me, it is certainly one that has the capability of growth, empathy, and larger understanding. With this in mind, he is the cinema cause I am looking to further, and that makes him more special to me than the others.

Steven Soderbergh, in his book about his own filmmaking hero, Richard Lester, categorized Lester's work under the banners of Masterpieces, Classics, Worthwhile Divertissements, and Really Fascinating Films. By that token, I would argue that Sidney J. Furie made five Masterpieces (*The Leather Boys, The Ipcress File, Hit!, The Boys in Company C, The Entity*), five Classics (*The Young Ones, The Ipcress File, Lady Sings the Blues, The Boys in Company C, The Entity*), five worthwhile divertissements (*The Boys, The Lawyer, Hollow Point, Going Back, Global Heresy*), and four Really Fascinating Films That Get Better with Age (*Wonderful Life, The Appaloosa, Little Fauss and Big Halsy, Sheila Levine Is Dead and Living in New York*). In addition to the Soderbergh categories, there are also three Bold Pioneering Efforts (*A Dangerous Age, A Cool Sound from Hell, During One Night*) and three Fascinating Failures (*The Naked Runner, Gable and Lombard, Purple Hearts*). This is not even to mention the unexpected pleasures that await (for viewers with discerning eyes) within films like *Doctor Blood's Coffin, The Snake Woman, Three on a Spree, Iron Eagle, In Her Defense,* and *The Circle*. I submit, how is it that this man has ever, even once, been called a hack? With hope, this book is the first step toward necessary reappraisal.

Postscript: *Drive Me to Vegas and Mars* went into production on June 21, 2015, and wrapped shooting on July 9. It is due for release in 2016.

Acknowledgments

Before I express my gratitude to anyone else, I would like to thank Sidney J. Furie himself, who is a director I grew up greatly admiring and who, throughout the writing of this book, grew to be a personal teacher, a cinema rebbe, a close friend, and an enthusiastic supporter—someone who bared his soul and always stayed honest about the span of history I covered. Without him and his *The Ipcress File,* film would be a mere hobby for me rather than an actual career . . . and so I owe a very happy life to him. Special thanks must also be extended to Sidney's family, including his wife, Linda, his sons Dan, Noah, Simon, and Chris, and his daughter, Sara. I would also like to thank the people who led me to Sidney, namely actors Jason Blicker and Saul Rubinek. There would be no book without them. Saul, you're a great friend and, alas, here is your "Book of Daniel"! I would also like to thank Margot Kidder, who was the first person to inform Sidney that I had written an article about his films—the article that proved to be the foundation on which this book was built. And also, a gigantic thanks to Paul Lynch, who pushed Sidney off the fence and first persuaded him to speak with me, and then do the book with me.

The book would not exist without the support of Patrick McGilligan, who believed in the project from the first time I e-mailed him proposing it (thanks here also goes to Marilyn Ann Moss and, once again, Paul Lynch, for putting the two of us in touch). Pat stuck with me and the book even during those difficult early stages when I (stubbornly) refused to weed out some rather neon-lettered hyperbole that I had ill-advisedly used to make it all look more appealing. Who knows what made him keep the faith? What a mensch! At the University Press of Kentucky, Anne Dean Dotson and Bailey Johnson made the whole process easy and even fun; thanks also to copyeditor Lois Crum.

I am also grateful to my best friend, the cinematographer on my own films, and the person with whom I discuss film-related topics the most, Aaron Hollander. Aaron's shared interest and enthusiasm for both this literary venture and the films I examined in this book proved invaluable, as a sounding board for ideas and the barometer of my film-by-film analysis. In many ways, we were discovering the brilliance of Sidney's work together, and our "Furie-thons" fostered the best discussions you could get from any friend or supporter on most any subject . . . and most found their way into this book.

Other major thank-yous go to the great Stephen Eckelberry and his daughter Celine Eckelberry, for opening up their sofa to me on my research trips out to Los Angeles. Sidney also thanks you! On a similar note, I would also like to thank William Cully Allen, his wife, Cynthia, and their kids Gabe and Emma, for providing occasional "writer's retreats" at their home in Moorestown, New Jersey.

I would like to thank my friend Sunrise Tippeconnie, whose enthusiasm and support proved equal to that of most anyone I encountered. When no one else could hold a substantive, "intellectual" conversation about *Iron Eagle* with me, Sunrise outdid himself. Also, I need to thank Deniz Demirer, a wonderful filmmaking collaborator who listened patiently and with interest as I ranted and raved about Sidney's career and aesthetics. Also: Deniz's guru (and another one of mine), Rob Nilsson, who likewise withstood my impassioned yammering.

I would like to also thank the people who granted me interviews and/ or provided useful input via cyber exchange, including Harry Basil, Stephen H. Burum, Michael Caine, Larry Cohen, Gray Frederickson, Daniel Furie, Linda Furie, Noah Furie, Simon Furie, Lou Gossett, Susan Hampshire, Piers Handling, Monte Hellman, Gary Howsam, Lauren Hutton, Henry Jaglom, Norman Jewison, Margot Kidder, Ted Kotcheff, David Labiosa, Paul Lynch, Melanie Mayron, Greg Mellott, Andre Morgan, Donald M. Morgan (double thanks), Diana Muldaur, Rick Natkin, Barry Newman, Phil Nimmons, Gail Parent, Nicolas Roeg, Mark Rosenthal, Albert S. Ruddy, Barry Sandler, Stan Shaw, Michael Snow, Kenny Solms, Dudley Sutton, Paul Sylbert, Edward Thorpe (longtime husband of Gillian Freeman, speaking on her behalf), Alan Trustman (and his assistant Saverio Mancina), Rita Tushingham, Jay Weston, Billy Dee Williams, and Joe Zito. Also, thanks to Jon Mulvaney and Charles Collier for connecting me with Nicolas Roeg, one of my top ten favorite filmmakers, a true master, one of my greatest influences. Mr. Roeg, if you're reading this, our brief phone call remains a big event for me. Hats off to you!

Thanks also goes to Dan Friedlaender, an old friend, for conversations about Furie's films, along with information and research materials about

Acknowledgments

Furie's early life with Dan's father at Carnegie Mellon. Indeed, what a small world we live in! I promised a well-deserved shout-out to fellow Furie nut Aaron W. Graham, from Winnipeg, who independently learned of my endeavor and tracked me down on social media to furnish me with a wide-screen viewing copy of *Little Fauss and Big Halsy* when one was completely unavailable otherwise. I must also give a shout-out to Wendel Meldrum, a generous and consistent supporter (both spiritually and often otherwise) of all my projects.

In terms of research, I extend thank-yous to Sandra Archer, Kristine Krueger, and Lea Whittington at the Margaret Herrick Academy of Motion Picture Arts and Sciences Library, who made my quest for information their own. Sandra, it was always comforting seeing your perennial smile above handfuls of reference material. Ditto to Rachel Burge at University of Toronto's Robarts Library, Julia Corrin at the Carnegie Mellon University Archives, and Jonathon Auxier at the USC Library–Warner Bros. Archive. At the British Film Institute, my gratitude goes to Lynn McVeigh, for her attention to excavating Sidney's long-thought-lost second film, *A Cool Sound from Hell,* which involved a year's worth of work and persistence. An archaeological dig requires diligence, and your patience was a virtue.

And last but not least, my beta-readers: Aaron Hollander (once again), Paul Sylbert, Elisa DeCarlo, Brad Balfour, and Kris Caltagirone. I hope it's everything you hoped it would be, guys!

And to my family in Pittsburgh—thanks for the support through my first three decades!

Baruch Hashem.

Appendix A

A Public Correspondence between Sidney J. Furie and Herb Aller

On October 9, 1966, the *Los Angeles Times* published the following editorial, written by Sidney J. Furie, for the Sunday Calendar section.

Hollywood Misses Its Cue, by Sidney J. Furie

The trouble with Hollywood is that it doesn't see enough TV. TV has made gargantuan strides, is light years ahead in terms of technique and equipment. And Hollywood, fountainhead of major feature productions, simply hasn't kept pace.

The industry is holding on to old rules, old formulas, the old way of doing things, because that is how it has always been done. Is it any wonder that so much of the excitement and enthusiasm has vanished from the Hollywood scene, only to crop out where the filmmaking climate is more salubrious? By failing to make use of new methods originated under its very nose, Hollywood is depriving itself of an opportunity to inject throbbing new vitality into its moribund acetate corpuscles. Basic moviemaking is practically the same today as at the advent of sound. There are cameras, cumbersome recording equipment, and an interlock system between them. That's it.

On the other hand, there are a number of TV shows which have had the resourcefulness and ingenuity to use a handheld camera for all photographic work, and to couple this with sound equipment called a "sync-pulse recorder," permitting stationing of such gear a great distance from the camera.

Needless to point out, such a combination gives a director, the actors and the technicians far great mobility and freedom. There is absolutely no reason why, with modern existing equipment, you cannot have a scene involving two people in a taxicab in which you cannot use a real cab moving through real traffic. It would take one man with a camera in the front seat next to the driver, and a sound truck a half mile away picking up the sound from body mikes. It isn't done that way in Hollywood. We go into the process stage and work hard at creating the entire illusion when we could achieve the same result—a better result—by going right out in traffic where the scene really belongs.

Examine one of the best of the New Wave pictures, Francois Truffaut's *The 400 Blows,* the film that launched a whole new trend, and you will find its impact derived in large measure from the fact that almost throughout it relied upon a handheld camera.

Through custom and habit the Hollywood cameraman has exercised a kind of tyranny on the set which has been accepted as the way to do things. To attempt something new, according to this time-worn concept, is to do things wrong. Why must the expected become the rule?

In shooting *The Appaloosa,* an outdoor movie, in the bright sunlight of Utah, where we went on location, you are expected to get as much sunlight into the scene as possible. Sunlight, they tell you, is why you went to Utah in the first place. Furthermore, it's the way westerns have been made in the past, and you are expected to follow the formula.

But I played a number of scenes in the shade with the hot-lighted background in the background where it belonged. I played scenes on the porch and in the shadow and in the dark, and the faces are almost black. When I first suggested the set-up, my technicians told me I would have to light the porch so that actors' faces could be seen. I said, "Don't light it. I want it dark. Because in real life, that is how it is." I got skeptical looks and expressions of doubt.

And this is one of the big problems in trying to approach old problems. Cameramen, purely and simply, are lighting men. This is what they do. In England, they do not have much to do with the camera. Most directors decide and construct their own camera set-ups, which is the way I work.

I say, "Put the camera here and aim it there," and that ends the cameraman's function as far as the director is concerned. He (the director) is responsible for the composition of the scene, the placement of his actors and the kind of camera angle he believes is essential for a particular scene.

In England, as I said, they call the cinematographer the "lighting cameraman" because that is what he does. After I have picked the camera angle and have rehearsed my actors and then the camera movements with the camera operator, the only thing left for the lighting cameraman to do is light. I hear that, in Hollywood, if you take on this kind of responsibility, you will be told, "I'm the cameraman, and you're the director; you do your job and I'll do mine." I've never heard that kind of reaction in England because if a cameraman ever said that to a director he'd be removed from the picture. On *The Appaloosa,* I had as a cameraman Russell Metty, an Oscar winner for *Spartacus.* He is a creative man who understood my viewpoint completely.

As I see it, filmmaking is a business which has some of the youngest old men in the world. They're the creative ones. And some of the oldest young men, too. They're the ones who have been stifled by the system. Where does the fault lie? Movie business is a creative business because it deals with magic and the world of make believe. Over the years, in some instances, certain phases of the work have been burdened with a union seniority system. Creative people need those experienced men and women. But sometimes the situation makes for unhealthy marriages.

If I had to guess a figure I'd say that 99% of Hollywood technicians are proficient and excellent and honestly interested in what they are doing. Unfortunately, the remaining 1% are very important to picture-making. Basic to the problem is that those who are willing to do the same things in the same timeworn ways never knew it could be done differently. Many members of a camera crew have a disdain for any camera that wasn't invented before 1930. Generally these are older men who, in any other industry, would face compulsory retirement by their own unions.

I dwell on this point because there have been some techniques which are held in contempt by some technicians simply because they are new. To me, filmmaking is a very special and demanding art. It withers without experimentation. But there can be neither excitement nor enthusiasm as long as the industry holds to old ways of doing things because it is how it has always been done.

Four days later, on Thursday, October 13, 1966, the *Los Angeles Times* published a rebuttal to Furie's editorial, written by Herb Aller, executive secretary of Local 659, International Alliance of Theatrical Stage Employees and Moving Picture Machine Operators.

Fuzzy Image of Cameramen Refocused, by Herb Aller

In the October 9 Calendar, Sidney Furie had much to say about making films in Hollywood. He seemed to find fault with the techniques and equipment employed and placed considerable stress on the problem of persuading cinematographers of feature films to change their patterns of photography. Furie emphasized the advancements to be accomplished with the handheld camera and the resistance he encountered to its use. At the same time, he said that cinematographer Russell Metty is creative and understood his views. Furie's first film in this country is *The Appaloosa*. He also seemed to resent cinematographers selecting the placement of the camera. It is his theory that the director is responsible for the composition.

There is great doubt that Furie speaks either with authority, knowledge or comprehensive understanding of making motion pictures. He deflates the English cinematographer to such an extent that were Freddie Fields, Jack Cardiff and Jack Hilyard to read the self-styled bravado applause of Furie, it might bring forth a meaningless civil war.

Time and time again, stage directors like Kazan, Logan and others have entered the motion picture industry and entrusted themselves into the hands of the many distinguished American cinematographers. The net result has been successful, artistically and monetarily. It is the varied knowledge of cinematography, art direction, editing and other component parts of picture-making that has resulted in the many interesting contributions the cinematographers have made to so many fine films. The working relationship of director and cinematographer has always been a team project.

Furie seems to be striving for control and respect based on his two films, *The Ipcress File* and *The Appaloosa*. It seems that he forgot to do his homework, for respect is earned, not muscled. Hollywood does not suffer from lack of techniques either photographically or otherwise. A handheld camera to get shots of a bouncy nature might be acceptable on a commercial where the frog or frug is being enacted to attract instantaneous attention—certainly not in a serious drama. An effort to do something different is hardly suitable to good picture-making.

Furie speaks of TV being far ahead of feature production. Almost the same people do the work one way or the other, except that TV directors have schedules and feature directors do not. It is a common event for a cinematographer to shift from TV to features. Curley Lindon, who just finished *Grand Prix* for John Frankenheimer (MGM), is a striking example.

It seems to me that not being able to cope with highly technical skills, Furie lays the blame on the cinematographer. Furie would be wise to devote his time to the script, for it may be that he'll go out the way he came in—with no class.

Appendix B

The Marcel Proust Questionnaire

Toward the end of Michel Ciment's book *Conversations with Losey,* Ciment subjects the director to a questionnaire originated by Marcel Proust. The answers to these questions are revealing about the man as director and individual. Since this will likely remain the authoritative text on Sidney J. Furie, it seemed logical and sensible to include such a supplement in this book. The questions are lifted in equal measure from both Ciment's Proust questions and television host James Lipton's *Inside the Actors Studio* questions (which were in turned adapted from French television personality Bernard Pivot's shows *Apostrophes* and *Buillon de Culture*).

My chief characteristic: Enthusiastic
The quality I prefer in a man: Sensitivity
The quality I prefer in a woman: Ballsiness
What I appreciate most in my friends: Loyalty
My favorite word: Great
Least favorite word: Can't
My favorite sound or noise: A movie or TV in the background
My main flaw: Superstitiousness
My idea of happiness: Dinner with my grandkids
My idea of misery: Stuck in the house for any reason
What I would like to be: Untroubled
The country where I'd most prefer to live: The U.S. of A
The color I prefer: Olive drab
Favorite writers in prose: Thomas Hardy and Aaron Sorkin
Favorite poets: The Canadian John McCrae, especially "In Flanders
    Fields"

Favorite painter(s): Modigliani

Favorite composer(s): The scorers for the films I saw growing up. I dearly love movie music.

Favorite filmmaker still working today: Woody Allen, I never miss any of his movies.

Favorite heroes in fiction: Noah Ackerman in Irwin Shaw's *The Young Lions*

Heroes in real life: The New York responders who died on 9/11

The military action I admire: Entebbe and D-Day

What I hate most of all: Negativity

Occupation other than your own you'd like to attempt: Ruler of the world

The gift I'd most like to have: Erudition, intellectual gab

I wouldn't mind being reincarnated as: No reincarnation, please.

Present state of mind: Hopeful

Faults I tolerate the most in others: Stupid, everyday prejudices of things that one should never be against

Faults I tolerate the most in myself: Thinking things aren't important, even if they're not.

My motto: Michael Caine said it first, "Life is not a rehearsal"

If heaven exists, what would you like to hear God say when you arrive at the pearly gates: "It's not my fault."

Filmography

Feature Films

A Dangerous Age, 1957. Screenplay, Sidney J. Furie. Cinematographer, Herbert S. Alpert. Editor, David Nicholson. Music, Phil Nimmons. Producers, Sidney J. Furie and Sean Sullivan. Caribou Productions, 35mm, color, 67 minutes. Cast: Ben Piazza (David), Anne Pearson (Nancy Michaels), Lloyd Jones (Old Postmaster), Claude Rae (Young Postmaster), Kate Reid (Nancy's Mother), Shane Rimmer (Nancy's Father), Aileen Seaton (Five-and-Dime Woman).

A Cool Sound from Hell, 1959. Screenplay, Sidney J. Furie. Cinematographer, Herbert S. Alpert. Editor, David Nicholson. Music, Phil Nimmons. Producer, Sidney J. Furie. Caribou Productions, 35mm, color, 72 minutes. Cast: Anthony Ray (Charlie), Carolyn Dannibale (Steve), Madeline Kronby (Debbie), Alan Crofoot (Milt), Ronald Taylor (Pete), Tom Harvey (Police Officer), Murray Westgate (Police Officer), Walter Massey (Pilot), Don Owen (Beat Poet).

Doctor Blood's Coffin, 1961. Screenplay, Jerry Juran (Nathan Juran). Cinematographer, Stephen Dade. Editor, Antony Gibbs. Music, Buxton Orr. Producer, George Fowler. Caralan Productions, Inc., 35mm, color, 91 minutes. Cast: Kieron Moore (Dr. Peter Blood), Ian Hunter (Dr. Robert Blood), Hazel Court (Nurse Linda Parker), Gerald C. Lawson (G. F. Morton), Kenneth J. Warren (Sergeant Cook), Fred Johnson (Tregaye), Paul Hardtmuth (Professor Luckman), Paul Stockman (Steve Parker).

The Snake Woman, 1961. Screenplay, Orville H. Hampton. Cinematographer, Stephen Dade. Editor, Antony Gibbs. Music, Buxton Orr. Producer, George Fowler. Caralan Productions, Inc., 35mm, color, 68 minutes. Cast: John McCarthy (Charles Prentice), Susan Travers (Atheris), Elsie Wagstaff (Aggie Harker), Geoffrey Denton (Colonel Clyde Wynborn), Arnold Marlé (Dr. Murton), John Cazabon (Dr. Horace Adderson), Frances Bennett (Polly the Barmaid).

Three on a Spree, 1961. Screenplay, Sigfried Herzig, James Kelly, and Wilkie Mahoney. Based on the novel and play *Brewster's Millions.* Cinematographer, Stephen Dade. Editors, Bert Rule. Music, Ken Thorne. Producers, George Fowler and David E. Rose. Caralan-Dador Productions and United Artists, 35mm, color, 92 minutes. Cast: Jack Watling (Michael Brewster), Carole Lesley (Susan), Renee Houston (Mrs. Gray), John Slater (Sid Johnson), Colin Gordon (Mitchell), John Salew (Mr. Monkton).

During One Night, 1961 (U.S. release title, *Night of Passion;* working title, *The 25th Mission*). Screenplay, Sidney J. Furie. Cinematographer, Norman Warwick. Editor, Antony Gibbs. Music, William McGuffie. Producers, Sidney J. Furie and Kenneth Rive. Galaworldfilm Productions, 35mm, color, 84 minutes. Cast: Don Borisenko (David), Susan Hampshire (Jean), Sean Sullivan (Major), Joy Webster (Prostitute), Graydon Gould (Mike), Tom Busby (Sam), Alan Gibson (Harry), Barbara Ogilvie (Mother), Jackie Collins (Girl), Michael Golden (Constable).

The Young Ones, 1961 (U.S. release title, *Wonderful to Be Young!*). Screenplay, Peter Myers and Ronald Cass. Cinematographer, Douglas Slocombe. Editor, Jack Slade. Music and songs, Peter Myers and Ronald Cass, with Stanley Black. Producers, Andrew Mitchell and Kenneth Harper. Elstree Studios, 35mm, color, 103 minutes. Cast: Cliff Richard (Nicky), Robert Morley (Hamilton), Carole Gray (Toni), Richard O'Sullivan (Ernest), Melvyn Hayes (Jimmy), Teddy Green (Chris), Annette Robertson (Barbara), Sonya Cordeau (Dorinda), Sean Sullivan (Eddie), featuring The Shadows.

The Boys, 1962. Screenplay, Stuart Douglass. Cinematographer, Gerald Gibbs. Editor, Jack Slade. Music, The Shadows, with Bill McGuffie. Producers, Kenneth Rive and Sidney J. Furie. Galaworldfilm Productions and Atlas Productions, 35mm, color, 123 minutes. Cast: Richard Todd (Victor Webster), Robert Morley (Montgomery), Dudley Sutton (Stan Coulter), Ronald Lacey (Billy Herne), Tony Garnett (Ginger Thompson), Jess Conrad (Barney Lee), Felix Aylmer (Judge), Wilfred Bramble (Robert Brewer), Roy Kinnear (Mark Salmon), Patrick Magee (Mr. Lee).

The Leather Boys, 1963 (copyright), 1964 (release). Screenplay, Gillian Freeman. Based on the novel by Eliot George (Gillian Freeman). Cinematographer, Gerald Gibbs. Editor, Reginald Beck. Music, Bill McGuffie. Producer, Raymond Stross. Garrick/British Lion/BLC Productions, 35mm, color, 108 minutes. Cast: Rita Tushingham (Dot), Colin Campbell (Reggie), Dudley Sutton (Pete), Gladys Henson

(Gran), Avice Landon (Reggie's Mother), Lockwood West (Reggie's Father), Betty Marsdon (Dot's Mother), Martin Mathews (Uncle Arthur).

Wonderful Life, 1964. (U.S. release title, *Swingers' Paradise*). Screenplay, Peter Myers and Ronald Cass. Cinematographer, Kenneth Higgins. Editor, Jack Slade. Music and songs, Peter Myers and Ronnie Cass. Producer, Kenneth Harper. Elstree Studios and Warner-Pathe, 35mm, color, 109 minutes. Cast: Cliff Richard (Johnnie), Walter Slezak (Lloyd Davis), Susan Hampshire (Jenny Taylor), Hank B. Marvin (Hank), Bruce Welch (Bruce), Brian Bennett (Brian), John Rostill (John), Richard O'Sullivan (Edward), Una Stubbs (Barbara Tate), Derek Bond (Douglas Leslie), Melvyn Hayes (Jerry).

The Ipcress File, 1965. Screenplay, Bill Canaway and James Dolan. Based on the novel by Len Deighton. Cinematographer, Otto Heller. Editor, Peter H. Hunt. Music, John Barry. Producers, Harry Saltzman and Charles Kasher. J. Arthur Rank Film (UK), 35mm, color, 104 minutes. Cast: Michael Caine (Harry Palmer), Guy Doleman (Ross), Nigel Green (Dalby), Sue Lloyd (Jean), Gordon Jackson (Carswell), Aubrey Richards (Radcliffe), Frank Gatliff (Bluejay), Thomas Baptiste (Barney), Oliver MacGreevy (Housemartin).

The Appaloosa, 1966. (UK title, *Southwest to Sonora*). Screenplay, James Bridges and Roland Kibbee. Based on the novel by Robert MacLeod. Cinematographer, Russell Metty. Editor, Ted J. Kent. Music, Frank Skinner. Producer, Alan Miller. Universal Pictures, 35mm, color, 98 minutes. Cast: Marlon Brando (Matt Fletcher), Anjanette Comer (Trini), John Saxon (Chuy), Rafael Campos (Paco), Miriam Colon (Ana), Emilio Fernandez (Lazaro), Frank Silvera (Ramos), Alex Montoya (Squint Eye), Larry D. Mann (Priest).

The Naked Runner, 1967. Screenplay, Stanley Mann. Based on the novel by Francis Clifford. Cinematographer, Otto Heller. Editor, Barrie Vince. Music, Harry Sukman. Producer, Brad Dexter. Warner Bros., 35mm, color, 100 minutes. Cast: Frank Sinatra (Sam Laker), Peter Vaughan (Slattery), Derren Nesbitt (Colonel Hartmann), Nadia Gray (Karen), Toby Robins (Ruth), Inger Stratton (Anna), Edward Fox (Ritchie Jackson), Cyril Luckham (Cabinet Minister).

The Lawyer, 1969 (copyright), 1970 (release). Screenplay, Sidney J. Furie and Harold Buchman. Cinematographer, Ralph Woolsey. Editor, Argyle Nelson. Music, Malcolm Dodds. Producer, Brad Dexter. Paramount Pictures, 35mm, color, 120 minutes. Cast: Barry Newman (Petrocelli), Harold Gould (Eric Scott), Diana Muldaur (Ruth Petrocelli), Robert Colbert (Jack Harrison), Kathleen Crowley (Alice), Warren Kemmerling (Sgt. Moran), Ken Swofford (Charlie O'Keefe), Booth Colman (Judge Crawford).

Little Fauss and Big Halsy, 1970. Screenplay, Charles Eastman. Cinematographer, Ralph Woolsey. Editor, Argyle Nelson. Music, Johnny Cash. Producers, Brad Dexter, Albert S. Ruddy, and Gray Frederickson. Paramount Pictures, 35mm, color, 98 minutes. Cast: Robert Redford (Halsy Knox), Michael J. Pollard (Little Fauss), Lauren Hutton (Rita Nebraska), Lucille Benson (Mom Fauss), Noah Beery (Seally Fauss), Ray Ballard (The Photographer), Linda Gaye Scott (Moneth), Erin O'Reilly (Sylvene McFall), Benjamin Archibek (Rick Nifty), Shara St. John (Marcy).

Lady Sings the Blues, 1972. Screenplay, Suzanne de Passe, Chris Clark, and Terence McCloy. Cinematographer, John Alonzo. Editor, Argyle Nelson. Music, Michel Legrand. Producer, Berry Gordy. Paramount Pictures/Berry Gordy Productions, 35mm, color, 144 minutes. Cast: Diana Ross (Billie Holiday), Billy Dee Williams (Louis McKay), Richard Pryor (Piano Man), James Callahan (Reg Hanley), Paul Hampton (Harry), Sid Melton (Jerry), Virginia Capers (Mama Holiday), Yvonne Fair (Yvonne), Ned Glass (The Agent), Harry Caesar (The Rapist), Isabel Sanford (The Madame), Scatman Crothers (Big Ben).

Hit!, 1973. Screenplay, Alan Trustman and David M. Wolf. Cinematographer, John A. Alonzo. Editor, Argyle Nelson. Music, Lalo Schifrin. Producer, Harry Korshak. Paramount Pictures, 35mm, color, 135 minutes. Cast: Billy Dee Williams (Nick Allen), Richard Pryor (Mike Willmer), Paul Hampton (Barry Strong), Gwen Wells (Sherry Nielson), Warren Kemmerling (Dutch Schiller), Janet Brandt (Ida), Sid Melton (Herman), David "Zooey" Hall (Carlin), Todd Martin (Crosby), Norman Burton (The Director), Noble Willingham (Warden Springer).

Sheila Levine Is Dead and Living in New York, 1975. Screenplay, Kenny Solms and Gail Parent. Based on the novel by Gail Parent. Cinematographer, Donald M. Morgan. Editor, Argyle Nelson. Music, Michel Legrand. Producer, Harry Korshak. Paramount Pictures, 35mm, color, 113 minutes. Cast: Jeannie Berlin (Sheila Levine), Roy Scheider (Sam Stoneman), Rebecca Dianna Smith (Kate), Janet Brandt (Bernice Levine), Sid Melton (Manny Levine), Charles Woolf (Wally), Leda Rogers (Agatha Horowitz), Noble Willingham (The Principal).

Gable and Lombard, 1976. Screenplay, Barry Sandler. Cinematographer, Jordan Cronenweth. Editor, Argyle Nelson. Music, Michel Legrand. Costumes, Edith Head. Producer, Harry Korshak. Universal Pictures, 35mm, color, 132 minutes. Cast: James Brolin (Clark Gable), Jill Clayburgh (Carole Lombard), Allen Garfield (Louis B. Mayer), Red Buttons (Ivan Cooper), Melanie Mayron (Dixie), Joanne Linville (Ria Gable), Carol McGinnis (Noreen), Noah Keen (Broderick), Alan D. Dexter (Sheriff Ellis).

The Boys in Company C, 1978. Screenplay, Rick Natkin and Sidney J. Furie. Cinematographer, Godfrey A. Godar. Editor, Michael Berman. Music, Jaime Mendoza-Nava. Producers, Andre Morgan and Raymond Chow. Golden Harvest, 35mm, color, 125 minutes. Distribution, Columbia Pictures. Cast: Stan Shaw (Tyrone Washington), Andrew Stevens (Billy Ray Pike), James Canning (Alvin Foster), Michael Lembeck (Vinnie Fazio), Craig Wasson (David Bisbee), Scott Hylands (Captain Collins), James Whitmore Jr. (Lieutenant Archer), Noble Willingham (Sergeant Curry), R. Lee Ermey (Sergeant Loyce), Santos Morales (Sergeant Aquilla).

Night of the Juggler (quit), 1980. Director, Robert Butler (some scenes, Sidney J. Furie). Screenplay, Bill Norton Sr. and Rick Natkin. From the novel by William P. McGivern. Cinematography, Victor J. Kemper. Editor, Argyle Nelson. Music, Artie Kane. Producers, Stephen Kesten, Arnold Kopelson, and Jay Weston. Columbia Pictures, 35mm, color, 101 minutes. Cast: James Brolin (Sean Boyd), Cliff Gorman (Gus Soltic), Richard Castellano (Lieutenant Tonelli), Abby Bluestone (Kathy Boyd), Julie Carmen (Maria), Linda G. Miller (Barbara Boyd), Sully Boyar (Larry), Mandy Patinkin (Allesandro the Cabbie).

The Jazz Singer (fired), 1980. Director, Richard Fleischer (some scenes, Sidney J. Furie). Screenplay, Herbert Baker. Based on the play by Samson Raphaelson. Cinematographer, Isidore Mankovsky. Music, Neil Diamond, with Leonard Rosenman. Producer, Jerry Leider. EMI Films, 35mm, color, 116 minutes. Cast: Neil Diamond (Jess Robin), Laurence Olivier (Cantor Rabinovich), Lucie Arnaz (Molly), Caitlin Adams (Rivka Rabinovitch), Franklyn Ajaye (Bubba), Paul Nicholas (Keith Lennox), Sully Boyar (Eddie Gibbs).

The Entity, 1982. Screenplay, Frank De Felitta. From the novel by Frank De Felitta. Cinematographer, Stephen H. Burum. Editor, Frank J. Urioste. Music, Charles Bernstein. Producer, Harold Schneider. 20th Century

Fox and American Cinema Productions, 35mm, color, 125 minutes. Cast: Barbara Hershey (Carla Moran), Ron Silver (Dr. Phil Sneiderman), David Labiosa (Billy), George Coe (Dr. Weber), Margaret Blye (Cindy Nash), Jacqueline Brooks (Dr. Cooley), Richard Brestoff (Gene Kraft), Michael Alldredge (George Nash), Alex Rocco (Jerry Anderson), Sully Boyar (Mr. Reisz).

Purple Hearts, 1984. Screenplay, Rick Natkin and Sidney J. Furie. Cinematographer, Jan Kiesser. Editor, George Grenville. Music, Robert Folk. Producers, Rick Natkin and Sidney J. Furie. Ladd Company, 35mm, color, 115 minutes. Distribution, Warner Bros. Cast: Ken Wahl (Don Jardian), Cheryl Ladd (Deborah Solomon), Stephen Lee (Wizard), Annie McEnroe (Hallaway), Paul McCrane (Brenner), James Whitmore Jr. (Bwana), R. Lee Ermey (Gunny), Drew Snyder (Lt. Col. Larimore), Lane Smith (Commander Markel).

Iron Eagle, 1986. Screenplay, Kevin Elders and Sidney J. Furie. Cinematographer, Adam Greenberg. Editor, George Grenville. Music, Basil Poledouris. Producers, Ron Samuels and Joe Wizan. Delphi Films and Tri-Star Pictures, 35mm, color, 107 minutes. Cast: Lou Gossett (Chappy), Jason Gedrick (Doug Masters), David Suchet (Akir Nakesh), Larry B. Scott (Reggie), Caroline Langerfelt (Elizabeth Masters), Jerry Levine (Tony).

Superman IV: The Quest for Peace, 1987. Screenplay, Lawrence Konner and Mark Rosenthal. Cinematographer, Ernest Day. Editor, John Shirley. Music, John Williams, with Alexander Courage. Producers, Menahem Golan and Yoram Globus. Cannon Films/Warner Bros., 35mm, color, 91 minutes. Cast: Christopher Reeve (Superman/Clark Kent), Gene Hackman (Lex Luthor), Margot Kidder (Lois Lane), Mariel Hemingway (Lacy Warfield), Jackie Cooper (Perry White), Marc McClure (Jimmy Olsen), Jon Cryer (Lenny), Mark Pillow (Nuclear Man).

Iron Eagle II, 1988. Screenplay, Kevin Elders and Sidney J. Furie. Cinematographer, Alain Dostie. Editor, Rit Wallis. Music, Amin Bahtia. Producers, John Kemeny, Jacob Kotzky, Sharon Harel, and Andras Hamori. Carolco Pictures and Alliance Entertainment, 35mm, color, 105 minutes. Cast: Lou Gossett (Chappy), Mark Humphrey (Captain Matt Cooper), Stuart Margolin (General Stillmore), Alan Scarfe (Colonel Vardovsky), Maury Chaykin (Sgt. Downs).

The Taking of Beverly Hills, 1991. Screenplay, Rick Natkin, David Fuller, and David J. Burke. Cinematographer, Frank Johnson. Editor, Antony

Gibbs. Music, Jan Hammer. Producers, Rick Finkelstein, Graham Henderson, and Barry Spikings. Nelson Entertainment, 35mm, color, 96 minutes. Cast: Ken Wahl (Boomer Hayes), Matt Frewer (Ed Kelvin), Harley Jane Kozak (Laura Sage), Robert Davi (Robert Masterson), Lee Ving James (Varney).

Ladybugs, 1992. Screenplay, Curtis Burch. Cinematographer, Dan Burstall. Editors, Tim Board, and John W. Wheeler. Music, Richard Gibbs. Producers, Albert S. Ruddy, Harry Basil, Gray Frederickson, and Andre Morgan. Paramount Pictures, 35mm, color, 91 minutes. Cast: Rodney Dangerfield (Chester Lee), Jackée (Julie), Jonathan Brandis (Matthew/Martha), Ilene Graff (Bess), Vinessa Shaw (Kimberly Mullen), Tom Parks (Dave Mullen).

Hollow Point, 1996. Screenplay, Robert Geoffrion and Stewart Harding. Cinematographer, David Franco. Editor, Yves Langlois. Music, Brahm Wenger. Producers, Nicolas Clermont and Elie Samaha. Nu Image, 35mm, color, 102 minutes. Cast: Thomas Ian Griffith (Max Parrish), Tia Carrere (Diane Norwood), John Lithgow (Thomas Livingston), Donald Sutherland (Garrett Lawton), Carl Alacchi (Alberto Capucci), David Hemblen (Oleg Krezinsky), Robert Ito (Shin Chan), Andreas Apergis (Ivan Krezinsky).

Top of the World, 1997. Screenplay, Bart Madison. Cinematographer, Alan Caso. Editor, Alan Jakubowicz. Music, Robert O. Ragland. Producers, Avi Lerner, Kevin Bernhardt, Danny Dimbort, Bob Misiorowski, and Elie Samaha. Nu Image, 35mm, color, 100 minutes. Cast: Peter Weller (Ray Mercer), Tia Carrere (Rebecca Mercer), Dennis Hopper (Charles Atlas), Joe Pantoliano (Vince Castor), David Alan Grier (Detective Augustus), Peter Coyote (Doc the Butcher), Martin Kove (Carl), Ed Lauter (Mel Ridgefield), Paul Herman (Valet), Eddie Mekka (Joe Burns).

In Her Defense, 1999. Screenplay, Marc Lynn and Jeffrey M. Rosenbaum. Cinematographer, Curtis Petersen. Editor, Denis Papillon. Music, Paul Zaza. Producers, Pierre Rene, Michael Mosca, Philippe Martinez, Jean-Marc Féiio, and Aziz Alaoui. Les Films St-Paul and Milagro Films, 35mm, color, 94 minutes. Cast: Marlee Matlin (Jane Claire), Daniel Pilon (Robert St. Laurent), Michael Dudikoff (Andrew Garfield), Sophie Lorain (Debra Turner), David Attis (Jeffrey Fishman).

Cord, 2000. (U.S. video title, *Hide and Seek*). Screenplay, Joel Hladecek and Yas Takata. Cinematographer, Curtis J. Petersen. Editor, Saul Pincus. Music, Robert Carli. Producers, Gary Howsam, Pieter Kroonenburg,

Gilles Paquin, and Mark Amin. GFT Entertainment, 35mm, color, 100 minutes. Cast: Daryl Hannah (Anne White), Jennifer Tilly (Helen), Vincent Gallo (Frank), Bruce Greenwood (Jack), Johanna Black (Emily), Sharon Bajer (Dr. Webster).

Going Back, 2001. (U.S. video title, *Under Heavy Fire*). Screenplay, Sidney J. Furie and Greg Mellott. Cinematographer, Curtis J. Petersen. Editor, Saul Pincus. Music, Amin Bhatia. Producers, Gary Howsam, Harel Goldstein, and Lewin Webb. GFT Entertainment, 35mm, color; director's cut, 149 minutes; video cut, 113 minutes. Cast: Casper Van Dien (Capt. Ramsey), Carré Otis (Kathleen), Jaimz Woolvett (Tex), Bobby Hosea (Ray), Joseph Griffin (Red Fuentes), Martin Kove (Father Brazinski), Jason Blicker (Fred), Austin Farwell (Doc Jordan).

Global Heresy, 2002. (U.S. video title, *Rock My World*). Screenplay, Mark Mills. Cinematographer, Curtis J. Petersen. Editor, David Ostry. Music, Jonathan Goldsmith. Producers, Gary Howsam, Mark Shorrock, Mark Thomas, Harel Goldstein, and Lewin Webb. Ballpark Productions, GFT Entertainment, and Ultimate Pictures, 35mm, color, 106 minutes. Cast: Peter O'Toole (Lord Foxley), Joan Plowright (Lady Foxley), Alicia Silverstone (Nat), Jaimz Woolvett (Leo), Keram Malicki-Sanchez (Flit), Christopher Bolton (Carl), Lochlyn Munro (Dave), Martin Clunes (James Chancellor).

The Circle, 2002. (U.S. video title, *The Fraternity*). Screenplay, Brian Hannan. Cinematographer, Curtis J. Petersen. Editor, Craig Webster. Music, Jonathan Goldsmith. Producers, Gary Howsam, Mark Shorrock, Mark Thomas, Harel Goldstein, and Lewin Webb. GFT Entertainment, 35mm, color, 100 minutes. Cast: Treat Williams (Spencer Runcie), Robbe Dunne (Alex Desineau), Gianpaolo Venuta (Jetson Harlow), Daniel Enright (Demian Carthy).

American Soldiers, 2005. Screenplay, Greg Mellott. Cinematographer, Curtis Petersen. Editor, Eduardo Martinez. Music, Varouje. Producers, Sidney J. Furie, Gary Howsam, Lewin Webb, and Christopher Petzel. Peace Arch Entertainment, 35mm, color, 103 minutes. Cast: Curtis Morgan (Spc. Tyler Jackson), Zan Calabretta (Sgt. Delvecchio), Jordan Brown (Spc. Cohen), Eddie Della Siepe (Pfc. Roy Pena), Paul Sturino (Pfc. Dowdy).

The Four Horsemen, 2008. Screenplay, Greg Mellott. Cinematographer, Curtis Petersen. Editor, Eduardo Martinez. Music, Varouje. Production designer, Valentin Nedialkov. Producers, Brenda Cogan, Joshua Howsam, Quincy Morgan, and Soo Luen Tom. Peace Arch Entertainment, 35mm, color, 118 minutes. Cast: Mark O'Brien (Eric Rollins), Curtis Morgan (Terry), Nick Abraham (Manny), Natalie Roy (Cathy), Joanna Douglas (Angie), Zan Calabretta (Sgt. Briggs).

Conduct Unbecoming, 2011. Screenplay, Greg Mellott and Richard Watson. Cinematographer, Curtis Petersen. Editor, Eduardo Martinez. Music, Simon Poole. Producers, Gary Howsam, Angelo Paletta, and Paul Paletta. E-One Entertainment, HD video, color, 118 minutes. Cast: Corey Sevier (Captain Nick Hawkes), Bridget Wareham (Molly), Michael Ironside (Colonel Dodd), Maury Chaykin (Colonel Fox), Nick Abraham (Mr. Richards), Curtis Morgan (Chaplain Ben).

A Pride of Lions, 2014. (U.S. video title, *The Dependables*). Screenplay, Richard Watson. Cinematographer, Curtis Petersen. Editor, Saul Pincus. Music, Craig McConnell. Producers, Gary Howsam, Bill Marks, and Julius Nasso. E-One Entertainment, HD video, color, 101 minutes. Cast: Bo Svenson (Mick Skinner), Margot Kidder (Jean Dempsey), Louis Gossett Jr. (Lou Jones), Seymour Cassel (Dominic Ackers), Cedric Smith (Paul Stasny).

Drive Me to Vegas and Mars, coming in 2016. Screenplay, Sidney J. Furie. Cinematographer, Jonas Klittmark. Editor, Stephen Eckelberry. Producers, Christine Akrey and Richard Watson. HD video, color. Cast: Stan Shaw (Cowboy), Beverly Todd (Maggie), Michael Lerner (Milt), Tony Todd (Frank), Googy Gress (Buddy Boy), Mackenzie Munro (Rachel), Alex Ho (Harold), Gareth Williams (Officer Mike), Melanie Hutsell (Tammy).

Additional Titles

Iron Eagle, On the Attack (1995)
The Rage (1997)
My 5 Wives (2000)
Partners in Action (2002)
Detention (2003)
Direct Action (2004)

Made-for-Television Films

Married to a Stranger (1997)
The Collectors (1999)

A Friday Night Date (2000) (aka *Road Rage*)
The Veteran (2006)

Television

Hudson's Bay (1959) (21 episodes)
"Thunder Guys" (1971) (pilot)
Lonesome Dove, the Series (1994) (3 episodes, including pilot)
V.I.P. (1998) (5 episodes)
Pensacola, Wings of Gold (1998) (8 episodes)
18 Wheels of Justice (2000) (2 episodes)
"Just Cause" (2001) (1 episode)

Unrealized Projects

Realized by Others

Summer Holiday (1963), Peter Yates
A Hard Day's Night (1964), Richard Lester
Dead Heat on a Merry-Go-Round (1966), Bernard Girard
Eye of the Devil (1967), J. Lee Thompson
Funny Girl (1968), William Wyler
A Matter of Innocence (1968), aka *Pretty Polly,* Guy Green
Planet of the Apes (1968), Franklin J. Schaffner
The Godfather (1972), Francis Ford Coppola
The Other Side of the Mountain (1975), Larry Peerce
Silver Streak (1976), Arthur Hiller
High Road to China (1983), Brian G. Hutton
Day by Day (1987), realized as *Triumph of the Spirit,* Robert M. Young

Never Realized in Any Form

Big Country, Big Man (1965)
Jack Bo (1967)
As Pretty Does (1970–1972)
Victory (1976–1977), a Western cowritten by Barry Sandler with Furie, after *Gable and Lombard.*
The Shipkiller (1978), based on a Book of the Month Club novel by Justin

Scott, adapted for the screen by Sidney J. Furie, with Jonathan Hales, then Clarke Reynolds.

Untitled trucking drama (1980–1981), "an artier version of Peckinpah's *Convoy*," the project Furie was developing when he was offered *The Entity.*

The Marvel of Haunted Castle (1984), full advertisement brochure printed for the trades on March 5, 1984. It was slated for principal photography in April 1984 for summer 1985 release. Screenplay by Lem Dobbs.

Tripwire (2000)

Americal, the story of an Army officer assigned to a unit whose past two commanders died under mysterious circumstances.

Carnival (1997), a Mario Puzo adaptation, to have been produced by Cine-Tel, by Paul Hertzberg and Lisa Hansen.

Notes

Unless otherwise noted herein, Sidney J. Furie quotes in the text originate from the author's audio-recorded sessions with Furie, from March to November 2013.

1. The Boy in His Own Company

Quotations from the following persons in chapter 1 are drawn from these interviews by the author, unless otherwise indicated:

Dan Friedlaender, interview, Philadelphia, June 2, 2013

Ted Kotcheff, telephone interview, June 11, 2014

1. Ben Hecht organized and wrote a "dramatic pageant" entitled *We Will Never Die,* which premiered at Madison Square Garden only a month after its groundbreaking publication in the *New York Times.* It was produced by Billy Rose and Ernst Lubitsch to raise public awareness about the ongoing mass murder of Jews in Europe. Kurt Weill wrote the music for the production.

2. Colonizing a Wilderness

Quotations from the following persons in chapter 2 are drawn from these interviews by the author, unless otherwise indicated:

Ted Kotcheff, telephone interview, June 11, 2014

Phil Nimmons, telephone interview, July 9, 2014

Anthony Ray, telephone interview, July 13, 2014

Michael Snow, telephone interview, September 3, 2014

Dudley Sutton, Skype interview, July 4, 2014

Epigraph: Véronneau, "Canadian Film," 213.

1. Knelman, *This Is Where We Came In,* 10, 11.

2. Piers Handling, "Canada," in *World Cinema since 1945,* ed. William Luhr (New York: Ungar, 1987), 93.

3. Wise, *Take One's Guide,* 18.

4. Handling, "Canada," 93.

5. Hill, "Furie's *A Dangerous Age*," 252.

6. Jack Karr, "*A Dangerous Age* Ready for Screens in Month," *Toronto Star,* November 26, 1957.

7. Ibid.

8. Piers Handling, email to the author, October 20, 2014.

9. Pratley, *Century of Canadian Cinema*, 54.

10. Gravestock, *Don Owen*, 3.

11. Ron Johnson, "Like Delayed Time Bomb, Drive Flings Furie Upward," *Toronto Star,* November 7, 1959.

12. Denton, "Furie Then and Now," 22.

13. Pratley, *Century of Canadian Cinema*, 48.

14. Gravestock, *Don Owen*, 4.

15. McGilligan, *Nicholas Ray,* 294.

16. Denton, "Furie Then and Now," 22.

17. Pattison, "Youth on Trial," 40. The exact quote: "What Furie looked for in films, no matter how silly the total effect might be (he instanced Kazan's *Wild River*) was the reality of human relationships. This was what excited him about the work of Kazan, Fellini, Bergman or Antonioni—a choice that is disappointingly square from the director of *A Cool Sound from Hell.*"

18. Pratley, *Century of Canadian Cinema*, 48.

19. Gravestock, *Don Owen*, 4.

20. Canuxploitation, a website devoted to Canadian cinema (mostly exploitation titles), which reviewed *A Dangerous Age,* also designated *A Cool Sound from Hell* as lost.

21. Eugene Walz, *Canada's Best Features: Critical Essays on 15 Canadian Films* (Toronto: Take One, 2002), 116.

22. Robert Fulford, as quoted in Knelman, *This Is Where We Came In,* 9.

23. Gerald Pratley, "Report from London: Second Budget Features Training for Big Time," *Toronto Star,* March 8, 1961.

3. Making a Name in London

Quotations from the following persons in chapter 3 are drawn from these interviews by the author, unless otherwise indicated:

Susan Hampshire, telephone interview, July 16, 2014

Nicolas Roeg, telephone interview, July 13, 2014

Dudley Sutton, Skype interview, July 4, 2014

Epigraph: Denton, "Furie Then and Now," 22.

1. Yule, *Man Who "Framed" the Beatles,* 56.

2. *The Young Ones* audio commentary, region 1 release.

3. "Making It in London," an episode in *Hollywood U.K.,* presented by Richard Lester, produced by Charles Chabot and Rosemary Wilton, BBC-TV, 1993.

4. Ewbank and Hildred, *Cliff,* 166.

5. Glynn, *British Pop Music Film,* 49.

6. *The Young Ones* audio commentary.

7. Ewbank and Hildred, *Cliff*, 169–70.

8. *The Young Ones* audio commentary.

9. Sheridan Morley obituary, *London Telegraph*, February 17, 2007.

10. Glynn, *British Pop Music Film*, 51.

11. Ewbank and Hildred, *Cliff*, 169.

12. "Making It in London."

13. Glynn, *British Pop Music Film*, 51.

14. Shail, *British Film Directors*, 76.

15. "Strangers in the City," an episode of *Hollywood U.K.*

16. Pattison, "Youth on Trial," 40.

17. Ibid.

18. Murphy, *Sixties British Cinema*, 127.

19. Peter John Dyer, review of *The Boys, Films and Filming*, September 1962, 196; review of *The Boys, Sight & Sound*, Fall 1962, 145.

4. Man's Favorite Sport

Quotations from the following persons in chapter 4 are drawn from these interviews by the author, unless otherwise indicated:

Susan Hampshire, telephone interview, July 16, 2014

Dudley Sutton, Skype interview, July 4, 2014

Edward Thorpe, telephone interview, July 11, 2014

Rita Tushingham, telephone interview, August 4, 2013

1. Pattison, "Youth on Trial," 40.

2. Murphy, *Sixties British Cinema*, 128.

3. "Phone Call Sets Police Squad on Leather Jackets: 'We're always blamed' Say the Ton-Up Boys," *London Express*, February 14, 1961.

4. The Ace Café Official Website, www.ace-cafe-london.com/.

5. "Strangers in the City," an episode of *Hollywood U.K.*

6. Ibid.

7. Review of *The Leather Boys, Variety*, February 5, 1964.

8. Peter Baker, review of *The Leather Boys, Films and Filming*, January 1964, 24.

9. Michael Arditti, foreword to *The Leather Boys*, by Gillian Freeman (Richmond, VA: Valancourt), vii.

10. Murphy, *Sixties British Cinema*, 129.

11. "Film Clips," *Sight & Sound* 34–35 (Winter 1964–1965).

12. *Fings Ain't Wot They Used t'Be* was never adapted into a film, despite its success on the London West End stage. In 1963 its stage director, Joan Littlewood, helmed her debut feature, *Sparrows Can't Sing*. Though offered a chance to direct the film version of *Fings . . .* after Furie's departure, she instead made a permanent return to the stage.

13. *The Young Ones* audio commentary.

14. Brian O'Brien, "Business as Usual," *Films and Filming,* March 1964, 48.

15. Ewbank and Hildred, *Cliff,* 168.

16. *Wonderful Life* audio commentary, region 1 release.

17. Ewbank and Hildred, *Cliff,* 173, 174.

18. "Film Clips," *Sight & Sound* (Winter 1964–1965): 34.

5. Through a Glass Refracted: The Wild Angles Picture Show

Quotations from the following persons in chapter 5 are drawn from these interviews by the author, unless otherwise indicated:

Michael Caine, telephone interview, October 23, 2013

Dan Furie, interview, Beverly Hills, CA, May 2013

Paul Lynch, interview, Beverly Hills, CA, May 2013

John Saxon, telephone interview, May 2013

1. The article in question was eventually published in the *London Evening Standard* on November 18, 1963, but did not quote Nat Cohen as calling Furie a "has-been," nor did it mention Furie at all.

2. Sangster, *Do You Want It Good,* 78.

3. Ken Adam, video interview, *The Ipcress File,* region 2 release.

4. Michael Caine, in "The Last Wave," *Hollywood U.K.*

5. Murphy, *Sixties British Cinema,* 222.

6. Roger Ebert, review of *Counterpoint, Chicago Sun-Times,* July 23, 1968.

7. Michael Caine, video interview, *The Ipcress File,* region 2 release.

8. Ibid.

9. Ibid.

10. Fiegel, *John Barry,* 122.

11. "The Last Wave," *Hollywood U.K.* The statement about Furie spiking his coffee with cognac is the only statement not contained in the documentary. Furie told this to the author.

12. Gary McMahon, "Harry Palmer, Michael Caine & *The Ipcress File,*" *Film International* 10, no. 2, issue 56 (June 2012).

13. "Film Clips," *Sight & Sound* (Winter 1964–1965): 34.

14. Caine, video interview.

15. Ibid.

16. Commentary with Sidney J. Furie and Peter Hunt, *The Ipcress File,* 2001, region 1 release.

17. "The Last Wave," *Hollywood U.K.*

18. Fiegel, *John Barry,* 122.

19. Ibid., 123.

20. *The Sound of Cinema: The Music That Made the Movies,* written and pre-

sented by Neil Brand, directed and produced by John Das, BBC television documentary, 2013.

21. Caine, video interview.

22. Robbe-Grillet was quoted in *L'Express* in an unknown 1965 issue of the magazine.

23. Fiegel, *John Barry*, 124.

24. This Caine quote from *Playboy* is requoted in *Modern Screen Magazine*, December 1965.

25. *Sight & Sound*, Spring 1965, 74.

26. The Billy Wilder sentiment about *The Ipcress File* has been quoted in so many places where the film is discussed that it is difficult to determine the original source.

27. Coursodon and Tavernier, *50 ans de cinéma*, 484.

28. Commentary with Furie and Hunt, *The Ipcress File*.

29. McMahon, "Harry Palmer, Michael Caine," 28.

30. Ibid., 17.

31. Sarris, *American Cinema*, 194.

32. Shirley MacLaine's official website, www.shirleymaclaine.com/.

33. Bart, "Furie-ous at Brando?"

34. Ibid.

35. Manso, *Brando*, 482.

36. Furie, "Hollywood Misses Its Cue."

37. Aller, "Fuzzy Image of Cameramen." See appendix A for the full correspondence between Aller and Furie.

38. Manso, *Brando*, 482.

39. Geist, "inter/VIEW with Furie," 5.

40. Bart, "Furie-ous at Brando?"

41. Manso, *Brando*, 484.

42. Marc Glassman, "Born to Film," *Montage*, 2010, 15.

43. Manso, *Brando*, 484.

44. Ibid.

45. Ibid.

46. Tony Thomas, *The Films of Marlon Brando* (New York: Citadel Press 1973), 202.

47. Schickel, *Brando*, 187.

48. Manso, *Brando*, 485.

49. "Conversations with Hiller and Furie," 16.

50. *Variety*, February 23, 1962.

51. Geist, "inter/VIEW with Furie," 12.

52. "Sinatra Enterprises Sets Second Film with Furie; It's Mitchell's *Jack Bo*," *Variety*, May 19, 1966.

53. Santopietro, *Sinatra in Hollywood,* 184.

54. Geist, "inter/VIEW with Furie," 12.

55. Coursodon and Tavernier, *50 ans de cinéma,* 485, my translation.

56. Murphy, *Sixties British Cinema,* 228–29.

57. Ibid.

58. Geist, "inter/VIEW with Furie," 5.

59. Mary Rourke, "Brad Dexter, 85, Dies: Sinatra Pal Often Played Villains," *New York Times,* December 12, 2002.

6. Professional Winners and Professional Losers

Quotations from the following persons in chapter 6 are drawn from these interviews by the author, unless otherwise indicated:

Gray Frederickson, telephone interview, April 12, 2013

Linda Furie, interview, Beverly Hills, CA, August 19, 2013

Diana Muldaur, telephone interview, May 2, 2013

Barry Newman, telephone interview, April 14, 2013

Albert Ruddy, interview, Hollywood, CA, May 24, 2013

1. Brad Dexter obituary, *Los Angeles Times,* December 14, 2002.

2. Dorothy Manners, "Attorney Bailey Offered Role in 'Sheppard Case,'" *St. Petersburg Times,* March 2, 1967.

3. "Atty. Lee Bailey Meets Coast Newsmen as Prelim to Sheppard Case Film," *Variety Weekly,* March 29, 1967.

4. Ibid.

5. John L. Scott, "Sheppard Attorney Will Appear in Film," *Los Angeles Times,* March 24, 1967.

6. Collins, "Newcomer Newman."

7. Luft, "Interviewing Sidney J. Furie," 4.

8. John L. Scott, "Sheppard Film Stalled." *Los Angeles Times,* August 24, 1967.

9. Luft, "Interviewing Sidney J. Furie," 4.

10. Geist, "inter/VIEW with Furie," 12.

11. Geist, "inter/VIEW with Furie," 12.

12. Evans, *The Kid Stays in the Picture,* 155.

13. Andrea Maletz, "*The Lawyer:* Law and Disorder," *Boston after Dark,* February 4, 1970.

14. Ibid.

15. An attendee at this screening of *The Lawyer* contacted the author with his account of the uproar but wished to remain anonymous.

16. Geist, "inter/VIEW with Furie," 12.

17. Luft, "Interviewing Sidney J. Furie," 4.

18. Geist, "inter/VIEW with Furie," 12.

19. Sarris, *American Cinema,* 194.

20. Monte Hellman to the author, August 19, 2013, e-mail.

21. Spada, *Films of Robert Redford,* 141.

22. Bart, *Infamous Players,* 183.

23. Robert Redford, video interview, in *Downhill Racer* (New York: Criterion Collection, 2009), DVD, region 1 release.

24. Geist, "inter/VIEW with Furie," 12.

25. Ebert, "Interview with Pollard."

26. Callan, *Robert Redford,* 202.

27. Spada, *Films of Robert Redford,* 142.

28. Ibid.

29. Bob Thomas, "Hell's Angels Not Plot of Cycle Picture," *Los Angeles Herald Examiner,* November 2, 1969.

30. Robert Redford, interview, December 1974, *Rolling Stone,* quoted in Callan, *Robert Redford,* 202.

31. Callan, *Robert Redford,* 165.

32. Ibid.

33. Coursodon and Tavernier, *50 ans de cinéma,* 485.

7. Idol Worship in Jazz

Quotations from the following persons in chapter 7 are drawn from these interviews by the author, unless otherwise indicated:

Gray Frederickson, telephone interview, April 12, 2013

Linda Furie, interview, Beverly Hills, CA, August 19, 2013

Noah Furie, interview, Beverly Hills, CA, May 2013

Henry Jaglom, interview, Santa Monica, CA, October 3, 2013

Paul Lynch, interview, Beverly Hills, CA, May 2013

Barry Newman, telephone interview, April 14, 2013

Albert Ruddy, interview, Hollywood, CA, May 24, 2013

Alan Trustman, telephone interview, October 12, 2013

Billy Dee Williams, telephone interview, October 7, 2013

1. Mario Puzo, "The Godfather Business," *New York Magazine,* August 1972, 22.

2. Evans, *The Kid Stays in the Picture,* 237.

3. *Easy Riders, Raging Bulls: How the Sex, Drugs and Rock 'n' Roll Generation Saved Hollywood,* directed by Kenneth Bowser, documentary, 2003.

4. Dick, *Engulfed,* 146.

5. Harlan Lebo, *The Godfather Legacy: The Untold Story of the Making of the Classic Godfather Trilogy* (Toronto: Fireside Publishing House, 1998), 28.

6. Evans, *The Kid Stays in the Picture,* 239.

7. Lanken, "If You 'want to be alone.'"

8. Jay Weston to the author, e-mail, September 23, 2013.

9. Lanken, "If You 'want to be alone.'"

10. Weston to the author, e-mail, September 23, 2013.

11. "Behind the Blues" featurette, in *Lady Sings the Blues* DVD.

12. Taraborrelli, *Call Her Miss Ross*.

13. Roger Ebert, review of *Lady Sings the Blues, Chicago Sun-Times,* October 1972.

14. Taraborrelli, *Call Her Miss Ross*.

15. Weston to the author, e-mail, September 23, 2013.

16. *New York Times,* July 20, 1971.

17. Taraborrelli, *Call Her Miss Ross*.

18. Audio commentary, in *Lady Sings the Blues* DVD, 2005, region 1 release.

19. Ibid.

20. "Behind the Blues" featurette, in *Lady Sings the Blues* DVD.

21. Richard Pryor, *Pryor Convictions, and Other Life Sentences* (New York: Pantheon, 1997), 97.

22. Audio commentary, in *Lady Sings the Blues* DVD, region 1 release.

23. Ibid.

24. Ibid.

25. Taraborrelli, *Call Her Miss Ross*.

26. Pryor, *Pryor Convictions*.

27. "Behind the Blues" featurette, in *Lady Sings the Blues* DVD.

28. Audio commentary, in *Lady Sings the Blues* DVD, 2005, region 1 release.

29. "Behind the Blues" featurette, in *Lady Sings the Blues* DVD.

30. Jay Weston to the author, e-mail, October 7, 2013.

31. Taraborrelli, *Call Her Miss Ross*.

32. Audio commentary, in *Lady Sings the Blues* DVD, 2005, region 1 release.

33. Weston to the author, e-mail, October 7, 2013.

34. Gordy, *To Be Loved*.

35. Storhoff, "Strange Fruit," 105.

36. Coursodon and Tavernier, *50 ans de cinéma,* 485, translation by the author.

37. Ibid.

38. Scott Saul, *Becoming Richard Pryor* (New York: Harper Collins, 2014), 279.

39. Geist, "inter/VIEW with Furie," 12.

40. Bart, *Infamous Players,* 106–7.

41. Saul, *Becoming Richard Pryor,* 299.

42. Review of *Hit!* DVD, *Sight & Sound,* May 2012.

43. Review of *Hit!, Combustible Celluloid* (Jeffrey M. Anderson), online at www.combustiblecelluloid.com/classic/hit.shtml.

44. Henry and Henry, *Furious Cool,* 142–43.

8. Sid & Carole & Clark & Sheila: The Romantic Fantasies

Quotations from the following persons in chapter 8 are drawn from these interviews by the author, unless otherwise indicated:

Larry Cohen, telephone interview, October 16, 2014

Gray Frederickson, telephone interview, April 12, 2013

Dan Furie, interview, Beverly Hills, CA, May 2013

Linda Furie, interview, Beverly Hills, CA, August 19, 2013

Paul Lynch, interview, Beverly Hills, CA, May 2013

Donald Morgan, telephone interview, April 4, 2013

Gail Parent and Kenny Solms, telephone interview, July 14, 2013

Barry Sandler, telephone interview, December 9, 2013

Paul Sylbert, telephone interview, December 10, 2013

1. Warga, "'Sheila' Writers Alive."

2. Gail Parent, *Sheila Levine Is Dead and Living in New York* (Woodstock, NY: Overlook TP, 2004), 43.

3. Warga, "'Sheila' Writers Alive."

4. Ibid.

5. Reed, *Valentines & Vitriol*, 236.

6. Don Morgan, interview by *American Cinematographer*, October 18, 2006, published online at www.theasc.com/asc_news/News_Articles/News_81.php.

7. Reed, *Valentines & Vitriol*, 236.

8. Don Morgan, interview by *American Cinematographer*.

9. Feldman, *Tell Me*, 126–27.

10. Ibid.

11. Denton, "Furie Then and Now," 23.

12. Scott Foundas, in conversation with the author, October 6, 2014.

13. Vincent Canby, review of *Sheila Levine Is Dead and Living in New York, New York Times,* May 17, 1975.

14. Leslie Halliwell, *Halliwell's Film Guide.*

15. Terry, "Gable & Lombard."

16. Jay Weston to the author, e-mail, November 3, 2013.

17. Barry Sandler, interview by Jeff Cramer on author's blog.

18. Terry, "Gable & Lombard," 21.

19. Ibid.

20. Dick Kleiner, "Forego Movie Accuracy for Drama," April 23, 1976.

21. Ibid.

22. Ibid.

23. Terry, "Gable & Lombard," 61.

24. Ibid.

25. Ibid.

26. Ibid.

27. "Gable's Back, and Clayburgh's Got Him: Jill Scores as the Ineffable Carole Lombard," *People Magazine* 5, no. 8 (March 1, 1976).

28. Terry, "Gable & Lombard," 21.

29. Ibid., 56.

30. Ibid., 21.

31. Ibid.

32. Terry, "Gable & Lombard," 63.

33. "Gable's Back."

34. *The Last Mogul,* documentary.

35. NEA, "Forego Movie Accuracy."

36. Ibid.

37. Ibid.

38. Ibid.

39. Dick Kleiner, "Dropping Historical Accuracy for Drama," *Syndicated Column,* April 23, 1976.

40. Audio commentary, in *An Unmarried Woman.*

41. NEA, "Forego Movie Accuracy."

42. Aretha Franklin, in a *Cosmopolitan* article. Author was notified of this by two interviewees but was unable to locate the precise source.

43. Denton, "Furie Then and Now," 23.

9. Cast Iron Jacket

Quotations from the following persons in chapter 9 are drawn from these interviews by the author, unless otherwise indicated:

Dan Furie, interview, Beverly Hills, CA, May 2013

Linda Furie, interview, Beverly Hills, CA, August 19, 2013

Melanie Mayron, telephone interview, July 2013

Andre Morgan, telephone interview, December 5, 2013

Rick Natkin, telephone interview, February 12, 2014

1. Peter McInerney, "Apocalypse Then: Hollywood Looks Back at Vietnam," *Film Quarterly* 33, no. 2 (Winter 1979–1980): 21–32.

2. Lee Grant, "Old Friends Spar over 'Angela,'" *Film Clips, Los Angeles Times,* October 27, 1976.

3. Ermey, *Gunny's Rules,* 40.

4. Audio commentary, in *The Boys in Company C,* region 1 release.

5. Berry, "Two of the Boys in Company C."

6. Audio commentary, in *The Boys in Company C.*

7. Berry, "Two of the Boys in Company C."

8. Audio commentary, in *The Boys in Company C.*

9. *Hearts of Darkness: A Filmmaker's Apocalypse*, directed by Eleanor Coppola, George Hickenlooper, and Fax Bahr, documentary, American Zoetrope 1991.

10. Audio commentary, in *The Boys in Company C*.

11. Ibid.

12. Berry, "Two of the Boys in Company C."

13. Roger Ebert, review of *Purple Hearts, Chicago Sun-Times*, January 1, 1984.

14. "*Full Metal Jacket:* Between Good and Evil," featurette in *Full Metal Jacket*, 2007, region 1 release.

15. Kellner and Ryan, "Vietnam and the New Militarism."

16. The Billy Wilder comment about *Full Metal Jacket* is semifamous by now. In Robert Horton's book *Billy Wilder: Interviews* (Jackson: University Press of Mississippi, 2001), 190, Wilder named "the first half of *Full Metal Jacket*" as a film he admires on its own.

17. Leonard Klady, "Outtakes," *Los Angeles Times*, August 2, 1987.

18. Dennis Schwartz, review of Samuel Fuller's *The Steel Helmet*, Ozus' Movie World Reviews (online).

19. Audio commentary with Jay Cocks, 2006, in *Full Metal Jacket*, region 1 release.

20. *Stanley Kubrick: A Life in Pictures*, directed by Jan Harlan, produced by Jan Harlan and Anthony Frewin, Warner Home Video, 2001, documentary, region 1 release.

21. Kellner and Ryan, "Vietnam and the New Militarism."

22. Brian J. Woodman, "The World War II Film Turned on Its Head: *The Boys in Company C*," in Eberwein, *The War Film*, 96.

23. Terry Christensen, quoted in ibid.

24. William P. McGivern, *Night of the Juggler* (New York: Putnam, 1975), 34.

25. Jay Weston to the author, e-mail, June 15, 2014.

26. *Variety*, August 9, 1978.

27. Gregg Kilday, "Furie Leaves 'Night of the Juggler,'" *Los Angeles Times*, August 9, 1978.

28. Weston to the author, e-mail, June 15, 2014.

29. Deborah Caulfield and Clarke Taylor, "'Jazz Singer': The Sound and the Furie," *Los Angeles Times*, March 9, 1980.

30. Ibid.

31. Ibid.

32. Wild, *He Is—I Say*, 153.

33. Caulfield and Taylor, "'Jazz Singer.'"

34. According to *The Official Razzie Movie Guide: Enjoying the Best of Hollywood's Worst*, by John Wilson, the *New York Daily News* reported overhearing Olivier denigrating the film at a restaurant. "This piss is shit" was the star's alleged curse. Whether this was during the shooting or before the premiere is unclear, as is whether Furie was still involved in the production at that point.

35. Wild, *He Is—I Say,* 154.

36. Fleischer, *Just Tell Me When to Cry,* 303.

37. Philip Ziegler, *Olivier* (London: MacLehose Press, 2014), 389. The author is quoting from Mark Amory's tapes of interviews with Laurence Olivier.

10. Cool Sounds from Hell

Quotations from the following persons in chapter 10 are drawn from these interviews by the author, unless otherwise indicated:

Stephen Burum, telephone interview, October 3, 2013

Michael Caine, telephone interview, October 23, 2013

Dan Furie, interview, Beverly Hills, CA, May 2013

David Labiosa, telephone interview, October 24, 2013

Rick Natkin, telephone interview, February 12, 2014

1. Wilson, "*The Entity,*" 19.

2. Barbara Hershey, interview in *Marquee Magazine,* January 1983, 51.

3. Wilson, "*The Entity,*" 19.

4. Ibid.

5. Ibid., 22.

6. Michael Atkinson, "Forgotten Pleasures of the Multiplex," *Sight & Sound,* http://old.bfi.org.uk/sightandsound/polls/forgotten-pleasures-of-the-multiplex-e-to-j.php.

7. David Pirie, review of *The Entity,* in *Time Out Film Guide 2011* (London: Time Out Guides, 2011), 319.

8. Janisse, *House of Psychotic Women,* 14.

9. Judah, "Attacked by Nothing."

10. Janisse, *House of Psychotic Women,* 14.

11. Mann, "Furie Leads the Cheer."

11. Matinee Buster

Quotations from the following persons in chapter 11 are drawn from these interviews by the author, unless otherwise indicated:

Linda Furie, interview, Beverly Hills, CA, August 19, 2013

Louis Gossett Jr., telephone interview, October 30, 2014

Margot Kidder, telephone interview, October 31, 2014

Paul Lynch, interview, Beverly Hills, CA, May 2013

Mark Rosenthal, telephone interview, March 29, 2013

Dudley Sutton, Skype interview, July 4, 2014

Joe Zito, interview, Sherman Oaks, CA, September 12, 2013

1. Mann, "Furie Leads the Cheer."

2. Ibid.

3. Marc Glassman, "Born to Film," *Montage,* 2010, 16.

4. Ibid.

5. Mann, "Furie Leads the Cheer."

6. Ibid.

7. Pratley, *Century of Canadian Cinema,* 108.

8. Coursodon and Tavernier, *50 ans de cinéma,* 485.

9. Edward Gross, "The Sound, the Furie & *Superman IV,*" *Starlog Magazine,* October 1987, 49.

10. Ibid., 48.

11. *The Go-Go Boys,* directed and produced by Hilla Medalia, produced by Roy Lev and Yariv Horowitz, feature-length documentary (Noah Productions).

12. Ibid.

13. Ross Plesset, "Time Tunnel: *Superman IV: The Quest for Peace,*" *Dream-Watch Magazine,* July 2006, 52.

14. Adrian Havill, *Man of Steel: The Career and Courage of Christopher Reeve* (New York: Signet, 1996).

15. Christopher Reeve, *Still Me* (New York: Random House, 1998).

16. Plesset, "Time Tunnel," 52.

17. Commentary Track with Mark Rosenthal, in *Superman IV: The Quest for Peace,* DVD (Burbank, CA: Warner Bros. Home Entertainment, 2006), region 1 release.

18. Plesset, "Time Tunnel," 53.

19. Havill, *Man of Steel.*

20. Christopher Reeve quoted in *Drama-Logue Magazine,* from Havill, *Man of Steel.*

21. Canadian Online Movie Database, Northstars.ca, Sidney J. Furie entry.

22. *The Go-Go Boys,* feature documentary.

23. Gross, "The Sound, the Furie," 50.

12. Housemaster

Quotations from the following persons in chapter 12 are drawn from these interviews by the author, unless otherwise indicated:

Harry Basil, telephone interview, April 29, 2013

Michael Caine, telephone interview, October 23, 2013

Gray Frederickson, telephone interview, April 12, 2013

Linda Furie, interview, Beverly Hills, CA, August 19, 2013

Gary Howsam, telephone interview, July 15, 2014

Margot Kidder, telephone interview, October 31, 2014

Greg Mellott, telephone interview, May 28, 2014

Phil Nimmons, telephone interview, July 9, 2014

Nicholas Roeg, telephone interview, July 13, 2014
Albert Ruddy, interview, Hollywood, CA, May 24, 2013

1. Edward Gross, "The Sound, the Furie & *Superman IV*," *Starlog Magazine*, October 1987, 50.

2. Untitled item, *Variety*, November 12, 1991.

3. "Dangerfield Lets Loose at Paramount's ShoWest Dinner," *Variety*, February 21, 1992.

4. Untitled item, *Variety*, November 12, 1991.

5. Ibid.

6. Pratley, *Century of Canadian Cinema*, 88.

7. Ibid., 87.

8. Peter Caranicas, "Furie's Death Cast Shadow on Agency," *Variety*, July 28, 2009.

9. Janice Laurie Kaye, "Certain Tendencies in Canadian Cinema: Temporary Insanity and the National Tax-Shelter Masquerade" (diss., University of Southern California Los Angeles, 2007).

Bibliography

Print Materials

Aller, Herb. "Fuzzy Image of Cameramen Refocused." *Los Angeles Times,* October 16, 1966.

Bart, Peter. "Furie-ous at Brando?" *New York Times,* January 23, 1966.

———. *Infamous Players: A Tale of Movies, the Mob (and Sex).* New York: Weinstein Books, 2011.

Berry, Jeff. "Two of the 'Boys in (and out of) Company C.'" *UCLA Daily Bruin,* May 18, 1978.

Bramley, Gareth, Geoff Leonard, and Pete Walker. *John Barry: The Man with the Midas Touch.* Bristol, UK. Redcliffe, 2008.

Caine, Michael. *What's It All About?* London: Arrow, 2010.

Callan, Michael Feeney. *Robert Redford: The Biography.* New York: Vintage/Alfred A. Knopf, 2011.

Clifford, Francis. *The Naked Runner.* New York: Coward-McCann, 1966.

Coleman, Terry. *Olivier.* New York: Holt, 2006.

Collins, Nancy. "Newcomer Newman: 'The Lawyer' Talks about Acting, Film and Himself." *Boston After Dark,* January 28, 1970.

"Conversations on Film with Arthur Hiller and Sidney Furie." *Canadian Cinematography* 26 (January–February 1966): 13–16.

Coursodon, Jean-Pierre, and Bertrand Tavernier. *50 ans de cinéma américain.* Paris: Omnibus, 1995.

Deighton, Len. *The Ipcress File.* London: Hodder & Sloughton Press, 1964.

Denton, Clive. "Furie Then and Now." *Cinema Canada* 26 (March 1976): 21–24.

Dick, Bernard F. *Engulfed: The Death of Paramount Pictures and the Birth of Corporate Hollywood.* Lexington: University Press of Kentucky, 2001.

Dyer, Peter John. "Independently Financed Canadian Feature Arrives in England." *Films and Filming* 4, no. 10 (July 1958).

Ebert, Roger. "Interview with Michael J. Pollard." *Chicago Sun-Times,* October 19, 1969.

Eberwein, Robert T., ed. *The War Film.* Chapel Hill, NJ: Rutgers Depth of Field Series, 2004.

Ermey, R. Lee. *Gunny's Rules: How to Get Squared Away like a Marine.* Washington, DC: Regnery, 2013.

Evans, Robert. *The Fat Lady Sings*. Burlington, VT: Phoenix Books: 2013.

———. *The Kid Stays in the Picture*. New York: itBooks, 1994.

Ewbank, Tim, and Stafford Hildred. *Cliff: An Intimate Portrait of a Living Legend*. London: Virgin Books, 2007.

Feldman, Edward S. *Tell Me How You Love the Picture*. New York: St. Martin's Press, 2005.

Fiegel, Eddi. *John Barry: A Sixties Theme: From James Bond to Midnight Cowboy*. London: Macmillan U.K., 2012.

Fleischer, Richard. *Just Tell Me When to Cry: A Memoir*. New York: Carroll & Graf, 1993.

Furie, Sidney J. "Hollywood Misses Its Cue." *Los Angeles Times,* October 9, 1966.

Geist, Kenneth. "inter/VIEW with Sidney Furie." *Interview Magazine* 1, no. 6 (1970).

George, Eliot [Gillian Freeman]. *The Leather Boys*. London: Anthony Blond, 1961.

Glassman, Marc. "Conversation with . . . Sidney J. Furie." *Montage Magazine,* October 2010.

Glynn, Stephen. *The British Pop Music Film: The Beatles and Beyond*. London: Palgrave and MacMillan, 2013.

Gordy, Berry. *To Be Loved: The Music, the Magic, the Memories of Motown*. New York: Warner Books, 1995.

Gravestock, Steve. *Don Owen: Notes on a Filmmaker and His Culture*. Bloomington: Indiana University Press, 2005.

Henry, David and Joe Henry. *Furious Cool: Richard Pryor and the World That Made Him*. New York: Algonquin Books, 2013.

Hill, Derek. "A Look at . . . Sidney J. Furie's *A Dangerous Age*." *Sight & Sound* 27, no. 5 (Summer 1958).

Jackson, Laura. *Neil Diamond: His Life, His Music, His Passion*. Toronto: ECW Press, 2005.

Janisse, Kier-La. *House of Psychotic Women: An Autobiographical Topography of Female Neurosis in Horror and Exploitation Films*. Godalming, Surrey, UK: FAB Press, 2012.

Judah, Tara. "Attacked by Nothing: Barbara Hershey and *The Entity* in Peter Tscherkassky's *Outer Space* and *Dream Work*." *cléo* 1, no. 3 (Doom) (November 28, 2013).

Kellner, Douglas, and Michael Ryan. "Vietnam and the New Militarism." In *Hollywood and War: The Film Reader,* ed. J. David Slocum. New York: Routledge, 2006.

Kellow, Brian. *Pauline Kael: A Life in the Dark*. New York: Viking Adult, 2011.

Kelton, Nancy. "Barry Sandler and the Making of *Gable and Lombard*." *After Dark,* January 1976.

Knelman, Martin. *This Is Where We Came In: The Career and Character of Canadian Film*. Toronto: McClelland & Stewart, 1977.

Lanken, Dane. "If You 'want to be alone' Don't Be an Oscar Nominee." *Montreal Gazette,* February 24, 1973.

Luft, Herbert G. "Director Series #9: Interviewing Sidney J. Furie." *Foreign Cinema,* May 31, 1968.

Luhr, William, ed. *World Cinema since 1945.* New York: Ungar, 1987.

MacLeod, Robert. *The Appaloosa.* New York: Fawcett Gold Medal, 1963.

Mann, Roderick. "Sidney Furie Leads the Cheer for 'Iron Eagle.'" *Los Angeles Times,* February 2, 1986.

Manso, Peter. *Brando: A Biography.* New York: Hyperion, 1995.

McGilligan, Patrick. *Nicholas Ray: The Glorious Failure of an American Director.* New York: itBooks, 2011.

McMahon, Gary. "Harry Palmer, Michael Caine & *The Ipcress File.*" *Film International* 10, no. 2 (June and September 2012).

Murphy, Robert. *Sixties British Cinema.* London: British Film Institute, 2008.

Parent, Gail. *Sheila Levine Is Dead and Living in New York.* New York: G. P. Putnam's, 1972.

Pattison, Barrie. "Youth on Trial." *Films and Filming,* June 1962.

Pratley, Gerald. *A Century of Canadian Cinema.* Toronto: Lynx Images, 2003.

Reed, Rex. *Valentines and Vitriol.* New York: Delacorte Press, 1977.

Robinson, David. "Film Clips: On the Set of *The Ipcress File.*" *Sight & Sound* 34 (Winter 1964–1965).

Ross, Lillian. *Picture.* Westminster, London: Penguin Group, 1952.

Russo, Gus. *Submob: How Harry Korshak and His Criminal Associates Became America's Hidden Power Brokers.* London: Bloomsbury USA, 2006.

Sangster, Jimmy. *Do You Want It Good or Tuesday? From Hammer Films to Hollywood! A Life in Movies.* Baltimore: Midnight Marquee Press, 1997.

Santopietro, Tom. *Sinatra in Hollywood.* New York: St. Martin's Griffin, 2009.

Sarris, Andrew. *The American Cinema: Directors and Directions, 1929–1968.* New York: De Capo Press, 1968.

Saul, Scott. *Becoming Richard Pryor.* New York, NY: Harper, 2014.

Scheuer, Philip K. "Another British Directing Genius." *Los Angeles Times,* September 7, 1965.

Schickel, Richard. *Brando: A Life in Our Times.* New York: De Capo Press, 2000.

Shail, Robert. *British Film Directors: A Critical Guide.* Carbondale: Southern Illinois University Press, 2007.

Spada, James. *The Films of Robert Redford.* Secaucus, NJ: Citadel Press, 1984.

Spoto, Donald. *Laurence Olivier: A Biography.* New York: Cooper Square Press, 2001.

Storhoff, Gary. "Strange Fruit: *Lady Sings the Blues* as a Crossover Film." *Journal of Popular Film and Television* 30, no. 2 (January 2002): 105–13.

Taraborrelli, J. Randy. *Call Her Miss Ross: The Unauthorized Biography of Diana Ross.* Secaucus, NJ: Carol, 1989.

Terry, Clifford. "Gable & Lombard & Dr. Kiley & Who?" *Chicago Tribune*, October 12, 1975.

Thomas, Bob. *Brando: Portrait of the Rebel as an Artist*. New York: W. H. Allen, 1973.

Véronneau, Pierre. "Canadian Film: An Unexpected Emergence." *Massachusetts Review* 31, nos. 1–2 (Spring 1990): 213–26.

Ward, James J. "Outlaw Motorcyclists They're Not: A Contrarian Reading of Joseph Losey's *These Are the Damned* (1961) and Sidney Furie's *The Leather Boys* (1964)." *Journal of Popular Culture* 43, no. 2 (April 2010): 381–407.

Warga, Wayne. "'Sheila' Writers Alive, Well and Living in Hollywood." *Los Angeles Times*, February 18, 1974.

Weaver, Tom. *The Return of the B Science Fiction and Horror Movies: The Mutant Melding of Two Classic Interviews*. Jefferson, NC: McFarland, 1999.

Wild, David. *He Is—I Say: How I Learned to Stop Worrying and Love Neil Diamond*. Cambridge, MA: De Capo Press, 2009.

Wilson, John M. "*The Entity*: High-Class Exploitation?" *Los Angeles Times*, March 13, 1983.

Wise, Wyndham, ed. *Take One's Essential Guide to Films and Filmmakers in Canada*. Toronto: University of Toronto Press, 1998.

Yule, Andrew. *The Man Who "Framed" the Beatles: A Biography of Richard Lester*. New York: Donald Fine, 1994.

Audiovisual Materials

The Boys in Company C. Audio Commentary with Andrew Stevens. DVD. Las Cruces, NM: Hen's Tooth Video/Granada International, 2008.

Full Metal Jacket. Audio Commentary with Adam Baldwin, R. Lee Ermey, Jay Cocks, and Vincent D'Onofrio, 2006. Includes featurette: "*Full Metal Jacket*: Between Good and Evil," 2007. DVD. Burbank, CA: Warner Home Video, 2007.

The Go-Go Boys. Directed by Hilla Medalia. Produced by Yaviv Horowitz, Roy Lev, and Hilla Medalia. Documentary. Noah Productions, 2014.

Harry Saltzman: Showman. Directed by John Cork. Produced by John Cork, David Naylor, and Bruce Scivally. Documentary. Los Angeles: MGM Home Entertainment, 2000.

The Ipcress File. Audio Commentary with Sidney J. Furie and Peter R. Hunt. Troy, MI: Anchor Bay Entertainment, 1999.

The Ipcress File. Featurette: "Michael Caine Is Harry Palmer: A Conversation with Sir Michael Caine" and video interview with production designer Ken Adam. DVD. London: Network U.K., 2006.

Lady Sings the Blues. Audio Commentary with Sidney J. Furie, Berry Gordy, and

Shelly Berger. Includes featurette: "Behind the Blues: The Making of *Lady Sings the Blues*." DVD. Hollywood, CA: Paramount Home Entertainment.

The Last Mogul: The Life and Times of Lew Wasserman. Directed by Barry Avrich. Produced by Nat Brescia and Tori Hockin. Documentary. New York: Kino Video, 2005.

Michael Caine: Breaking the Mold. Directed by Gene Feldman and Suzette Winter. Produced by Gene Feldman, Suzette Winter, and Stephen Janson. Documentary. Janson Media, 1994.

"Strangers in the City" and "The Last Wave." Episodes in *Hollywood U.K.: British Cinema in the Sixties.* Produced by Charles Chabot, Kim Evens, and Rosemary Wilton. Narrated by Richard Lester. Documentary miniseries. BBC-TV, 1993.

An Unmarried Woman. Audio Commentary with Paul Mazursky. DVD. Beverly Hills, CA: 20th Century Fox Home Entertainment.

Wonderful Life. Audio Commentary with Sidney J. Furie, Paul Lynch, and Waylon Wahl. DVD. Troy, MI: Anchor Bay Entertainment, 2001.

The Young Ones. Audio Commentary with Sidney J. Furie, Paul Lynch, and Waylon Wahl. DVD. Troy, MI: Anchor Bay Entertainment, 2001.

Index